THE CIVILIZATION OF THE AMERICAN INDIAN SERIES

The Aztec Arrangement

THE AZTEC ARRANGEMENT

The Social History of Pre-Spanish Mexico

By Rudolph van Zantwijk

Foreword by Miguel León-Portilla

UNIVERSITY OF OKLAHOMA PRESS : NORMAN

By Rudolf van Zantwijk

Los Indígenas de Milpa Alta, herederos de los aztecas (Amsterdam, 1960)
Informes de Sociología Rural (Crefal, Pátzcuaro, Mexico, 1961-63)
Las Ciencias Sociales y el Desarrollo de la Comunidad: una introducción (Pátzcuaro, 1963)
Leyendas Nahuatlacas (Mexico City, 1963)
Servants of the Saints: The Social and Cultural Identity of a Tarascan Community in Mexico (Assen, Netherlands, 1967)
Zeven dromen over Latijns-Amerika (Amsterdam, 1971)
Los Servidores de los Santos: la identidad social y cultural de una comunidad tarasca en México (Mexico City, 1974)
La Organización social de la México-Tenochtitlan naciente (Mexico City, 1976)
Handel en Wandel der Azteken: de Sociale Geschiedenis van Vóór-Spaans Mexico (Amsterdam, 1977)
(Editor) *Los Anales de Tula: Introducción y comentarios* (Graz, Austria, 1978-79)
The Aztec Arrangement: The Social History of Pre-Spanish Mexico (Norman, 1985)

Library of Congress Cataloging in Publication Data

Zantwijk, R. A. M. van (Rudolf), 1932-
  The Aztec arrangement.

  (Civilization of the American Indian series; no. 167)
  Bibliography: p. 325.
  Includes index.
  1. Aztecs—Social conditions. 2. Aztecs—History. 3. Indians of Mexico—Social conditions. I. Title. II. Series.
F1219.76.S63Z36   1985   972'.01   84-21927
ISBN 0-8061-1677-3

This expanded and enlarged work based on *Handel en Wandel van de Azteken: de Sociale Geschiedenis van Vóór-Spaans Mexico*, the original Dutch language edition, published 1977 by Van Gorcum Ltd., Assen, The Netherlands. Copyright © 1977 Van Gorcum & Comp. B.V. P.O. Box 43, 9400 AA Assen, The Netherlands.

The paper in this book meets the guidelines for permanence and durability of the Committee on Production Guidelines for Book Longevity of the Council on Library Resources, Inc.

Contents

Illustrations and Maps

Foreword

Miguel León-Portilla

How HISTORY, literally, was depicted anew to induce a functional
integration of a hetereogenous society is the theme of this book.
As sagaciously perhaps as King Itzcoatl, who around 1431 ordered
the burning of the ancient historical records in Mexico-Tenochtitlan, Rudolf van Zantwijk seeks to unveil the origins and structuring of an Aztec society that was apparently in great need of a
new historical consciousness.

This may prove to be a controversial book, but one thing I take
as true: it is a work rich in new insights, a valuable piece of
research based on firsthand knowledge of indigenous testimonies
derived from the pre-Hispanic tradition. I take as an honor indeed
the author's invitation to write this preface. In it I want to sketch
Rudolf van Zantwijk's academic personality and also attempt a
critical recapitulation of the conclusions he reaches in the present
work.

It was in 1957 that I first met Rudolf van Zantwijk, my *"hol-
lantecatl"* friend and colleague. Through several letters he had
written to me in Nahuatl, I already knew something about him.
He was born in Amsterdam, and when he was very young, he
became deeply attracted to the indigenous history of Mexico. I
could also infer from his letters, and better still when I met him,
that he had read widely on the subject, including some of the
primary sources in Nahuatl and other texts in Spanish—as well
as important monographs in French, English, German, and Dutch
dealing with Mesoamerican cultures.

The young scholar, who had taught himself Nahuatl, came to
Mexico to spend several years first as a student and then as a
teacher. He improved his knowledge of Nahuatl until he became
fluent in it. He also learned Tarascan (the Phorhépecha language

of the indigenous group of Michoacan) and, above all, succeeded in becoming what he wanted to be, a specialist in the ancient history of Mexico.

A large number of articles in professional magazines, papers presented at various congresses, and several books are a tangible consequence of his persevering research. As lecturer and professor he also awakened interest in Mesoamerican cultures not only at the University of Amsterdam, his alma mater, but in the Netherlands in general.

Among the several aspects of Mexico's indigenous past that have attracted his attention two stand out: the literary legacy of the Nahuas and the Tarascans and the complexities of Aztec social and political structures. His first contribution, published in 1957, dealt with the Aztec hymns as the expression of the Mexican philosophy of life. Some of his studies related to Tarascan literature, including legends and poems, have been published in various issues of *Tlalocan,* the Mexican journal devoted to the compilation and analysis of ancient and contemporary Mesoamerican texts. Van Zantwijk has also prepared a manuscript on the grammar of the Nahuatl language, as well as a good number of Dutch, English, and Spanish translations of various texts of the pre-Hispanic tradition. One example is his "Hartbloemen: Azteekse liederen" (Flowers of the Heart: Aztec Songs), an anthology of Nahuatl poetry addressed to the Dutch reader, published in an Amsterdam journal in 1972. Another publication of particular importance is his Spanish edition, with commentaries, of *The Annals of Tula* (Graz, Austria, 1980).

Even more numerous are his contributions whose aim is to analyze and clarify the complexities of the social and political organization developed by the ancient Mexicans. His persevering research in this matter has covered such aspects as "The Organizing Principles of Aztec Society and State" (1963), "The Division in Fifteen Parts of Aztec Society" (1965), "The Organization of Eleven Aztec Garrisons" (1967), "The Socio-Economic and Religious Forms of Organization of the Corporate Groups of Aztec Merchants" (1979), and "Politics and Ethnicity in a Pre-Hispanic Mexican State" (1973).

His most recent publications, following the same research, anticipate some of the viewpoints which are given concrete form in this book. I restrict myself to mention of two of his papers: "Social Organization in the Beginnings of Mexico-Tenochtitlan," presented at the Forty-first International Congress of Americanists (Mexico

City, 1974), and "Ordination of Tenochtitlan; The Interrelation of the Gods, Temples, Dates, Cosmic Directions, and Places with the Social Entities of the Aztecs" (University of Erlangen, Nürnberg, 1980).

I consider it necessary at this point to mention his *Handel en Wandel van de Azteken: De Sociale geschiedenis van Vóór-Spaans Mexico* (The Comings and Goings of the Aztecs: The Social History of pre-Hispanic Mexico, Amsterdam, 1977). As its title indicates and an analysis of its contents confirms, this work anticipates what is discussed at length in the present book.

After almost twenty-five years of uninterrupted research in the social history of ancient Mexico, Rudolf van Zantwijk now offers us the present work, an original approach he labels the "Aztec Arrangement." A concise description of his conclusions is presented in the following paragraphs. Here, as in all his previous contributions, he also follows and analyzes the primary sources (ancient native books, Nahuatl texts transcribed after the Conquest, and early Spanish chronicles) to reconstruct the social history of the Mexicas, or Aztecs. He provides evidence of the often-divergent ethnic backgrounds of the groups who came to integrate Aztec society. To him the original calpollis—described by various authors as "kinship as well as residential units," social ensembles organized into hereditary clans whose members claimed to descend from a common ancestor—actually had diverse ethnic origins. With the passage of time, as other *calpollis* joined those who had left Aztlan, the place of departure of the Aztecs, the multiethnic character of the social entity increased.

A closely related question, basic to Van Zantwijk's approach, is how these different groups were integrated into the structures of a new society. Looking for an answer, the author develops an original thesis. He initiates his approach by studying the myths that are at the core of the Aztec world view. He stresses the importance of the many references to Tollan, the "Place of Reeds" and, as he puts it, "Where Authority Originates." The ancestors of the sixteenth-century Aztecs were exposed in different ways to the influence of those who, like the Culhuacans, had inherited Toltec culture, that is, the culture which had flourished in Tollan. Everything Toltec, including, of course, the source of authority, wisdom, the arts, and nobility, was a prototype to the Aztecs. Thus, when in their "pilgrimage" they entered into contact with peoples of diverse origins, they learned to distinguish between what belonged to them and what was an attribute of the Toltecs. According to

Van Zantwijk, a "Toltecized" tendency in the hierarchical organization of Aztec society is perceptible from the days of the founding of Mexico-Tenochtitlan. At the same time, however, the multiethnic character of this society subsisted in the calpollis.

The scrutiny of the sources of Aztec tradition—depicted anew in the days of Itzcoatl, soon after the Aztecs won their independence from the Tecpanecs—reveals a number of changes in the social organization of this people. According to Van Zantwijk's interpretation, the ability of the calpollis to play an important political role declined with the rise of a new "state nobility" as a result of military achievements. From that time some members of the original calpollis—that is, commoners—were allowed to take part in the privileges of the nobility. The rest, who constituted the major part of the society structured in the calpolli units, maintained their unity above all through their various occupations: horticulture; crafts such as ceramics, featherwork, and manufacture of other ceremonial or utilitarian objects; commercial enterprises; and other activities. It was in this manner that, according to the author, corporate professional groups gained strength.

Van Zantwijk believes that there is enough evidence in the sources to assert that, with the passage of time, kinship and class distinctions determined the structuring of Aztec society to a far less extent than did the various corporate groups. He discusses how these groups achieved their own integration and how they participated in the political, economic, and religious spheres of Aztec society. He concludes that the often conflicting interests and rivalry of the various corporate groups more than once threatened the balance of power and even the existence of Aztec society.

Challenging other viewpoints, such as those that make use of the Asiatic model of production or those that insist upon the primary importance of class distinctions, the author arrives at a new interpretation. As already noted, from the time of the Aztecs' victory over the Tecpanecs of Azcapotzalco and even before, changes in their socioeconomic organization had taken place. Kinship remained important in the succession of the rulers, as well as in other areas of political and economic affairs, such as property. But other factors overshadowed the differences implied by the divergent ethnic backgrounds. Shifts in the functions and socioeconomic participation of the various groups occurred in the process of growth and strengthening of a central nucleus of political power. According to Van Zantwijk, the various calpollis, even those originally integrated by the nobles, lost some of their power to a group which was rising as an elite and in whose hands rested the duty and the right to make the most important decisions. The priests too lost some of their previously enormous political power to the military, the merchants, and corporate entities devoted to the manufacture of a great variety of products.

To integrate in an efficient way the many corporate groups, which were often of different ethnic origins, several changes were necessary. To deal with the consciousness of their past, a "new history" had to be devised and depicted. In that new history, the main goal was to portray how all the various groups belonged to a predestined people, chosen by their god to accomplish many great things, including the conquest of the world—the Cemana-huac—all the lands they knew about. To depict anew such a version of Aztec history, King Itzcoatl ordered the burning of the ancient books.

Closely related to the new historical consciousness that began to be developed and transmitted in various forms, a new adaptation of the Toltec world view was conceived to affect the sphere of social organization. Each corporate group was to have its own symbols, its destiny determined by the calendar, its particular situation in space and time, its specific participation in the feasts and ceremonies, and obviously, as a final and extremely important consequence, its own role in the total social reality. A clever arrangement was thus achieved, closely linked to a history officially depicted anew which ultimately represented the historic development of the Aztecs, among other things the rise of corporate groups and their struggles for power among themselves.

This is the core of what the author describes as the "Aztec Arrangement." Within that structure all the groups, regardless of their ethnic backgrounds, could form and integrate a new hierarchical social, economic, religious, and administrative system.

A preface is not the place to accept or reject a historical interpretation. My intention has been to describe the most significant aspects of this provocative, indeed stimulating, new view of the development and integration of Aztec society. I can add that I am familiar with most of the indigenous texts my friend and colleague adduces here in support of his thesis. I have employed many of these same testimonies to let the Aztecs speak for themselves, as was my aim in *Aztec Thought and Culture* and *The Ancient Mexicans Through Their Chronicles and Songs*. Rudolf van Zantwijk goes much further. He is entitled to do so. His persistent research and his knowledge of the texts are his credentials.

The reader, whether specialist or generalist interested in Meso-american culture, will discover here a work that challenges some of the prevailing interpretations. Applying a critical eye, he may disagree with the author's ideas, but I am inclined to believe that he will welcome as a refreshing contribution this new study of the social history of ancient Mexico.

Institute of Historical Research
National University of Mexico
April, 1982

Preface

WHEN I began writing this Preface, seeking to describe the origin of my work and place it in the context of Aztec studies, I realized that the remote origin of this book lies in a personal experience I had as a child. In 1941, after receiving what was then the normal preparation of European youth in the cultural anthropology of the New World by way of the books of Karl May, I happened to read an article about the conquest of Mexico and Aztec culture in an old illustrated magazine that I found in my grandmother's house. Modern forms of human sacrifice were beginning to be practiced in our new and alarming European order of things of that time. Thus there was a double shock: it became clear to me that Indians could be quite different from and more culturally developed than the romantic heroes of Karl May, and at the same time they resembled in some respects the German conquerors of my youth. An enduring interest had been aroused.

In secondary school I began studying Spanish and Nahuatl, the Aztec language. I had to teach myself, and I was the first to cut the pages of old Spanish colonial grammars and more recent French grammars of Nahuatl that for years had been stored unnoticed in the library of the University of Amsterdam. At the same school, a few classes more advanced than I, was R. Thomas Zuidema, now a member of the faculty of the University of Illinois. As a boy Tom and I lived in the same quarter of the city of Haarlem. We did not realize then that the future had something in common for us.

In the early 1950s, Zuidema was finishing his preparation in cultural anthropology at the University of Leyden, and I was a student in the same field at the University of Amsterdam. Zuidema was prepared in the tradition of the so-called structural school of Leyden, and I received my preparation in the framework of the dominant trend in Amsterdam: the comparative-functional method in cultural anthropology enthusiastically advocated by A. J. F. Köbben. Yet the quite different emphases of our theoretical preparation did not prevent Zuidema and me from collaborating intensively. He introduced me to his structural analysis of the Inca social system when he was preparing his famous study about the *ceque* system of Cuzco. Although I never shared completely his enthusiasm for Claude Lévi-Strauss, Zuidema had a decisive influence on my own interest in the field of Mexican studies. We were both convinced that the real meaning of a culture could be captured only by considering it from the inside, which meant that in our opinion knowledge of the native language related to the culture in question was essential. Apart from that we both recognized the importance of *versunkenes Kulturgut* (that part of the cultural heritage that is maintained either unconsciously or in secret) and the possibility of using dates obtained in modern field-work as important contributions to ethnohistorical investigations. I was aware of the concept of *versunkenes Kulturgut* from my childhood. Once I angered my mother when I innocently hung two ornamental balls near the top of the Christmas tree, where she had just placed a pointed silver ornament (in fact a phallic symbol belonging to the Teutonic fertility god Frey).

At first I was particularly interested in modern Aztec, or Nahua, culture and society, but my interest was always related to the historical background. From 1955 I maintained regular contact by correspondence with important Mesoamericanists, such as Miguel León-Portilla, Ángel María Garibay, and Paul Kirchhoff, in Mexico; with Rafael Girard, in Guatemala; and with Ernst Mengin, Gerdt Kutscher, and others, in Europe. In 1957, I did my first anthropological fieldwork in Milpa Alta and Tlacotenco, two Nahuatl-speaking villages south of Mexico City, where I gained my experience with spoken Nahuatl and my first face-to-face contacts with bearers of the remnants of Aztec cultural tradition. They had a great influence on the further development of my interest, for men like Miguel Vilchis Mancera and particularly his elderly mono-lingual female relatives informed me about the real subjects of the ancient Aztec world view. The same was done in their own way by Miguel León-Portilla and Ángel María Garibay, and I feel myself indebted to them all for the instruction and the enormous support I received from them. From that time I became a regular contributor to *Estudios de Cultura Nahuatl,* a journal of the Universidad Nacional de México.

After finishing my academic preparation in Holland, I returned to Mexico for a second period of fieldwork, this time in the Tarascan area, where I carried out investigations from the summer of 1960 until the end of 1963. During that time I served on the faculty of the Centro Regional de Educación Fundamental y del Desarrollo de la Comunidad (Regional Center of Fundamental Education and Community Development) in Pátzcuaro, a school for government workers from throughout Latin America. Also during those years I received the helpful support of Mesoamericanists Wigberto Jiménez Moreno, Pedro Carrasco, Fernando Horcasitas, Alfredo López Austin, Demetrio Sodi, and many others.

At the end of 1963 I returned to Europe and presented my doctoral dissertation, on the Tarascan community of Ihuatzio, at the University of Amsterdam, where J. van Baal was my sponsor.

In 1965 I became an "entrepreneur," inheriting the commercial enterprises of my father. I mention this here only because this circumstance stimulated my interest in Aztec merchants and the economic bases of Aztec society. In the same year I was appointed to the Center for Latin American Studies and Documentation, in Amsterdam, where I collaborated with H. Hoetink, the famous Caribbean specialist, who gave me active support. After serving for a few years as Hoetink's successor as director of the center, on January 1, 1971, I was appointed professor of Latin-American studies in the University of Amsterdam. Soon afterward I began writing this book. I had observed that in our knowledge about the Aztecs there was an enormous gap between historical studies and the theories about Aztec social organization. It was my ambition to fill this gap.

During a number of visits and attendance at international congresses, Zuidema and I discussed many parts of this manuscript, which was originally written in Dutch. At the same time there were exchanges of views about the topics of this study with Nigel Davies, Pedro Carrasco, Gerdt Kutscher, Horst Hartung, Franz Tichy, Bodo Spranz, Ulich Köhler, Rafael Girard, and Henry Nicholson. Together with my wife and our four children, they contributed much to the critical attitude in relation to my own work, and I consider theirs an indispensable contribution to an almost entirely individual undertaking. I thank them all for their important direct and indirect support.

Finally, I feel myself very obliged to Mrs. W. H. P. M. van Es-Jacobs and to Mrs. Suzan Boot-Caolo for their translations of the Dutch texts and to Mrs. Rosina de Koning-Gomes for her help in the preparation of the definitive manuscript for this enlarged American edition of the book.

Garderen, Holland   RUDOLF VAN ZANTWIJK

The Spelling and Pronunciation of Nahuatl, the Aztec Language

A BOOK on the social history of the Aztecs necessarily contains many words derived from Aztec language and culture. Apart from the fact that some of them may sound unusual to us, the repeated use of literal translations would evoke reminiscences of wild West films or the romantic Indian stories of our youth, and in this context I prefer to avoid such identification. Another, even greater, disadvantage in the use of translated terms and concepts is that they would make it extremely difficult to compare this book with other literature on the subject. These are the reasons why, as a rule, Aztec names and concepts are translated at their introduction but afterward are used in the original language.

To enable readers to gain some idea of the pronunciation of Nahuatl, the first thing they must realize is that the spelling of this language was created by Spaniards and their Indian apprentices in the sixteenth and seventeenth centuries. Therefore, Nahuatl is generally pronounced in agreement with the rules valid for the Spanish language of that time. However, compared with modern Spanish there are some notable exceptions:

The spelling *"ll,"* for instance, as in *pilli* ("son," "noble"), is not pronounced "ly," as would be the rule in Spain nowadays, but is pronounced more or less as in the English word *will.* Nor is *x,* as in *xochitl* ("flower"), pronounced as in actual Spanish, but just as before the sixteenth century the actual *jota* was spoken; this means that the word *xochitl* sounds like "shootshyeetl" in an English spelling.

There were a few sounds in Nahuatl that had no equivalent in Spanish. Therefore, the Spaniards had to create approximations in their spellings. Thus they spelled the Nahuatl sound *w* (more or less as in English *water*), as *hu, u,* or *uh. Huitzil* ("hummingbird") was spelled this way, or as *uitzil,* and pronounced "weet-seel."

Aztecs do not clearly distinguish between the vowel sounds *o* (as in *rose*) and *u* (as in *roof*). In any case, this difference in pronunciation never leads to a difference in meaning, but is merely recognized as a local or even personal speech variant. Therefore, one may find the spellings *xuchitl* as well as *xochitl* ("flower"), *teutl* as well as *teotl* ("god"), *calpulli* as well as *calpolli* ("ward"), and so on.

Another Spanish approximation of Aztec sounds uses two characters for the representation of a single sound. Examples are the Nahuatl consonants *tl* and *tz,* as in the words *tletl* ("fire") and *itztli* ("obsidian").

A meaningful and therefore important element in the pronunciation of Aztec words is the "glottal stop," called *saltillo* ("little jump") in Spanish. Unfortunately, most colonial and modern writers do not indicate this glottal stop in their spellings. Therefore, we sometimes have to guess whether the *saltillo* had to be written. Study of modern Nahuatl dialects gives us a number of solutions, but not in every question, because of some notable differences among the dialects. Because of the importance of the glottal stop with respect to the meaning of a word, I have tried to indicate the *saltillos* in the Aztec texts and concepts that I have included in this book. Various annotations of the *saltillo* were developed by authors who took the trouble to indicate this sound. The most general one uses the circumflex (ˆ) over the vowel preceding the *saltillo,* or, in vowels written in capital letters the apostrophe (') after the vowel in question. In this way the spelling *âtlacatl* (inhuman being, evildoer) means that the *saltillo* is pronounced immediately after the first *a.* At the beginning of a sentence the same word is spelled *A'tlacatl.* I have adopted this system in this book. The reader will better understand the great importance of the *saltillo* when he learns that *atlacatl* (= seaman), without the *saltillo,* has a quite different meaning. Other examples are *hue-huetlan,* which means "place of drums," and *huehuêtlan,* which means "place of old men"; *cemehua,* which means "of the same age," and *cemêhua,* which means "of the same personality, of the same skin"; and *ma ehua,* which means "may he, or she, rise," and *mâ ehua,* which means "may he, or she, not rise." There are many more examples.

One of the main problems with the *saltillo* is that its use is not, and probably was not, consistent in different dialects or even in different places within the same dialectic region. Actually *âmo* (= no) is spoken with the *saltillo* in many villages in central Mexico, but the same word is pronounced *amo* ("no") without the *saltillo* in other communities. More frequent in modern dialects is the pronunciation *ahmo* ("no"), when the *saltillo* developed into a guttural *h*. Probably this pronunciation already existed in pre-Spanish times side by side with the other forms *(amo* and *âmo),* for some Spanish authors used the *h* in the colonial period; *êecatl* ("wind"), for instance, is more often spelled as *ehecatl.* The same problem as with the word *âmo* exists in relation to the word *têuhctli, têcuhtli,* and *têctli,* which in all three instances means "lord" or "sir," and also "chief." The different ways of spelling this word demonstrate that its pronunciation was difficult for the Spaniards. The main reason is that the word is variously pronounced in different regions. Nowadays *teuhctli, têctli,* and *tecuhtli* are more frequently heard, but *tecohtli* also exists. I opted for the spelling with the *saltillo,* because this sound is predominantly heard in the short form *têctli,* and while this pronunciation is logical in relation to the root of the verb *tequi* ("to cut"), the word pronounced without the *saltillo,* has a quite different meaning.

Three Aztec words gained worldwide acceptance: *tomatl* ("tomato"), *chocolatl* ("chocolate" to drink) and *cacahuatl* ("cocoa," chocolate to eat).

The Aztec rule for accenting is very simple: word stress is always on the next-to-last syllable.

Abbreviations Used in Tables, Figures, and Notes

AC	*Annals of Cuauhtitlan (Anales de Cuauhtitlan*, ed. Lehmann, 1938)
ATl.	*Annals of Tlatelolco (Anales de Tlatelolco*, ed. Berlin, 1948)
CF	*Florentine Codex* (ed. Anderson and Dibble, 1950-69)
CFM	*Codex Fejérváry-Mayer* (ed. Seler, 1906)
CM	*Codex Mendoza* (ed. Cooper Clark, 1938)
CMex.	*Codex Mexicanus* (ed. Mengin, 1952)
CTR	*Codex Telleriano-Remensis* (1964)
CVB	*Codex Vaticanus B* (1972)
CVR	*Codex Vaticanus-Ríos* (1964)
ECN	*Estudios de Cultura Náhuatl*
ENE	*Epistolario de la Nueva España* (ed. Paso y Troncoso, 1940)
HMP	*Historia de los Mexicanos por sus Pinturas* (1941)
HT-Ch.	*Historia Tolteca-Chichimeca* (1942)
IS	*Informants of Sahagún* (ed. Garibay, 1958; ed. León-Portilla, 1958; ed. López Austin, 1961)
LS	*Leyenda de los Soles* (ed. Lehmann, 1938)

The Aztec Arrangement

CHAPTER 1

The Historical Sources as Starting Points

IN THE sixteenth and seventeenth centuries many Spanish colonial administrators and priests from Spain, and other European countries who had lived in the New World wrote histories of pre-Spanish Mesoamerica.[1] These European historians, of course, organized their works according to the standards of their own contemporary cultures. Some of them, Bernardino de Sahagún and Alonso de Zorita, for example, using data provided by indigenous informants, produced systematic works far superior to the usual histories of their time. Sahagún's informants, as a result of his studies, formed a close, enthusiastic group of native scribes who were interested in preserving the cultural history of their people.

In the second half of the seventeenth century interest in the indigenous cultures of the New World declined, and writings about them decreased in number and quality. During the eighteenth century a revival took place that for Mexico was represented especially by the Jesuit Francisco Javier Clavijero. Clavijero was of Spanish-Mexican descent, but, having been expelled from Mexico with the Jesuits, he first published his great work, the first complete history of ancient Mexico, *Storia antica del Messico*, in Italian. The original Spanish manuscript still exists in the Jesuit Archives in Mexico (personal communication from Miguel León-Portilla). The Spanish version, *Historia antigua de Mexico*, was published in 1958. Another revival of interest in the native cultures of Mesoamerica took place in Mexico during the second half of the nineteenth century. This new concern about the early history of Mexico accompanied the growth of strong national feelings engendered by the wars against the North Americans and the French. It was in those days that Alfredo Chavero and Manuel Orozco y Berra wrote their detailed histories of pre-Spanish and colonial

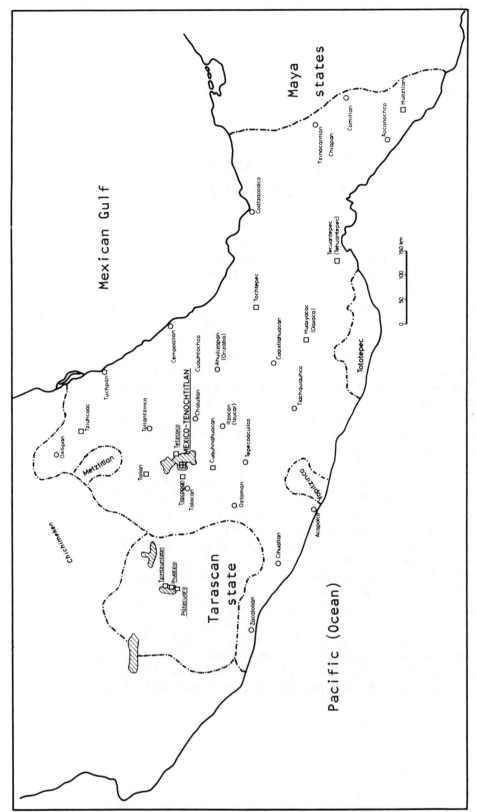

Fig. 1.1. *The Aztec empire.*

times. Also in France, England, and especially Germany a number
of Mexican studies were published. The development of Mexican
studies and the impression thus formed of Aztec society have been
comprehensively and penetratingly described by Benjamin Keen.[2]

Since about 1950 there has been a marked increase in Mexican
studies. In Mexico, Wigberto Jiménez Moreno, Alfonso Caso, Paul
Kirchhoff, Ángel María Garibay, Miguel León-Portilla, and others
began studying the indigenous historical sources, thus laying the
foundation for a new form of historiography and a new ethnohistory
of pre-Spanish Mesoamerica. Although these studies were closely
connected to the simultaneous development of a new approach
to the problems of the present-day Indian minorities of Mexico,
historians were evidently more interested in the study of calendars,
philosophy, linguistics, and culture in general than in the social
histories of the indigenous populations. Meanwhile, the works of
the more recent generation of Mexican historians and anthropologists have shown considerable development. Unlike their predecessors, these scholars have not occupied themselves exclusively with
the Aztecs but have studied them as one of many groups who
shared in Mesoamerican culture. According to these later historians, the Aztecs manifested Mesoamerican culture in their own
special way. Modern historians have also shown more interest in
the Toltec and Chichimec population groups, who had made great
contributions to the cultural progress of central Mexico before
the rise of the Aztecs. These later studies have stimulated new
questions about the origin of the Aztecs, for the explanation given
in the colonial sources has increasingly been found unsatisfactory.

About ten years ago two books appeared that are of the greatest
importance to our understanding of the Aztecs' early history.
Both works offer important new perspectives and can unquestionably be regarded as the first works that clearly describe the time
when Aztec state and society were formed. They are unique because they are based on close, systematic analysis of indigenous
historical sources. One of these works is *Hombre Dios (Man God)*,
by Alfredo López Austin.[3] López Austin, a Mexican anthropologist
and ethnohistorian, describes the development of Mesoamerican
religion, especially in the early days of the Aztecs. The other work
is *The Aztecs*, by Nigel Davies, which deals with the political
aspects of early Aztec society.[4] Davies's study gives a thorough
description of that period based on a wealth of indigenous historical data. Such data had previously presented problems to Mesoamericanists because of their many apparent contradictions, but

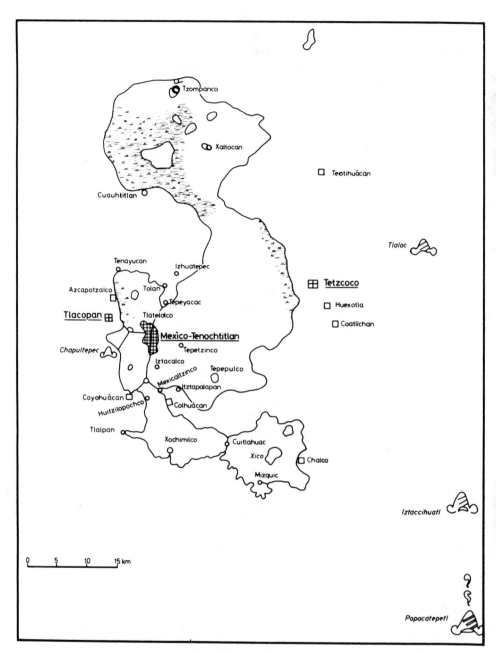

Fig. 1.2. *The Valley of Mexico.*

Davies has been able to resolve many of these conflicts and has thus considerably broadened our understanding of early Aztec political development.

Although both of these books deal with two different but equally important aspects of Aztec history, namely, the religious and the political, they contain little about the complex sociostructural processes which led to the development of the Aztec state. These early relationships form the main theme of this book. While the subject has been studied with much enthusiasm by Kirchhoff and others, their efforts have yielded only modest results. Others, possibly of a more practical mind, have avoided this complex topic, occupying themselves with more accessible subjects. The new approach presented here has been made possible by the two works mentioned above, as well as many years of detailed examination of the original Aztec hieroglyphic documents and chronicles. When this book was already in press Jerome A. Offner published his *Law and Politics in Aztec Texcoco* (1983). His provocative study gives ample attention to sociostructural processes in the area of Acolhuâcan and thus offers a very useful amplification of the conclusions presented here, based principally on data about Mexîco-Tenochtitlan.

To determine the range and nature of Aztec social history, such concepts as "Toltecs," "Chichimecs," and "Aztecs" must be dealt with. Until now, these terms have generally been interpreted as references to specific ethnic groups. In anticipation of my conclusions in this book, I wish to say now that there are good reasons for a new interpretation of these names. As will be explained later, historical documents show that, in spite of vague connections with certain ethnic groups, these terms have been used in historic times to signify certain interethnic conceptual systems. These systems were closely connected with the ambitions of specific peoples who aspired to develop socioreligious or sociopolitical organizations based on the collaborative efforts of a number of social groups, comprising "tribes," "clans," or communities of both a local and a regional nature. The above remarks do not apply to the same degree to the terms "Mexitin" and "Mexîcâ," which more clearly imply ethnic relationships and for which a more detailed description will be given below.

This work is based on four kinds of historical documents: (1) pre-Spanish documents in picture writing (codices), (2) colonial documents in picture writing (codices), (3) tales and chronicles by Indians or *mestizos* based on the codices or on information provided by native informants, and (4) tales and chronicles by Spanish and other European writers based on codices and information from informants.

Some documents in the third and fourth groups contain pictographic sections done in indigenous style. Many of the documents of the second group are "enriched" with explanatory texts written in roman script, either in an Indian language or in Spanish. These "explanatory" texts, which were evidently added at a later time, were sometimes erroneous and caused confusion rather than aiding in the correct interpretation of a codex.

These four kinds of sources together form the historical material that can be regarded as "original" in the broadest sense of the word. Unfortunately, pre-Spanish documents that deal directly with our subject are rare. Only three of the codices in the first group are valuable for this study: the *Borbonicus*, the *Boturini*, and the *Fejérváry-Mayer*.

Fortunately, the second group of sources is much larger and is, moreover, rich in data important to the subject. Many of these documents are copies of pre-Spanish codices that were lost during the Spanish conquest or during the first decades of the colonial period. The most important works among these are the *Aubin*, the *Azcatitlán*, and the *Izhuatepec*, followed by the *Magliabecchiano*, the *Mendoza*, the *Mexicanus*, the *Sigüenza*, the *Telleriano-Remensis*, the *Vaticanus A* or *3738* (also called the *Codex Ríos*), the *Xolotl*, and, finally, Diego Durán's *Atlas*, the *Mapa de Tepechpan*, and the Otomi *Códice de Huichapan*.

The third group of sources provides us with a wealth of complementary data. The works may often be confusing and seemingly contradictory, yet they are essential to the study of the Aztecs' social development. The most important documents of this group are *Anales de Cuauhtinchan* or *Historia Tolteca-Chichimeca,* *Anales de Cuauhtitlan* or *Codex Chimalpopoca, Anales Mexicanos, Anales de Tlatelolco, Crónica Mexicana* and *Crónica Mexicayotl,* both written by Tezozomoc; the historical works of Ixtlilxochitl; the *Relaciones* of Domingo Francisco de San Antón Muñón Chimalpahin Cuauhtlehuanitzin; and, of course, the many different texts provided by Sahagún's native informants found in the *Florentine Codex* and among the manuscripts in the Royal Palace in Madrid.

The fourth group of sources is also rich in relevant historical data. Here, however, Western influence is much stronger, and most of the original data have been adapted by the authors and included in a European system of interpreting historical data. The most important of these are by José de Acosta, Bartolomé de Las Casas, Javier Clavijero, Diego Durán, Henrico Martínez, Gerónimo de Mendieta, Toribio de Benavente Motolinía, Juan Bautista Pomar, Bernardino de Sahagún, Juan de Torquemada, Juan de Tovar, Mariano Veytia, Alonso de Zorita, the anonymous documents known as *Historia de los mexicanos por sus pinturas*, and the *Codex Ramírez*. These sources have been used cautiously and with restraint. This work is based primarily on documents of the first three groups.

The consideration that led me to establish the four categories above also led to a further subdivision of the historial data based on the important consideration of their origin. We can distinguish among sources deriving from the Tenochcas, the Tlatelolcas, the Têcpanecs, the Acolhuas (or Tetzcocans), and the Chalcas and non-Aztec writings dealing with the Aztecs. Depending on their origin, these accounts often differ in perspective and the importance given to particular historic events. For instance, the rivalries between and contrasting interests of Mexico and Tetzcoco and even those of the twin cities Tenochtitlan and Tlatelolco, have produced more or less contradictory data, which, by virtue of their inconsistancies, can be extremely illuminating.

The writings of Tezozomoc, Durán, and Tovar and the *Codex Ramírez*, for example, represent the Tenochca concept of history. The works of Ixtlilxochitl and Veytia and the *Codex Xolotl* were written from a Tetzcocan perspective. The works of Chimalpahin, Torquemada, Motolinía, and others take intermediate positions. Moreover, these contrasting historical perspectives do not simply vary from region to region or from place to place. As I shall explain later, occasionally widely differing traditions and ideas about the past appear to have existed within a single community. Sometimes these contradictory traditions were maintained for many generations as a valuable part of the individual heritage of corporate groups (*calpollis*, guilds, and so on) or extended families belonging to one community.

Of course, not all historical sources were written independently of each other. Some clearly show the influence of another known source; others can be assumed to have been based on a source that has been lost. Therefore, the repetition of data in more than one source must not be taken alone as confirmation of their validity.

Like all other products of human culture the Mexican historical sources have had their own history. Two events had a far-reaching influence on their contents and even their survival. One was the policy implemented by the Tlâtoani Itzcoatl following the revolution of 1426 to 1433, which gave rise to the Aztec state. Itzcoatl ordered the destruction of many historical documents that had to do with previous rulers in the Valley of Mexico. At that time Mexican history as it has come to us began to be written. Less than a century later another even more catastrophic event took place when the Spanish conquerors burned the state archives in each of the three Aztec capitals, Tenochtitlan, Tetzcoco, and Tlacopan, thereby destroying the temple libraries. Throughout the sixteenth century the Spaniards burned every surviving codex that they found. This destruction was a result of the religious fanaticism of the Spaniards, or in some instances it was done simply out of ignorance of the significance of the documents.

Once again historians attempted to rewrite the history of Mexico, basing it on the few surviving remnants of a rich cultural heritage that colonial administrators, soldiers, and priests had tried to destroy. Along with the material limitations facing these colonial historians, their efforts were considerably hampered by restrictions of a spiritual and philosophical nature. These restraints may have been self-imposed or may have been forced upon them by the spiritual and temporal authorities or by existing social control. Whatever the causes, the colonial historiographers were forced to express pronounced "antiheathen" biases in their works. They were so constrained by the church that a great deal of essential and revealing information about the Aztecs' social organization was ignored or even deliberately omitted. Invariably the data that were left out had to do with indigenous ritual or religious organization. The Spaniards wanted to eliminate the strong conceptual identifications that the Indians made in social groups, their indigenous patron deities, and the rituals that honored them. For that reason clear data about the relationships between Aztec social and religious organizations are almost nonexistent. None of the historical sources explain the complex of ritual connections between, for instance, such basic social units as the calpollis, their patron gods, and their priests. Data about these mutual identifications are rare and scattered; nevertheless, the few that are available enable us to trace the essentials of pre-Spanish Aztec social organization.

Besides the problem of insufficient data, which is always present in historical research, there is another difficulty peculiar to indigenous Mexican documents that puts us in the domain of ethnohistory, a broad and relatively new field of study born of the need to explain the historical materials of non-Western cultures. The "historians" of such cultures may have had a concept of history markedly different from our own. Myths, sagas, and legends about ancient periods are recognized as the precursors of modern Western history. So, might many of the Aztec "historical" records detailing the events of their past be perceived by Westerners. This would pose no particular problem if the nature of the accounts could be shown to be the expression of a certain evolutionary stage in the development of historical thinking in general. However, this all-too-easy explanation must be rejected. Among these apparently mythical data about the Aztecs are found other data that must be considered truly historic because they fit within a known chronological framework and refer to peoples and leaders, often related by kinship, who are represented as historic figures. For instance, Chimalpahin begins "Aztec history" in A.D. 50, which corresponds with a year, I Tochtli (I Rabbit), of the official Tenochtitlan calendar. According to him, the Aztecs were then still living in Aztlan (or Aztatlan, the White Land or the Land of the White Herons), the country of their origin.[5] Chimalpahin says that some of the Aztecâ (they who have come originally from Aztlan) and a group of their tributaries, the Mexitin, left Aztlan in I Tecpatl (I Flintstone).[6] That year more or less corresponds to the year A.D. 1064. Other historical sources, however, mention A.D. 1090, a later I Tochtli (I Rabbit), as the year of the exodus.[7]

It is well known that in Mesoamerican calendrical systems fifty-two-year periods are generally accepted units of time that had great ritual significance. Moreover, it appears that in Mesoamerica numerical units of twenty were also very important in ritual and organizational matters. Units of twenty days, twenty feasts, twenty social groups, twenty officeholders, and so on are commonly found in various contexts.

Still another common phenomenon in this culture area is the cyclical succession of units of time and space, which also appear to be closely related to each other and to social groups and their gods. From A.D. 50 to 1090 is a period of 1,040 years, which is exactly twenty times a "bundle" of 52 years. In view of these facts, Chimalpahin's "historical" data about the Aztecs' settlement in Aztlan in the year A.D. 50 raises some questions. These data fit a structural model that was common in Mesoamerica too neatly to be considered actual historic dates. For this and other reasons Aztlan has been regarded by many Mesoamericanists as a purely mythical land of origin.[8] For the present I accept their view, but

I shall indicate below where some historical authenticity may be found with regard to Aztlan.

Many of the myths and legends, in which tribal gods, their priests, and varying numbers of tribal chiefs are the most important characters, pertain to the period between the Aztec "exodus" from Aztlan and their "arrival" in the Valley of Mexico. The subject of these stories and descriptions is usually referred to in Spanish as the *peregrinación* ("pilgrimage" or "trek"). The historical validity of references based on such myths and legends is doubtful, however.

According to Walter Krickeberg, Aztec history begins in Coatepec, near Tollan or Tullan, but Kirchhoff sees the possibility that it goes further back to a time before the Aztecs' arrival at Tollan.[9] Some sources give rather elaborate descriptions of water control and irrigation works that are assumed to have been constructed in Coatepec by the migrating Azteca-Mexitin. They elaborate on the conflicts that developed among the Azteca-Mexitin as a result of these constructions; however, the Mesoamericanist López Austin does not consider these data to be historically correct.[10] Which of the scholars is right? Can it be that each of them is correct in a special way? Is it possible that each has dealt with a different aspect of the same question? These questions are discussed in the following two chapters. For now, let us look at the part of the so-called pilgrimage that most Mesoamericanists regard as "historic."

The historic part of the pilgrimage was the thirteenth-century migration of the Mexitin from Tzompanco, in the northern part of the Valley of Mexico, to Chapultepec, in the middle of the valley. During that period the first *tlâtocayotl* (autonomous administration) of the Mexitin was formed under the leadership of a chief who was descended from a marriage alliance between an immigrant Mexitin family and a noble family of Tzompanco.[11] An even more important reason to give special consideration to the Mexitin's stay in Tzompanco is found in the indigenous historical sources. Evidently the native historians regarded that period as a decisive turning point in Aztec history. All the sources agree that subdivisions within the Aztec group and the secessions from larger entities that may have existed during an earlier stage of the migration preceded their stay in Tzompanco. After describing the events in Tzompanco, however, the indigenous sources emphasize a great many administrative and social relationships, for example, kinship alliances entered into with other groups in the Valley of Mexico and conflicts with foreign tribes and peoples. The traditional tales of that later period refer primarily to relations between the new-comers and the indigenous population groups, whereas the earlier historical traditions relate mainly to internal affairs. Before I explain the significance of the Mexitin stay in Tzompanco, it is necessary to consider the circumstances under which Aztec history was formed. To do this, we must understand the historical models applied by indigenous historians.

There are three clearly recognizable periods in which the Mexitin (Mexîcâ) and the Aztecs felt the need to create their own history. The first was during their stay in and around Chapultepec at the end of the thirteenth century, after their migration from Tzompanco. This period coincides with their first attempt to form an independent political entity in the Valley of Mexico. Their efforts soon failed.

The second period began with the so-called foundation of Tenochtitlan, or perhaps with the rule of Ilancueitl and Acamâpichtli during the second half of the fourteenth century and lasted until the violent overthrow of Chimalpopoca and his military chief in 1427. This was a period of partial independence under the supremacy of the Têcpanecs—a Nahuatlized people from the western part of central Mexico, who probably were of Matlatzinca origin.

The third period (1433–1521), the imperial period, began after the revolution led by Itzcoatl, which lasted from 1427 to 1433. This was the most important period for Aztec historiography as we know it, if we succeed in eliminating recognizable Spanish colonial influences.

These three periods should be studied within the larger framework of Mesoamerican history. After the late-eleventh-century disintegration of the Toltec empire—the first important Nahua state in Mexico—the political aim of the remaining centers of power must have been to restore a central authority that had been dispersed. In their efforts to achieve their aim, all the groups involved claimed "Toltec" backgrounds to legitimize their "historic right" to play the dominant role in the larger system. The groups that were led by male or female chiefs who could prove Toltec ancestory had few problems in achieving this end. The others often employed one of two alternatives: their chiefs acquired the necessary Toltec ancestors by establishing kinship ties with Toltec families, or they "adopted" such desirable ancestors by forging their genealogies or the records of their ancestry.

The Aztecs probably made ample use of both methods to legitimize their political aims. It seems, however, that they applied them more often during the second and third periods of their political and social development; during the first period their political aims must have been modest and almost exclusively directed at obtaining autonomy over a very small area. The suggestion that they had far-reaching political and religious ambitions during that period must be attributed either to the politically inspired historiographical reform introduced by Itzcoatl or to Spanish chroniclers, who, influenced by their Roman Catholic world view, were inclined to represent the Aztecs as a "chosen people" comparable to the ancient Jews.

So far I have used the names Mexitin, Mexîcâ, and Aztecâ interchangeably, as different names for the same social group, a common practice in many historical sources. At this point, however, it is useful to distinguish among them. According to Kirchhoff, Aztatlan was the most northwesterly of the twenty provinces which made the Toltec Empire.[12] The name Aztecatl (plural, Aztecâ) refers to all peoples who regarded Aztlan, or Aztatlan, as their ancestral homeland. The name Aztecatl was also applied in a more restricted sense to the group that had cultural and political dominance in that region. In that context the Aztecâ probably represented the more elite ethnically "Toltec" segment of the population.[13]

The Mexitin were then subservient to this Aztec social elite and could be distinguished from them both ethnically and religiously. The Mexitin, viewed as a people belonging to a village or an area called Mexîco, were called Mexîcâ by historians. Thus the name Mexîca (singular, Mexîcatl) came into general use after the founding of the twin cities Mexîco-Tenochtitlan and Mexîco-Tlatelolco.

The explanation accounts for the simultaneous use of such names as Aztecs and Mexicans. Yet the basic problem in Aztec history remains that the "real" or "original" Aztecs are a mythical people, whereas the Mexitin gradually mixed with other groups and thus greatly altered their social system so that the people known later as Mexîcâ cannot be regarded as ethnically identical to the early Mexitin. Moreover, it is not certain that the peoples who were later called Mexîcâ formed an ethnically homogenous group. As I have explained elsewhere, the so-called Aztec founders of Mexico City were a heterogeneous population that included Chinampanecs, Otomis, and Chichimecs.[14] Tenochtitlan was named for Tenoch, who was an Otomi or whose name denoted one of the lineages of Otomi chiefs.[15] From the time of the founding of Tenochtitlan the name Azteca was apparently used to represent an interethnic communal relationship. This community was based to a great extent on religious and administrative organization in which the ties between religion and politics were very strong. Every increase in administrative power was inevitably accompanied by an expansion of the religious system through the addition of foreign deities and the ancestors of the social groups who claimed them.

Histories of Mexico written in colonial times and even more modern ones invariably represent the Aztecs as people who maintained their own identity from the time they left Aztlan, or at least from their arrival in Tzompanco, until the coming of the Spaniards. It is clear, however, that until the founding of Tenochtitlan there is no question of homogeneous Aztec society as a historic phenomenon. As we shall see in the following chapters, the god Huitzilopochtli, the true symbol of the Aztec ethic, was not the same deity as the tribal god of the early Mexitin but rather a Toltec god who was adopted by the "founders" of the City of Mexico.[16] The important deities of the migrating Mexitin, Tetzauhteotl (Wonderful God) as God of the Moon and Underworld[17] and Mexîtli as God(dess) of the Earth,[18] are the all-too-logical predecessors of the heavenly god Huitzilopochtli of imperial times. These three gods represent the three vertical subdivisions of the cosmos as conceptualized by the Mesoamericans.[19]

On the basis of what I have said above, I have arrived at an interpretation of Aztec history that differs in some respects from generally accepted theories. In this introductory chapter I give a provisional chronological survey of the formation of the Aztec social system. The details and the most relevant data about this development are given in the chapters that follow.

The growth of Aztec society to the beginning of the imperial period around 1487 centers on five important changes or reforms in the social system. They coincide with successive periods from pre-Aztec to Aztec times that emerge from the historical material, each with distinct characteristics. By the end of pre-Aztec times there were several Nahua-speaking Toltec groups in the Valley of Mexico,[20] as well as some groups of Mixtec origin, all of whom were bearers of traditional Mesoamerican culture. This means that they had an institutionalized polytheistic religion; a strictly hierarchical structure of priestly, administrative, and military organizations; and well-developed intensive agriculture and trade. Among the members of these groups were specialists who applied themselves to the study of calendars, picture writing, education, commerce, and high-quality arts and crafts. Their main centers were previous Toltec capitals, such as Colhuâcan, Coatlichan, and the Chalco area. The economic basis of these population groups was intensive chinampa horticulture[21] and irrigation agriculture; the yields from both allowed for a dense population with a standard of living far above subsistence level. All of this made possible the development of a remarkable division of labor (to be discussed in chapters 7 and 8).

Besides the groups with traditional Mesoamerican culture or those that had Mesoamerican elements, there were many marginal groups in pre-Aztec central Mexico. Beginning in the twelfth century, while the Toltec Empire was gradually disintegrating, these peripheral peoples penetrated into the heart of the empire. Some, such as the Têcpanecs and the Acolhuas, were numerous and had already adopted traditional Mesoamerican culture. The Otomis, another large population group, were scattered throughout the area; however, on the whole they displayed little political or social coherence. The Otomis represented the most ancient population in the area, but by Toltec standards they were rather ignorant. Amid these large population groups were smaller ones that were viewed as semicivilized or even "barbaric." Most had come from the northern border areas of the Toltec Empire or from even more remote regions little influenced by Mesoamerican culture. These peoples, of various origins and descent, are known in Mexican history as Chichimecs (in Nahuatl: Chichimecâ).[22] One of the smaller of these groups who succeeded in penetrating into the Valley of Mexico was the Mexitin. Most of the Chichimec migrants admired Mesoamerican culture and tried to emulate it. Those who stubbornly clung to their own ways of life and continued to be hostile to the "Toltecized" groups were eventually overcome by their acculturated relatives.[23] Few details of Chichimec social organizations are known. Probably there were a great many differences among them, and it is possible that a kind of clan organization was common.

The calpolli was the basic unit of the Nahua-Toltec social organization. There are various theories about the nature of the calpolli. It has been variously described as a clan, a town, a village ward, a parish, an agriculture-based cooperative, and so on. As will be seen in chapter 4, the indigenous historical sources describe the calpolli as a group of families related by kinship or proximity over a long period of time. This group of families was connected to one or more families of local chiefs who were the traditional officeholders in the dual secular administration characteristic of Mesoamerica. The elite families provided the members of the calpolli with arable land or with nonagricultural occupations. In return, the nonelites of the calpolli performed various services for their chiefs. The most important historical sources on the calpollis of precolonial times are the studies by Pedro Carrasco and the work of Zorita, both of which confirm this interpretation.[24] A study by Luis Reyes García (1977) on the social organization of southern Puebla in early colonial times emphasizes the links between the Toltec tradition and the calpolli system, which was absent from areas not subject to Toltec influence. Typically the calpollis were ethnically homogeneous; however, there is evidence that some were not.

By the end of the thirteenth century the efforts of the Mexitin to create a small, independent state in and around Chapultepec had failed. Before their defeat they had fought a hard battle against the Chinampanec population of the lake district. That battle must have been the origin of the myths and legends about the struggle between the Mexitin priest and at the same time military chief called Cuauhtlequetzqui and the priest of the Chalmecâ named Copil.[25]

Some calpollis of Chinampanecs, Otomis, and refugee Toltecs had previously settled in the lakeshore swamps near Chapultepec, Coyohuâcan, and Azcapotzalco, where they lived in a "culture of poverty." They named the swamp area Toltzalan-Acatzalan (Between Rushes and Reeds).[26] When the alliance of several powerful groups including the Têcpanecs, the Colhuas, and the inhabitants of Xaltocan put an end to the Mexitin's struggle for power, some of the defeated chiefs, accompanied by kinsmen and followers, went into hiding in the swamps of Toltzalan-Acatzalan. There they found refuge with the indigenous population. Another, probably larger, group of defeated Mexitin was deported to Colhuâcan, where they occupied subservient positions in society. Yet even in this previously Toltec capital city the Mexitin resumed their struggle for independence. Many of them escaped from Colhuâcan and joined the other Mexitin living in the swamps. Thus in the first half of the fourteenth century an entirely new community came to be formed in the lakeshore swamps of Lake Tetzcoco. The original calpollis of the Toltecs, Chinampanecs, and Otomis accepted into their midst some homogeneous calpollis of Mexitin and others consisting of Mexitin and related Colhuas. The families of the chiefs of all these calpollis allied themselves through the marriages of their sons and daughters, and these marriages contributed to the formation of a new political and social system that can be called "Aztec."

During this early stage the "Chichimec" element of the population was evidently powerful, for the Chichimecatêuhctli (Chichimec chief) Acacihtli (Reed Hare) held the important office of Têcpanecatl (Man of the Palace, the head of the external administration).[27] This was one of the two highest ranks in the oligarchic administration of the community at that time. The calpolli leaders and the priests of the two Aztec communities of Mexîco-Tenochtitlan and Mexîco-Tlatelolco were the local administrators but had little or no authority outside their very restricted territories and were themselves subject to the authority of others. From the beginning Tlatelolco was, in fact, dominated by the Têcpanec administration in Azcapotzalco, while Tenochtitlan, which had at first tried to maintain close relations with the former Toltec capital cities Colhuâcan and Coatlichan, was soon obliged to accept the same Têcpanec supreme authority. The scarcity of economic resources in the two communities made it necessary for the Aztecs to offer their services as military mercenaries to the Têcpanec administration. This led to a marked improvement in the Aztecs' military skill, while making the Têcpanec government more and more dependent on the support of Aztec warriors. Thus the Aztecs gained political influence. Tlatelolco tried to increase its political influence by establishing close relations with the court at Azcapotzalco and by accepting Têcpanec princes as governors. Tenochtitlan preferred to conduct a more autonomous, yet more dangerous, policy. It established its own *tlâtocayotl* (state government) by joining a princess of Toltec blood, Ilancueitl, who was made ruler, with a chief of mixed Aztec and Colhua descent named Acamâpichtli, who was given authority over internal affairs.

Thus the communities entered the second stage of their social and political development, the first Aztec era. Tenochtitlan and Tlatelolco developed into cities with strong economic bases; there was considerable expansion of chinampa horticulture, as well as growth in trade and military power. Acamâpichtli, who became the first Aztec ruler of Tenochtitlan, also married daughters of all the calpolli chiefs and with them created a new line of nobles. These Aztec elite were no longer subject to the internal administrations of the calpollis, whose political influence diminished. The important chiefly lineages lost their traditional power, and the reckoning of descent through both lines to determine status became less important. At the same time opportunities for social mobility through military achievement increased. Accompanying these processes was the continuing adaptation to Mesoamerican culture whereby Aztec society became more and more "Toltecized." The Toltec and Chinampanec elements in this society, represented by Ilancueitl and her ties with Tlacatêcpan's calpolli and by Acamâpichtli and his ties with Chalman's calpolli, came to receive greater emphasis.[28] The Otomi and Mexi elements lost their dominant positions as the Tenoch, Mexitli, and other noble families of Otomi and Chichimec origin lost much of their former influence. The political suicide of Chimalpopoca in 1427 marked the end of the second stage.[29]

A violent revolutionary movement managed to bring about drastic political changes in the Têcpanec Empire. Within a period of six years Itzcoatl, Tlacayelel, Nezahualcoyotl, and Motêuhczoma Ilhuicamina emerged as leaders of a new state that soon equaled and later surpassed the power and extent of the former Toltec Empire. This powerful new administration accelerated Aztec social development to a degree never before achieved. Three of the four highest-ranking leaders of the new regime lacked the ancestors required by traditional Toltec standards for the legitimate execution of their offices. Although all four of them supported a policy of "restoration" of Toltec administrative institutions, they permanently excluded from the highest government offices the descendants of Chimalpopoca, who were the legitimate heirs to them. That was reason enough to rewrite their history and burn the old chronicles.

There was yet another motive for changing the old histories. The political pretensions of Tenochtitlan as the center of the restoration movement and as the most important capital of the new empire made it necessary for the new administration to manifest its own clearly recognizable identity that could serve as a bridge to the Toltec past. This connection was to be found in the "history" of the Mexitin. The important ties to the Toltecs were made by inventing the particulars of the "trek" from the mythical border area, Aztlan, by way of Tollan and Coatepec, to Tzompanco and the Valley of Mexico. One might say that the Toltecs of Tenochtitlan allowed the Mexitin to adopt the appropriate ancestors from the more legitimate Toltec calpollis, thus making their own political ascendancy more acceptable in comparison with that of other quasi-Toltec groups in the Valley of Mexico. This adoption of ancestors by fiat was "explained" in the newly cast history by legendary tales of "secessions" that had taken place during various stages of the "pilgrimage." In this context it is significant that the highest Aztec governmental leaders, Tlacayelel and Motêuhczoma Ilhuicamina, sent an expedition of priests north to Tollan with orders to "visit" Aztlan.[30]

The fourth stage of Aztec social development began after the unsuccessful rebellion of Tlatelolco. One result of that civil war was a drastic change in the socioeconomic organization of the Aztec capital. Tenochtitlan became a center for the production of luxury goods, making the social position of the merchants semiofficial and well regulated.[31] The ancestral gods of the calpollis lost their prominence and were reduced to *petlacontzitzquiquê* ("keepers of the mats and urns"), meaning that they had to stand in subjugation at the sanctuary of the god Huitzilopochtli.[32] In this respect they symbolized the servitude of the ordinary calpolli folk, who were *macehualtin* ("subjects") of the new empire with its strongly stratified social system.

During the imperial era, which actually began during the rule of Ahuitzotl (1486–1502), the predominant theme of the Aztec histories was that the Aztecs were the bearers of Toltec culture and were to a large extent descendants of the Toltecs. When viewed within the greater framework of all people possessing Toltec background, however, the Aztecs actually derived their identity through the Mexitin. The Mexitin, led by their god Huitzilopochtli, were destined to play a decisive role in the restoration of the Toltec Empire, which had been destroyed in the war between the followers of Huemac and those of Quetzalcoatl. In this historical context the Aztecs were the heirs of Huemac and his followers.

The Spanish conquest brought about drastic changes in the conditions that had enabled Aztec imperial historiography to develop with almost unchecked freedom. During the first half of the colonial era the Spanish conquerors promoted "anti-Aztec" historical interpretations with the political aim of destroying the indigenous imperial institutions. Thus it was possible to revive or popularize histories of a parochial and often chauvinistic nature typical of the first stage of Aztec social development. The tales belonging to these early histories had probably survived the Aztec imperial era only because they were handed down by word of mouth in the family circles of old calpolli nobility. Many of these families had lost their respected status before the arrival of the Spanish conquerors, and after the Conquest new conditions offered them opportunities to regain some influence as the right of their former high status.

The Spanish rulers encouraged the families of local native chiefs to liberate themselves from Aztec administrative institutions. That is why colonial chronicles contain a great many private histories written by groups that had opposed the Aztec regime and retained their own historical traditions.

For these reasons some calpollis in the northern section of Tenochtitlan handed down to posterity an early history of the Mexitin that differed from that of the calpollis in its southern sections. The social development, the legends, and the myths are similar in structure, but those taking the leading roles are different. It goes without saying that the internal contradictions in this complex of histories have greatly hampered the work of Mesoamericanists. On the other hand, they have enriched the body of historical materials, which yielded, for example, nearly two hundred different names of families and individuals said to have been involved in the Aztec "founding" of Tenochtitlan and Tlatelolco. By associating these names with those of gods, officials, social groups, occupations, directions, territories, and calendar dates, we can describe in detail the social organization of Tenochtitlan, the most important Aztec capital. Through knowledge obtained in this manner, we can gain essential new insights into the development of Aztec society and the Aztecs' concept of their own history. Achieving that goal is the aim of this book.

CHAPTER 2

"From the Mists, from the Clouds, from the Seven Caves": History or Myth?

To GIVE a correct description of the indigenous Mexicans' view of their past, it is necessary first to explain some ideas basic to the world view of the Mesoamerican civilizations. In all these societies there were specific identifications with time, direction, place, color, one or more deities, and social groups. These elements served as parts of a rigidly structured world order, and in turn, this world order was part of a similarly structured cosmic system.

Three organizational principles formed the basis of these structured conceptions: (1) a dual principle, through which the male and the female aspects of deities were associated, as were the internal and external aspects of society—matters concerning peace and war or civil and military affairs and all matters concerning the nuclear part of an empire and its relationship to the outlying provinces; (2) a triple principle, which was associated with the vertical structure of the universe, consisting of underworld, earth, and heaven (or sky); and (3) a quadruple principle, connected with the four quarters of the compass in the sense that each of the four sectors of the earth faces one of those directions. These three principles were woven into a total system and applied to the organization of the state.

The state usually had three major cities, which were seats of regional government, and four territorial parts. Each of these seven areas was ruled by a dual chieftainship. Naturally, these simple organizational features were developed into much more complex systems, but even then the basic principles are easy to recognize.

The geographical shape of Mexico and Central America resembles a funnel that narrows on the south, making central Mexico and southward the inevitable meeting place of the many peoples and population groups who migrated from north to south. They en-

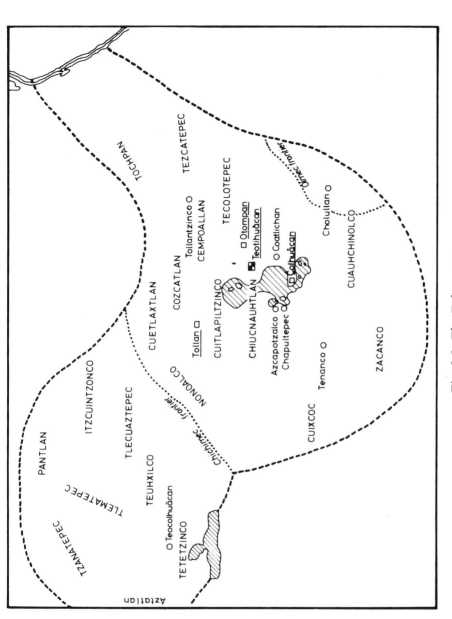

Fig. 2.1. *The Toltec state.*

tered the funnel over a broad stretch of land; however, as they moved south, they came in closer proximity to each other. Consequently, central and southern Mexico and Central America, farther south, have from time immemorial been scenes of intensive interethnic contacts. Even today on the isthmus of Tehuantepec it is possible to hear ten different languages and to meet population groups with ten different cultures within a distance of sixty miles. One can imagine that such diversity must have been more pronounced before the introduction of Hispanic and Western influences.

Perhaps one result of so many ethnically different peoples coexisting in a relatively small area was the Mexicans' early acceptance of the view that the "government" of an area should be composed of representatives from the various ethnic groups inhabiting that region. This did not, however, imply general interethnic fraternization or even a desire for equal rights for all ethnic groups. It meant only that no official discriminatory measures were taken against minorities. They were not harassed, and no ethnically alien groups were destroyed. On the contrary, such actions were clearly abhorred. This interethnic "tolerance," or tendency to accept ethnic differences, was closely related to the three principles of organization.

During the times of the so-called historical Olmecs and the Toltecs of the fifth and eleventh centuries, respectively, communities already consisted of two or more ethnically distinct groups under one system of leadership. These multiple structures of leadership naturally offered representatives of various ethnic groups many possibilities for unification under one administrative system. The late-Olmec state Tlachihualtepetl was governed by warlords of the Xicalancas and Olmec priests.[1] The Toltecs shared with the Nonoalcas the most important government posts in their celestial capital, Tollan, and all twenty provinces of the Toltec empire had an ethnically heterogeneous population.

As long as things went well, each ethnic group had its own social, political, and religiously organized niche in the system. As a result of the associations of place, direction, social group, and relevant deity or deities, each played a predesignated role. Often it was arranged for a particular ethnic group to undertake military functions and other priestly functions, while a third group was assigned the responsibility of the agricultural or economic life of the community. Thus usually one or more ethnic groups were specifically connected with military and economic affairs, while others were relegated to the service sectors. However they were arranged, these assignments always directed the performance of important communal tasks according to a rotation system that enabled each group to be, at some time, at the top of a specific hierarchy. In this way the dominant groups often managed to temper the resentment of the subservient groups. On the other hand, the subject groups were allowed to keep their own corporate institutions, as well as a functional organization that made them permanent potential rivals for offices of highest authority.

These interethnic institutions were, in fact, mechanisms that maintained the balance of power in a government that could easily disintegrate if high-level cooperation was disrupted. The indigenous Mexican empire builders reduced the risk of such a split by making their interethnic systems of government mutually complementary. That is to say, they divided government operations among the various ethnic groups in such a way that the state could function only through their cooperation. Each group was responsible for only a part of the system; therefore, no segment could independently regulate it.

Another, no less binding, force was the kinship relationships that resulted from interethnic marriages between aristocratic families. Marriages among the elites were directly connected to the dual structure of governmental institutions in two ways. First, such exogamous marriages expressed some cooperation between two ethnic groups in a single dual system and formed interethnic bonds between aristocratic families through which the husband's family was usually connected with the external authority of the chieftain. Second, there were endogamous marriages that confirmed the commitment of an aristocratic family to the internal government. Since descendants of these endogamous couples were related in both the male and the female lines to persons who had held internal government positions, they would also be eligible for those offices in the future.

Nearly all Mexican peoples had traditional rules, which combined hereditary succession with election, for the selection of principals. A chief was not automatically succeeded by a son or daughter; the successor was elected on the basis of personal qualities from among the legitimate candidates produced by the family. Through these relationships the concepts of ethnic identity or social and cultural identity acquired a meaning that to us may seem somewhat strange. A particular ethnic group was always associated with the same public offices, particular gods, important calendar dates, orientation of place, a certain cosmic direction, and specific aristocratic families. Under such circumstances there was little chance for gross ethnic discrimination; each group had a clearly defined place, and each had the important psychological satisfaction of exaggerating the importance of the role it played in the system.

The world view discussed above had, of course, a considerable effect on a people's ideas about its past, and subsequently these ideas pervaded histories of these ancient Mexican peoples. It is clear that each historic period was always associated with certain social groups whereas in Western history periods are associated with certain historic persons. Kings, queens, priests, and warlords in ancient Mexican histories were mainly representatives of and often merely symbols for social groups and their gods. Therefore, an unquestionably correct interpretation of such historical sources by Mesoamerican ethnohistorians can never be achieved. In indigenous histories the Mesoamerican political structures, which were composed of a number of corporative units usually with varying ethnic origins, were given symbolic roles that sometimes differed considerably from their actual historic roles. Histories originating from such a structure were mainly written for the purpose of giving a "historical" explanation for the interrelationship of such groups involved.

All great Mesoamerican peoples have produced myths and legends describing a migration from an often vague land of origin to the historically known place where the wanderers eventually settled. Several Mayan peoples, as well as the Toltecs, Chichimecs, Tarascans, and Aztecs, had such traditions. In pre-Spanish times these tales of origin were — certainly in the more important centers of power in Mesoamerica — recast and incorporated into the "official history" of the people in a way that gave legitimation to the rulers.

In colonial times this practice was continued by native as well as Spanish chroniclers. Therefore, these sources contain many myths and legends presented as true accounts of real events. In itself this practice is not surprising, but the remarkable thing is that until well into the twentieth century a great many Mesoamericanists uncritically accepted this form of historical presentation as an accurate representation of Mesoamerican history. Of course, all myths and legends may be based on real events to a certain degree, but as historical sources they should be used carefully and critically. The necessity of such critical analyses is clearly shown in Ixtlilxochitl's description of the Toltec migration to central Mex-

ico, in which he claims that "during the first twenty-three years
of their trek there was no sexual intercourse between the men and
their wives because on leaving their country of origin they had
sworn an oath that it should be so."[2]

It is clear that such "data" cannot be interpreted literally. In
general, such statements did not lead to serious misunderstandings
for the reason that they were obviously unworkable. These far-
fetched statements were either left unexplained or simply mentioned by scholars as strange phenomena. Much more deceptive
are data that in essence are similar to the above example but
resemble Western historical data in form. Because such data had
a familiar shape to Mesoamericanists, they were therefore placed
within a framework that fit the Western concept of the past. To
avoid making similar errors, present-day Mesoamericanists must
first acquire a thorough understanding of the nature of pre-Spanish
and colonial Mexican historiography. This understanding can be
achieved by comparing various historical tales from indigenous
Mexican cultures and by testing these data against findings from
a comprehensive cultural study. Of course, such a thorough study
cannot be included in this book, but a summary of some features
common to all indigenous tales about Mexico's early history can
be given here. Such a summary, however brief, reveals a great deal
about the nature of the tales.

The early histories of the Quiché Mayas, the Toltecs, the Chichimecs, the Tarascans, and the Aztecs share the following characteristics:

1. The land of origin is far away and usually said to be somewhere in the north.

2. The departure from the land of origin takes place by the order
of a god or goddess, in consequence of a civil war or the suppression of one or more groups by another.

3. The people whose history is described always leave the homeland accompanied by other groups.

4. During the migration "secessions" take place, sometimes by
one group after another, sometimes by several groups simultane-
ously, as recounted in the "dispersion myths."

5. The departure from the land of origin always takes place at a
date that is the beginning of a new era (for example, one of the
so-called year-bearers, accompanied by the numeral I; see chapter
10).

6. The route to be taken during the migration is pointed out by

a god or a divine messenger, or by leaders possessing superhuman powers.

7. Final settlement is ordained by supernatural omens and sometimes accompanied by elaborate ritual ceremonies.

Pre-Spanish Mesoamerican literature has many impressive myths and legends, among which the origin myths and the sagas are the finest. In the ancient chronicles exciting, almost intoxicating passages revealing wonderful worlds have been preserved in these early histories of Indian peoples and in their precious traditions of ancient wisdom and knowledge. Such descriptions of diverse peoples' lands of origin exist for the whole of Mesoamerica. Although only a few of these many tales of origin can be dealt with in this book, the selected examples illustrate the many others that could not be included.

For the Quiché Mayas of the Guatemalan highlands the history of origin is found in *Popol Vuh,* their holy book. It follows their tales of the creation and the gods and begins:

Balam-Quitzé was the grandfather and the father of the nine great houses of the Cavec; Balam-Acab was the grandfather and the father of the nine great houses of the Nimhaib; Mahucutah, the grandfather and the father of the four great houses of Ahau-Quiché.

   Three families existed but they did not forget the name of their grandfather and father, those who propagated and multiplied there in the East. The Tamub and Ilocab also came, and the thirteen branches of peoples of Tecpán, and those of Rabinal, the Cakchiquel, those from Tziquimahá, and the Zacahá and the Lamaq, Cumatz, Tuhalhá, Uchabahá, those of Chumilahá, those of Quibahá, of Batenabá, Acul-Vinac, Balamichá, the Canchahel and Balam-Colob.

   These are only the principal tribes, the branches of the people which we mention; we shall speak only of the principal ones.

   And having heard of a city, they went there.

   Now then, the name of the place where Balam-Quitzé, Balam-Acab, Mahucutah, and Iqui-Balam and those of Tamub and Ilocab went was Tulán-Zuivā (Cave of Tullan), Vucub-Pec (Seven Caves), Vucub-Zivan (Seven Gorges). This was the name of the city where they went to receive their Gods.[3]

Place of the Tules (Tullan, or Tollan) and Seven Caves or Seven Gorges (Chicomoztoc in Nahuatl) are mentioned again and again by many peoples as their place of origin. Mexican peoples speak of another, Colhuâcan Place of Possessors of Ancestors, sometimes also called Teocolhuâcan, (Divine or Real Colhuâcan), to make a clear distinction between this legendary place and the later historical city Colhuâcan, on Lake Xochimilco. The *Historia Tolteca-Chichimeca,* written in the Cuauhtinchan area, near the modern city of Puebla, mentions Tollan and Colhuâcatepec (Mountain of the Possessors of Ancestors) as places of origin.[4] The place is described as follows:

Izcatqui in coliuhqui tepetl	Here was the crooked mountain,
in catcâ in atl xoxouhqui imancan,	the place of the extensive emerald waters,
in iztac tolin imancan,	where the white tules grow,
in iztac acatl imancan,	where the white reed is found,
in iztac huexotl in ihcacan,	where the white willow stands upright,
in iztac axalli imancan,	where the white river sands lie,
in tlapapalichcatl in yonocan,	where differently colored species of cotton grow,
in tlapapalatlacuezonan in yonocan,	where the multicolored water-lilies live,
in nahuallachtli in yonocan,	where the magic ball court lies,
in zacuan miztli imancan.[5]	where the yellow puma lies outstretched.

The *Annals of Cuauhtitlan,* also called *Codex Chimalpopoca,* tells this about the origin of the Chichimecs:

In l-Acatl ipan quizquê	In (the year) One-Reed the
Chicomoztoc in Chichimecâ,	Chichimecs left the Seven Caves,
omîto omoteneuh	that is the tradition, that
in imîtoloca.[6]	is told in their history.

Ixtlilxochitl also says in one place that the Chichimecs of Xolotl left Chicomoztoc for Tollan,[7] but elsewhere he calls their country of origin Oyome,[8] a name that is not Nahuatl. The same Tetzcocan historian mentions Huehuê Tlapallan (Old Land of Colors) or Hueyi Tlapallan (Great Land of Colors) as the oldest known homeland of the Toltecs. But he projects even further back in history when he says that the Toltecs passed through several areas during a period of 104 years (2 × 52) before they settled in Huehuê Tlapallan in a year I Tecpatl (I Flintstone.)[9]

After a battle against the related population of Tlaxicoliuhcan, in a year I Tecpatl, they fled from this area (led by seven chiefs and a priest called Huemâtzin (Great Hand). Two of the seven chiefs were of higher rank than the other five: Acamâpichtli (Hand Full of Arrows) and Chalcatzin (Jade Man). The other five chiefs

were Ceêcatzin (One Wind), Cohuatzon (Serpent's Beard), Xiuhcoatl (Blue Snake), Tlapalmetzin (Colored Agave), and Mexotzin
(Agave Stalk). During this migration each of the seven chiefs in
turn founded towns.

For eight years the inhabitants of Tlaxicoliuhcan pursued and
fought the fugitives. Only after that time did Chief One Wind
found the first town, called Tlapallantonco (Little Land of Colors), where they stayed three years. When they moved on, Serpent's Beard founded Hueyi Xallan (Great Sands), where they
lived for four years. After that Blue Snake founded Xalixco (Opposite the Sands), where they stayed eight years. Then Colored Agave
founded Chimalhuâcan Atenco (Where People Have Shields, On
the Shore), and they lived there five years. Next Agave Stalk
founded Tochpan (Place of Rabbits), and there they also stayed for
five years. Then the supreme chief Acamâpichtli (Handful of Arrows) founded Quiahuixtlan Anahuac (In the Face of the Rain,
near the Water), and they lived there six years. The other supreme
chief, Chalcatzin (Jade Man) in his turn founded Zacatlan (Place
of Grass), where they stayed for seven years. Thus in the first
thirty-nine years (3 × 13) of their migration each of the seven
chiefs founded one town.

During the next seventy-eight years (6 × 13) the process was
repeated. Following the same order, they founded Tuchapan
(Rabbit River), where they remained six years; Tepetla (Mountain Range), seven years; Mazatepec (Deer Mountain), eight years;
Xiuhcoac (Place of the Blue Snake), eight years; Iztachuexucan
(Place of the White Willow), twenty-six years; Tollantzinco (Little
Place of Tules), sixteen years; and finally Tollan (Place of Tules).
They arrived there in a year I Calli (I House).[10] Ixtlilxochtitl believed that the legendary town Hueyi Tlapallan was situated in
northern present-day Mexico, near the Gulf of California.[11] It is
interesting that Colhuâcan and Chicomoztoc are not mentioned in
this migration tale but are named in the *Historia Tolteca-Chichimeca*.

According to Muñoz Camargo, the "Chichimec" ancestors of the
Tlaxcaltecs also migrated on the order of a tribal god, Camaxtli.
They crossed water and came to the Seven Caves, whence they
proceeded to Mazatepec (Deer Mountain), Tepenenec (Mountain
of Dolls), Teotlacochcalco (Divine, or Real, House of Spears),
Teohuitznahuac (Divine, Real, or Original Place by the Thorns),
Colhuâcan (Where One Has Ancestors), and then the Valley of
Mexico.[12]

After this brief description of Mesoamerican origin tales pertaining to peoples other than the Aztecs, we now direct our full attention to the latter. Table 1 is a brief record taken from seventeen of the indigenous and early-colonial pictorials and chronicles. It includes the most important dates, starting places, places where they stayed for some time, and the most crucial events during the migration of the Aztecâ-Mexitin. Of these seventeen documents two, the *Codex Telleriano-Remensis* and the *Codex Vaticanus Ríos,* are in fact only one source; the second is a complete copy of the first. Since, however, part of the original *Codex Telleriano-Remensis* has been lost, both documents have been studied. It did not seem useful to include an eighteenth source, the work of Cristóbal del Castillo, since the fragments that have been preserved are only accounts of the beginning of the migration from Aztlan-Chicomoztoc to Teocolhuâcan. Of these eighteen sources thirteen say that the migration started in Aztlan or Aztatlan (Heron Land, Land of the White Herons, or, in a figurative sense, perhaps White Land). In the *Codex Azcatitlan* the depiction of the island of origin is captioned "Azcatitlan" in roman letters, but at the foot of the mountain a pyramid or altar is shown with the hieroglyph for Az(ta)tlan.

In the *Telleriano-Remensis* and the *Vaticanus-Ríos* the story begins with Chicomoztoc; however, probably the first one or two pages have been lost. The only other source that gives a description of the Mexitins' migration that does not mention Az(ta)tlan is the work of Sahagún's informants. Here the migration is said to start in the area referred to as Chichimecapan-Teutlalpan, the dry prairies in north-central Mexico, where in early times the seminomadic Chichimec tribes lived. Most of the sources give I Tecpatl (I Flintstone) as the year of departure. The *Annals of Tlatelolco,* however, say that the year was I Acatl (I Reed) and gives the day of departure as l Cipactli (l Crocodile). The *Annals of Cuauhtitlan* and the *Codex Vaticanus-Ríos* claim that the year was I Tochtli (I Rabbit).

According to the *Codex Aubin,* the *Codex Azcatitlan,* and one version given by Chimalpahin, those who migrated were organized into four calpollis. According to other data given by Chimalpahin, Tezozomoc, and many other chroniclers, the migrants were divided into seven calpollis. The *Codex Boturini* says six calpollis. To add to the confusion, in other sources the tribes or population groups that supposedly accompanied the Aztecs during the early part of the migration are also referred to as calpollis. There are also vari-

Table 2.1. The Aztec Trek

(A comparative survey of the most important historical sources with regard to 26 stopping places of the Aztecâ-Mexitin during their trek from their place of origin to Chapoltepec. (The sequences vary in different sources)*

	Chimal-pahin	Tezo-zomoc	A.C.	Codex Botu-rini	Codex Sigüenza	Codex Azca-titlan	Codex Mexi-canus	CVR CTR	HMP	Codex Aubin	CF, MS Royal Palace of Madrid	A.Tl	HTCh.
Az(ta)tlan	X	X	X	X	X	X	X	X	X	X		X	X
(Teo)Colhuácan	X	X		X		X	X	X	X	X		X	X
Chicomoztoc	X	X			X	X	X	X	X			X	
Quinehuayan	X	X								X	X	X	
Cuextecatlichocayan	X	X		X									
Coatlicamac	X	X	X	X		X	X		X			X	
Cuahuitlicacan	X	X											
Acahualtzinco	X	X			X								
Coatepec	X	X	X	X		X	X		X			X	
Tollan	X	X	X	X		X	X		X		X	X	X
Atlitlalacyan	X	X		X	X		X		X		X	X	
Apazco	X			X	X	X	X		X			X	
Atotonil(ton)co		X							X			X	
Tequixquiac							X		X			X	
Citlaltepec			X		X								
Tzompanco	X	X	X	X	X	X	X	X	X	X	X	X	X
Cuauhtitlan			X		X	X	X		X	X			X
Ehecatepec	X	X	X	X		X		X	X	X		X	
Tolpetlac		X	X	X	X	X		X	X	X	X	X	
Huixach(ti)tlan		X	X	X		X		X		X			
Tecpayocan	X	X	X	X		X	X	X		X		X	
Azcapotzalco	X			X†		X		X		X			
Pantitlan	X		X	X	X	X	X			X			
Popotlan	X		X	X						X			
Atlacuihuayan	X	X		X								X	
Chapoltepec	X	X	X	X	X	X	X	X	X	X	X	X	X

*For abbreviations of codices, see list of abbreviations preceding notes.   †Amalinalpan, a ward of Azcapotzalco, is mentioned here.

ous traditional stories about those groups, which the pictographs *Boturini* and *Azcatitlan* show as the Matlatzincas, the Têcpanecs, the Tlahuicas, the Acolhuas, the Cuitlahuacas, the Xochimilcas, the Chalcas, and the Huexotzincas, eight in all. The *Annals of Tlatelolco* say that the Têcpanecs of Azcapotzalco, the Xochimilcas, the Chalcas, the Acolhuas, the Huexotzincas, the Colhuas, the Cuitlahuacas, the Mizquicas, the Cuauhnahuacas, the Cohuixcas, the Matlatzincas, and the Malinalcas—that is twelve groups with their leaders—left Aztlan before the Mexîcâ. The Mexîcâ are said to have remained behind with the Cuaochpanmê (the later Huacúxecha-Chichimecs of Michoacán) and the Matlactezcahuâquê (who were related to the Cuaochpanmê).[13] The *Codex Mexicanus* shows the secession of seven accompanying groups in Chicomoztoc-Quinehuayan. These are the Xochimilcas, the Malinalcas, the Acolhuas, the Cuitlahuacas, the Têcpanecs, the Mizquicas, and the Chalcas.[14] The route that the Aztecs are supposed to have followed from Aztatlan-Chicomoztoc also differs in the various sources, but they agree on a northern origin, and it is generally assumed that the route ran without many deviations from Coatlicamac (near Acahualtzinco) to Coatepec and Tollan and then by way of Tzompanco to Chapultepec. Only Tezozomoc, who describes a western detour by way of Pátzcuaro in Michoacán, and Sahagún, who suggests a long eastern detour by way of Tamoanchan through central Mesoamerica, show much divergence from other sources.

The foregoing accounts of the origin of the Aztecs differ in many respects but agree in several particulars. The points of agreement however, also coincide with events and places in the origin tales of other Mesoamerican peoples. Clearly the Seven Caves, the Place (or Mountain) of One's Ancestors, and the White Land, or Land of Herons, are mythical places, which might be situated anywhere and might belong to different peoples. In other words, these names might well have been given to more than one place. While Colhuâcatepec (Mountain of One's Ancestors) is certainly acceptable as a place-name, Chicomoztoc (Seven Caves) may have been used symbolically to represent many places in Mesoamerica. The number seven expresses the unification of the quadripartite surface of the earth and the tripartite celestial axis; therefore, a population group consisting of seven parts may serve as a model for one of the simplest socioadministrative organizations. Anyone with doubts about Az(ta)tlan should read Chimalpahin, who says of the Mexitin: ". . . mixtitlan ayauhtitlan in oquizacô" (". . . they emerged from a foggy land, a land full of mists"),[15] an expression used verbatim by the Aztec high priest Coatzin in 1524, when, at the conference with the first twelve missionaries from Europe, he described his concept of the origin of the Spaniards, who in the eyes of the Aztecs came from an unknown, mysterious world.[16] The detailed descriptions given especially by Chimalpahin, Tezozomoc, and Castillo are in apparent contradiction with this mythical nature of Aztlan and its inhabitants. They say that Az(ta)tlan is a land surrounded by water, as can be seen in the ancient pictorial writings; and they also give details about the inhabitants and their rulers. The Aztecâ, who dominated this land, lived on the island or peninsula Az(ta)tlan proper. They had many gods (indicating a Mesoamerican or "Toltec" culture), and they were ruled by a king whose name was Motêuhczoma (Grave, or Angry, Lord). In their region the Mexitin, who were lakeshore people and occupied themselves with fishing and shooting waterfowl, lived as their vassals. The Cuextecâ (Huaxtecs), who had only to a degree adapted to Mesoamerican culture, also lived there. The Aztecâ were thought to have oppressed and exploited the Mexitin, who practiced a different religion. They worshiped, above all, the Tetzauhteotl (God of Magic, or Imposing God), an aspect of the Moon God. The water on the shore where they lived was called Metzapan (Moonwater), and some chroniclers even try to find an association between their name, Mexitin, and the word Metztli (Moon).

Other, very different explanations for the meaning of Mexitin or Mecitin are also common. When King Motêuhczoma of the Aztecs died, he was succeeded by his two sons. The elder became king of the Cuextecâ, and the younger, whose name was Chalchiuhtlatonac (Brilliant Jade), became king of the Mexitin. The elder brother wanted to rule over the whole population as his father had. This led to a civil war, which resulted in the exodus of Chalchiuhtlatonac and his followers.[17] This story, though a legend, is one of the least mythical of the traditional tales that explain the reason for the migration.

According to a different, more widely known legend, the Mexitin had a chief, Tecpatzin (Flintstone) and a priest chief, Huitzil (Hummingbird). The tribal god Tetzauhteotl "spoke" regularly with Huitzil in response to the meticulously performed divine ritual that the priest and his followers continued to hold. One day the god told the people, through his representative Huitzil, to leave the country. According to another version, still current in modern folklore, Huitzil received this divine order through the tiny bird whose name he bore. It called to him again and again from the same tree,

"Tihuî, tihuî!" ("We are going, we are going!"), which is indeed how the song of the hummingbird might be interpreted. When the priest Huitzil had heard it over and over, he consulted with his coruler Tecpatzin. The two men decided to obey the order. The *Codex Sigüenza,* among others, depicts this legend.[18] In other traditional tales the god or at times the person who leads the migration away from Aztlan is called Mexitli or Mecîtli (Agave Navel or Agave Hare) and is supposed to have given his name to the people, who were then called Mexitin.[19]

In some instances, however, Iztac Mixcoatzin (White Cloud Snake)[20] and Chalchiuhtlatonac, mentioned earlier, are identified as the original leaders. Tezozomoc says that Chalchiuhtlatonac and Mexitli were the same man.[21] The *Annals of Tlatelolco* names Tlotepetl Xiuhcoatl (Falcon Mountain Blue Snake) as the first leader.[22] In the *Codex Boturini* the original leader is nameless; however, the name of his wife or female consort is given as Chimalman (Resting Shield).

The names mentioned so far belong to various ethnic groups. As has been said before, the widely cited places of origin are of a mythical nature and can be found in the traditions of many different peoples. In a way, the same can be said of Tollan (Place of Tules), the great Mesoamerican center of government and culture, which was held in great esteem by the whole region. The *Mapa Quinatzin* tells us that the name Tollan was even applied to Teotihuâcan. Cholullan also was sometimes called by that name, as was Cuitlahuac. The Mixtecs called Tenochtitlan Ñuucoyo, which also translates as Place of Tules. Since the chiefs' seats were usually woven of tules, the Place of Tules may well have been used symbolically to refer to the "foundation of government" or the "beginning of law and order and government." Thus the name Tollan may refer to a concept as well as to a real geographical place. The same can be said of the word Az(ta)tlan. There was a province called Az(ta)tlan in the northwestern part of a great Toltec empire, one of its twenty parts. This led Kirchhoff to assume that it was the land of Aztec origin,[23] but, however convincing his arguments may be, that interpretation can never contain more than a fraction of the whole truth. The frequent contradictions and the constantly changing combinations of characters in the sources allow for only one explanation. Because of the pan-Mesoamerican trait of correlating gods, groups, times, and directions and placing them within one well-arranged system, the various traditional tales of disparate population groups that

PEREGRINACION DE LOS AZTECAS

CODICE BOTTURINI

Fig. 2.2. *Departure from Aztlan for (Teo)Colhuâcan.* Codex Boturini.

belonged to increasingly interethnic societies were integrated into a single history. When in colonial times the indigenous imperial Aztec system, which had always played a leading role in the unification of these groups, had been destroyed, the different traditional tales were recombined in various ways, depending on the ethnic biases and the special interests of the native historiographers.

Of all the traditions described so far, the version told by Sahagún's informants probably most closely approaches the Aztecs' "official" history. This is plausible for two reasons: first, because most of the informants were former Aztec nobles and high administrators and, second, because it is the only description that consistently integrates the Toltec (and probably the even older Olmec) and Aztec traditions into one continuous history. This is exactly what we would expect of the Aztec government and its "Toltec" political pretensions. The grounds on which this "official" Aztec view of their history can be challenged are scattered throughout the works of the regionally chauvinistic, native chroniclers and pictographers of colonial times. In chapter 3 I shall disclose all the evidence and use it to compose a revised short "social history of the Mexitin."

CHAPTER 3

The Social History of the Mexitin

WHO WERE the Mexitin? Most historians agree that they were originally a Chichimec group. This does not clarify their identity, however, for the meaning of Chichimec is extremely broad and vague, including populations of very different ethnic origins. Mesoamerica knows few greater differences in culture and origin than those among the Tarascans, Otomis, and Toltecs. Yet each of these peoples is called Chichimec. What, then, are the common elements of all Chichimecs? The major criteria for identifying Chichimec peoples are a northern origin and descent from semi-nomadic groups of hunters and primitive farmers whose religion gave the deities of the sun and the moon major importance, and whose most common form of ritual sacrifice was deer offerings. Sometimes the deer offerings were replaced or supplemented by a form of human sacrifice in which the victims were hanged from scaffolds and then shot with arrows. This form of sacrifice was different from that common among the more highly developed Mesoamerican cultures, in which the victims were laid on their backs across a sacrificial stone and their hearts cut out.

All sources agree that the Mexitin satisfied these conditions: they were of northern origin, and Tetzauhteotl, their original tribal god, was evidently a moon god(dess).[1] The myths and legends about the migration show, however, besides these typically Chichimec features, a number of distinctly Mesoamerican traits that seem to appear almost immediately after their departure. These traits include their method of sacrifice and, with their arrival in the region of Tollan, their skill in the construction of hydraulic works. A tentative conclusion might be that the Mexitin descended from Chichimecs, who had adapted to Mesoamerican culture before leaving Az(ta)tlan. Such an interpretation would fit Kirch-

Fig. 3.1. *The Four* teomamas *and the eight accompanying tribes.* Codex Boturini.

hoff's view that Az(ta)tlan was an outlying Toltec province inhabited mainly by semiacculturated Chichimecs (including the Mexitin) but dominated by a local Toltec elite (the Aztecs).

Now let us take a look at the principal myths and legends about the migration of the Aztecâ-Mexitin to see whether they contain data on which to base further studies. When the migrants left Teocolhuâcan, they were led by several chiefs and four god bearers. One of the god bearers was a woman named Chimalman (Resting Shield). Her three colleagues were Apanecatl (Hailing from the Place of the Water Banner), Cuauhcoatl (Eagle Serpent) —so he is called in the *Codex Boturini,* but Tezozomoc calls him Iztac Mixcoatzin (White Cloud Snake)—and Tezcacoacatl (Hailing from the Place of the Mirror Snake). In the *Codex Boturini,* Tezcacoacatl is the god-bearer *(teomama)* of Huitzilopochtli. Although the pictorials and chronicles seem to agree about the god bearers, they often disagree about the number of chiefs.

The first important myth about the events that took place after the departure from Teocolhuâcan concerns the dispersion of the other population groups said to have accompanied the Aztecâ-Mexitin. In the *Codex Boturini* five leaders of the Aztecâ-Mexitin are depicted gathered in front of a small Huitzilopochtli temple behind which stands a huge tree with a severed crown. The number five associated with the tree refers to the five years that they stayed in that place. Nearby a sixth Aztec is talking to the chief of the Cuitlahuacas, who weeps upon hearing the Aztec's message. On either side of a pictograph of a house, which represents the calpolli of the Cuitlahuacas, are seven other houses. On the left are those of related Huexotzincas, Chalcas, and Xochimilcas; on the right are those of the Acolhuas, the Tlahuicas, the Têcpanecs, and the Matlatzincas. On the far right side of the folio we see the same six Aztec leaders weeping and encircling the statue of Huitzilopochtli. Huitzilopochtli addresses them, and they reply. Then their migration resumes. Chimalpahin tells this traditional story as follows:

Huitzilopochtli quimilhui	Huitzilopochtli told them:
"xiquinnahuatican in anmech	"Order those who accompany you,
huicâ in chicuei altepemê	the eight communities
in Colhuâquê,	of the Colhuas,
xiquimilhuican,	declare to them
câmo tiyazquê	that we shall not go
in campa otiyazquiâ	to where we were supposed to go,
ca zan nican	but that we shall
titocuepazquê."	change here."[2]
Auh niman oquinnahuatiquê	And then they gave the order
in Colhuâquê in chicuei	to the eight communities of the
altepemê.	Colhuas.
Auh in oiuh quimilhuiquê	And when they had told them all,
cenca ic tlaocoxquê	they were very sad . . . .
niman ic achto hualpeuhquê	therefore then they began first to come
	here, those said eight communities
inin in omoteneuhquê	of the Colhuas.
chicuei altepemê in Colhuâquê,	They left the place at the
quimoncauhquê	foot of the great tree,
in oncan hueyi cuahuitl itzintlan	which broke down above their
in ipan poztec.[3]	heads.

In the *Codex Boturini* the great tree is shown with two human arms and many roots. It seems safe to regard this tree and its branches as a symbol of the originally close relationship that had

Fig. 3.2. *Dispersion of the tribes.* Codex Boturini.

existed among the Chichimec groups and was suddenly broken by
order of a god to cause their dispersal. Moreover, the myth provided the Aztecs with an explanation for their late arrival in the
Valley of Mexico that would show that they were not inferior
to—less Toltec than—the other groups.

In another myth, however, the tree is depicted in a very different way. This story and the following one seem to be part of
a much more generally accepted and probably very old Chichimec
myth, which may be found, for instance, in the *Annals of Cuauhtitlan,* which describes the creation of Chichimec rule through the
divine interposition of the Earth Goddess Itzpapalotl (Obsidian
Butterfly, or Butterfly of the Sacrificial Knife).[4] This myth can
be found in its most nearly complete form in the original translation of a pictorial known as *Leyenda de los soles.* In this elaborate
tale about the Cloud Snakes we are told that Cuauhtli Izohuauh
(Wife of the Eagle)—one of the many names given to the earth
goddess, who was also called Itzpapalotl—hides in a tree with
three brothers and a sister. They are being pursued by their kinsmen, the many Cloud Snakes, who, unlike Cuauhtli Izohuauh and
her siblings, refuse to worship the sun god. When they are encircled by their innumerable enemies, the tree breaks above their
heads, and Wife of the Eagle—that is, Wife of the Sun—emerges.
Her three brothers leave their hiding places to work such miracles
as causing an earthquake, a mountain to collapse, and a seething

flood. By means of these disasters they kill the Cloud Snakes and offer them to the Sun God as "food and drink."[5] Itzpapalotl is one of the names for the Mother, or Earth Goddess in the song to the Mother of the Gods, one of the ancient sacred hymns that Sahagún's informants reported, which also mentions her brothers Xiuhnel (Genuine Turquoise) and Mimich (Fish).[6]

Torquemada gives another version of this myth, which is probably based on a pictorial that has since been lost. He tells how a "witch," Quilaztli (She Who Makes Vegetables Grow), joined the Aztecâ-Mexitin in their migration. Quilaztli is another name for the Earth Goddess; here it refers to her as the eagle's wife, the wife of the Sun, and a warrior like her husband.[7] According to Torquemada, the "witch" Quilaztli could assume various shapes, and to mock them she appeared before the warlords Mixcoatl (Cloud Snake) and Xiuhnel (Genuine Turquoise) in the guise of a beautiful eagle perched atop a huge cactus.

The warlords, believing the eagle to be an ordinary though exceptionally large one, shot at her. At that moment she spoke to them, saying: "To mock you, I have done with it: do not shoot, for I am your sister Quilaztli." The two lords became very angry but turned aside. Later, when the migration had been resumed and they had arrived at Chimalco (In the Shield), she challenged them again, saying: "You know me as Quilaztli, but I have four other names: first Coacihuatl (Snake Woman), further Cuauhcihuatl (Eagle Woman), moreover Yoacihuatl (Warrior Woman), and my fourth name is Tzitzimincihuatl (Spirit Woman) and these names reveal my qualities and the power I possess." The two leaders were not frightened, but because they did not want to fight a woman, they turned away again.[8]

It is apparent that this traditional tale as recorded by Torquemada, the myth of the Cloud Snakes, was confused with that of Prairie-Grass Flower, which we shall examine closely below. Tezozomoc, in his *Crónica Mexîcayotl*, tells the same myth as follows:

Auh ye omîto	And, as has been said before
in cuahuitl itzintlan	the Aztecs stayed
huêcauhtica in oc ompa	there a long time
catcâ in Aztecâ.	at the foot of the tree.
Zahtepan in ohualpeuhquê	Afterwards, on their way to this place,
in ôtlica inpan oâcicô	they were attacked by
in tlatlacatecollô,	the man-owls (demons),
hueyi comitl itla	by the side of the globular cactus

huehuetztoquê
ihuan cequintin mizquitl
itzintlan huehuetztoquê.
Yêhuantin in quintocayoticâ
mimixcoâ
chicomentin;
in ce tlacatl
itoca Xiuhneltzin
inic ome itoca Mimichtzin,
inic ei in cihuatl,
inhueltiuh,
itoca Teoxahual;
auh in oc nahuintin
âmo huel nomati
in intoca tlatlacatecollô[9]

they fall down again and again,
and some of them fell down
at the foot of an acacia.
They were called:
cloud snakes
there were seven of them;
one man was called
Genuine Turquoise,
The second was called Fish,
the third was a woman,
their sister, who was called
Divine Array;
but of the other four
it is not known with certainty
what the names of those man-owls
were.

Huitzilopochtli then called his priests and the supreme chief Chalchiuhtlatonac (Brilliant Jade) and ordered them to sacrifice the Cloud Snakes up on the globular cactuses:

Xiquimonanacan
in on hueyi comitl
itlan huehuetztoquê
ca yêhuantin in acachto
tequitizquê[10]

Seize them in that place,
who fell down there
beside the globular cactus,
they shall be
the first tribute we pay.

These were, according to Chimalpahin, the words spoken on that occasion by the Aztec high priests.

When this divine order had been carried out, there was another, no less remarkable sacred edict:

Auh zan niman
oncan oquincuepili
in intoca in Aztecâ
oquimilhui:
"in axcan aocmo
amotoca in amaztecâ,
ye anmexitin."
Oncan no
quinnacazpotoniquê,
inic oquicuiquê
in intoca Mexitin,
inic axcan ye mîtoâ
Mexîcâ
ihuan oncan no

And then immediately
in the same place he [Huitzilopochtli]
changed the name of the Aztecs.
He said to them:
"Now your name will
no longer be Aztecs,
you are already Mexitin."
In that place they also stuck
feathers on their ears,
therefore they were given
their name of Mexitin,
and therefore they are now
called Mexicans,
and there he also

quinmacac in mitl,	gave them the arrows,
ihuan tlahuitolli	and the bows,
ihuan chitatli, [perhaps *chilatli*],	and the nets to catch [perhaps bird arrows]
in tle âco yauh	so that all things flying above,
huel quiminâ	will be successfully shot
in Mexitin.[11]	by the Mexitin.

We can now return to the *Codex Boturini* with a more nearly complete background with which to explain the pictures. We see the three Cloud Snakes lying on the cactuses ready for sacrifice. An Aztec wearing Toltec headdress bends over the third cactus performing the sacrificial ceremony according to Mesoamerican rites. Above this scene a speaking member of the Mexitin group is depicted. He wears a Chichimec headdress, is decked with feathers, and holds a bow and arrow. In front of him lies a *cacaxtli,* a carrier bag, which was commonly used by Chichimec seminomads. Obliquely above him is a flying eagle that has been struck by an arrow. The meaning of the picture is now clear. The essence of the myth, however, still contains many internal contradictions. The "Toltec" Aztecs are forced by their god to become "Chichimec" Mexitin, but at the same time they perform a typically Mesoamerican, perhaps Toltec, ritual sacrifice. Even after this event, in the *Codex Boturini,* they are shown wearing the Toltec headdress and clothes. In the *Codex Azcatitlan,* however, throughout the migration some chiefs are depicted in Toltec dress, while others wear Chichimec costume. In the *Codex Telleriano-Remensis,* on the other hand, they are all shown in Chichimec clothing for the duration of the migration.

The following myth about the migration concerns the abandonment of Malinalxochitl (Prairie Grass Flower) and her kin by the followers of Huitzilopochtli. It is a most interesting story and beautifully told by Tezozomoc. He describes how Huitzilopochtli decided to abandon his sister Malinalxochitl and her kindred while they were asleep, because she was an evil witch and sorceress who deluded people with false promises. Huitzilopochtli called the four god bearers to him and said:

Notâhuanê, ca âmo notequiuh	Oh, my uncles, as you know it is
in quimotequiuhtia	not my task, that which Prairie Grass
in Malinalxoch;	Flower considers to be her task;
in ompa inic oniquizaco,	I left that place
inic onihualihualoc	and set out for this place

ca mitl ca chimalli	because I was given
in onimacoc,	arrow and shield
ca yaoyotl in notequiuh	for war is my business
auh ca nelchiquiuh,	and with my breast and head
ca notzontecon,	[with all my powers]
inic niquittaz	I shall behold
in nohuian in altepetl	all lands
auh ca nitechiaz	and wait for people there
ca nitenamiquiz	and meet people
in nauhcampa,	in the four directions,
ca niteatlitiz	and I shall give the people
ca nitetlamacaz,	food and drink,
ca nican niquinnechicoz	for here I shall unite
in nepapan tlacâ.	all the different peoples.
auh ca âmo zannen	But my subjection of them
ca niquinpehua,	will not be in vain,
inic niquittaz	for it will make me behold
in chalchiuhcalli	the jade house,
in teocuitlacalli	the house of noble metal,
in quetzalcalli,	the house of green feathers
in quetzalitzcalli,	the beautiful obsidian house,
in tapachcalli	the shell house
in tlapaltehuilocalli[12]	the house of coloured rock crystal.

Huitzilopochtili and his followers then traveled quickly to Oco-pipillan (Place of the Torch Sons), then to Acahualtzinco (Behind the Dry Land), and from there to Coatepec (Snake Mountain), which was near Tollan.

Malinalxochitl was very angry when she found that she had been left behind. With her kinsmen she fled for safety to Malinalco (In the Prairie Grass), where the king, Chimalcuauhtli (Shield Eagle), offered her a loving home. A son was born to them, whom they called Copil (Crown).[13] From the "song of the Female Serpent," one of twenty ancient hymns recorded by Sahagún's informants, it is clear that Malinalxochitl (Prairie Grass Flower) is another name for the Mother, or Earth, Goddess called Quilaztli, Itzpapalotl, Teteô innan, and so on:

Malinalla nomac temi,	Prairie Grass fills my hands,
centli teumilco	the corn cob in the divine field
chicahuaztica motlaquechizca	is protected by rattles.
Aomey cuauhtli ye tonan,	Thirteen-Eagle, our mother,
chalmecatêcuhtli,	the chief woman of Chalman,
a itzihuac imahuiz.	takes a pride in her cactus.
Tla nech ya tetemili	May he fill me,

yêhua nopiltzin Mixcoatl,	he, my prince, Cloud Snake,
ya Tonan Yoacihuatzin.	our mother Warrior Woman.
Tonan Yaocihuatzin	Our mother Warrior Woman,
in mazatl Colihuâcan	the deer of Colhuâcan
iîhuitla ipotoca.[14]	is arrayed with feathers.

Close to Malinalco lies Chalman, the famous place of pilgrimage. But from ancient times the name Chalman also represented the entire southern part of the Valley of Mexico with its fresh water lakes and chinampa horticulture. Muñoz Camargo reckons the Chalmecâ (People of Chalman) to be among the oldest population groups in Mexico.[15] Thus the name Chalmec is synonymous with the Chinampanec, which became more commonly used in later times; like Chinampanec it refers to the populations of Chalco, Mizquic, Cuitlahuac, Xochimilco, Colhuâcan, and their subject areas, which, in fact, included Malinalco.[16]

The following important migration myth is the well-known story about the reincarnation of Huitzilopochtli on Snake Mountain, near Tollan. Special mention is made of the fact that, upon the arrival of the Mexitin, Coatepec (Snake Mountain) was already inhabited by Otomis, who did not at first welcome the newcomers.[17] In spite of the friction with the alien Otomi, so the myth says, a new conflict began among the Mexitin.

On Snake Mountain the Centzon Huitznahuâ (Innumerable Southerners) lived with their mother—or aunt—named Coatlicue (Serpent Skirt) and their sister, Coyolxauhqui (Face Painted with Bells). One day while Serpent Skirt was sweeping her place of offering to the gods, a feather ball fell out of the air and landed just in front of her. She concealed it in her skirt but later could not find it. When she learned that she had become pregnant, the Innumerable Southerners became very angry and asked: "Who brought this about? Who made her pregnant? She has brought misfortune and shame upon us." Their sister Face Painted with Bells suggested killing their mother. Serpent Skirt was very frightened when she discovered the plot, but her unborn child spoke to her saying: "Do not worry. I know what to do." The Innumerable Southerners led by Face Painted with Bells pursued Serpent Skirt to the top of the Snake Mountain. But she was not alone, for one of the Innumerable Southerners, Cuahuitlîcac (Upright Tree), assisted her along with Tochancalqui (He of Our House), who was her faithful servant. Cuahuitlîcac informed the unborn child of the progress made by their pursuers: "They have reached the

Skull rack; they are approaching Snake sand; now they are arriving at the top." At that moment Huitzilopochtli (Left or Southern Hummingbird) was born in full armor. Tochancalqui lit Huitzilopochtli's *xiuhcoatl* (Blue Snake). With this irresistible weapon he decapitated Face Painted with Bells and destroyed the Innumerable Southerners.[18]

Beginning with Seler, this myth has generally been given a cosmological interpretation. The Sun (Huitzilopochtli) was born of the Earth (Coatlicue) and drove the stars (Innumerable Southerners) before him, while the Moon (Coyolxauhqui) faded away. Without rejecting this interpretation, I would like to point out that, as is so often the case in Mesoamerica, a sociohistoric explanation is also possible from the data and may be the correct one. Tezozomoc related this myth in a very different way:

When the Mexitin had arrived at Coatepec, they constructed a temple for Huitzilopochtli, as well as a *cuauhxicalli* (eagle vase), a sacrificial vessel to hold human hearts. Then they built fifteen calpolli temples, one for each of the patron gods of the groups into which they were divided. Among these fifteen sanctuaries was one belonging to the Huitznahuâ (Southerners), one of the fifteen previously mentioned calpollis. Huitzilopochtli also laid out his *tlachtli* (ball court) and built a *tzompantli* (skull rack), on which the skulls of human sacrifices were displayed. Then they built a water reservoir, and the land was made fertile, full of willow trees, tules, water lilies, and useful water animals, among which was the red waterworm *izcahuîtli,* which Huitzilopochtli claimed to be "his flesh and his color." Then there were dances, and the familiar Huitzilopochtli hymn was sung:

Huitzilopochtli in yahquetl	Huitzilopochtli the warrior,
âco in ai in yôhuihuîhuia,	he is active up above, where again and again he follows his daily course,
ânen niccuic in tozquemitl	it is not in vain that I have put on my garment of yellow feathers.
ca ya noca oyatonac.[19]	For with me the sun has risen!

It is remarkable how Mesoamerican—even more so, how Chinampanec and Chalmec—this picture is. The artificial lake and its products, its temples, the skull rack, the sacrificial vessel, and the ball court are all manifestations of an older Toltec culture, not of Chichimec culture. According to Tezozomoc, the Mexitin, and in particular the Huitznahuâ, were so satisfied with their community that they wanted to stay on Snake Mountain permanently. The priests of Huitznahuac asked Huitzilopochtli to allow his subjects, the Aztecâ-Mexitin, to remain there since what had been foretold on their departure had been realized in this place. Huitzilopochtli, greatly angered, prepared himself for a fight. On the sacred ball court he attacked his aunt and uncles, the Innumerable of Huitznahuac. He beheaded Face Painted with Bells and ate her heart. Then he sacrificed his uncles and consumed their hearts. Afterward he destroyed their artificial lake and forced the terrified Mexitin to continue their journey.[20] This version implies a conflict among the charismatic priest-leader of the migrants, the priests, and a female calpolli chief, thus suggesting that we have indeed touched upon the social history of the Aztecs.

Later we shall return to this myth, but for now we shall deal with another migration tale, the legend of Tzompanco, which is found in two totally different versions in the *Annals of Tlatelolco* and the *Crónica Mexîcayotl*. The first source tells us that on Citlaltepec (Mountain of Stars) the Mexitin fought a battle against Tlahuizcalpotonqui (Feathered Dawn), the leader of their enemies. They killed him, beheaded him, and placed his head on a skull rack erected on the spot where the battle had been fought. Since then that place has been called Tzompanco. After this victory the indigenous people gave a woman to the Mexicans, who continued on their trek. Then the Mexicans lost their way in a fog that lasted eighty days; one group found itself in Chalco; another, the largest, in Cuauhtitlan; and others, in Huexotzinco and Matlatzinco.[21]

Tezozomoc described the arrival of the Mexicans at Atenco, on the present Lake Zumpango (Tzompanco):

In oncan chanêquê,	The people living there,
in tlâtoani itoca	who had a king,
Tlahuizcalpotonqui teuhctli	whose name was Lord Feathered Dawn,
cenca quintlazohtlaquê	accepted the Mexicans
in Mexîcâ;	with loving hearts;
quinnamictiayâ	They invited them to meet the jar
in comitl in caxitl.	and the bowl [they invited them to join their meals].
Niman oncan quimanquê	Then they built there
in intzompan,	their skull rack,
oncan oquîtoquê,	and so it is still
inic axcan itocayocan:	called:

Tzompanco.	Place of the Skull Rack.
Oncan quimacac	There Lord
in iichpoch	Feathered Dawn gave
in Tlahuizcalpotonqui teuhctli,	them his daughter,
in iichpoch itoca	whose name was
Tlaquilxochtzin;	Transplanted Flower;
yêhuatl quinchiuh,	she gave birth to,
oncan ye tlacati,	who were born successively,
inic ce cihuatl	first a woman,
itoca Chimallaxochtzin,	who was called Flower of Shields,
inic ome câ yêhuatl	the second was he
in itoca Huitzilîhuitl,	whose name was Hummingbird Feather,
inic ei itoca Tozpanxochtzin.[22]	and the third was Yellow Flag Flower.

In other versions, such as that of Torquemada, the migrants were given a friendly reception, but the king bore another name and gave not a daughter but a son to the Mexicans.[23] This son became the father of Hummingbird Feather (see chapter 9).

The following myth is an interesting sequel to that of Quilaztli-Malinalxochitl. When the Mexicans arrived on Chapultepec (Locust Mountain), not far from what was to be Tenochtitlan, they were attacked by Copil (Crown), the son of Malinalxochitl (Prairie Grass Flower). This is one of the most beautifully told Aztec myths; we might even call it a saga. It has been recorded in many different ways. Below are summaries of the most important versions.

According to the *Annals of Tlatelolco:* Tozcuecuex was still supreme chief of the Aztecâ-Mexîcâ when Copil, who lived in Teticpac, arrived. For three days Copil applied his magic against the Mexicans. Then the tribal god addressed the high priest Cuauhtlequetzqui (Eagle going into the Fire), saying: "Copil has been clouding your brain for three days now; send for Tenoch [Stone Cactus]." The two leaders consulted with one another and decided to go to Acuezcomac and Cuauhximalpan. There Cuauhtlequetzqui took Copil prisoner. Copil told Cuauhtlequetzqui that they were related and belonged to the same tribe but had been separated at Tzompanco. He also said that he had been ordered to fight by the chief Acxocuauhtli (Fir Eagle) of Colhuâcan. Copil told his daughter Xîcomoyahual (Busy Bee), who was with him, "Accompany Cuauhtlequetzqui, for he is your uncle." Cuauhtlequetzqui then decapitated Copil, took his head and heart, and buried the body at Acopilco (In the Water of Crown). He proceeded to Tlatempan, where he built a fire and ordered Tenoch to bury Copil's head at Tlatzinco. He himself buried the heart at Acatzalan Toltzalan (Between Reeds and Tules), on the very spot where the stone cactus of Tenochtitlan later grew.[24]

According to *Historia de los Mexicanos por sus Pinturas,* Copil was the son of the woman whom the Chichimecs of Michoacan (the Huacúxecha) received from the Mexicans. Copil was taken prisoner near Chapultepec when he went there to take revenge on the two Mexican chiefs. Ordered by Huitzilîhuitl (Hummingbird Feather) to do so, he dueled with Cuauhtlequetzqui. He lost the combat and was sacrificed. The victor buried Copil's heart at Temestitan and his head at Tluchitongo.[25]

Acccrding to the *Cronica Mexîcayotl,* in the year I Calli (I House, 1285), the wicked wizard Copil, son of Malinalxochitl and Chimalcuauhtli of Malinalco, decided to do battle with the Mexitin at Zoquitzinco, Atlapalco, and Itztapaltemoc. Copil, disguised as Itztapaltetl (God of the Sacrificial Knife), then returned to Malinalco. With his daughter Azcatlxochtzin (Ant Flower) he came to the Mexîca at Têcpantzinco (In the Little Local Administration Center). Thereupon Huitzilopochtli called his followers to arms, and the god (that is, his deputy, the high priest) met Copil on the little island of Tepetzinco (In the Little Mountain), killed him, decapitated him, and took his heart. He left Copil's head on the island where it fell, which is called Acopilco; he hurled the heart into the reeds and tules at Tlalcocomolco (Where the Ground Is Full of Holes). He then married Copil's daughter, who gave birth to Coatzontli (Serpent's Beard).[26]

According to the *Annals of Chimalpahin,* in the year X Calli (1281), Tenoch warned the high priest Cuauhtlequetzqui that Copil would lead the inhabitants of Texcaltepec, Malinalco, and Tolocan (modern Toluca) against Chapultepec, accompanied by his daughter Xîcomoyahual (Busy Bee). Cuauhtlequetzqui killed Copil at Tepetzinco, removed his heart, and ordered Tenoch to bury it at Toltzalan Acatzalan (Between Tules and Reeds). Tenoch did so on the exact spot where the great church of Mexico City was later to be built. There he made a sacrificial fire to Huitzilopochtli. Cuauhtlequetzqui married Xîcomoyahual, and a son was born to them who was named Coatzontli (Serpent's Beard). Cuauhtlequetzqui prophesied to Tenoch that on the spot where Copil's heart lay a stone cactus would grow, on which an eagle would alight tearing at a snake (still the insignia of modern Mexico). That place would ultimately be the permanent home of the Mexicans.[27]

The *Codex Ramírez*, the Tovar manuscript, and the chronicles of Durán and Acosta all include versions of the Copil saga similar to those of Chimalpahin and Tezozomoc.

The *Codex Mexicanus* dates the struggle with Copil at the year I Calli (I House, 1285), as does Tezozomoc in his *Crónica Mexîcayotl*. In this rendition Copil wore the pointed hat that was also worn by Quetzalcoatl and the Xipe priests.[28]

Early in the fourteenth century, when the Mexicans suffered a crushing defeat at the hands of the surrounding population, some of them escaped to Toltzalan-Acatzalan, the lakeshore swamps near Chapultepec. The *Codex Sigüenza* depicts this defeat in a striking way. The victors carried away men, women, and children to many places in the Valley of Mexico, and the largest group of defeated Mexicans were made serfs to the inhabitants of Colhuâcan.

The last legend that we shall examine took place before the founding of Tenochtitlan. The Mexicans had lived at Colhuâcan for a long time and had been partly assimilated by the local population, and more than once they had served as auxiliary military forces for the ruling chiefs. But, because they had been obstinate and troublesome subjects, the Colhua chiefs allowed them to settle as an independent group in an undesirable area of dry lava soil. There, at Tizaapan (Chalk Current), they built a temple for Yaocihuatl (Warrior Woman), who was another aspect of Quilaztli-Itzpapalotl-Malinalxochitl and represented the warlike form of the Mother, or Earth Goddess. Huitzilopochtli ordered the Mexicans to ask the Colhua chief, Achitometl, to relinquish his daughter to the temple. The poor father, believing that she was to become a priestess to Yaocihuatl, complied, but the Mexicans sacrificed and flayed her. A priest, wearing her skin, performed a dance at the dedication feast for the temple, to which her father had been invited and given a seat of honor. This act brought on a civil war at Colhuâcan and the flight of the Mexicans, who joined the earlier refugees from Chapultepec in the marshes of Toltzalan-Acatzalan.[29]

An examination of the myths shows the following consistencies: the deities in the myths appear in both Chichimec and Toltec forms; the population groups in these stories consist of Chichimecs, Otomis, Chalmecs, and Toltecs; the historical nature of these traditional tales becomes more pronounced as the migration proceeds; the first close contact with a foreign group took place at Tzompanco, which, whatever the nature of the contact may have been, resulted in an important marriage; and all the decapitation myths

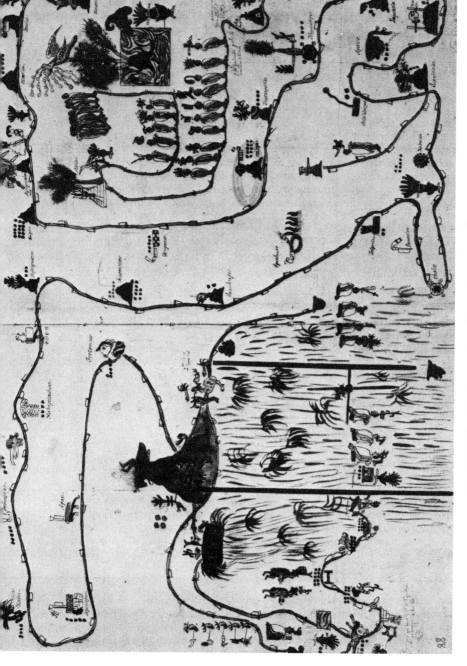

Fig. 3.3. *The Mexitin trek to Chapultepec.* Codex Sigüenza.

Fig. 3.4. *The defeat of Copil. Codex Mexicanus, pl. 38.*

deal with relationships between kin. These similarities lead us to conclude provisionally that the makeup of Aztec society was reflected in the picture that they composed of their distant past. It was a society that consisted of several population groups, each having its own pantheon, legendary heroes, and heroines.

In the next chapter we shall see just how Tenochtitlan and Tlatelolco grew into societies composed of several sometimes ethnically different corporate groups (calpollis). The migration stories mention the most important of these, though their number varies and they are sometimes called by different names. In a former article I have explained that the historical sources lead to the assumption that the Aztecs regarded the four calpollis of Aztlan as the typically "Aztecatl" ones and considered the calpollis Izquitlan, Yopico, and Huitznahuac on the opposite shore to be "Mexîtli."[30] In complete accordance with the dualistic nature of Mesoamerican social organization, there existed between the two groups a division of functions that cut across the whole population. Each of the two groups supplied certain chiefs and priests who were relevant to the whole society.

How can we arrive at the "real" history of the Mexitin? There is no doubt that they were originally Chichimec. Their tribal god was Tetzauhteotl, a moon god, identified with night and the underworld. The light of Mesoamerican civilization had not yet or had barely reached them. Moreover, it is certain that these Mexitin came from the north. I dare go no further regarding their early beginnings. I am inclined to distrust theories that Aztecs had a Toltec religion and culture before the trek, though I recognize early Toltec influences in the north. Nevertheless, such traditional migration tales are unreliable because they contain many elements that reflect conditions of a later time.

The four god bearers and Chimalman symbolize the four central calpollis in Tenochtitlan: Tezcacoac, Acatliacapan, Cuauhquiahuac, and Têcpantzinco. The last was situated next to the western causeway leading into the town, and Chimalman (Resting Shield) was a goddess of the west, where the sun set. These four central calpollis, in which the imperial nobles had a considerable share, appear to have been formed at a comparatively late date (See chapters 4, 10, and 11).

The *Historia de los Mexicanos por sus Pinturas* tells us that when the Mexicans arrived at Huitzilopochco they created the god Huitzilopochtli. He was a combination of Huitzil, the deified priest of the Huitznahuac Mexitin calpolli, and Opochtli (Left, or Southern God), one of the various forms of the rain god, worshiped by the Chinampanecs.[31] Opochtli and Quilaztli-Malinalxochitl, as well as various forms of Mixcoatl, were the principal deities of the Chalmecs who inhabited the chinampa areas. When Copil paid his first visit, he changed himself into (or dressed as) Itztapaltetl, god of the *tlaxilacalli* Huitznahuac (see chapter 12). But Copil himself was a Chalmec. The struggle between these two calpollis is, in fact, the basis of the Malinalxochitl and Copil myths. The historic struggle between these two calpollis, however, took place entirely in the lake district, not at Coatlicamac and Tzompanco. References to these last two locations are based on projections of important more recent events onto past history. Probably the Aztecs incorporated these references into their history at an early stage to provide their Mexitin forebears with "Toltec" characteristics. It is likely that the Mexitin remained culturally Chichimec until after their success at Tzompanco and their invasion of the lake district. Once settled there, they became more "Toltecized" through their contacts with the indigenous population.

But what about Aztlan and the "real" Azteca? Although Kirchhoff's hypothesis cannot be dismissed altogether, I am more inclined to think that the land of origin, the Aztlan mentioned in the myths, was situated not far in the north but much nearer home. In present-day folklore Cuitlahuac (modern Tlahuac) is still called the White Island. On the opposite shore of the now-dry Lake Chalco is still a place called Iztayopan (On the Whiteness). In pre-Spanish times Cuitlahuac was an island situated where Lake Chalco passes into Lake Xochimilco. It was a chinampa village and remained so until recent times. Cuitlahuac occupied a special status in the Aztec empire, because an aristocratic family who lived there, the Tzompan, was supposed to have descended from Mixcoatl. The Tzompan family was notorious in the region for witchcraft and prophecy.[32] Furthermore, it is notable that each of the four calpollis of Cuitlahuac—Têcpan, Tizic, Atenchicalcan, and Teopancalcan—had achieved the status of *tlâtocayotl*—an administrative unit headed by a *tlâtoani*—which usually occurred only on a broader regional level. It also appears that Cuitlahuac's calendrical system had predominated for some time in central Mexico, which indicates a long period of strong administrative influence.[33] A number of place and township names found in Cuitlahuac, such as Atempan, Atenchicalcan, Aticpac, Calpilco, and Cihuatêcpan, were also found in Tenochtitlan.[34] Even more important is that personal or family names such as Tzompan and Chalchiuhtlatonac were common in both cities.[35] The early importance of Cuitlahuac is also apparent from the fact that in its foundation legend it is called Tollan-Cuitlahuac.[36] Mixcoatl was the tribal god of the Cuitlahuacas, who like Huitzilopochtli and Mexîtli was called Tetzauhteotl (Impressive God).[37] The close relationship between Mixcoatl, Camaxtli—the god of the Tlaxcaltecs—and Huitzilopochtli is well known.

The following enumeration of events clarifies the special importance of Cuitlahuac to the Aztecs:

1. In some of the earliest tales of the Aztecâ-Mexitin, as well as in those which tell of the Tzompan family among the Cuitlahuaca, Mixcoatl Xocoyotl, the youngest Mixcoatl god, more commonly called Iztacmixcoatl (White Cloud Snake), is depicted as a tribal ancestor and leader of the migration.[38]

2. As we have seen in the *Codex Boturini,* the leader of the Aztecs spoke to the Cuitlahuaca chief alone, just before the dispersal of the several population groups represented by the broken tree.

3. In the days of the Aztec king Itzcoatl, Cuitlahuac was conquered by an unusual force consisting of only young men; that had never happened before, and was never again repeated.[39]

4. During the reign of Motêuhczoma Ilhuicamina (in the year I Calli, 1441) a civil war broke out in Cuitlahuac between the calpollis Tizic and Atenchicalcan. It happened that while the men of Tizic were engaged in a war against Chalco the men of Atenchicalcan attacked those of Tizic who stayed behind and took their houses. When they returned, the warriors of Tizic took revenge and forced the population of Atenchicalcan to abandon their own calpolli. The Atenchicalcanecs complained to Motêuhczoma, who, in spite of the fact that the warriors of Tizic had aided him in the Chalco war, sent his supreme war chiefs with an army to return the people of Atenchicalcan to their calpolli. In the ensuing fight, the temple of Mixcoatl Xocoyotl (the Youngest, or White Cloud Snake) was burned down, which decided the battle. The Aztec war chiefs demanded the statue of the god, but Tezozomoc, the king of Tizic, gave them instead the statue of Teuhcatl, the tribal god of Tizic (He from the Place of Dust), who was another aspect of Mixcoatl. This statue was placed in the great Mixcoatl temple in Tenochtitlan.[40]

5. The Tzompan in Cuitlahuac was so distinguished a family that a daughter of Motêuhczoma Ilhuicamina, the princess Yohuatzin, was married to one of its members.[41]

6. When Motêuhczoma Xocoyotzin, the Aztec emperor who reigned from 1502 to 1520, desired to have the Huitzilopochtli temple overlaid with gold on the outside and jade on the inside, and again, when he heard the first reports of the Spaniards, he consulted with the head of the Tzompan family in Cuitlahuac.[42]

All these data support the claim that Cuitlahuac was of great importance to the Aztecs. "Official" history has almost ignored the role this city played in the Aztec past, but it would seem fully justifiable to examine the possibility that some of the population of Tenochtitlan who had Chimpanec ancestors originated in Cuitlahuac. It is, therefore, likely that the origin legends of these Chinampanecs or Chalmecs were incorporated in the Aztlan complex of later "official" histories. Thus, to recreate the old Toltec image, they depicted Huitzilopochtli, who was in essence a "Toltec" god, as impatient to reach his final destination, the palaces of Quetzalcoatl — the jade house, the noble metal house, the green feather house, the shell house, and so on.[43]

CHAPTER 4

Aztec Social Organization at the Founding of Mexîco-Tenochtitlan

AN understanding of the structural-functional relationships among Mesoamerican corporate groups is indispensable in penetrating further into the ethnohistory of the region. It was on these relationships that the solidity of the indigenous societies depended. Where the Aztecâ-Mexitin are concerned it is crucial to know the socioeconomic as well as the ceremonial and administrative functions of the calpollis. Much is known about the economic functions of the calpollis; much less is known, however, about the other aspects of their social activity. Many chronicles from the first century of colonial rule stress their social importance, saying that within each calpolli members of specific noble families held most of the administrative and religious offices. An ethnohistorian intending to study the connections between social functions of calpollis and the noble families associated with them confronts difficulties since colonial chronicles contain little information on this subject.

A surprising, but also discouraging, fact is that at first the colonial as well as the pre-Spanish pictographs seem vague and appear to contain little information on these connections. Of the many historical sources dealing with the Aztecs, not one contains direct information about the relationships between the leaders at the time of the founding of Tenochtitlan and their calpollis, though the leaders and the calpollis are frequently mentioned. Information about the spatial distribution of the calpollis is also very rare. One exception in this respect is the *Codex Izhuatepec*,[1] which contains valuable data about the location of the five important calpollis in Tenochtitlan during the second half of the fourteenth century.

This pictorial also shows the ties between Acamâpichtli (Hand

Full of Arrows) and the calpolli Chalman as well as those between Ilancueitl (Old Women's Skirt) and the calpolli Tlacatêcpan.
This information is very important and will be discussed below.

In spite of the fact that, at first, the available material seems
somewhat discouraging, the time of Tenochtitlan's founding is the
most appropriate period to begin the study of Aztec social structure. At least here it is possible to separate the historical from
the legendary elements in the material. The principal historical
sources that deal with the foundation period of Tenochtitlan are
the *Codex Mendoza*,[2] the *Codex Mexicanus*,[3] the *Codex Sigüenza*,[4]
the *Crónica Mexicana* and the *Crónica Mexîcayotl* (both by Tezozomoc),[5] the *Relaciones of Chimalpahin*,[6] the *Codex Ramírez*,[7]
the *Tovar Manuscript*,[8] and the works of Fray Diego Durán.[9] By
comparing the data in these sources with the indigenous structural systems as described, for example, in the codices *Fejérváry
Mayer*[10] and *Vaticanus B*,[11] we can trace a number of relations
between chiefs and their calpollis. Once this has been done, we
can study the social importance of the calpolli and the impact of
calpolli nobility more closely.

The best-known rendition of the founding of Tenochtitlan is
seen on the first leaf of the *Codex Mendoza*. Here Tenochtitlan
is represented as a "city" divided diagonally into four parts by
two canals that cross in the center. Within the city quarter depicted on the left are four of the "founders," namely, the chiefs:
Tenoch (Stone Cactus), Acacihtli (Reed Hare), Mexitzin (Agave
Navel), and Xocoyol (probably not derived from *xocoyolli*, "sorrel,"
since the hieroglyph suggests that it is a compound of *xotl*, "foot,"
and *coyolli*, "little bell," thus Foot Bell). In each of the other three
city quarters are two representations of chiefs: in the lower quarter,
Xiuhcaquê (He Who Has Turquoise, or Blue Sandals) and Atototl
(Waterbird); in the right quarter are Xomimitl (Foot Arrow) and
Ahuexotl (Water Willow); and in the upper quarter, Tzompan
(Beard Banner) and Ocelopan (Ocelot Banner).

Two of my translations of the hieroglyphs disagree with the
captions written on the leaf by the colonial interpreter. Instead of
Mexitzin he wrote Tetzineuh (He Who Expels), and instead of
Tzompan he put down Cuâpan (Eagle Flag). The latter interpretation is easily explained in that eagles and ocelots were symbolic of a select Aztec military corps, and the colonial scribe,
being aware of this, interpreted the names accordingly. Furthermore, he transposed the word Ocelopan for the hieroglyph representing Acacihtli and Acacihtli for the hieroglyph of Ocelopan.

This mistake, too, will be explained later in this chapter. The names Tetzineuh and Cuâpan occur in no other source dealing with the founding of the city. The hieroglyph that the colonial scribe interprets as Tetzineuh, moreover, is the well-known symbol for the frequently mentioned Mexitzin, an agave *(metl)* and the lower part of a human being, used to represent the concept of foundation *(tzintli)* and indirectly the polite suffix *(tzin)*. In fact, in the last century Orozco y Berra gave the same interpretation to this hieroglyph.[12]

Orozco y Berra and Chavero[13] in the last century and Moreno, Monzón, Caso, and others[14] in more recent times have believed that the *Codex Mendoza* showed the associations of the founders to the four well-known later divisions of Mexîco-Tenochtitlan: Moyotla, Teopan-Zoqui(a)pan-Xochimilcâ, Atzacoalco, and Cuepopan-Tlaquenchiuhcan. It is indeed surprising that this hasty and too-obvious conclusion has not been questioned before. There are two good reasons to do so now.

First, the stories about the founding of Tenochtitlan show that its center was first situated somewhere in what would be the southern part of the later and, of course, much larger city. Hence the four parts that existed at the time of the city's founding could not have been located in the same places as the later city quarters.[15] Second, and more important, is that the quartering of the later city was achieved by two causeways that crossed in the center. These causeways continued in three directions as far as the shores of the mainland; only the eastbound causeway ended in Tenochtitlan and did not cross Lake Tetzcoco.[16] The directions of these causeways do not agree with those of the canals shown in the *Codex Mendoza.*

What, then, does the division into quarters by canals mean? The answer to this question can be found in the *Crónica Mexîcayotl* and the *Codex Fejérváry-Mayer.* When Tezozomoc describes the founding of Mexîco-Tenochtitlan in the *Crónica Mexîcayotl,* he relates, among other things, the following legend:

Auh in no ipan quizatô	And then, when they also prepared to depart,
in oquittaquê cenca	they saw many different wonderful
miectlamantli in tlamahuizolli	things there
in oncan câ in acaihtic,	in the reed beds,
ca yehica ipampa innahuatil	just as it had been foretold,

iuh quimilhui in Huitzilopochtli
in teomamaquê in itâhuan
in Cuauhtlequetzqui anozo
in Cuauhcoatl,
in Axolohuâ tlamacazqui,
ca quinnahuati ca iuh quimilhui
in ixquich in oncan in onoc

in tolihtic in acaihtic,
in oncan ihcaz, in oncan tlapiez,
in yêhuatl in Huitzilopochtli,
ca itencopa quimilhui,
ca iuh quinnahuati
in Mexîcâ;
auh niman oquittaquê
iztac in ahuehuetl
iztac in huexotl in oncan ihcac,

ihuan iztac in acatl, iztac in tolli

ihuan iztac in cueyatl,
iztac in michin,
iztac in coatl,
in oncan nemi atlan.
Auh niman oquittaquê
nepaniuhtîcac
in texcalli in oztotl.
Inic ce texcalli in oztotl
tonatiuh iquizayan itztoc
itoca Tleatl Atlatlayan.

Auh inic ome in texcalli in oztotl
    mictlampa itztoc,

inic nepaniuhtoc,
itoca Matlalatl
ihuan itoca Toxpalatl.
Auh in oquittaquê
niman ye chocâ in huehuetquê,
quîtoâ: "Anca ye nican yez,
ca otiquittaquê in techilhui
in ic technahuati
in tlamacazqui in Huitzilopochtli,
in quîto: 'in iuhqui anquittazquê
in tolihtic in acaihtic

as Huitzilopochtli had told
his god bearers, his uncles
Eagle Who Goes into the Fire
or Eagle Snake and
the priest He Who Has Axolotls,
for he told and explained to them
everything that lived there and in-
    habited
the tule grounds and reed beds,
there he will take his stand, there he
will keep watch, he, Huitzilopochtli,
for from his lips came his
statement to them, for thus
he had foretold it to the Mexicans:
and then they saw,
that the weeping willows and
the willows that stood there were
    white,
and also the reeds and the tules
    were white
and the frogs were white,
the fish were white,
the snakes were white,
which lived there on the shores.
And they saw,
that rocks and caves
stood face to face.
The first rock and cave were
seen where the sun rises
and is called: Fire Water, Where
    the Water Is Burning.
And the second rock and cave were
    seen in the direction of the realm
    of the dead [the north]
— therefore they cross each other —
it is called Blue Water
and its name is Yellow Water.
And when they had seen that,
the old people cried, and said:
"So this will be the place,
for we have seen what
has been told and explained to us
by the priest Huitzilopochtli,
when he said: 'As you will see,
there are in the tule-grounds

miectlamantli in oncan câ.'

Auh in axcan coatiquittaquê
oticmahuizoquê,
ca ye nelli ca omochiuh,
ca oneltic in itlâtol
in ic technahuati."
Niman oquîtoquê:
"Mexîcayê, ma oc tihuiyan,
ca otitlamahuizoquê,
ma oc titlâtolchiecan
in tlamacazqui;
yêhuatl quimati quenin mochihuaz."
niman ohuallâquê motlallicô
in oncan Temazcaltitlan.[17]

in the reed-beds many different
things.'
And now here we have all
beheld and admired it.
for it has truly happened
and the word has proved to be true,
that he spoke to us."
Then they said:
"Oh, Mexicans, let us still go away,
for we have seen miracles,
let us wait still for
the word of the priest,
for he knows what will happen."
Then they came and settled
there, Beside the Steam Bath.

This text reflects the same things that the pictographer of the *Codex Mendoza* showed on the famous first leaf. There were two sacred waters. One ran from east to west and was called Tleatl-Atlatlayan, and the other, the Matlalatl-Toxpalatl, ran from north to south, and so they crossed each other.

The symbolic meaning of the intersection of these sacred waters is explained in the *Codex Fejérváry-Mayer*. The first leaf of this beautiful pictorial, which is as famous as that of the *Codex Mendoza*, shows two integrated levels of the Aztec cosmos, each divided into four parts on the surface of the earth. Combined, the two levels have eight parts. The first and most striking of these two systems is composed of four holy trees that are symbols of the four cardinal points and, therefore, belong to eight important gods and goddesses. These deities are represented on either side of each of the four trees. This depiction corresponds with the well-known division of Tenochtitlan into four city quarters, sectioned by the four causeways. The second conceptual division of the Aztec city into four parts as shown in the *Codex Fejérváry-Mayer* is made by four streams of blood running from the east, the north, the west, and the south to meet in the center. This division is meant to connect spatially the twenty thirteen-day periods of the *tonalpoalli* (calendar) as shown in pictographs. The spatial quartering corresponds with the four parts of the young city of Tenochtitlan as depicted in the *Codex Mendoza*. This interpretation is, in fact, quite plausible, because at that time there were no causeways.

Thanks to the *Codex Fejérváry-Mayer*, among other sources,

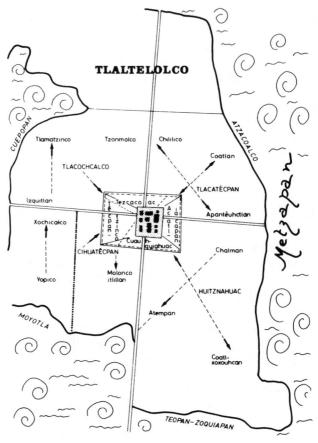

Fig. 4.1. *Tenochtitlan.*

the symbolism is quite clear. From each of the four cardinal points the sacrificial blood flows to the ceremonial center, where the rites of worship are performed for important gods, who feed on the sacrificial offerings brought by the people. Only with this nourishment can they discharge their cosmic tasks. A depiction of the founding of Tenochtitlan occurs on page 37 of the *Codex Ramírez.* It expresses the same idea when it says about the sacred waters:

[The Mexicans] came back to visit this spring they had seen the day before, and they saw that the water, that previously had welled up from the earth clear and clean, was now red like blood and that it divided itself into two streams and where the second started the water came up in such a deep blue color that it was terrifying to see.

Fig. 4.2. *Gods, time, and space.* Codex Fejérváry-Mayer, *leaf 1.*

Fig. 4.3. *Acamâpichtli and Ilancueitl as rulers of Tenochtitlan.* Codex Izhuatepec.

Each of the intersecting waters of the *Codex Mendoza* is given a name in the *Crónica Mexîcayotl.* Each canal cuts diagonally across two of the four parts of the city formed by the imaginary lines connecting the cardinal points. Later these imaginary lines were delineated by the causeways in the enlarged city of Tenochtitlan. It is clear now that the sacred waters pictured in the *Codex Mendoza* did not divide the imperial city of Tenochtitlan into four large city quarters. On the contrary, they were the real or conceptual bisectors of each of those four quarters (see map, fig. 4.1). Therefore, the chiefs pictured between the canals did not belong to the same city quarters, but those pictured on opposite sides of the canal belonged to the same quarter (fig. 4.5.).

The location of five important calpollis is shown in the *Codex Izhuatepec.*[18] It places Chalman and Huitznahuac in Zoquipan; Tlacatêcpan (indicated by the *têcpan* and the office of *tlacateccatl,* which was said to be held by Ilancueitl) lies in Atzacoalco, Tlacochcalco in Cuepopan, and Cihuatêcpan in Moyotla. Unfortunately the calpollis of Yopico and Izquitlan, mentioned in the migration story, are not depicted on this map of Tenochtitlan. But some colonial maps show Yopico situated in Moyotla.[19] Data about ritual and ceremonial functions in Izquitlan lead to the assumption that together with Tlacochcalco it was part of Cuepopan.[20] The spatial division of Tenochtitlan is that only one of the seven original calpollis is in Atzacoalco; each of the other three quarters of the city has two of the original calpollis.

We would find the connection we seek between the "founders" and the calpollis if we could relate the data above to the *Codex Mendoza*. However, there is one more difficulty: the *Codex Mendoza* does not indicate the cardinal direction in which each of the four parts lies; it shows only their spatial relationship to one another. We might interpret the simple building shown between the chiefs Ocelopan and Tzompan as the *têcpan* (the government building), but there is no glyph to confirm this. The pictographic representation of the foundation myth is in the center of the folio. The eagle perched on the cactus, however, is clearly supported by the section where the chiefs Xiuhcaquê and Atototl are shown. There we also see the well-known shield *(tehuehuelli)* of Huitzilopochtli with its arrows and the seven downy eagle feathers (the real Aztec "coat of arms" of Tenochtitlan).

Another striking object that might provide a clue to orientation is the *tzompantli* (skull rack), situated opposite the chiefs Xomimitl and Ahuexotl. Unfortunately, none of these objects has any firm relationship to cardinal points. Therefore, we must find the solution to our problem elsewhere.

Two other historical sources from the sixteenth century mention eight chiefs as leaders of the seven most important calpollis. These sources are the *Codex Mexicanus*[21] and the works of Durán.[22] The problem is that neither names the calpollis. The *Codex Mexicanus* shows the symbol for calpolli seven times but does not show the hieroglyph for a name. Six of the calpollis are represented by a single chief; the seventh calpolli, which occupies the fourth and central place, is shown with two chiefs. The first calpolli is led by Tenoch; the second, by Aatl (Water), which other sources give as a second name for Mexitzin; the third, by Ahuexotl; and the fourth, by two chiefs, one of whom is Ocelopan. The name of the other is indicated by an uncommon symbol that appears to be an *acaxitl,* a water container. This might well be a hieroglyph for the phonetically similar name Acacihtli, since such approximate symbols are by no means rare in old Mexican pictographs. The fifth calpolli is led by Xomimitl, the sixth by Tzompan, and the seventh by Xiuhcaquê. Thirteen other chiefs who played a role in the founding are depicted, but they are not shown to be connected with any of the calpollis. Among them is Atototl, who, like the eight chiefs mentioned above, also appears in the *Codex Mendoza.*

Durán also mentions eight chiefs among the founders of Tenochtitlan:

> those who left this place [Aztlan] were Tenzacatetl [Lip Ornament], Acacihtli [Reed Hare], Ocelopan [Ocelot Flag], Aatl [Water], Xomimitl, [Foot Arrow], Ahuexotl [Water Willow], Huicton [Little Planting Stick], Tenoch [Stone Cactus], and they were seven [*sic*] brave men and these seven men were the chiefs of each separate barrio [calpolli].

Durán speaks of only seven chiefs of seven calpollis, but he gives eight names. The difference here from the enumeration found in the *Codex Mexicanus* is that Durán mentions Tenzacatetl instead of Tzompan and Huicton instead of Xiuhcaquê.

A comparison between the data found in both sources shows the striking proximity of Acacihtli and Ocelopan, and the inversion of their positions by the colonial interpreter of the *Codex Mendoza.* In the *Codex Mendoza* the two chiefs are found on either side of the same canal and occupy the space of one entire future quarter of the city. This quarter must be Atzacualco, for it is the only one that contains just one of the seven original calpollis, and we have already seen that Ocelopan and Acacihtli belonged to the same calpolli. Now we may conclude that this calpolli is Tlacatêcpan and that the small building pictured in front of Ocelopan (or Acacihtli?) is evidently the *têcpan.* This also implies that the top of the first leaf of the *Codex Mendoza* represents east. But who made the error, the pictographer or the writer of the text? In the *Crónica Mexîcayotl,* Acacihtli is called by the official title *têcpanecatl chichimecatêuhctli* ("Chichimec chief in charge of the government building").[23] In any case, this confirms the relationship of Acacihtli with the *têcpan.* It does not mean, however, that Ocelopan had nothing to do with the *têcpan,* because he may have been the "Aztec" or "Chinampanec" chief of the government building. Unfortunately, all we know is that Ocelopan was of "Toltec" descent.[24] Another difference between these two chiefs is shown in the legend of the secession of Tlatelolco from Tenochtitlan, thirteen years after the founding. As the *Codex Sigüenza* shows, Ocelopan left the city with the Tlatelolcas, but Acacihtli stayed in Tenochtitlan. These particulars explain, to a certain extent, why

Fig. 4.4. Eight chiefs and founders of Tenochtitlan and their seven calpollis. Codex Mexicanus, pl. 44.

it would be easy for the colonial scribe who wrote the explanatory text to transpose the positions of the two chiefs, since both of them had a relationship with the *têcpan*.[25]

On the other side of the *têcpan* is depicted a chief whom the caption identifies as Cuâpan (Eagle's Flag), though other codices and chronicles identify the chief in that position as Tzompan (Beard Flag, or Skull Rack).[26] A comparison of the placement of this chief with the positions of the calpollis in the *Codex Izhuatepec* shows that he must have belonged to Chalman. Acamâpichtli was a Chalmec when he held the office of *cihuacoatl* ("chief of the administration of internal affairs"). Therefore his grandson Tla-cayelel, who inherited the same office, also belonged to that cal-polli, in particular to a subordinate part of it called Atempan.[27] A grandson of Tlacayelel was also called Tzompantzin,[28] which helps confirm the connection between the "founder" of that name and the calpolli Chalman. There is another piece of evidence that supports this connection. According to Durán, Tzompan was replaced by Tenzacatetl. Tenzacatetl is also found in the *Codex Mexicanus* and in other sources. In the *Codex Mexicanus* he is said to be the father of Acamâpichtli and therefore is likely to be the person referred to as Opochtli Iztahuâtzin in other sources.[29] Later in this chapter we shall show that Opochtli was a *calpolteotl* (calpolli god) of Chalman.

We have not identified the important calpollis of the eastern half of the city and their chiefs. They are associated with the *cuauhtlehuanitl* (rising sun), and they formed that half of the city which in a symbolic as well as structural sense dealt with external affairs, such as the expansion of power, administrative autonomy, offensive warfare, and so on. Since these were matters of little importance at the time of the founding, the overall influence of these calpollis was limited. Under such circumstances this was (and still is in some places) the usual way in which Mesoamerican societies maintained a latent organization for the administration of external affairs. This system functioned as a kind of shadow gov-ernment concomitant with the regime in power, and it was ready to play a more active part when circumstances changed. For the time being, however, the administration of the young Aztec com-munity of Tenochtitlan was dependent on the supremacy of the Têcpanec government in Azcapotzalco and had not even reached the status of *tlâtocayotl* (administrative unit ruled by a *tlâtoani*, its own external ruler).[30]

The central authority of that young community, then, could be

Fig. 4.5. *The Aztecs' "founding" of Tenochtitlan and their first conquests.*
Codex Mendoza, *leaf 1.*

Fig. 4.6. *The Aztecs' "founding" of Tenochtitlan.* Manuscript Tovar, *pl. 4.*

situated only in the western half of the city, associated with the *cuauhtemoc,* the setting sun. This administrative sector was for the most part in charge of internal affairs, was associated with military defense, and functioned with necessary political flexibility and a dependence on higher authority. In the *Codex Mendoza* six chiefs are shown in the western half of the city. Four of them are identified in the *Codex Mexicanus* as the calpolli chiefs Xomimitl, Xiuhcaquê, Aatl-Mexitzin, and Tenoch. A fifth chief, Atototl, is shown as one of the twenty-one "founders," but no connection with a calpolli is given for him. The sixth, Xocoyol, is also mentioned in other sources. These chiefs are always shown as individuals, but it should be remembered that these names might refer to noble or aristocratic families rather than to historic persons. The names of important personages were sometimes given to their entire families. Moreover, it was a custom in aristocratic families to use certain personal names again and again, so that after several generations the deeds of one or more ancestors might easily be ascribed to a descendant of the same name, and it was uncertain how many bearers of a single name were involved.

We may assume that the chiefs Mexitzin and Tenoch or the families whose names were used to give the new Aztec community the name Mexîco-Tenochtitlan, held the two highest administrative positions. Like any other Mesoamerican administration, that of the young Aztec community was headed by a pair of chiefs, in accordance with the traditional dualistic principle. Of course, the native pictographer may have put the two chiefs in the center of his idealized representation of the newly founded city, but he evidently rejected this placement to put the symbol of the foundation myth—the eagle perched on a cactus growing from stone—in the center of his map. Furthermore, he needed room for the community coat of arms—the *tehuehuelli* (shield) of Huitzilopochtli. It is logical for the shield to be pictured under the symbol of the founding. Tenoch is shown with a "speech scroll," symbolizing "ruler" or "administrator." Pictured behind him is his coruler, Mexitzin. In my opinion the position of these two chiefs here is meant to represent their relationship to the central government.[31] Therefore, they have been shown adjacent to the symbols representing the founding and the community. That they have been placed in the city quarter on the left, need not have any direct significance in terms of their relationship with a particular calpolli.

Fig. 4.7. *The "founding" of Tenochtitlan. Durán*, Atlas, trat? *1*, lam? *32.*

With the help of the *Codex Izhuatepec* and the investigations
made by Alfonso Caso, the four remaining chiefs depicted on the
western half of the map can be associated with four particular
calpollis. Xomimitl was the chief of Yopico, and the glyph for
"skull rack" is appropriate to this calpolli because it is certain
that a *tzompantli* existed near the Yopico temple.[32] From data
provided by the *Codex Izhuatepec* we can conclude that Atototl
was a chief of Cihuatêcpan, Xiuhcaquê a chief of Izquitlan, and
Xocoyol a chief of Tlacochcalco. Since the two supreme chiefs were
given a central position in this pictograph, Xocoyol and Atototl
were evidently chiefs of lower rank. They are shown in the *Codex
Mendoza* merely to indicate the position of their calpollis, not as
calpolli chiefs. Nor are they said to be calpolli chiefs in the *Codex
Mexicanus* or by Durán. This means that the two supreme chiefs
must have belonged to the calpollis Cihuatêcpan and Tlacochcalco. In view of the conditions that existed at the time of the
founding, one can hardly expect anything else, for, as the name
indicates, Cihuatêcpan, the "female administrative building" was
associated with the administration of internal affairs, and Tlacochcalco, the spear house, or arsenal, was the seat of the high
command of the armed forces for defense.

We would especially like to know the calpolli to which each of
the two supreme chiefs belonged, but unfortunately this question
is almost impossible to answer. The *Codex Izhuatepec* and the
Codex Santa Isabel Tola vaguely indicate that the Tenoch family

Fig. 4.8. *The "founding" of Tenochtitlan.* Codex Aubin, *p. 48.*

was from Tlacochcalco. Mexitli, as the name of a god, is easily
associated, with Cihuatêcpan because, as we shall see below,
Cihuatêcpan's calpolli goddess was Itzpapalotl, another aspect of
the Earth Goddess. These data are important indications, but not
certainties. What is known about the descendants of these two
highest-ranking founders families provides no useful information
in this respect. Cuâtlecoatl (Eagle's Fire Snake), a grandson of
Mexitzin, was *tlacochcalcatl* during the rule of Huitzilíhuitl II and,
therefore, connected with the calpolli Tlacochcalco; but some time
later, after the conquest of Coyohuâcan, he became one of the
four high-ranking imperial dignitaries with the title *tlillancalqui*
("chief of the black house"), an office connected with a dependency of Cihuatêcpan. A grandson of Tenoch, Epcoatl (Shell
Snake) held the office of *temilotli tiacauh,* a military rank with
no clear connection to any one calpolli. (See chapter 6.) In the
days of the founding, the two calpollis to which the supreme
chiefs belonged were very important. In any case, Cihuatêcpan
was obliquely opposite Tlacatêcpan, and Tlacochcalco lay in the
same relationship to Huitznahuac. In Mesoamerican systems such
oppositional pairs were either mutually complementary, as were
the first two calpollis, or they were competitive, as were Huitznahuac and Tlacochcalco.

The data we have gathered so far lead to the following conclusions about the social organization of the young state of Mexîco-
Tenochtitlan:

1. The seven important calpollis spatially arranged according to
eight ideal-typical sectors each of which was responsible for a
distinct function in the community.
2. Varying hierarchic structures, both between aristocratic families and within a single aristocratic family, were integrated. This
closely corresponded to differences in the status of entire calpollis.
3. The functions of the hierarchies and their mutual relations
changed over time in accordance with the administrative, social,
economic, and religious development of the society.

These remarks will become clearer as we go more deeply into
some matters. The famous and heroic words spoken by the high
priest Cuauhtlequetzqui (Eagle That Goes into the Fire) in one
version of the Copil saga symbolize the hierarchical relationship
between two of the most important chiefs:

Auh occeppa oquîto	And once more
in Cuauhtlequetzqui	Eagle That Goes into the Fire said,
oquilhui in Tenuch:	once more he said to Stone Cactus:
"Tenuchê, itla ye huêcauh	"Oh, Stone Cactus, we have been here
nican ticatê,	too long,
niman tiyaz titlachiatiuh	go now and have a look
in Tulzalan in Acatzalan,	in Between Tules and Reeds,
in oncan otictocato	where you buried
in iyollo tlaciuhqui Copil,	the heart of Crown (Copil), the magician,
quen tlamamanitiuh;	and look how things are there;
iuh nechilhuia in toteouh	as our god Huitzilopochtli
Huitzilopochtli,	explained to me,
oncan ixhuaz	there the heart of Crown
in iyollo Copil,	will sprout,
auh têhuatl tiyaz	and you will go,
in ti Tenuch	you, Stone Cactus,
in tiquittatiuh	you will go and see
oncan oixhuac in tenuchtli,	that there the stone cactus has sprouted,
yêhuatl in iyollo Copil;	that is the heart of Crown;
oncan icpac in oquetztîcac	and on top of it stands upright
in cuauhtli,	an eagle,
quicxitzitzquitîcac,	there he stands with outstretched claw,
quitzotzopitztîcac	with his beak he rips open
in coatl quicua.	the snake that he will eat.
Auh inon tenuchtli yez	And on this stone cactus it will be,
ca têhuatl in ti Tenuch,	for you are Stone Cactus,
auh in cuauhtli tiquittaz	and the eagle that you will see,
ca nêhuatl;	that is me;
yêhuatl totenyo yez,	it will be our fame
zan in quexquichcauh	and as long as
maniz cemanahuatl,	the whole ring (the world) exists,
aic pollihuiz	they will never be lost,
in itenyo in itauhca	the fame and the heroism
in Mexîco-Tenochtitlan."[33]	of Mexîco-Tenochtitlan."

The text above refers to three chiefs who played an important part in early Aztec history. We may assume that Cuauhtlequetzqui, as high priest of Huitzilopochtli, belonged to that god's calpolli, Huitznahuac, or to a subsidiary of it. This assumption is strengthened by the fact that a grandson of this high priest held an office connected with Huitznahuac. Tenoch probably belonged to Tlacochcalco, and Copil, the son of Malinalxochitl (Prairie-grass Flower) —according to the *Crónica Mexîcayotl*, he was also one of the god bearers and a founder of Tenochtitlan—belonged to or was associated with the calpolli of Chalman.

The symbolic representation in the center of the first folio of the *Codex Mendoza*, which is so beautifully expressed above, can be directly related to the social organization of the young state of Tenochtitlan. The eagle symbolizes Cuauhtlequetzqui as well as the celestial order and the animal counterpart (*nahualli*) of Huitzilopochtli that led the migrating Mexîtin to their promised land. It also stands for the sun as ruler and creator and the military offensive and religious functions of the Huitznahuac calpolli. The stone cactus, Tenoch, is the defensive military leader and a symbol of the earth. The snake represents Copil, the priest of the alien religion, magician, son of the witch of Chalman, and symbol of the underworld and of the indigenous Chinampanec population, which was connected with the underworld. All of this indicates a tripartite hierarchy of calpollis and their chiefs that played a part in the formation of the Aztec community.

This particular tripartite structure, however, was not the only one to which these three chiefs belonged. On the contrary, it forms only one part of a much more complicated system of cross-cutting hierarchies, by which all mutual relations between chiefs and calpollis were organized. Tenoch, for instance, was also the symbol of the *tepetl* ("mountain"), while Aatl-Mexitzin represented *atl* ("water"). Thus the two together formed the concept of *altepetl* (*atl + tepetl*), "water and mountain,"[34] which in Nahuatl means "town," "village," or "community." In Aztec religious organization Cuauhtlequetzqui, as high priest of Huitznahuac and Huitzilopochtli, was closely connected with Axolohuâ (*axolotl* owner), a rain priest of the Otomis.[35] In this context Cuauhtlequetzqui represented the sun, and Axolohuâ represented water from heaven. Thus the two formed a dual spiritual leadership for agriculturalists, who depended on the nourishing effect of sun and rain for prosperity. The legend told in the founding myth of Axolohuâ's "drowning" in one of the holy springs should be understood within this context. After a day he emerged and said:

Ca oniquittato   For I went to see
in Tlaloc,   Tlaloc (the Rain God),
ca onechnotz, ca quîtoa: for he called me and said:
"oquimihiyohuilti   "He has taken the trouble,

ca oâcico	for he is arrived,
in nopiltzin	my venerable son
in Huitzilopochtli,	Huitzilopochtli,
ca nican ichan yez,	and here will be his home,
ca yêhuatl ontlazôtiz,	for he will be worth that we live together,
ca tonehuan."[36]	we, both of us."

The two priests who represent the sun and the rain occupy opposite positions. On one hand, they are like "water and fire"; on the other, they are complementary. Symbolically they also represent the reconciliation of the Chichimec (Mexitin) newcomers and their sun cult with the indigenous Chinampanecs, who worshiped Quetzalcoatl and Tlaloc in their various aspects, as supreme. Ocelopan and Tzompan were a complementary pair, and their calpollis, Tlacatêcpan and Chalman, provided the most important complementary chiefships in the days of Ilancueitl and Acamâpichtli.

I have repeatedly emphasized the "symbolic" nature of the spatial representation of Mexîco-Tenochtitlan to explain why this spatial order should not be seen as a true picture of the geographic position of the calpollis or of the actual homes of their members. Although there may be some general correspondence between the two, we cannot regard it as a fact that could be used as a basis for further studies. We shall return to this point below.

Tezozomoc, Durán, and Veytia provide us with the names of the gods of the calpollis at the time of the founding, and the *Codex Fejérváry-Mayer* enables us to find their positions in the symbolic spatial order so that each of them can be associated with a specific calpolli.[37] The eight gods and goddesses who in the codex mentioned above surround the god of fire, Xiuhtêcuhtli, are not identical with those of the eight sectors in Tenochtitlan. Yet there are so many characteristics in which they are alike that this source is most useful in establishing the relationship between the gods and calpollis in the Aztec capital city.

Tezozomoc says about the migrating Aztecâ-Mexitin:

. . . and as many of them came from seven "wards" [calpollis], each group brought the name of its own god, such as: Quetzalcoatl (Precious Twins), Xocomoco [this should be Oxomoco, an ancestral god], Matla(l)xochiquetzal [Feather Ten-Flower or Blue Flower], Chichiltic Centeutl [Red-Maize God], Piltzintêcuhtli [Prince-Lord, a name for the young Sun God], Metêuhctli [Lord or Lady of the Agave], Tezcatlipuca [Bril-

liant Mirror]; see Chap. 7, note 7, Mictlantêcuhtli [Lord of the Dead]
and Tlamacazqui [Priest in Charge of Sacrificial Ceremonies] and other
gods; all these came, because although each of them from the seven
"wards" [calpollis] carried the symbol of his own god, they brought other
gods as well, and those who appealed most to the Indians were Huitzilopochtli, Tlazolteutl [Goddess of Filth, a form of the earth Goddess and
the Goddess of women in child-bed] and Mictlantêcuhtli [Lord of the
Dead].[38]

In his version of the migration Durán mentions the seven gods
of the seven calpollis, but he simply gives them titles derived from
the names of the calpollis, and this information does not help us
much.[39] Fortunately, he later gives us relevant data in his description of the ritual of the feast of Tlacaxipehualiztli (Flaying
of Men):

> Forty days before the feast they dress an Indian in the same array
> as the figure of the god, so that to the people he might represent the living
> idol. During those forty days this Indian, a purified slave, was treated
> with the same attention and reverence shown to the figure of the god,
> and he was continually shown to the public. The same thing was done
> in every ward [calpolli]. These wards were parishes, each of which had
> names dedicated to a god and its special sanctuary. The special sanctuary
> served as a temple for the ward so that during a feast each one could
> array a slave to represent its own god, just as was done in the main
> temple. This was done for no other feast of the yearly calendar, but on
> this occasion, if there were twenty wards, twenty Indians might be seen
> walking about, representing their universal god [Xipe Totêc, Our Lord
> the Flayed One]. Every ward honored and venerated its Indian represen-
> tative of the god, just as was done in the main temple. My impression
> of this feast is that in one god they worshiped all gods. To help us
> understand this concept, they brought out the Indian in the early morn-
> ing of the feast day itself [after he had represented the living god for
> forty days]; and after him [Xipe] they brought out the image of the Sun;
> then that of Huitzilopochtli, then that of Quetzalcoatl; then that of
> the god Macuilxochitl [Five Flower], and that of Chililico [In the Fire
> of the Pepper], and that of Tlacahuepan [Royal Wooden Beam or Clear
> Great Banner, a form of Tezcatlepoca], and that of Ixtliltzin [Black
> Eye], and that of Mayahuel [Mighty Green Snail, the goddess of the
> agave], those were the gods of the nobles in the important wards [cal-
> pollis].[40]

Veytia mentions the names of seven gods of the original and
most important calpollis: Quetzalcoatl, Tlazolteotl, Macuilxochi-
quetzalli, Chichiltic Centeotl, Piltzintêcuhtli, Tezcatlepoca, and
Mictlantêcuhtli.[41] At first examination the data given by the three

historians appear to be confused and contradictory. Sometimes the confusion arises because they refer to different aspects of a single god or goddess. At other times there are more complicated reasons.

The old religious song of the "Warrior of the South" (Huitzna-huac Yautl) clearly expresses the intimate ritual relations between Huitznahuac and Tlacochcalco.[42] Evidently gods and calpollis, oc-cupying as they did opposite sectors in the ideal-typical spatial order of the community, are significantly related to each other. In the following general survey I have shown how the data provided by the three authors I have quoted can be combined into one unifying system. (See fig. 4.9).

We must first consider a number of relationships between op-posite pairs of calpollis and the economic, administrative, and military bases of the Aztec community. Tlacochcalco and Huitzna-huac, for example, had strong ties to the military establishment as well as to the religious concepts of fire and human sacrifice. Tlacatêcpan and Cihuatêcpan were generally involved in matters of administration and authority. Yopico and Coatlan, a subsidiary of Tlacatêcpan (see below) were associated with the fertility of the fields and the cultivation of maize. Another subsidiary of Tlacatêc-pan, Chililico, was probably responsible for the cultivation of chilis. Chalman was generally associated with horticulture, fishing, and shooting of waterfowl while its opposite calpolli, Izquitlan, was associated with the making of agave wine (= pulque). It also appears that four of the eight sectors of Tenochtitlan were connected with certain activities of the nobles (chiefs and warriors), and the other four with the economic life of the *macehualtin*, the common people and farmers. Evidently priests and merchants carried out their activities in all sectors.

The social organization of Tenochtitlan is gradually coming into perspective. The picture becomes even clearer when we read in the *Codex Ramírez*: One night Huitzilopochtli spoke to one of his priests and helpers as follows: "Tell the Mexican congregation of believers that the chiefs, each with his relatives, friends, and de-pendents, divide themselves into four large city quarters; in the middle they should take the house that you build for me to rest in, and after that each quarter may build whatever it like." These are the city quarters that still exist today in Mexico City, now called San Pablo (Teopan), San Juan (Moyotla), Santa María la Redonda (Cuepopan) and San Sebastián (Atzacualco).[43]

After the Mexicans had been divided into four sectors, the gods

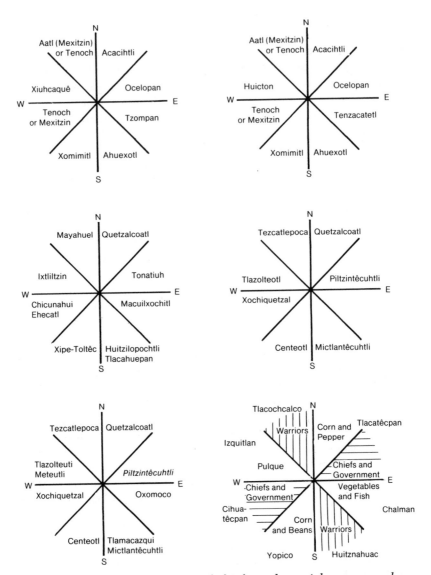

Fig. 4.9. *Various identifications of chiefs, gods, social groups, and economic activities with eight directions or sections in Tenochtitlan.*

ordered them to divide the subordinate gods and goddesses whom he would allot to each of the city quarters. He would then designate special, smaller wards within each quarter in which those gods were to be individually worshiped. Thus the people of those large quarters subdivided themselves into several smaller wards according to the number of gods and goddesses that their supreme god had instructed them to worship. These lesser deities were called *calpulteteô* ("calpolli gods").[44]

In this way the seven original calpollis subdivided themselves, or adopted dependencies of different origins, and became the seven ceremonial subcenters within the community of twenty calpollis. This number corresponds with the ritually important daily calendar, which had twenty different names for days. The people who belonged to these twenty calpollis formed the actual community of Mexîco-Tenochtitlan. Besides these calpollis, probably many more lay within the territory of the future city. But these did not take part in the ceremonial life, or at least not fully, and their members remained, in a sense, alien outsiders.

Thus the population of the city was divided into three groups: members of the seven original calpollis; members of the thirteen subsidiaries of the seven calpollis, also called calpollis; members of calpollis that did not fully take part in the ceremonial life, and inhabitants who were not of any calpolli.

This is another instance of the well-known established Mesoamerican tripartite hierarchy, which is, for instance, also found in the calendrical system of the *Codex Vaticanus B*. Such a tripartite form is the basic model for the conceptualization of the vertical structure of the Mesoamerican cosmos, consisting of underworld, earth, and heaven, as well as for the structure of Mesoamerican society.[45]

The Aztec god Huitzilopochtli, god par excellence, manifested himself on each of the three levels of this cosmic order. As Tetzauhteotl he was a moon good of night and the underworld. As Mexîtli he had the qualities of an earth god(dess), as the *Anales of Cuauhtitlan* say clearly: ". . . yehuatl in Tlalteuhctli in Mecîtli" ("This Mecîtli is the Lord or Lady of the Earth").[46] As Huitzilopochtli (Left of Southern Hummingbird) he became Sun and Ruler of Heaven, who was also called Ilhuicatl Xoxouhqui (Blue Heaven).

Following is a summary of what we have learned about the nature and the structure of Aztec society at a time during and soon after the founding at Mexîco-Tenochtitlan:

1. The population of Mexîco-Tenochtitlan formed a pluralistic and multiethnic society organized in a system of cross-cutting social hierarchies. The bases for social stratification were sometimes to be found in the different ethnic backgrounds in the society. In other instances social stratification had nothing to do with ethnic relationships but rather was founded on ritual or functional associations.

2. The calpolli was no longer a clan, if it had ever been one. Nor was it a community based on any other form of kinship, as many anthropologists and historians have thought. The calpollis were communities of people who were connected in various ways with one or two specific noble families or with one or more individual chiefs from such families; furthermore, they belonged to a local ceremonial center at which a particular god or goddess was worshiped. It had a stratified structure comparable to that of the larger community of twenty calpollis. Members of some single calpollis may have been of different ethnic origins.

The above conclusions make it necessary to reject two assertions about the Aztecs commonly found in the literature. The first is the view that Aztec history is the history of a nation. As we have seen, there may be a slight chance that during Toltec times the Azteca-Mexitin were a single population composed of two groups of different ethnic origins. However, the chiefs of the seven calpollis who took part in the foundation of Mexîco-Tenochtitlan were also of various ethnic derivations. According to the *Codex Ramírez*, Tenoch and Axolohuâ were Otomis.[47] The calpolli of Chalman was of Chinampanec origin and probably had claimed the more indigenous inhabitants of Toltzalan-Acatzalan. The Yopicas came from the region near Tollan, not from Aztlan. Two calpollis, which are believed to have originated in Aztlan, became no more than minor subsidiaries in the later imperial capital.[48] Now we can understand why some sources mention eight original calpollis and others seven, six, or four. The *Codex Boturini*, which gives six, may have left out the Chalmecs. The data on which Veytia based his views evidently had the same starting point, for when he enumerated the gods of the original calpollis he too ignored the sector belonging to Chalman.

In short, we can say that the population of Mexîco-Tenochtitlan was of various ethnic backgrounds and that chiefs of different origins "with their relatives, friends and dependents" found safety in the lakeshore marshes along Moon Lake, where they joined those who had preceded them. It seems that those of Otomi origin allowed the new arrivals to live in peace among them but that the Chinampanec peoples were at first hostile toward the new-comers. Apparently then, the term "Aztec" referred not to one particular people or nation but rather to a religious and cultural current with a political ideology of its own that had certain social and administrative implications and followers among the different ethnic groups.

The second view, which is the result of European interpretations of the subject, and which must also be rejected, is concerned with the nature of administrative and social relationships within the calpolli. Many Mesoamericanists have believed and still accept that the original political structure at calpolli level was demo-cratic. In some instances the structure in modern Indian communi-ties has influenced their thinking. In my opinion this, too, is the result of erroneous interpretations of observations made in these communities, since modern Mexican communities usually have a corporate structure and are, in essence, still stratified. The im-poverishment of their cultural and social life during and after Spanish colonial domination has made socioeconomic differences less obvious. Moreover, it can be rather confusing for the un-initiated who observe the frequent instances of social mobility in such stratified systems. But then, this social mobility was also a feature of pre-Spanish Mexico. Democracy, however, is quite a dif-ferent thing. Many have described the calpolli as a tribal clan that lost its democratic character in the efforts for centralization made by the imperial administration of Motêuchzoma Xocoyotzin (1502-20). The material I have gathered leads only to the conclusion that the original calpollis were hierarchically organized in the same structure as was the larger society. What did happen was that over the course of time more contrast developed between the traditional calpolli nobility and the new imperial nobility with its allegiance to the central institutions of the Aztec empire.

As described above, in theory Tenochtitlan was divided into eight sectors, each with its own supreme god and predominant social group(s) associated with that god. These eight sectors were symbolically formed by a diagonal line made by the four sacred waters, which were represented as running from the four cardinal points to the main ceremonial center through each of the four large sectors of the city. It has already been noted that these four sacred waters were a symbolic representation with a mythical basis, and although they may have had some connection with existing natural springs, they were probably not representational of actual canals or waterways in Tenochtitlan. Therefore, the diagonal division of the large quarters of the city cannot be regarded as a geographical reality, but it is, of course, extremely important to know the real territorial division of Tenochtitlan and the exact location of each calpolli temple.

Old maps and descriptions of Tenochtitlan and early colonial Mexico City give us some clues with which to speculate on the locations of the earliest seven calpollis.[49] Data taken from Durán have already shown that the populations of these seven important wards was further "divided" to form a total of twenty calpollis.[50] We can assume that many of these so-called divisions were in fact newcomers who were combined with the original settlers. Nevertheless, the result was that two or more calpollis were formed from each of the seven original ones. The names of the twenty calpollis are given by Tezozomoc in his two historical works *Crónica Mexicana* and *Crónica Mexîcayotl.* For reasons to be explained below, Tezozomoc cites these names in more than one context in several series of fifteen calpollis or calpolli temples. This is probably the reason why so few Mesoamericanists have discussed these twenty in their studies.[51]

In the following list of twenty calpollis the seven original calpollis are indicated by an asterisk:

1. Tlacatêcpan*	11. Cihuatêcpan*
2. Chililico	12. Molonco itlillan
3. Coatlan	13. Têcpantzinco
4. Apantêuhctlan	14. Yopico*
5. Acatliacapan	15. Xochicalco
6. Tlacochcalco*	16. Huitznahuac*
7. Tzonmolco	17. Coatlxoxouhcan
8. Tezcacoac	18. Cuauhquiahuac
9. Izquitlan*	19. Chalman*
10. Tlamatzinco	20. Atempan

Probably these twenty calpollis did not include all the people who lived in the vicinity of Tenochtitlan. Nor is it correct to assume that this list contains all the calpolli names used in Tenochtitlan. As I have said in an earlier work, many calpollis could be called by more than one name, depending on their territorial, social, religious, or other characteristics.[52] It is also likely that, besides the people who belonged to these twenty calpollis, there were among the inhabitants of Tenochtitlan people organized in similar but different corporate units. These were probably not regarded as real Mexîcâ-Tenochcâ and were excluded from an active role in the ceremonies that were part of the sanctified communal life of the recognized Tenochcas. Finally, several early-colonial censuses show that the Aztecs and other Mexican population groups often referred to subdivisions of calpollis as "calpolli" too. Because these twenty names are the only ones mentioned by Tezozomoc in connection with the consecration rite of the great temple of Huitzilopochtli in 1487, of the large number of calpolli names, names of groups, and names of localities in Tenochtitlan they can be regarded as the most commonly used for the calpollis in their socioreligious role. Moreover many of these names occur in other historical sources, for instance, in the material from the informants of Sahagún.[53]

The location of the twenty calpollis in the four large city quarters becomes a problem when we read in the *Florentine Codex* that four of the twenty calpollis were immediately outside the four city gates, in the *coatepantli* ("snake wall"), on either side of one of the four main thoroughfares that formed the boundaries of the large quarters. These four are Acatliacapan, Tezcacoac, Têcpantzinco and Cuauhquiahuac. These gates gave access to the ceremonial center where the great temples stood and at the same time separated the center from the four major avenues. From accounts of the fights in Tenochtitlan against the Spaniards in 1520 and 1521 it appears that Têcpantzinco was situated on the western causeway, and Cuauhquiahuac on the southern.[54] Caso is clearly mistaken when he places Acatliacapan on the northern thoroughfare and consequently Tezcacoac on the eastern thoroughfare.[55] There are many indications of the connection between Tezcacoac and the large quarter of Cuepopan. Tezozomoc lists five officials who represented the four large city quarters: *tlacateccatl, huitznahuac tiacauh, cihuatêcpan tiacauh, tezcacoac tiacauh,* and *yopicâ tiacauh.*[56] The *tlacateccatl* represents Atzacualco, just as Ilancueitl did in the *Codex Izhuatepec,* and particularly the calpolli Tlacatêcpan. As his title indicates, the *huitznahuac tiacauh* belonged to the calpolli of Huitznahuac and consequently to the city quarter of Teopan-Zoqui(a)pan. The *cihuatêcpan tiacauh* and the *yopicâ tiacauh* were connected with the calpollis Cihuatêcpan and Yopico, both of which, as has been said before, belonged to the city quarter of Moyotla. Thus only the city quarter of Cuepopan was left for the *tezcacoac tiacauh.* Below we shall see that these four central calpollis occupied a special position among the twenty calpollis. Although they were situated on either side of the main causeways, each was associated with one of the four city quarters. Moreover, their specific location indicated their central function in the overall organization of Tenochtitlan.

Let us leave these four important central calpollis for the moment and look at the other sixteen. The dual character of Mesoamerican forms of organization suggests that they might be considered a doubling of the eight groups that existed when the city was founded, namely, the two parts of Tlacatêcpan and the other six earlier calpollis.

Early colonial chronicles and maps of Mexico City contain data about the locations in which some of the listed calpollis settled. We should take into account, however, that the colonial locations may not have been the same geographically as pre-Spanish ones of the same name and that the nature of colonial settlement may have been quite different from that of the pre-Spanish population. By the second point I mean that we are not quite certain about the nature of the pre-Spanish calpolli-settlements in Mexîco-Tenochtitlan. It may be assumed that, in view of the urban character of this society, people who belonged to the same calpolli lived in a closely built section of the city with boundaries clearly defined, but we do not know that for certain. It is also possible that only the calpolli temples, as organizational centers, had fixed locations, while the people who belonged to them lived scattered over the city among members of other calpollis. This was a common settlement pattern in some rural areas. Leaving the resolution of the problem of settlement pattern until later, now at least we can conclude that each of the calpolli temples always belonged to a specific large city quarters and that any colonial remains or continuations were regarded as also belonging to the same city quarters.

Colonial sources show that Coatlan belonged to the city quarter of Atzacoalco.[57] In an earlier study it has already been shown that Tzonmolco was a calpolli temple, which stood in the area with the territorial name Copolco and was therefore regarded as belonging to Cuepopan.[58] In the ritual ceremony of the fourteenth annual feast of Quecholli, Tlamatzinco appears to be closely associated with Izquitlan.[59] Furthermore, this calpolli had a Tlamatzinco *calmecac*, a boarding school for training priests and administrators. Since the seven *calmecac* schools were evidently connected with the seven original calpollis of Tenochtitlan, of which Izquitlan was one, there must have been a direct connection between Izquitlan and Tlamatzinco, also making it quite likely that Tlamatzinco was in Cuepopan. Atempan's location is also easy to establish.

Sahagún's informants mention the goddess Tocî-Teteoinnan as *calpolteotl* of Atempan,[60] and Durán places the temple of this goddess on the east side of the southern main street, south of Huitznahuac in Teopan.[61] In an earlier work I pointed out that Atempan was evidently associated with the calpolli of Chalman, because the famous *cihuacoatl Tlacayelel*, who, as we know from the *Codex Izhuatepec*, derived his title from Chalman, had been *atempanecatl* before assuming the higher office.[62] Since Chalman was located in Teopan, it is not at all surprising to find Atempan in that quarter of the city.

Now we have established the approximate locations of fifteen of the twenty calpolli temples. It is more difficult, though not impossible, to place the other five. According to Sahagún's informants, both Chililico and Molonco Itlillan were associated with the calendrical symbol of Chicunahui Ehecatl (Nine Wind),[63] who was considered as an aspect of Quetzalcoatl.[64] We know that Quetzalcoatl was a god of the east as well as of the west because of, among other things, his association with both the morning and the evening star.[65] This leads one to expect that the worship of this god was connected with a calpolli temple situated in the east, that is, in Atzacualco, as well as with one in the west, in Moyotla. Furthermore, from a myth about the founding of Tenochtitlan it appears that, when the city was established, within its territory was a red as well as a black seat of Quetzalcoatl.[66] Therefore, it is justifiable to associate the meanings of the two calpolli names we have just discussed with the red and black seats of Quetzalcoatl. For Chililico (which is meaningful only as a combination of *chili* and *tlico*) signifies "In the Fire of Red Pepper," and Molonco Itlillan means "Black Place of the Pool."

The red seat of Quetzalcoatl would have been associated with his place as morning star. Therefore, Chililico should be regarded as part of Atzacoalco and a dependency of Tlacatêcpan. Molonco Itlillan should then be considered to lie in the west and belong to Moyotla. It seems reasonable to assume that the Tlillancalco (Black House) and the Tlillan Calmecac (School of the Black Place— for the training of priests and administrators) also belonged to Moyotla. The hypotheses that each of the seven *calmecac* schools in Tenochtitlan lay in one of the seven important original calpollis leads to the conclusion that Molonco Itlillan was a dependency of Cihuatêcpan. For the other *calmecac* in Moyotla was that of Yopico, which was the only other calpolli of the original seven situated in that quarter section of the city.[67] The name indicates a connection between the Yopico *calmecac* and this temple.

It is now left to discover to what quarter the three remaining calpolli temples belonged. To summarize, the distribution of the other seventeen calpolli temples was five in Cuepopan and four in each of the other three quarters of the city. Therefore, it seems reasonable to assume that the division of the city into four large parts with a central ceremonial complex, which can be regarded as a fifth city section, is repeated in each of the four quarters of the city. This would mean that the three remaining calpolli temples, Coatlxoxouhcan, Apantêuhctlan, and Xochicalco, were in three different city quarters and that none were in Cuepopan. This supposition goes along with our previous assumption that the sixteen noncentral calpolli temples were the result of a doubling of the eight original sacred places belonging to the eight sectors in the city.

The above historical representation may also be found in a brief but almost complete summary told in simple narrative style by the Spanish conqueror Bernal Díaz del Castillo, who says: "I have lingered on my account of that great temple of Tlatelolco and its inner courts, for, as I said, this was the largest temple in the whole of Mexico [City] where there were so many temples, very luxurious and imposing, so that between four or five parishes or city wards they always had a sanctuary with their idols."[68]

Coatlxoxouhcan means literally "Place of Coatlxoxouhqui," the Green or Emerald Snake. He is mentioned in the *Florentine Codex,* where he is directly associated with Omacatl (a calendrical name of Tezcatlepoca) and Yecatzintli.[69] The name Emerald Snake possibly identifies this calpolli god with Huitzilopochtli and, therefore, with Huitznahuac and the city quarter of Teopan-Zoqui(a)pan. Of the many names given to Huitzilopochtli one of the best known is Ilhuicatlxoxouhqui (Emerald Sky), which evidently refers to this preeminent Aztec god in his heavenly aspect.[70] As calpolli god of Huitznahuac he was often referred to as Tlacahuepan Cuexcochtzin, a name sometimes also given to Tezcatlepoca.[71] Therefore, the association made above with Omacatl-Tezcatlepoca can be viewed as another connection with Huitznahuac. Also, the element "snake" in the name has a powerful symbolic meaning. As has been said before, the snake was a symbol of the underworld. If Emerald Sky refers to the heavenly aspect of Huitzilopochtli, it seems altogether likely that Emerald Snake is a name for his aspect as a god of the underworld, which is largely associated with original, ancient gods and population.

The name of the god Coatlxoxouhqui (Green Snake) seems to refer to the concept that life (symbolic color: green) springs from the
creative force of the underworld (symbol: snake). Coatlxoxouhqui
may therefore be regarded as one of the names given to the very
ancient creative force, Ometêuhctli (Couple Lord, Lord of Duality),
also called Tonacatêcuhtli-Tonacacihuatl (Lord and Lady of Our
Existence). In Mexican mythology this ancient creative force was
also expressed in a special aspect of Huitzilopochtli referred to
as Omitêuhctli (Lord of Bones).[72] This form fits in well with a
dependency of Huitznahuac, and in chapter 9 we shall see that
the priest of this Omitêuhctli actually took part in an important
ritual ceremony that was held in the Huitznahuac temple. All
these data taken together justify the conclusion that, as a calpolli,
Coatlxoxouhcan was hierarchically subordinate to Huitznahuac
and that, like this original calpolli of the Mexitin, it belonged to
the city quarter of Teopan-Zoqui(a)pan.[73]

Sahagún's informants said that during Ochpaniztli feast three
gods were worshiped in the calpolli temple of Xochicalco (In the
Flower House). They were Iztac Cinteotl (White Maize God),
Tlatlauhqui Cinteotl (Red Maize God), and Atlatonan (Our Mother
of the Waters). As the name says, Xochicalco was associated with
fertility, especially with the fertility of the main food crop, maize.
Fertility and rejuvenation were also the main focus in the worship
of the god Xipe Totêc, whose major temple was in the calpolli
of Yopico. Therefore, it is probable that Xochicalco was the dependency of Yopico and was, like Yopico, connected with the city
quarter of Moyotla.

The only location, then, for Apantêuhctlan is as a dependency
of Tlacatêcpan in Atzacualco. The god Apantêuhctli was on the
one hand an aspect of the rain god Tlaloc;[74] on the other he
was one of the Mimixcoâ.[75]

It will probably be impossible to say precisely where each of
the twenty calpollis was situated, but we can determine whether
the structure of each of the four quarters of the city reflected
typical divisions of the city as a whole.

Let us begin with Cuepopan. Here Tlacochcalco was the most
important calpolli and had, moreover, two important dependencies: Tzonmolco and Tezcacoac. We know that Tzonmolco was
in the northern part of Cuepopan while Tezcacoac was in the
middle of the city. Therefore, Tlacochcalco must have been situated between these two calpollis. Izquitlan was somewhere along
the causeway to Popotla and Tlacopan, which meant that it was

situated exactly opposite to Chalman, which was in Teopan, south of the main road leading to the lakeshore. We have already said that calpollis placed opposite each other in two facing quarters of the city often had important ritual relationships. A well-known example was that of Tlacochcalco and Huitznahuac. Their ritual associations are clearly expressed in the ancient religious song "Huitznahuac Yautl."[76]

This important organizational principle was evidently also applied in Teopan-Zoqui(a)pan. For Atempan, which was opposite Chalman, was Chalman's dependency, and Cuauhquiahuac, Huitznahuac, and Coatlxoxouhcan were approximately on a line perpendicular to one connecting Chalman and Atempan. In Cuepopan and Moyotla, however, things were different. Tlacochcalco must have been somewhere in the center of Cuepopan, just as Huitznahuac was in the middle of Teopan-Zoqui(a)pan. Tzonmolco and Tezcacoac, then, were east and Izquitlan and Tlamatzinco were west in this quarter of the city. From data provided in the ritual for the second annual feast of Tlacaxipehualiztli, we know that Yopico, in Moyotla, and Coatlan, in Atzacualco, were in ritual opposition to each other.[77] This makes it likely that the two calpollis were in the southwest section of Moyotla and in the northeast section of Atzacualco, respectively. This probability is somewhat confirmed when we actually find the calpollis in those locations on colonial maps.[78] This means, however, that Têcpantzinco, Cihuatêcpan, and Yopico lay more or less in a straight line, while Molonco Itlillan and Xochicalco were more or less in a line perpendicular to it and opposite each other. But because Molonco Itlillan was a dependency of Cihuatêcpan and Xochicalco a dependency of Yopico, clearly the boundaries between the ranges of influence of Cihuatêcpan and Xochicalco ran approximately north to south, not diagonally through Moyotla, and were different from those in Zoqui(a)pan. Molonco Itlillan must have been situated opposite Atempan, on the west side of the southern causeway leading into the city. The Tlillancalli (Black House) also stood on that side of the southern causeway, and the temple of Tocî-Teteôinnan, the calpolli god of Atempan, opposite it. Xochicalco, then, must have been situated on the south side of the west causeway. This agrees with the fact that Tzapotlan was also situated there, as seen on colonial maps.[79] According to Sahagún's informants, Tzapotlan was a ceremonial place, which like Xochicalco was a dependency of Yopico.[80]

The situation for Atzacualco was different because it had only one of the original calpollis, Tlacatêcpan. The other four subordinate calpollis were dependencies of Tlacatêcpan. What was the location of these four dependencies? According to the principle of opposition described above, the question is not a difficult one. Chililico lay opposite Molonco Itlillan and therefore east of the northern road leading northwest into the city. Acatliacapan was adjacent to the center of the city. Since Coatlan was opposite Yopico, it was in the northeastern part of Atzacualco. Tlacatêcpan was between these three. Apantêuhctlan must have been somewhere on the north side of the city's eastern thoroughfare and therefore opposite Xochicalco. The relationship between the gods Apantêuhctli and Atlatonan would make this interpretation likely.

The ideal typical division of the city of Tenochtitlan is now complete. It was divided into twenty calpollis, which comprised the entire citizen population that could participate fully in the religious and social life of the city. Besides the Tenochcas there must have been many other inhabitants of the city who did not belong to any of those calpollis. These persons who, as a rule, would have been of foreign origin, had three kinds of relationships with the citizen Tenochcas. First, they held lower- and middle-rank offices in the civil service and the army without connection to any calpollis except perhaps the four central ones. They were servants and debtor-slaves to the upper classes in the capital city, which consisted of nobles, high-ranking soldiers, priests, and merchants. Finally, they were servants to the calpollis in the capital.

The lower- and middle-rank offices of the first relationship were often held for a limited period of time, one to two years at most. Imperial civil servants and soldiers of high rank who had come from a rural area would nearly always have joined a calpolli in the capital by adoption or by taking a vow to a calpolli god. Sometimes such memberships were granted to non-Tenochcas as a reward.[81]

Those who worked as servants to members of the upper class in the capital had, as a rule, direct association only with their individual male or female employer, though some may have been assigned by the government to serve distinguished noblemen, military men, or merchants.

Those who served the calpollis would mostly have been so-called *mâyequê* ("right hands"). They were farm workers or tenant farmers who cultivated the calpolli's fields, which were rarely cultivated by the Tenochcas themselves. A calpolli such as Tzonmolco, which had a large number of members employed in trade and commerce, either leased out their lands or acquired

Fig. 4.10. *General view of Tenochtitlan and Tla(1)telolco on the eve of the Spanish conquest, as seen from the western side. In the background are the volcanoes Iztaccihuatl and Popocatepetl, and on the right, where the causeway ends, Huixachtepetl can be seen.* La Civilización Azteca, *p. 41 (National Museum, Mexico City).*

workers to cultivate them. Under Aztec rule either alternative came much to the same thing. In the pages that follow, attention will be given to the mutual ritual associations of the twenty calpollis in Tenochtitlan and their relationship with the other two imperial capitals. Only then will it be possible to give a more detailed description of the affinity between the twenty calpollis and their gods. Details for this analysis have been derived from Tezozomoc's extensive description of the consecration ceremony of the great temple of Huitzilopochtli and Tlaloc, Coatepetl (Snake Mountain).

CHAPTER 5

Incorporation and Development Within the Framework of the Têcpanec Empire

BEFORE continuing our description of Aztec social development in the Valley of Mexico, we must return to the events of the last days of the Toltec empire, when dissension was rife in that society. Such disagreement may have occurred earlier in Mesoamerica, for instance, among the Mayas and Olmecs, but at any rate it was clearly a factor among the Toltecs. In one way such internal discord was a natural consequence of traditional Mesoamerican dual organization found in all the societies of the region. Therefore, it is not surprising that it was still operating in Aztec times. It is no exaggeration to say that the essential functions performed by the government of every Mesoamerican group were, on the one hand, to exploit the tension in the dual social system and, on the other, to manipulate it and keep it within certain bounds.

The leadership was not always successful. For example, when Huemac (Big Hand) and Quetzalcoatl (Feathered Serpent or Magnificent Twin) ruled Tollan in its last days, the situation became critical. The names of these two leaders are actually the titles of the two highest-ranking leaders of an oligarchic Toltec state, rather than personal names. Huemac, from the Toltec-Chichimec population, represented a religious ceremonial in which Tezcatlepoca-Tezcatlanextia (Radiant Mirror-Brilliant Mirror) was the most important God in a large pantheon. Most of Huemac's functions were of a military or administrative nature. Quetzalcoatl, from the Nonoalca population, was foremost a priest who worshiped the god Quetzalcoatl as well as the rain god Tlaloc (Wine of the Earth or He Who Became Earth).

The celestial identifications of the two are very interesting. Huemac and his major god, Tezcatlepoca-Tezcatlanextia, were associated with the star-filled sky in general: the Black Radiant Obsidian Mirror is the symbol of the nocturnal sky, in which the name Big Hand may refer to the Moon. Quetzalcoatl is Venus as both morning star and evening star. Venus, called Great Star in the Nahuatl language, is a spectacular dual and dominating phenomenon in the sky at night which could not fail to appeal to the people of Mesoamerica. The translation Magnificent Twin is an unusual one, but quite justifiable, because besides "snake" *coatl* means "twin" (think of the *cuates* in modern Mexican Spanish) and *quetzalli* means "feather of the green quetzal bird," but because this is the most precious kind of feather, the word was also used in the sense of "precious" or "magnificent."

There probably has been nothing in Mexican history so widely misinterpreted as Quetzalcoatl's part in it. This misunderstanding can be attributed to the fact that the Spaniards, in their boundless aversion to the fierce Huitzilopochtli philosophy, found themselves attracted to what they believed to be a more benign view; some of them even identified Quetzalcoatl as a stray Christian Apostle. Because of their aversion to Huitzilopochtli and their more sympathetic attitude toward the cult of Quetzalcoatl, adherents of the latter sect were allowed greater freedom of speech than were the followers of Huitzilopochtli.

As we have seen, Huemac, in a celestial sense, stood for the large constellation of stars that, according to northern religious views, represented the many dead ancestors of the northern Chichimec tribes.[1] In a terrestrial sense Huemac was the representative of the common people. Quetzalcoatl was, in his celestial sense, the predominant, the extraordinary one. In a terrestrial sense he represented the hereditary nobility and the highest priesthood.

The effect of these attitudes was that Quetzalcoatl was represented as a beneficent civilizer, a great spiritual leader, one who hated human sacrifice and who was eventually driven away by demonical powers which also brought about his moral deterioration.[2]

In reality there is no doubt that the followers of Quetzalcoatl practiced human sacrifice.[3] The sect, moreover, was responsible for the introduction of the Mexican form of human sacrifice to the Mayan area.[4] In mythology the god Quetzalcoatl was shown as having a constructive as well as a destructive effect on people, just as were all the other great gods. His negative influences are described at great length in the *Annals of Cuauhtitlan.*[5]

It is unclear what actually caused the violent struggle between the two factions in Tollan. The available sources suggest the following possibilities:

1. A serious prolonged drought had affected the arable land and other resources of the population in and around Tollan, and the followers of Huemac and Quetzalcoatl quarreled over the best way to deal with the situation in religious terms. The followers of Quetzalcoatl started a kind of polytheistic iconoclasm.[6]

2. Ethnic rivalries between Toltecâ-Chichimecâ and Nonoalcâ played a part in the struggle, and Huemac tried without success to bridge the animosity by encouraging marriages between the two groups. According to the *Historia Tolteca Chichimeca,* however, the ethnic boundaries did not exactly coincide with those of the two religious factions.[7]

3. The growing power of the military nobility, led by Huemac, caused increasing resistance in the established aristocratic class of priests, which eventually led to an outburst of violence.

In any case, it was Quetzalcoatl who called upon his followers to leave Tollan, and by doing so, against the will of Huemac, he destroyed the traditional dualistic system of the community as well as the society itself.

In his latest work on the Toltecs, Nigel Davies says that external influences may also have stimulated the acts of violence that ultimately led to the fall of the empire. In this connection he especially mentions the Huaxtecs.[8] His explanation of the internal struggle of the Toltecs, however, seems to be open to question, especially his opinion that it was the Nonoalcas who were the adherents of Tez-catlepoca and that the entire Tolteca-Chichimecâ group followed Quetzalcoatl.[9] A few pages farther on he is less certain of this interpretation and tries to make the civil conflict seem less important by noting the strong resemblance between the gods of the two groups.[10] He overlooks the fact that history knows of many violent struggles over minor religious differences.

It is difficult for Westerners, unaccustomed as they are to "encapsulating" tendencies in their own society, to understand why Huemac considered the flight of his opponent a personal defeat. To a Toltec chief, however, the breaking up of the dual system of administration meant the end of his regime. Therefore, Huemac went after Quetzalcoatl to bring him back. When he failed, he committed suicide in the Cincalco cave near Chapultepec.[11]

The Aztecs considered themselves heirs of Huemac's policy. Therefore, their political and social attitudes took into account the minority position to which the Toltec population had been reduced; moreover, within that minority the state had to reconcile the two traditional Toltec themes into a new, unified system. The identification of the Aztec leaders with Huemac was clearly evident in the visions of the grand ruler Motêuhczoma Xocoyotzin when the Spaniards were first seen off the Mexican coast. In his dreams Motêuhczoma spoke with Huemac in the Cincalco cave and heard his dire prophecies.[12] His centralizing and increasingly aristocratic policy had led Motêuhczoma a long way toward the Quetzalcoatl current, and his conflict with the Tzompan family of Cuitlahuac was a consequence of this.[13] The reader who is interested in this subject, which falls outside the scope of this book, should remember that the priests and corporate groups attached to the god Quetzalcoatl need not adhere to the so-called Quetzalcoatl philosophy but could very well be loyal to the Aztec regime.

The founding of Tenochtitlan and Tlatelolco produced two "Aztec" sister towns, in which a new Toltec, or in any case Mesoamerican, society was formed from many ethnic elements. At first the Têcpanecs, who had little interest in this swampy area bordering on Colhuâcan, left the earlier inhabitants as well as the newcomers alone.

In contrast with later times, when the construction of hydraulic works had drastically changed ecological conditions in this area, at first most of it was unsuitable for chinampa horticulture, because it was saturated with water from Lake Tetzcoco, which contained saltpeter. Yet the early population managed to provide for itself by hunting, fishing, trading, and sending men out to serve as military mercenaries. Since Tlatelolco specialized in trading, it was forced, more than Tenochtitlan, to maintain good relations with the Têcpanec government. This resulted in the appointment of a Têcpanec prince as *tlâtoani* (ruler, or chief of the external administrative system) of Tlatelolco. Thus Tlatelolco was generally recognized as an administrative unit separate from Tenochtitlan, which pursued a more independent policy. The Tenochcas did not ask a Têcpanec prince to be their king and to rule above and alongside of their own traditional calpolli chiefs but instead asked the Toltec princess Ilancueitl and her nephew Acamâpichtli, who was of mixed Mexican-Toltec blood, to act as supreme rulers. From a sociohistorical perspective this event is a direct consequence of the superior position that the more "Toltec" calpollis of Tenochtitlan had gained over those of the Mexitin. According to the *Codex*

Izhuatepec, five of the calpollis held most of the administrative power in those days: Chalman, Huitznahuac, Tlacatêcpan, Tlacochcalco, and Cihuatêcpan.

The historical nature of the Acamâpichtli (Handful of Arrows) as chief of Chalman and *cihuacoatl* (female companion, or highest internal administrator) for the entire city of Tenochtitlan is vague. Many backgrounds are ascribed to him. His father may have been an Opochtli priest.[14] He himself is sometimes referred to as Itzpapalotl (Obsidian Butterfly), a priest of the goddess by the same name.[15] In chapter 9 we shall come back to Acamâpichtli's uncertain descent. The most questionable part of his identity is his name. We have already seen that one of the first Toltec chiefs, the founder of Tollantzinco, was also named Acamâpichtli. The name suggests an association with the traditional Chichimec rite for taking possession of land, shooting arrows in the directions of each of the four quarters of the compass.[16] Therefore any independent community with a complete or partial Chichimec tradition could call the founder of its administration by that name. This and the fact that the founder of Tenochtitlan's royal house is referred to by several entirely different names indicates that Handful of Arrows was a symbolic name or title given to that personage in later times.

Tezozomoc says of his name Obsidian Butterfly:

yêhuatl in piltzintli	He is the prince,
in conetzintli	the noble child,
in tocozqui in toquetzal	our gem, our precious feather;
in itoca in iteheca	his name, his personal wind-blown acquisition,
in Itzpapalotl	is Obsidian Butterfly,
in Acamâpichtli.	is Hand Full of Arrows.

That is what was said by the representatives of Tenochtitlan, who had been sent to Colhuâcan to ask permission to lead the prince to their city, before Acamâpichtli ascended the throne. At the time he may have held a priestly office connected with the worship of the goddess Itzpapalotl, and for that reason her name was mentioned. Itzpapalotl was one of the main goddesses of the Colhuas.[17] The expression *iteheca* ("his personal windblown acquisition") suggests that a magic wind once destined him for this high office. Two other chronicles give some corrupted forms of Acamâpichtli's personal name, for example, Xilechoz, Gilechoz, and Pilethoc.[18] Both sources state emphatically that he bore this name before he was selected to assume the government post. Veytia, on rather

vague grounds, says that he was also called by the name or nickname Matlalîhuitzin (Blue Feather).[19]

The problem of conflicting dates given for his rule has been
thoroughly and convincingly dealt with by Davies.[20] For the establishment of the beginning date of his reign, it is necessary to realize
that chronological conflicts arise from the fact that a number of
historical sources make indiscriminate use of different calendric
systems. Moreover, they do not agree on the nature of the administrative offices held by this Acamâpichtli. The documents give
different data:

1. Acamâpichtli came to Tenochtitlan as the husband of his
aunt Ilancueitl and did not immediately assume a government
office. Ilancueitl was the supreme external administrator of the
Tenochca community.[21]

2. While Ilancueitl was the supreme administrator of Tenochtitlan, Acamâpichtli held the office of *cihuacoatl,* which was the
highest administrative rank of the internal system.[22]

3. The historical sources that describe the beginning of the royal
house of Tenochtitlan as a "condominium" of Ilancueitl and Acamâpichtli probably refer to the situation mentioned under number 2
above, or something similar to it.[23]

4. From the first, Acamâpichtli was *tlâtoani* (supreme administrator in the external system) of Tenochtitlan, perhaps accompanied by his aunt and wife, Ilancueitl.[24]

The historical sources based on the lost *Codex X*—such as the
works of Durán, the *Codex Ramírez,* and the Tovar manuscript—
say that Ilancueitl was barren and that the children of Acamâpichtli had been born to the daughters of the chiefs of the twenty
calpollis. These women had been offered to the king when it appeared that his marriage to the Toltec princess would remain
childless.[25] Furthermore, Durán relates that Ilancueitl was so
deeply grieved and found it so difficult to resign herself to this
state of affairs that she tried to find a more acceptable solution.
She proposed that Acamâpichtli bring all the babies born to the
daughters of the calpolli nobles and lay them in her bed, so that
she could make the citizens believe that she had given birth to
them. And so it happened. Whenever a child was born, all the
high dignitaries and representatives of the neighboring communities came to congratulate Ilancueitl on the birth of a royal child,
which again and again many thought to be her own.[26]

Fig. 5.1. *The four "Aztec" calpollis in Aztlan.* Codex Azcatitlan, *pl. 2.*

Torquemada gives two contradicting versions of the traditional
story. He also cites the barrenness of Ilancueitl and goes on to say
that, according to some sources, she was sent back to her parental
home in Coatlichan—a version he rejects—and that other, more
reliable sources say that Acamâpichtli, after consulting Ilancueitl,
took another wife. Ilancueitl took such great interest in the education of the children born from this second marriage that many
looked upon her as the children's mother.[27]

To summarize, most of the historical sources emanating from
Tenochtitlan emphasize the aristocratic descent and the political
significance of Ilancueitl but also mention her barrenness and consequently do not represent the later members of the Aztec royal
house as her descendants. Since the Aztec aim was to restore the
Toltec empire, to say that the new royal family was descended
from Toltec royal ancestors in both the matrilineal and the patri-

Fig. 5.2. *The coronation of Acamâpichtli.* Codex Azcatitlan, *pl. 13.*

lineal lines would give it strong legitimation. Evidently to do so the Aztec historians would have had to stretch historical reality too far. Most chronicles emphasize that Ilancueitl was of an older generation than Acamâpichtli and call her his aunt, his "mother" (probably in the sense of mother's sister), his wet nurse, or his foster mother. The *Annals of Cuauhtitlan* indicate that she died in 1383 and that, according to the people of Cuitlahuac, royal rule in Mexîco-Tenochtitlan was not established until that time.[28] However, the year symbol VIII Acatl (VIII Reed), which in the Tenochtitlan calendar coincides with the year 1383, coincides with the year 1371 in the Cuitlahuac calendar. If Ilancueitl had died an old woman as early as 1371, it is indeed almost unthinkable that she could have been the mother of Acamâpichtli's children, whether or not she was fertile in her productive years. It seems possible that

she was past childbearing age when the so-called marriage with
her younger kinsman Acamâpichtli was arranged.

What part Ilancueitl played in the formation of the new local
government of Tenochtitlan during the second half of the fourteenth century remains an essential question. It seems necessary
to understand Ilancueitl's role in order to acquire clear insight
into the change from the traditional government of the islands of
Toltzalan-Acatzalan into the new *tlâtocayotl* (the semi-indepen-
dent administrative unit with its own external chief, the *tlâtoani*)
of Mexîco-Tenochtitlan. The sources quoted above do not contain
enough material to provide the necessary understanding. Therefore, it is more profitable to use the *Codex Azcatitlan* as a starting point for the study of Acamâpichtli's function and his place
in history. This codex is the only pictorial that gives many particulars about the coronation of Acamâpichtli and his accession to the
throne. It is also one of the historical sources that completely ig-
nores the existence of Ilancueitl. The left side of folio 13 of the
codex shows the accession to the throne and the coronation of the
first *tlâtoani* of Tenochtitlan (fig. 5.2). He is pictured in the center
seated on an *oceloicpalli* (a reed stool covered with ocelot hide),
and around him are twelve other personages. Among them is one
who occupies a prominent place, for he sits on a high throne directly opposite the new *tlâtoani.* According to his glyph he is Acacihtli (Reed Hare), the *têcpanecatl chichimecatêcuhtli* and one of
the two supreme chiefs of the calpolli of Tlacatêpan at the time
of Tenochtitlan's founding. At Acacihtli's right, seated on an *oceloicpalli,* is the other chief of Tlacatêcpan, recognizable from the
glyph of that calpolli, but his personal name is not given. He may
be Ocelopan or one of his successors. Opposite the two chiefs are
the new *tlâtoani* and three other personages who hold the symbols
of coronation. The figure in the middle holds both the Aztec crown
(xiuhhuitzolli) and the royal staff *(tlâtocatopilli);* the other two
carry the royal robe and the royal necklace. Surprisingly, the name
glyph identifying the new *tlâtoani* is not that of Acamâpichtli. It
is a smoldering arrow piercing a foot. In the Nahuatl language the
elements of that symbol may mean arrow (*mitl* or *chilatl*), fire
(tletl), and foot or lower part of leg (*icxitl* or *xotl*). Therefore, it
is reasonable to render this hieroglyph as Chilatlexotl or its polite
form, Chilatlexotzin. The name could easily have been corrupted
to Xilechoz in the Spanish colonial chronicles; as we have seen,
it was Acamâpichtli's personal name before he was appointed to
high office in Tenochtitlan.

At the bottom left of the folio are four calpolli chiefs, all of whom are seated on *oceloicpalli*. They are, from left to right, Epcoatl (Shell Snake), Xomimitl (Lower Part of Leg Pierced by an Arrow), Xiuhcaquê (He Who Has Turquoise Sandals), and finally a chief designated by a glyph to be read as Calpilcatl (He Who Is of Calpilco). The last symbol consists of three elements: a house *(calli)*, a rope or a cord wrapped around with some other article *(tlapiloni)*, and a globular cactus *(comitl)*, forming the name Calpilco, which, connected with a relevant office holder, expresses the idea Calpilcatl. According to Chimalpahin, Calpilco was one of the original calpollis of the legendary Aztlan, or Aztatlan.[29] The same glyph appears on the second sheet of this codex (Azcatitlan) accompanying one of the four chiefs from the original island of the Aztecs. The other three chiefs are designated by the place glyphs of Tlacochcalco, Tlacatêcpan, and Contzalan. If we assume that Tlacochcalco and Tlacatêcpan were located in the same relative positions as were the later calpollis of the same names in Tenochtitlan, namely, in the northwest and northeast, we can conclude that Calpilco belonged to the southwestern part. This was the area which, in Tenochtitlan, was called Moyotla and where Cihuatêcpan and Yopico were the most important calpollis. In the previous chapter we have seen that Xomimitl was chief of Yopico. Therefore Calpilco was likely to have been part of Cihuatêcpan, so that the Calpilcatl can be regarded as representative of that calpolli in Moyotla. We know that Xiuhcaquê was the chief of Izquitlan, and Epcoatl, who was said to be a grandson of Tenoch,[30] probably represented his grandfather's calpolli, Tlacochcalco.

On the far left of the picture are three more individuals seated on *oceloicpalli*. The bottom personage bears the name Cuahuitzcoatl (Eagle Thorn Snake), a priest and *teomama* (god bearer), who is also mentioned in other historical sources and who belonged to the calpolli Huitznahuac.[31] Depicted above him is a chief called Memexoch (Agave Flower), and at the top is a god bearer of Tezcatlepoca who carries, on his back an image of this god, recognizable by his headdress of heron feathers. I interpret his name as Huemac (Big Hand or Old Hand), for the accompanying hieroglyph consists of a hand *(maitl)* on a mountain *(tepetl)*. The last element may also indicate the concepts big, original, old, and important.

The *Codex Azcatitlan* shows that the coronation took place in a year VII Tochtli (VII Rabbit), which immediately preceded VIII Acatl (VIII Reed), the year in which, according to the *Annals of*

Cuauhtitlan, Ilancueitl died and the "reign in Mexico began." According to the *Codex Mendoza,* Acamâpichtli undertook the administrative office of *cihuacoatl* ("female companion") in a year I Tecpatl (I Flint), that is, six years before the coronation date mentioned above. Also, according to the same codex, he became *tlâtoani* ("ruler") in the year VIII Reed, which is the date mentioned in the *Annals of Cuauhtitlan.*[32] In this way the *Codex Mendoza* reconciles seemingly contradictory data from two groups of historical sources that mention the years 1376 and 1383 as the beginning of the reign of Acamâpichtli. A much earlier date, around 1366, is given by a third group of historical sources, among which are such important ones as the *Annals of Tlatelolco;* the *Florentine Codex;* the *Tovar Manuscript;* the *Crónica Mexîcayotl,* by Tezozomoc; and one of the traditional stories recorded by Chimalpahin.[33] Probably they refer to the year that Acamâpichtli first moved to Tenochtitlan, before he filled a central government position. He may have held a post in the calpolli of Chalman, just as his father, Opochtli, had once held a priestly office there.

Viewed against this background, Acamâpichtli's coronation, as it has been pictured in the *Codex Azcatitlan,* seems to rest on a firm foundation. But a closer look at the personages involved in this ceremony reveals that the depiction could not have been a "historical" one in the Western sense of the word, though it was meant to be a historical scene according to Aztec conceptions. Acacihtli (Reed Hare), who figures prominently as master of ceremonies, was one of the chiefs of the migration that took place more than a century before this coronation and one of the founders of Tenochtitlan.

The same *Codex Azcatitlan* gives on its second folio the chief Calpilcatl as one of the four calpolli chiefs in Aztlan at the end of the eleventh century. On the third folio of this codex Cuahuitzcoatl, Memexoch, and Huemac are represented as chiefs and god bearers leading the tribes from the mythical place Teocolhuâcan in the year I Tecpatl (I Flint Knife, A.D. 1168). Other historical sources give Memexoch and Huemac as officials or kings of the Toltecs.[34]

In fact the only undeniable contemporaries of Chilatlexotzin-Acamâpichtli are Tezozomoc of Azcapotzalco and Cuacuapitzahuac of Tlatelolco, who are depicted on the right side of folio 8, plus the three nameless persons pictured on the left side of folio 1 holding the ceremonial attributes of the coronation. The other figures are apparently only symbolic of the most important corporate groups that were involved in the establishment of the new government. Acacihtli occupies a predominant position as the symbol of the family that had provided the most important official in the external administration of the previous government made up of calpolli nobles. Furthermore, his family supplied the new king's most important spouse, who was to be the mother of his future successor, Huitzilîhuitl (Hummingbird Feather).[35] The fact that two Toltec kings have been included in the scene is most notable. It is not likely that they represent groups in the community of Tenochtitlan, though it is possible that there were one or more small groups of Toltec origin in the city.[36] It is more likely, however, that the presence of the Toltec kings at Acamâpichtli's coronation only served as a legitimation for the political efforts of the Aztecs, as heirs of the Toltecs, to undertake the restoration of the Toltec empire. Other chronicles and pictorials present the Colhua-Toltec princess Ilancueitl as an important personage, whereas the *Codex Azcatitlan* does not even mention her. Yet it is the only codex to mention two Toltec kings as participants in Acamâpichtli's coronation ceremony. It seems logical to conclude, then, that these kings and the princess Ilancueitl in other historical records serve the same purpose: to provide legitimate claim to the historic right of the Aztecs for the Toltec imperial heritage.

All this may raise doubts about the actual presence of Ilancueitl in the political life of Tenochtitlan. The two Toltec kings, at any rate, did not play any personal role in it. It is nevertheless likely that the princess Ilancueitl had something to do with the Mexitin at the time that they occupied the territory of Colhuâcan. Furthermore, there are many indications of her symbolic importance in Tenochtitlan. It is possible that she was still alive when Chilatlexo-tzin-Acamâpichtli began his administration. She may even have had some special relationship with the *têcpan* of Tenochtitlan, as the *Codex Izhuatepec* indicates. But in that same *têcpan*, the office of supreme external leader, the *têcpanecatl-chichimecatêcuhtli*, was held by a member of the Acacihtli family. It is highly probable that the two traditions, one including Ilancueitl, the other not including her, are in perfect agreement in a historical sense that was conceptually meaningful to the Aztecs. Both are concerned with the important social developments connected with the termination of the struggle and the friction between the newly arrived Chichimecs and the indigenous population, which consisted of Chinampanecs or Chalmecs as they were presented for posterity in the legends about Malinalxochitl and Copil. When at last the hostilities came to an end in the second half of the fourteenth century, a *pax azteca* was brought about and resulted in the new regime of Acamâpichtli. The most prominent aristocratic family in the community of Aztecâ-Mexitin, designated by the name Acacihtli, offers the new regime its indispensable support, as shown in the prominent place occupied by a representative of this family at the coronation.

It is nevertheless significant that by picturing Acamâpichtli as chief of Chalman the *Codex Izhuatepec* records that the later dynasty of supreme administrators came from that calpolli and therefore had Chalmec, that is, Chinampanec, backgrounds. Subsequently an overall administrative system was developed in Tenochtitlan, accompanied by the intermarriage of Chalmec nobility with the aristocracy in the other calpollis. Meanwhile the military and trading power of the two sister towns steadily increased as a result of the growing need of other cities to use their military forces, giving them a large number of contacts over extensive areas.

Thus the Aztecs managed to gain so much influence within the Têcpanec empire that they succeeded in forcing upon it a typically "Toltec" administrative system. The sister towns Tlatelolco and Tenochtitlan became the two other administrative centers after Azcapotzalco. At the beginning of the fifteenth century the newly organized Têcpanec empire succeeded in conquering the only important power left in the Valley of Mexico, the empire of Acolhuâcan.[37] For the first time since Toltec times all lakeshore lands in the Valley of Mexico had one central authority. It was true that the Chichimecs of Xolotl previously had achieved almost the same thing, but they had not been able to gain a firm footing in the southern sections of the valley. Then, in 1419, the entire area, with its valuable chinampas, was united with four more supreme chieftainships to form one state. Three capitals taken from among the conquerors were Azcapotzalco, ruled by Tezozomoc; Tlatelolco, governed by Tezozomoc's grandson Tlacateotzin; and Tenochtitlan, where Acamâpichtli's son (or grandson) Huitzilîhuitl had just been succeeded by his brother Chimalpopoca.[38]

Four new capital cities were created in the conquered area. They were Coatlichan and Otompan, which had been two Toltec administrative centers; Acolman and Chalco, the important lakeshore town in the south. The administration of these four towns remained in the hands of noble families from the former state of Acolhuâcan, which even before it was conquered numbered

among its inhabitants large minority groups of Têcpanecs and Aztecs. An interesting tax system was introduced. The tributes levied
in the conquered territory were divided into eight parts. One-
eighth of the taxes consisting in the contribution from Huexotla
went to Tlatelolco; one-eighth of the tributes delivered by Tetzcoco,
the seat of the former independent government of Acolhuâcan,
went to Tenochtitlan; each of the four new jurisdictions in the
conquered territory also received one-eighth part of the total tribute
to maintain their own administrative apparatus; the remaining two-
eighths went to the Têcpanec capital city, Azcapotzalco.[39] It is
understandable that the Aztec sister towns, which together received
as much of the total tax revenue as Azcapotzalco, prospered. They
began building causeways to connect the Aztec islands with each
other and with the mainland. The causeways also served as dams
to regulate the influx of fresh water from the rivers so that the
saltpeter content in some parts of the lake was permanently reduced. Thus, chinampa horticulture flourished around the Aztec
sister towns and contributed to the economic progress of the area.[40]

As long as Tezozomoc was the ruler—and he must have grown
very old by this time—this empire continued unchanged. Yet there
were always those in the Têcpanec upper classes who tried to
withdraw or change the concessions made to groups with Aztec
neo-Toltec political aspirations. Again and again these factions
tried to select Têcpanecs for administrative offices which, in accordance with Toltec hereditary traditions, should have been held
by members of local noble families. The Aztec political leaders—
male and female—opposed this tendency, sometimes with success,
sometimes in vain. The rehabilitation of the Tetzcocan prince Nezahualcoyotl (Hungry Wolf), who had survived the Conquest, and
the partial return of offices and goods to him, was in any case
largely the work of his Aztec aunts. The mother of this prince was
a sister of Chimalpopoca, and her sisters—the prince's aunts—
lived at times in the court at Tenochtitlan and at regular intervals in Azcaptozalco. They successfully exercised their influence
on Tezozomoc to grant their nephew extensive privileges. Since
Nezahualcoyotl had for many years waged a guerrilla war against
the Têcpanec military, it is indeed surprising that his aunts succeeded in doing so much for him. Thanks to their influence, he
was allowed to live in the Cillan palace in Tetzcoco and obtained
the right to stay in Tenochtitlan.

Once this had been arranged, Nezahualcoyotl had every opportunity to devise political intrigues with his Aztec relatives, the

Fig. 5.3. *Nezahualcoyotzin, prince of Tetzcoco.* Codex Ixtlilxochitl, *fol. 106; Bo-ban, pl. 76.*

army chiefs Itzcoatl, Motêuhczoma Ilhuicamina, and the latter's half-brother, Tlacayelel. These four began serious consultations about how to stop the centralizing policy of certain factions in Azcapotzalco, which they regarded as too radical. They decided to overthrow the regime after the death of Tezozomoc, at which time these groups might be most likely to win the struggle to succeed him. Nezahualcoyotl began recruiting soldiers from the east and south, especially from among the Tlaxcaltecs, Huexotzincas, and Chalcas. The Aztecs, who were mercenary warriors highly experienced from many past wars and had the best troops to be found in all of Anahuac, were joined by the Chichimec inhabitants of Cuauhtitlan, who had been allies of the Mexicans since ancient times.

The generally accepted histories of Mexico represent the complicated situation that arose around 1427 as follows. There were difficulties in connection with the succession of Tezozomoc, and as a result Nezahualcoyotl was able to liberate his father's empire from Têcpanec domination. Then with his relatives in Mexîco-Tenochtitlan he unceasingly attacked the enemy in their own territory until they were totally defeated. In the histories the second war is presented as a continuation of the first, but it is doubtful that this is accurate. What, in fact, did happen? Tezozomoc had several sons, but before his death he designated Quetzalayatzin as his successor. It was necessary for this choice to be confirmed by the Têcpanec imperial council. Although the Aztec members of the council were in favor of Quetzalayatzin, the majority of Têcpanec members supported his brother, or half brother, Maxtla, who was governor of the important Têcpanec town Coyohuâcan. Maxtla and his followers intervened, making Quetzalayatzin governor of Coyohuâcan, where Maxtla's reliable staff could keep an eye on him. Maxtla was then proclaimed Tezozomoc's successor.

At that time a plot that Chimalpopoca of Tenochtitlan had entered into with Quetzalayatzin against Maxtla, was discovered. In a surprise attack Têcpanec troops took the king of Tenochtitlan prisoner, and he and Quetzalayatzin were eliminated. After that the *tlacochcalcatl*, who was responsible for the defense of the city, committed suicide. Maxtla soon took the dominant position, and things did not look too promising for the neo-Toltec Aztecs. All the sources show that Maxtla received strong support, especially from the occupied area on the eastern shores of Lake Tetzococo, where Têcpanec officials had held posts in the internal administration from ancient times. Opposition to his regime was found only in

Fig. 5.4. *Cihuacoatl Tlacayelel and King Axayacatl assisting at a sacrificial ceremony. Durán*, Atlas, trat⁰ 1, lam⁰ 8a.

Cuauhtitlan and the two Aztec sister towns. A civil war broke out within the Têcpanec empire, and the factions involved fought with varying degrees of success.

Evidently it was specifically due to the great political as well as military qualities of Tlacayelel (Bright Spirit) that the Aztec party was the ultimate victor. Tlacayelel succeeded in winning the Colhuas to his side. Then, united with them and part of the Tenochtitlan population, he went to war.

He proclaimed to the rest of the population of Tenochtitlan that his warriors would be elevated to noble status if they were victorious. Thus he confronted them with the realities of the political situation; those who took part in the war would either be raised to the peerage or blamed for the defeat and thus sacrificed, whereas, the onlookers would be unharmed.[41] With this, a new element had been introduced by which the Aztec social hierarchy was no longer based exclusively on descent but was also based to a great extent on military achievement. Thus a new institutionalized mechanism was created for social mobility, for improving one's position in society. It is understandable that the insurgent princes approved of this change because, except for Nezahualcoyotl, none of them were eligible to rule in accordance with Toltec tradition since they were not descended from the appropriate mothers.

After four years of warfare Azcapotzalco was conquered, but only after the Têcpanecs had occupied Cuauhtitlan, one of the few towns entitled to have a slave market. Since the slave market was the only place where merchants could acquire victims for human sacrifices, the town that had it also had prestige. After they had conquered Cuauhtitlan, the Têcpanecs planted agave in its market-place, an act that caused deep humiliation, and then moved the slave market to Azcapotzalco.[42] Later, even after the conquest of Azcapotzalco by the Aztecs, the slave market remained there, probably because their merchants preferred the shorter distance to Tenochtitlan. However, they deprived the town of its function as an administrative center and moved it to Tlacopan. All this took place about halfway through the war. First in Coyohuâcan and then in the Matlatzinca area the Têcpanecs held out as well as they had in the former state of Acolhuâcan.

In 1433–34 the Aztec troops had to conquer this territory once more, this time to restore the offspring from the original royal family to the throne from which they had helped drive him away. When Tetzcoco had been reconquered, a new "Toltec" tripartite administration was established with Mexîco-Tenochtitlan, Tetzcoco, and Tlacopan as the three capital cities. Tenochtitlan was given the supreme power over military affairs; Tetzcoco was given authority over certain juridical and cultural affairs, while Tlacopan became a kind of subsidiary to Tenochtitlan with special and very dangerous tasks in external relations, such as presenting declarations of war on behalf of the empire. In this way one government had again been created for the whole lake area, and for the time being no other political power in Mexico or Central America as a whole was able to withstand the strength of this young empire.

Of course, the four leaders of the rebellion took the key positions in the new government. Itzcoatl became Hueyi Tlâtoani (Grand Ruler) of Tenochtitlan. His cousin Tlacayelel became first Tlacochcalcatl (Chief of the Spear House) and afterward Cihua-coatl (Female Companion). Tlacayelel is given relatively much attention not only in the sources which are directly or indirectly based on the lost so-called *Codex X,* such as the works of Acosta, Durán, Tovar, Tezozomoc, the *Codex Ramírez,* and to a less extent in the works of Chimalpahin, but also in the *Codex of Huichapan.*

This is important because there seems to be no connection at all between this Otomi document and the sources of the *Codex X* group. The Mexican ethnohistorian Jesús Monjarás Ruiz recently discovered a bilingual colonial manuscript from the Chalco region that also gives ample attention to Tlacayelel and his family. Motêuhczoma Ilhuicamina became Tlacateccatl (a high military and juridical office), and Nezahualcoyotl, of course, became Tlâtoani (Ruler) of Acolhuâcan. All four of them, together with the Tlâtoani of Tlacopan, became members of the Tlâtocan (Imperial Council) of Tenochtitlan. The philosophical content of the regime is attributed mainly to Tlacayelel. His ideas were first and foremost based on the old Toltec-Aztec view: "We, the people of Huitzilopochtli, are responsible for the maintenance of the order of the fifth Sun, and our task will be to regulate all earthly matters in accordance with the cosmic order only." But to this he added: "No one who belongs to the nobility will, for that reason only, be allowed to rule; everyone aspiring after a high social position, whether he is of noble birth or not, will first have to gather the necessary sacrifices for the gods, preferably on the ceremonial battlefield of the war of flowers. The wars of flowers will be like markets where respect and honor may be bought with blood and effort."[43]

Thus arose what Miguel León-Portilla calls a mystical-military view of life. The position of women too was included in this philosophy. A woman who gave birth to a child for the Aztec society was making a "prisoner." The idea gave a woman a higher status in accordance with the number of live babies she gave birth to.

In religious matters an encapsulating policy was pursued. All the gods of other peoples were regarded as appearances of their own gods, and in the Coateocalli (the Temple of Unification) of Tenochtitlan each of them had his own place. The greatly increased power and the consequently increased tax revenues brought about new economic and social changes in Tenochtitlan. Industry grew, making necessary the immigration of several alien groups into the city because the original population lacked the necessary skill and training. This influx rapidly increased the size of the city and the number of its inhabitants; the calpollis grew larger and larger, and their populations may have increased as well. Merchants became more numerous and more important as a group in Tenochcan society.

CHAPTER 6

The Social Organization of Tenochtitlan During the Têcpanec War (1426–1433)

DURING Acamâpichtli's administration a new elite began to develop, some members of which intermarried with the old calpolli nobility while others settled in Tenochtitlan as an independent aristocracy. The establishment of a new elite continued despite the resistance to Têcpanec supreme authority. Before the rebellion this development had been considerably strengthened by the Têcpanec themselves. However, at the same time this development tended in another direction. Opportunities for social mobility were provided by the new government, possibly because the three principal leaders of the rebellion (Itzcoatl, Tlacayelel, and Motêuhczoma Ilhuicamina) had genealogies that were not entirely in accordance with the established requirements for legitimate appointment to the administrative offices they had seized. Social promotion, as a reward for exceptional military achievement, became one of the pillars of the new regime.[1] Perhaps an even more important fact was that no one despite his belonging to a high-status family, could ever be considered for high office unless he had performed great services for the community (or the regime).[2] The Tenochca historical sources attribute this novel social policy to the personal influence of Tlacayelel; other sources mention Itzcoatl as its creator. It would be incorrect, however, to conclude that under the new regime the community became more egalitarian. The strictly stratified vertical social structure remained, but social mobility was enhanced since an individual's social position could be determined not only by the proper kin relationships but to an even greater extent by personal achievement.

The interplay between the old and the new institutions is apparent in the lists naming the conquerors of Azcapotzalco and Coyohuâcan and their respective offices, preserved by Tezozomoc in his *Crónica Mexicana.* These data enable us to form a general picture of the social organization of Tenochtitlan around 1430 after they have been compared with complementary data from other sources. Tezozomoc mentioned thirteen Tenochca chiefs who were directly involved in the capture of Azcapotzalco. Twelve of these, along with the offices they held, were also named in another list of twenty-six chiefs who had taken part in the capture of Coyohuâcan.

Ingham considers each of these twenty-six chiefs to be the representative of a calpolli in Tenochtitlan.[3] He bases his conclusions mainly on fieldwork done in the present-day village of Tlayacapan, once a dependency of Xochimilco, which had twenty-six calpolli temples. This interpretation is untenable, as I shall demonstrate.

The list of thirteen conquerors of Azcapotzalco consists of two parts: first, four sons and another relative of Acamâpichtli are given, followed by eight sons of Huitzilîhuitl; all thirteen chiefs were noblemen. The list of twenty-six conquerors can be divided into three or four parts. First, four supreme chiefs are mentioned, each of whom was a high functionary in one of the four large town districts, and apparently each held a high office in what was then the *tlâtocan.* Two were sons of Huitzilîhuitl, and two were sons of Acamâpichtli. Then there was a second group of seventeen nobles at least nine of whom were sons or grandsons of Acamâpichtli. Finally there was a group of five warriors who did not belong to the Tenochca nobility. This group consisted of two subgroups. The two men mentioned first were *macehualtin* from Tenochtitlan; the three others were probably *macehualtin* too, but from Colhuâcan. All five had distinguished themselves in the battle for the capture of Coyohuâcan by performing great military feats while fighting on the side of Tlacayelel.[4] Before drawing any further conclusions, we shall take a closer look at those mentioned in the two lists and their respective offices.

The thirteen conquerors of Azcapotzalco were as follows:

1. Cuauhtlecoatl was a son of Acamâpichtli and Xiuhcuetzin, the daughter of Aatl-Mexîtzin,[5] who, after the capture of Coyohuâcan, was made one of the four high-ranking imperial dignitaries with the title *tlillancalqui.* According to Chimalpahin, he held the office of *tlacochcalcatl* during Huitzilîhuitl's regime.[6]

2. Tlacahuepan was also a son of Acamâpichtli, but his mother was a daughter of Cuauhtlequetzqui and was therefore descended from the most important family of Mexitin priests.[7] After Coyo-

huâcan he too became one of the four imperial noblemen and held the title *ezhuahuacatl.*[8]

3. Tlâtolzaca was a son of Acamâpichtli and the daughter of Tenzacatetl, who was probably the Tezcatlamiahuatl mentioned in the *Codex Mexicanus.*[9] After the distribution of offices following the fall of Coyohuâcan, Tlâtolzaca was not mentioned again, probably because he died about that time. His son Cahualtzin was given the office of *acolnahuacatl* (see below), which had probably been held by his father. It is possible, however, that, as a younger brother *(iteicauh)* of Huitzilîhuitl, Tlâtolzaca held an even more important office.

4. Epcoatl was also a son of Acamâpichtli. His mother was a daughter of Tenoch.[10] After the capture of Coyohuâcan he was made *temilotli tiacauh.*[11]

5. Tzompantzin was a name that occurred in the chiefly noble family of the calpolli of Chalman.[12] Because we know that Acamâpichtli, in his function of *cihuacoatl,* originally belonged to that calpolli, we can infer that Tzompantzin in this instance probably refers to one of Acamâpichtli's close relatives, because of the place where the name was mentioned. After the capture of Coyohuâcan, Tzompantzin became *hueyi tiacauhtli.*[13]

The following are the eight sons of Huitzilîhuitl. The name mentioned first in this list of eight is sixth in the list of thirteen conquerors, the famous future *cihuacoatl:*

6. Tlacayelel, whose mother, Cacamacihuatzin, came from Teocalhuiacan. According to Chimalpahin, he was born on the same day as his half brother Motêuhczoma Ilhuicamina.[14] When the Têcpanec war started, he held the title *atempanecatl.*[15] After the capture of Coyohuâcan he became one of the four high-ranking imperial dignitaries and at the same time one of the two supreme army leaders with the title *tlacochcalcatl.*[16] Later he gave up this office to devote himself, as *cihuacoatl,* to the internal administration of the new Aztec empire.

7. Huehuêzacan became *tezcacoacatl* after Coyohuâcan.[17] Later, during the reign of his brother Motêuhczoma Ilhuicamina, he held the even higher office of *tlacateccatl,* one of the two supreme commanders of the military. When a general appeal was made for forces to construct a dam in the Lake of Mexico, he refused to cooperate, whereupon he was burned, in his own house, by order of his brother.[18]

8. Motêuhczoma Ilhuicamina (Chalchiuhtlatonac) was one of the three supreme leaders of the Aztec rebellion against the Têc-

Fig. 6.1. *Motêuhczoma Ilhuicamina (left), with Tlacayelel behind the throne.* Codex Azcatitlan, *pl. 18.*

panec regime. He was a son of Miahuaxihuitl, a princess of Cuauhnahuac.[19] After Coyohuâcan he became one of the four high-ranking dignitaries with the title *tlacateccatl,* a position that he had previously held.[20]

9. After the capture of Coyohuâcan, Citlalcoatl was given the office of *atempanecatl,* which had been held before him by Tlacayelel.[21]

10. After Coyohuâcan, Aztacoatl was given the high military rank of *tocuiltecatl.*[22]

11. Axicyotzin was appointed *teuhctlamacazqui*[23] after the fall of Coyohuâcan, which meant that he acted as the high priest of Huitzilopochtli.

12. Cuauhtzitzimitl was given the office of *huitznahuacatl*[24] after Coyohuâcan.

13. Xiconoc was appointed *atempanecatl,* as was his brother Citlalcoatl.[25]

After the capture of Azcapotzalco, Itzcoatl, the *tlâtoani*, was first granted extensive compulsory services, as well as rights to tributes and landed property. Evidently these were not private privileges but rather institutional rights since Tezozomoc emphasized that "aunque venian a darlo a Itzcoatl, era para todos los mexicanos en común" ("although they had come to give them to Itzcoatl, it was a gift meant for the whole community of Mexicans").[26]

The thirteen "conquerors" mentioned above, who had commanded the Tenochca military forces during the siege of Azcapotzalco, received many individual privileges, including the usufruct of important landed estates. The *atempanecatl* Tlacayelel alone was allotted no fewer than ten landed estates.[27] Cuauhtlecoatl, Tlacahuepan, and Tlacateccatl Motêuhczoma Ilhuicamina also received considerable landed rights. The other nine men received less. Unlike the aforementioned nobles, who had evidently acquired their rights at the expense of the Têcpanec nobility, the "old, established citizens" of Mexico were allotted a single piece of land from the communal property of Azcapotzalco. They did not gain private rights since these were allotted to their calpollis, which, moreover, had to reserve a part of this small allotment for the calpolli gods and the ceremonies of their worship.[28]

More interesting than the above list of the thirteen conquerors of Azcapotzalco is the list of the twenty-six chiefs and warriors who distinguished themselves in the war against Coyohuâcan.[29] It is particularly interesting not only because of the greater number of persons represented but also for the descriptions of personal functions and titles, which in most cases indicate an association with a ritually important place and its corresponding social group in Tenochtitlan. Table 6.1 gives, whenever possible, the relationships of titles, functions, ritual places, social groups, and classes. It shows that in twelve instances titles were derived directly from calpolli names. Three of these twelve, however, are repeated, so that only nine calpollis are actually involved. They are Tlacochcalco, Tlacatêcpan, Tezcacoac, Atempan (twice), Huitznahuac (twice), Cuauhquiahuac (twice), Coatlan, Yopico, and Izquitlan. By comparing these titles with other data, we can connect a number of other titles with specific calpollis, although the titular names do not imply any direct connections.

The survey shows, for instance, that Ezhuahuacatl Tlacahuepan was one of the four high-ranking imperial dignitaries mentioned first in the list. The other three from this group of the highest-ranking personages in the Tlâtocan represent the calpollis of Tla-

Table 6.1. The Twenty-six Conquerors of Coyohuácan, Their Functions and Social Background
(Based on Tezozomoc)

No.	Names	Titles of Functions	Nature of Functions			Ritual Places	Calpollis	Nobles	Commoners
			Military	Priestly	Official				
1	Tlacayelel	Tlacochcalcatl	X			Tlacochcalco	Tlacochcalco	X	
2	Motéuhczoma Ilhu	Tlacateccatl	X			Tlacatêcpan	Tlacatêcpan	X	
3	Tlacahuepan	Ezhuahuacatl			X	Ezhuahuaco	Huitznahuac	X	
4	Cuauhtlecoatl	Tlillancalqui		X	X	Tlillancalco	Molonco itlillan	X	
5	Huehuêzacan	Tezcacoacatl	X		X	Tezcacoac	Tezcacoac	X	
6	Aztacoatl	Tocuiltecatl	X			Tocuillan	Huitznahuac	X	
7	Cahual(tzin)	Acolnahuacatl		X	X	Acolnahuac		X	
8	Tzompantzin	Huey Tiacauhtli	X			—	Chalman	X	
9	Epcoatzin	Temilotli tiacauh	X		X	—		X	
10	Citlalcoatl	Atempanecatl			X	Atempan	Atempan	X	
11	Tlahueloc	Calmimilolcatl			X	Calmimilolco		X	
12	Ixhuetlantoc	Mexîcatl têuhctli			X	Mexîco	Cihuatêcpan	X	
13	Cuauhtzitzimitl	Huitznahuacatl	X			Huitznahuac	Huitznahuac	X	
14	Xiconoc	Atempanecatl			X	Atempan	Atempan	X	
15	Tlazolteotl	Quetzaltoncatl		X		Quetzaltonco		X	
16	Axicyotzin	Têuhctlamacazqui		X		—	Huitznahuac	X	
17	Ixnahuatiloc	Tlapaltecatl		X		Tlapallan	Chililico	X	
18	Mecatzin	Cuauhquiahuacatl	X			Cuauhquiahuac	Cuauhquiahuac	X	
19	Tenamaztli	Coatecatl		X		Coatlan	Coatlan	X	
20	Tzontemoc	Pantecatl		X		Pantitlan		X	
21	Tlacacochtoc	Huêcamecatl		X		Huêcaman	Atempan	X	
22	Machiocatl	Cuauhnochtli	X		X	—			X
23	Telpoch	Cuauhquiahuacatl	X			Cuauhquiahuac	Cuauhquiahuac		X
24	Acaxacal	Yupicatl	X	X		Yupico	Yupico		X
25	Atamal	Huitznahuacatl	X			Huitznahuac	Huitznahuac		X
26	Quillaoyo	Izquitecatl		X		Izquitlan	Izquitlan		X

cochcalco, Tlacatêcpan, and Molonco Itlillan (Tlillancalco is, as we know, the *calpolco* of this calpolli).[30] These titles would also have represented those city quarters as a whole, not just the three calpollis, which lie in different city quarters. Therefore, the only possibility is that Ezhuahuaco was in Teopan and that the other three belonged to Cuepopan, Atzacoalco, and Moyotla, respectively. Other sources also suggest a connection between the *ezhuahuacatl* and Teopan-Zoqui(a)pan.[31] Tlacahuepan's mother was a daughter of Cuauhtlequetzqui, and this title may well have been given to him because Ezhuahuaco was a dependency of the important calpolli Huitznahuac, to which Tlacahuepan's grandfather belonged.

Tlillancalco has already been discussed; this "Black House" belonged to Molonco Itlillan and was in Moyotla.[32]

Tocuillan, in its archaic form of Tocuilitlan, was mentioned in the *Huitznahuac Yautl icuic*, the holy song of the calpolli god of Huitznahuac.[33] Other sources show that the office of *tocuiltecatl* was connected with the city quarter of Teopan-Zoqui(a)pan.[34] Thus Tocuillan may be considered part of Huitznahuac.

Although Tzompantzin's title, *huey tiacauhtli* ("grand officer" or "chief officer"), does not give any indication of a particular connection to a calpolli, the name and descent of this chief suggest that he represented the calpolli of Chalman.

The *mexîcatl têuhctli* Ixhuetlantoc can be reckoned to belong to Moyotla and to the most important calpolli in that city quarter, Cihuatêcpan. Moyotla was Mexîco in particular, and the Moyotecâ, more specifically, were members of Cihuatêcpan; so they appear in the *Codex Izhuatepec*.[35] This city quarter, which was identified with the west, was usually associated with the autochthonous and popular aspects, the origins, and the people as a whole.[36]

The *têuhctlamacazqui* Axicyotzin received the title of one of the two high priests of Huitzilopochtli. He must, therefore, have been connected with Huitzilopochtli's calpolli, Huitznahuac.[37]

The *tlapaltecatl* Ixnahuatiloc derived his title from the holy town of Tlapallan (Red Land or Red Place). In the earlier interpretation of the foundation myths, this "red place" corresponded to the "red seat" of Quetzalcoatl, and, in Tenochtitlan, evidently also to the calpolli of Chililico.[38]

So far we have traced the connections with calpollis for nineteen of the twenty-six titles. These nineteen titles are connected with twelve different calpollis, since Molonco Itlillan, Chalman, and Chililico could be added to that original list of nine. It is possible, of course, that Tocuillan was more directly connected with a dependency of Huitznahuac, for instance, Coatlxoxouhcan or Cuauhquiahuac. If the former possibility is correct, we have found connections with thirteen calpollis.

Seven titles remain for which no connection with a calpolli is known: *acolnahuacatl, temilotli, calmimilolcatl, quetzaltoncatl, pantecatl, huêcamecatl,* and *cuauhnochtli.* In some of these there is, indeed, a connection with a particular city quarter. For others there is a vague indication of a possible connection with some calpolli. The *acolnahuacatl* Cahualtzin was a son of Tlâtolzaca, a grandson of Acamâpichtli, and a great-grandson of Tenzacatetl Chiauhtototl and Opochtli Iztahuâtzin.[39] Since all these forebears were connected with the calpolli of Chalman, it seems reasonable that Cahualtzin would have also held an office from the city quarter of Teopan. It is no more than a probability because it was possible for important leaders like Tlacayelel and Cuauhtlecoatl to transfer their associations from one city quarter to another. Tlacayelel, for example, was first *atempanecatl* (a Teopan office), then *tlacochcalcatl* (a Cuepopan office), and after that *cihuacoatl* (a Teopan office). Cuauhtlecoatl was first *tlacochcalcatl* (a Cuepopan office) and later *tlillancalqui* (a Moyotla office). The reader should be reminded that a position might be connected with a certain social group without its execution being restricted to that particular group. Usually any office, even one associated with a single group, implied involvement with the whole community of cooperating calpollis. However, the connection of the office of *acolnahuacatl* with the city quarter of Teopan-Zoqui(a)pan-Xochimilcâ seems highly probable not only from what has been shown but from other data as well. Tezozomoc mentions the office several times in relation to other administrative or ritual functions. For instance, the imperial council in charge of the preparations for the military punishment of the Tlatelolcâ in 1473 consisted of the following ten officials: *cihuacoatl* (Teopan), *tlacochcalcatl* (Cuepopan), *tlacateccatl* (Atzacoalco), *cuauhnochtli, tlillancalqui* (Moyotla), *tecocyahuacatl* (Moyotla), *ezhuahuacatl* (Teopan), *acolnahuacatl, tocuiltecatl* (Teopan), and *tezcacoacatl* (Cuepopan or center).[40] Eight of the ten were undoubtedly connected with only one of the city quarters.

The *tecocyahuacatl*'s connection with Moyotla can be deduced from the *Codex Izhuatepec* and the *Codex Mendoza.*[41] As we shall see, the *cuauhnochtli* was probably associated with Acatliacapan

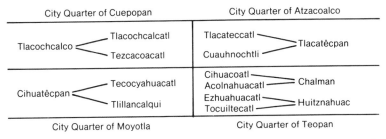

Fig. 6.2. *Organization of the special council for the punishment of the Tlatelolcâ in 1473.*

and thus with Atzacualco or the center considering the four central calpollis as a fifth city quarter. For reasons of symmetry then, we must conclude that the title *acolnahuacatl* was indeed viewed as belonging to Teopan, as is shown in Fig. 6.2. The council was apparently composed of office bearers from the same five important calpollis mentioned in the *Codex Izhuatepec,* each of which was represented by two officials. Finally, the connection between the *acolnahuacatl* and Teopan is also shown by Garibay and Caso. Garibay places Acolnahuac in Candelarita and San Jeronimito,[42] and Caso gives these as the Spanish names for the calpollis of Ometochtitlan and Atlixco, in Teopan.[43]

The *temilotli tiacauh* Epcoatzin was a grandson of Tenoch, who probably would have been connected with Tlacochcalco or a dependency of it, or, if we assume that Tenoch and not Aatl-Mexitzin was chief of Cihuatêcpan, with Cihuatêcpan or of one of its dependencies. The question, therefore, is whether it was a Cuepopan or a Moyotla office. The office of *temilotli,* however, also had a civil-administrative function since it was responsible for poetry and music.[44] It would then be associated with one of the four central *calpoltin,* perhaps Tezcacoac, or more likely with Tlamatzinco, to which belonged the Mixcoacalli (House of Mixcoatl), the Aztec House of Songs and Dances. Both *calpoltin* were in Cuepopan.

The *calmimilolcatl,* as a functionary, is designated by Garibay as having charge over the supervision of building and town planning.[45] This interpretation seems to be based on no more than one, disputable, "literal" translation of the term.

The *quetzaltoncatl,* as a functionary of Quetzaltonco, may have been associated with the small temple of Quetzalcoatl there.[46] Whereas connections with the typical Quetzalcoatl calpollis of

Chililico and Molonco have already been mentioned, Tzonmolco, being an old Toltec calpolli, might also be considered a suitable place for that office.

The *pantecatl* corresponded to Pantitlan, a lakeshore area in Atzacualco,[47] or to one of the gods of pulque, which belonged to Izquitlan, Tezcacoac, and Cuepopan. Therefore, responsibilities of the office must have belonged to the northern half of the city.

Presently I have no reliable or relevant data about the *huêcamecatl* or the ritual place Huêcaman.

Cuauhnochtli is a title often mentioned in other sources, such as the *Florentine Codex* (Sahagún), and the *Codex Mendoza.* The *Florentine Codex* gives the *cuauhnochtli* as one of the fifteen *têcuhtlâtoquê* forming the council of the *cihuacoatl.*[48] Sahagún mentions this title as one of six *achcacauhtin*, the other five being the *tezcacoacatl*, the *tecocyahuacatl*, the *ezhuahuacatl*, the *atempanecatl*, and the *mazatecatl.*[49] The *Codex Mendoza* mentions the *cuauhnochtli* in a group of four *executores,* the others being the *tlillancalqui*, the *atempanecatl*, and the *ezhuahuacatl*, in connection with another group of four military leaders.[50] Of these seven additional office bearers two were from Cuepopan, two from Moyotla, and three from Teopan. It would thus seem reasonable that the *cuauhnochtli* came from Atzacualco, or, more specifically, from Acatliacapan, owing to the complex executive nature of the office.

This argument is strengthened by comparing it to the many references made by Tezozomoc to this functionary as a member of many diversely composed committees of army leaders or administrators. We are even more convinced by Tezozomoc's description of the marching order of officers and their army detachments. First came the *cuauhnochtli* and his troops (Tlacatêcpan), then the *tlillancalqui* and his warriors (Cihuatêcpan opposite Tlacatêcpan), then the *ezhuahuacatl* and his troops connected with Huitznahuac, and finally the *tezcacoacatl* and his men from the opposite city quarter.[51]

Given this detailed examination of the data, we may now conclude, first, that, in spite of the ideology of status by achievement held by the new rulers, a substantial majority of the new elite were of noble descent, particularly from the great noble family of the *tlazôpipiltin.* This noble family, probably known as the Chalchiuhtlatonacs, was descended from Acamâpichtli and produced many rulers in Tenochtitlan.

The titles reveal the pervasive effect the old calpolli system had on the new social order; many are old titles that had been held by chiefs in the calpultin. The offices that they represented were given new content, however, and accession to the offices was no longer dependent on strict rules of inheritance. Of the twenty-six conquerors of Coyohuâcan it was specifically the three strangers among them who received three indisputable calpolli titles. It does not seem coincidental that these titles should have been connected with the three calpollis of Izquitlan, Yopico, and Huitznahuac, for, as I have said before, these were the three of the seven "original" calpollis of the mythical Aztlan model that were believed to be associated with the external system.[52] Therefore, they are, in fact, calpollis of immigrants, which proves once again that the entire social order of Tenochtitlan was still viewed from an original Toltec or Chinampanec perspective. In general, the Tenochcas applied some kinship criteria with regard to their duties, but the really great heroes, such as Tlacayelel, may have followed a completely different course. The two brave *macehualtin* who were allowed to climb the social ladder to high positions were given offices in central calpollis, which in practice meant that they were among *têcpanpouhquê*, or foreign nobility who were mobilized for middle-rank administrative duties. Probably it was still necessary to show consideration for the traditional calpolli nobles by not confronting them with such upstarts in their own ranks.

In the survey of the twenty-six conquerors shown in table 6.1, I have tried to represent the nature of their offices. Owing to the close interdependence of religious and administrative spheres of Aztec social life, many official roles were rather complex. In the survey above I have attempted to indicate the major responsibilities of each office with regard to the religious or administrative spheres. Where that proved to be impossible, both concerns have been indicated. It is worth noticing that the three spheres are almost equally represented among the twenty-six office bearers. Even a superficial examination of the twenty-six offices shows that they could not possibly have represented twenty-six groups in Tenochtitlan as Ingham says. The three repetitions of Atempan, Huitznahuac, and Cuauhquiahuac reduce the theoretically possible number to twenty-three. My investigations have proved that even this number should be further reduced and that no more than twenty calpollis were represented by the twenty-six holders.

It is worth noting that each double or multiple representation of the same calpolli always occurred in relationship to the calpollis of Teopan-Zoqui(a)pan. It is true that Teopan was the largest of the four city quarters, but I believe that the explanation of this phenomenon is to be found in the very important position taken by the calpollis of Chalman and Huitznahuac in the Tenochca collaboration and in the relatively large contribution which they and their dependencies made to the struggle against the Têcpanec regime.

After the fall of Coyohuâcan, just as after the capture of Azcapotzalco, a redistribution of land took place. Tlacayelel again received ten landed estates because in those ten places he had "killed Têcpanecs and cut off limbs and heads of enemies."[53] Each of the other conquerors received only one or two estates. The community of Tenochtitlan was faced with considerable change. Differences in power and wealth among the population became rapidly more apparent, but, at the same time, opportunities to acquire power and wealth also grew. Tenochtitlan's military might, which had been formidable for a long time was strengthened by a considerable increase in the city's political influence. Its greatly expanded economic base then enabled Tenochtitlan to play a major role and it was not the Tenochcas' nature to waste advantageous opportunities.

The *Annals of Cuauhtitlan* neatly summarizes the situation for the year V Tecpatl:

Mâcuilli Tecpatl ipan inin xihuitl huel hualixnez in Tenochtitlan Tlâtoani Itzcoatzin inic nohuian	V Flintstone (1432): in this year the King of Tenochtitlan, Itzcoatzin, attracted universal notice because he reigned everywhere
tlâtocat in impan ahuâcan tepehuâcan tlâtoanimê. Oncan in cemmanca ompeuh in immahuizyo Mexîcatl Tenochcatl.[54]	over the kings of the communities. There the high respect in which the Tenochcâ-Mexicans were held began to increase steadily.

CHAPTER 7

The Social and Economic
Development of the Aztec Merchants

IN THE sixteenth century Fray Bernardino de Sahagún collected material on Mexican society and wrote an important work about the spectacular civilization and socioeconomic system of the Aztecs in which he discussed at great length the so-called merchants' guilds. Several students of the Mexîcâ have made studies of these particular guilds using Sahagún's work as their primary source. Seler, Schultze-Jena, Garibay, Acosta Saignes, Miguel León-Portilla, Caso, Anderson and Dibble, López Austin, Alba, Soustelle, and Katz have all published interpretations and translations of relevant parts of the material copiously supplied by Sahagún's informants.[1] After so many studies one might suppose that the subject had been sufficiently dealt with. With the exception of Acosta Saignes, however, none of these scholars has attempted a comprehensive survey of the merchants' social and religious institutions as an integrated system to determine their place in Aztec society. Acosta Saignes's attempt largely failed because of a lack of data on Aztec social structure. His study, nevertheless, is a pioneering work of great value. Other writers have confined their studies, in most cases, to either the sociological or the economic aspects of the merchant's life. Some interpretations of the Nahuatl text supplied by Sahagún's informants are superficial. Many of the works were based on Sahagún's frequently imperfect translation into Spanish done many years after the Nahuatl texts had been set down. Even so, the writers came to different conclusions regarding the status of organized merchants in Aztec society. One writer describes the merchants as rapidly gaining in influence and would have become the most powerful group in the society had it not been for Spanish interference.[2] Another writer depicts Aztec merchants as small businessmen who, in their attempts to rise socially, had great difficulty overcoming the strong resistance of the ruling elite, the military, and the priests.[3] Both authors based their interpretations on European social models, applying the Western concept of social and economic class. In my opinion such a procedure is not unconditionally applicable, and may easily lead to a misunderstanding of pre-Spanish conditions. Therefore, I try to avoid the use of such models as much as possible. By a comparison of the merchants with other institutions and groups in Aztec society, by structural analysis, and by new interpretations of existing texts, I hope to be able to explain four important features of these merchants: their socioeconomic organization, their *cargo*, or "task-related," hierarchy, their ritual ceremonies, and in part their ethical principles.

The last two features cannot be adequately described without an explanation of the first two. Moreover, the *cargo* hierarchy of the pre-Spanish merchants shows notable points of similarity to the *cargo* systems found among modern Indian communities, and so that a study of it will also benefit those interested in the religious and ceremonial systems in contemporary Mexico and Central America.

Before we consider the social and religious life of that remarkable group of merchants who occupied such an important niche in the Aztec imperial regime, it is necessary to understand the two basic premises of Aztec religious thought: the responsibility of man in general and of the Aztecs in particular for the preservation of a well-balanced cosmic system and the concept of *teotl*, or god.

The basic idea on which the entire upper spiritual strata and the ideology of the Mexican regime was founded was that in four past eras the universe had gone through four so-called suns, that is, four different forms, each ruled by its own special constellation of gods. Following these four suns came the fifth, the sun of motion, during which human life began. Each change from one sun to the next, or, one might say, each radical change in the cosmic structure, was always accomplished by an enormous catastrophe that destroyed the greater part of the existing one. Therefore, in the fifth sun man's main task was to serve the gods of this constellation and thus to contribute to their preservation and to the maintenance of balance in the universe. This is a fundamental concept in Mexico that is both ancient and widespread. It existed as early as the Toltec empire (6th–11th century) and probably even earlier among the Huixtotin and the Olmecs. Even to the present day this world view can be found among the Aztecs, Hopis, Tarahumaras, Huicholes, and other groups north of the Valley of Mexico as well as the Mixtecs and the Mayan peoples on the south. But it was never used as the organizing principle of a social system to the extent that it was by the Mexican, or Aztec, society of the fifteenth and sixteenth centuries.[4]

In the first half of the fifteenth century the preeminent Mexican empire builder, the *cihuacoatl* (female attendant) Tlacayelel I developed an ideology from this originally Toltec principle that became the motive force of the Aztec imperial regime.[5] In accordance with this new doctrine the Aztec Mexican tribal god Huitzilopochtli was made the principal deity in the Pantheon constellation of the fifth sun. Thus the Aztecs were charged to organize life on earth accordingly by guiding and coordinating the united efforts of all humanity. Mexican society was to serve as a model for the harmonious structure of all earthly matters, in which controversies must be controlled lest they disturb the balance between the worldly and heavenly orders. Driven by this belief, the combined armies of the three united Aztec central states set out in all directions "to unite the different peoples of the world." Inspired by this belief, they waged their ceremonial wars against specially selected, closely related population groups belonging to the same Aztec civilization to gather the most appropriate human sacrifices for blood to be offered as food for the gods of the fifth sun. Sometimes far less valuable prisoners captured in wars against peoples that refused to be subsumed in the structure of Huitzilopochtli were added to these sacrifices. It was this creed that compelled the organized Aztec merchants, too, to march out into the world as explorers in advance of the armies and sometimes to engage in fiercer battles than those of the regular military. Because the great distances they traveled usually precluded the taking of prisoners, they spent most of their riches on slaves, whose hearts and blood were sacrificed to the gods.

The important Aztec concept of *teotl* or god can best be explained from texts supplied by Sahagún's informants. The oldest Nahuatl texts collected by Sahagún were from the village of Tepeapulco and are extremely valuable since they contain clear descriptions of the principal *teteô* (plural of *teotl*).[6] These include one text about the supreme *teotl* Tezcatlipoca, or rather Tezcatlepoca,[7] who is also frequently referred to metaphorically as Tloquê Nahuaquê (Ruler of the Adjacent, the Nearby Things, that is, that which prevails everywhere, here and a short distance away), Ipal-

nemoani (That Which Makes Life Possible), and many other names.
In 1528 the Aztec informants at Tepeapulco spoke about this
teotl:

Tezcatlepoca	That which makes the black mirror shine,
inin huel teotl	a real god,
ipan machoya;	it was considered;
nohuian in nemiya	it lived everywhere,
mictla[n],	in hell [the realm of the dead],
tlalticpac,	on earth,
ilhuicac,	in heaven;
in ihcuac nemiya tlalticpac	when it lived on earth,
yêhuatl quiyolitiaya	it brought dust
in teuhtli tlazolli;	and dung to life;
cococteopouhqui	it caused sorrow and
quiteittiaya	trouble among men;
tetzalan tenepantla	it settled among them
motecaya	and divided them;
ipampa in mîtoaya	therefore, it is said,
necoc yaotl;	to be hostile toward either side;
mochi quiyocuya,	it created everything;
quitemohuiaya	it caused all things to befall them;
quiteêcahuiltiaya,	it caused everything to rage over them;
quitecuitiaya	it made itself recognized as their master
in ixquich âcualli	through all the misfortunes
tepan mochihuaya	that came over them.
tequequeloaya.	It mocked the people.
Auh in quemman quitemacaya	But occasionally it gave them
in necuiltonolli, in tlatquitl,	riches and ownership,
in oquichyotl, in tiacauhyotl,	courage and heroism,
in têuhcyotl, in tlâtocayotl,	command and power to rule,
im pillotl, im mahuizotl.[8]	nobility and high respect.

This interesting text clearly shows that the Aztecs looked upon
their supreme *teotl* as a capricious god, a god who was not particularly concerned with the fate of men, but bestowed favor or
disfavor, whimsically, a god who was distinguished by his seemingly unlimited power. He was cosmic and clearly a pantheistic
god; he was best known as That Which Makes the Black Mirror
Shine, which means that he caused the stars to appear in the
nocturnal skies. In other texts he is also called Tezcatlanextia,
He Who, or That Which, Causes the Mirror To Shine Brightly,
which means that he caused the sun to shine. He was also the

creator. Thus in him were combined the chief elements of the supreme gods of the great religions of the ancient world; but his relationships to man were of a slightly different nature.

The above text does not provide a clear picture of the concept of *teotl*. In other texts the word implies an entirely different idea:

Tlaloc	Wine of the earth,
tlaloquê tlamacazqui	priest of the rain gods,
ipam machoya in quiahuitl;	meaning the rain,
ca yêhuatl quiyocoaya,	for he [this god] created
quipixoaya in quiahuitl ihuan	rain and hail
tecihuitl; quixotlaltiaya	and scattered them over the earth;
quitzmolinaltiaya	he caused to wither
quixoxohuialtiaya	or to germinate
quicueponaltiaya	or to become green
quizcaltiaya	or to sprout
in cuahuitl in zacatl,	or to grow
in tonacayotl,	the trees and the grass,
ihuan no itech tlamiloya	our means of life [maize],
in teilaquiliztli,	and he also caused
in tlahuitequiliztli.	death by drowning and death by lightning.

Here we have a *teotl* that merely resembles a nature god of any polytheistic religion. The next text about the *teotl* Huitzilopochtli, however, prevents us from identifying the concept of *teotl* with, for example, the Greek, Roman, or Germanic concepts of god. Regarding the most important Aztec *teotl*, Huitzilopochtli, Sahagún's informants from Tepeapulco said:

Huitzilopochtli,	Hummingbird of the left [of the south],
zan macehualli	he was but subject
zan tlacatl catcâ,	and monarch [the people],
nahualli, tetzahuitl	[yet] a fascinating, bewildering phenomenon,
âtlacacemellê teixcuepani,	a superhuman being, creating illusions;
quiyocoyani in yaoyotl,	he as the creator of war;
yaotecani,	it was he who regulated war;
yaotlâtoani;	he controlled the battle;
ca itechpa mîtoaya	for it was said of him
tepan quitlaza	that he cast over the people
in xiuhcoatl	the fire snake
in mamalhuaztli,	and the fire drill,
quîtoznequi; yaoyotl,	which means: war,
teoatl tlachinolli.	holy water and fire.

Auh in ihcuac	And when his feast
ilhuiquixtililoyâ	was celebrated,
malmicoayâ,	they sacrificed war captives,
tlaatilmicoayâ	then also those who had been bathed
	were killed,
tealtiloyâ	those who had been bathed ritually
im pochtecâ.	by the merchants.

One reference in this text would have been most welcome to Emile Dürkheim. Using a stylistic phrase commonly found in Nahuatl (termed *difrasismo* by Garibay), the text refers to the Aztec tribal god as one who is "but subject and monarch."[9] In other words, Huitzilopochtli was incarnate in the Aztecs themselves. The Aztec informants who provided this text already had some knowledge of the Spaniards' way of thinking and the Spanish concept of God. They tried to explain to Sahagún that Tezcatlepoca was indeed a "real god" *(inin huel teotl)* but that Huitzilopochtli was not a god in the Spanish sense, since he was no more than the people. These informants worded their explanation in rather exaggerated terms, which serves to make it all the more illuminating. Another text, written by Aztec students at Tlatelolco in the early part of the second half of the sixteenth century, concerns a religious service held by itinerant merchants. It contains a description of the deification of a collective body of men:

Auh in tla cana	And when during the night
ôimpac yoac,	somewhere on their way,
cana cuahuitl itzintlan	somewhere at the foot of a tree,
ahnozo atlauhcamac	or finding shelter in a gorge,
omololoâ	they wrap themselves up,
omocemololoâ	entirely wrap themselves up well,
omotepeuhtitlaliâ	huddling together,
monechicoâ quicuitlalpiâ,	crowding side by side,
quicencuitlalpiâ	pressing shoulder to shoulder,
quicemilpiâ	then they bind their staves together,
quicemmanâ in intopil.	and stand them bundled together.
In ipan quixehuayâ	In this way they represent
inteouh in Yacatêcuhtli.	their *teotl*, the Lord of the Vanguard.
Oncan ixpan tlamacehuâ,	There in his presence they do penance,
mizoh,	sacrificing their blood,
monacaztequi,	then they cut their ears,
tlaquixtiâ,	drawing blood from them,
zan quimocemmacatoquê	thus preparing themselves completely
in tlein impan yê mochihuaz.	for the things awaiting them.[10]

A comparison of these four texts enables us to form a clearer idea of the concept of *teotl*. Tezcatlepoca is *teotl*, and so are Tlaloc, Huitzilopochtli, and Yacatêcuhtli. What do they have in common? All of them represent supernatural forces in the universe, but they differ greatly in importance, ranging from the supreme god and creator to the collective unity of a group of merchants. All of them are more powerful than any one person and, even more important, they are more permanent than any individual. A possible linguistic explanation of the word *teotl* is that it is a derivative of the root *tetl* ("stone") plus *yotl* (suffix for an abstract noun), which metaphorically implies "something permanent," "something unassailable." Other instances of Aztec imagery, such as *yollotetl* (literally, "heart of stone"), used to refer to firmness of character, seem to confirm this interpretation. Modern linguists, such as Juan Hasler, however, derive the word *teotl* from a proto-Uto-Aztec word, *tawit*, which expressed the concepts of light and fire.[11]

Are we, then, to assume that the Aztecs and other related groups defied collective bodies of men because as a unit they were more enduring than were individual human beings? This would be too simple an explanation, for it should be remembered that the primary foundation of their religious beliefs was their cosmic involvement. To the Aztecs a so-called god of the people was not so much a deification of a superindividual as an embodiment of the entire cosmos that enabled the collective to exist. Explanations are no simpler if we consider that the Aztec world view also encompassed a complex and elaborate system of magic and, further, an unseen level of reality. The *nahualli* concept is part of that other reality in which each individual is associated with an animal counterpart that either determines or simply takes part in that individual's destiny. Drugs were sometimes used to gain entrance to that other reality, especially hallucinatory mushrooms. The merchants' rituals should be examined against this background since they were part of a comprehensive cultural tradition that permeated the whole society (compare the recent studies of Alfredo López Austin and the introduction of Michael Coe and Gordon Whittaker to the *Treatise on Superstitions*, by Hernando Ruiz de Alarcón.

In general we can distinguish two types of Aztec merchants. First, there was a large group of male and female market vendors. Trade was not their sole occupation, for most of them were also farmers, horticulturists, or artisans. Some of them even had a "profession," such as that of calendar reader or physician (male or female). Their wares were predominantly the usual consumer goods, such as food, clothes, flowers, and products of home crafts, some of which could be viewed as luxury goods. As a rule they operated within small areas, leaving their villages for only a few days at a time. They were not organized into a collective body of merchants but usually belonged, with other free citizens *(mace-hualtin)*, to a calpolli.

The merchants of the second group were of higher status. They carried on trade in different parts of the empire and in far-off foreign areas. Their goods consisted for the most part of luxury items, such as rare decorative feathers, gold, precious stones, expensive beverages, foodstuffs, and costly textiles. These merchants were situated in twelve towns in the center of the Aztec empire, where they formed local as well as regional socioeconomic units that had a high degree of autonomy in Aztec society. This stratum of merchants and their religious life are treated below.

In addition, there were warriors and nobles who had received mantas as gifts, tribute, or bounty and who occasionally traded or sold their excess in the markets.

The twelve towns which had the local merchants associations were in the three central states of the empire: Mexîco, Acolhuâcan, and Tepanecapan, or Tepanohuâyan (fig. 7.1). Together these three central states formed the prestigious core of the Aztec imperial state, most of the others outside this region were no more than tributaries with a markedly lower status within the empire. Other provinces that enjoyed almost the same prestige as the three dominant central states were those that had joined the empire of their own volition, such as Teotitlan, and those designated as enemies in the "flower wars" (ceremonial wars in which the military captives were considered to be those most desirable for human sacrifice), such as Tlaxcallan, Tliliuhquitepec, Cholullan, and Huexotzinco. This may perhaps be accounted for by the fact that the populations of these areas were closely related ethnically to dominant factions in the Aztec population.

On the other hand, the Aztecs seldom discriminated among the ethnically different populations in the empire and were usually quite tolerant of them. The three central states contained large non-Aztec populations, such as the Otomis, who spoke their own language and had their own religion and culture. On the whole such populations lived in peace amid the ruling Aztecs. The Aztec social order, which, as we have seen, had dual and multiple forms of organization, offered many opportunities for their incorporation. Culturally or socially different peoples could easily find a niche

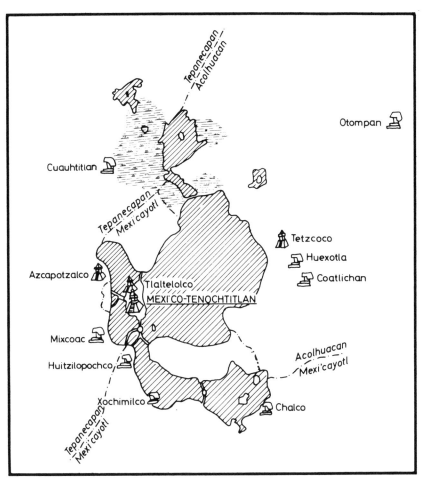

Fig. 7.1. *The twelve towns belonging to the imperial organization of merchant guilds.*

and a function of their own within a society that gave them a large measure of internal autonomy. Various Aztec texts indicate that the local merchant groups were not twelve separate trade organizations of equal standing but formed one "national" organization with a decidedly hierarchical structure.[12]

The status of the twelve local associations was recognized according to four criteria: the federal state to which they belonged (and were closely associated), their ethnic groups, their authority within the national organization, and their trading rights. Table 7.1 shows the twelve towns and their relative status based on these four criteria.

Tenochtitlan and Tla(l)telolco were sister cities that formed the City of Mexico, the capital. There were institutionalized ceremonial oppositions and other forms of rivalry between the two cities, but externally they shared many interests. Together they controlled and thus monopolized almost the entire trade in tropical products. When their merchants traveled with their retinues of hired carriers to the tropical coastal regions, they were accompanied by Mexican merchants from Huitzilopochco and by Têcpanec merchants from Cuauhtitlan and Azcapotzalco, who went as helpers or "followers" *(inhuicalhuan)* in a subordinate position and probably received only a relatively small share of the proceeds of the trade. The merchants from the other seven towns had no direct contact with the tropical regions and could acquire tropical products only through their colleagues in Tenochtitlan or Tla(l)telolco, who made sizable profits as middlemen. The chiefs of the merchants' guild of Tenochtitlan administered the affairs of the entire regional organization. One of the chiefs may even have been looked upon as a minister of economic affairs in the imperial government. Therefore, the domination of the imperial capital over ten of the eleven other towns was founded on its powerful economic as well as administrative position; as far as Tla(l)telolco was concerned, Tenochtitlan's domination was of an administrative nature only.

The larger regional association of merchants maintained a large commercial center in Tochtepec, the strategic garrison town in what is now the state of Oaxaca. There each of the twelve local organizations had its own hostel, storehouse, and small temple. From Tochtepec the caravans set out to the tropical lowlands along both the Pacific and Atlantic coasts, and to Tochtepec they returned before going back to their home. These traveling merchants could trade for their own profit, but often they traded on a commission basis. The merchants who did not undertake expeditions

Table 7.1. The Relative Status of the Twelve Merchant Towns (Divided into Ranked Groups)

Five towns with trading rights in the tropical lowlands; the last three were helpers of the first two	1. Tenochtitlan	The merchant chiefs of Tenochtitlan exercised authority over the entire national organization Ethnically Mexîcâ	State of Mexîco
	2. Tlaltelolco 3. Huitzilopochco		
	4. Cuauhtitlan 5. Azcapotzalco 6. Mixcoac	Ethnically Têcpanecâ	State of Têcpanecapan
Seven towns without trading rights in the tropical coastal regions of Anahuac Xicalanco and Ayotlan	7. Texcoco 8. Huexotla 9. Coatlichan 10. Otompan	Ethnically Acolhuâ	State of Acolhuâcan
	11. Xochimilco 12. Chalco	Ethnically Chinampanecâ	State of Mexîco

themselves, especially women merchants, invested their "capital" (mantles and so on) in these expeditions, which were led by experienced men in the prime of life. The central government also frequently invested part of the tax revenues in these undertakings.

This information about the association of merchants can be deduced from the texts supplies by Sahagún's informants. Further interpretation of the texts is needed to understand the local structure of merchants in the imperial capital, and some of the explanations below must be of a hypothetical nature.

The organized merchants in the capital including Tenochtitlan and Tlatelolco and probably those in the other ten towns were referred to by two different terms: *pochtecâ,* "people from the land of the ceibas" (large shade trees, *Bombax ceiba*); and *oztomecâ,* "people from the extensive cave." A superficial reading of the texts suggests that the two terms were interchangeable, that they referred to the merchants as a whole. Close analysis of the texts has shown that this is too easy an explanation and that perhaps the most widely accepted interpretations in the scholarly literature should be rejected. A detailed account of my study of the texts on this point is not within the scope of this book, yet the conclusions are of fundamental importance for a true understanding of the merchants' participation in the religious and social life of that city.

In its social and religious aspects the merchants' organization in the capital city belonged to the calpolli of Tzonmolco, in Cuepopan. Cuepopan lay in the northwest quarter of the city, but it was associated with the north.[13] This calpolli is not mentioned among the seven original *calpoltin* of the Aztecâ-Mexîca in Aztlan and may have been added at a later time. The calpolli god of the Tzonmolcâ was Xiuhtêcuhtli Ixcozauhqui, the god of fire, also called Huehuêteotl (Old God). He was one of the chief gods of the Aztec pantheon, which made the ceremonial religious center of Tzonmolco an important one in Tenochtitlan. One of the seven *calmecac,* or priests' schools, in the capital was in Tzommolco, and it was one of the six *calpoltin* to which a special function in the worship of Huitzilopochtli had been assigned.[14]

The ceremonial-religious name of Tzonmolco was connected with the strictly local territorial name Copolco. It was the priest of Copolco who, at the beginning of every new cycle of fifty-two years, drilled the new fire on Mount Huixachtepec, an extinct volcano near Colhuâcan. From there it was carried to all the temples in the empire.[15] It was said that the ashes of all the

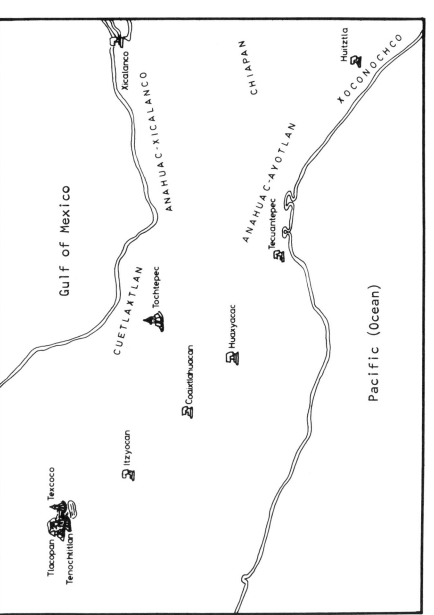

Fig. 7.2. *The towns and regions most important to the Aztec organized merchants outside the three central states.*

huehueintin tlâtoquê, the supreme rulers of the empire, were laid to rest in a vault in Copolco.[16]

I have emphasized that the merchants were associated with Tzonmolco; however, it is uncertain that all of them lived there. In fact, there are strong indications to the contrary. Nor were all the people who had social and ritual connections with Tzonmolco merchants by profession. For example, the *amantecâ,* the feather-mosaic workers, also had a relationship to this large calpolli.[17]

The merchants in the capital city were divided into six local administrative units, each with its own ceremonial subcenter. This conclusion is based on a passage in the text of Sahagún's informants that has puzzled many Mesoamericanists:

niman ye ic quicuepiliâ	Then answer was made to his speech
in itlâtol in puchtecâtlâtoquê	by the chiefs of the *puchtecâ,*
in izquipetlamê inic cecen	who, in their individual seats,
calpulpan teyacanâ	are the administrators of every calpulli:
Puchtlan, Ahuachtlan,	[in] Puchtlan, Ahuachtla[n],
Atlauhco, Acxotla,	Atlauhco, Acxotlan,
Tepetitlan, Itztulco,	Tepetitlan, Itztulco,
Tzonmolco,	Tzonmolco,
in chicuacen petlamê	the six [*sic*] seats where
cecenmê teyacanquê	each of them acts as chief,
tlapachoâ.[18]	where they rule.

Seven names are given, though the text speaks of only six seats. This has been interpreted in different ways. Acosta Saignes and Schultze-Jena simply assume that the word *chicuacen* ("six") is a mistake in writing and should have been chicome ("seven"). Garibay thinks that two names have been used for one group. In the light of what I have said about Tzonmolco, however, there seems to be only one tenable explanation. There was no mistake in writing; the list is indeed an enumeration of the six administrative and ritual locations of the merchants' guild in the capital. To these the informants added a seventh, the name of their major religious center, Tzonmolco. These six groups were also parts of a hierarchy. Two of them, Pochtlan (Puchtlan) and Acxotlan, were of a higher status than that of the other four. Pochtlan was the seat of the *pochtecâtlailotlac,* who was one of the two chief executives of the regional merchants association and a member of the imperial government. Pochtlan was also the residence of the *pochtlan teo-huâ,* the high priest of the god of the organized merchants. It was also the center for the *calpulteotl* (calpulli god) of this group in the capital city, whose name was Yacatêcuhtli (Lord of the Vanguard).

Pochtecâ (People from Pochtlan) was one of the two names for the merchants, as explained above.

Acxotlan was the seat of the Acxotecatl, the other chief executive in the dual system of the merchants' guild.

Assuming that Sahagún's informants listed the gods of the six groups in the same order as they did their locations, the following associations may be observed:

Petlatl ("mat" or "seat")	*Teotl* ("god")
1. Pochtlan (Place of the Ceiba Tree)	1. Yacatêcuhtli (Lord of the Vanguard)
2. Ahuachtlan (Place of Dew)	2. Chiconquiahuitl (Seven Rain) and Chalmecacihuatl (Woman of the Chalmecâ)
3. Atlauhco (In the Gorge)	3. Acxomucuil (Waterbird?)
4. Acxotlan (Place of the Fir Tree)	4. Nacxitl (Four Foot)
5. Tepetitlan (Beside the Mountain)	5. Cochimetl (Sleeping Agave)
6. Itztulco (In the Obsidian Reed)	6. Yacapitzahuac (Pointed Nose)

The area distribution of the six groups was probably as shown in fig. 7.3.

According to the *Florentine Codex* (9:37) there were five temples in which the merchants performed sacrificial rituals:

5. Tlamatzinco temple	1. Tlacatecco (Calpolli temple of Tlacatêcpan)	3. Pochtlan temple (In Coatlan)
(Cuepopan)		(Atzacualco)
(Moyotla)		(Teopan)
4. Yopico temple	2. Huitznahuac temple	

The name Ahuachtlan is associated with two gods. The explanation is that Sahagún's informants mentioned six male deities and then added one female, Chalmecacihuatl. At first this seems to lend support to the idea that a mistake in writing had been made and reopens the question of the possibility of seven groups. In another place in the text, however, Chalmecacihuatl is said to be another name for Chiconquiahuitl.[19] Chalmecacihuatl was prob-

Petlatl ("mat" or "seat")	*Teotl* ("god")
1. Pochtlan (Place of the Ceiba Tree)	1. Yacatêcuhtli (Lord of the Vanguard)
2. Ahuachtlan (Place of Dew)	2. Chiconquiahuitl (Seven Rain) and Chalmecacihuatl (Woman of the Chalmecâ)
3. Atlauhco (In the Gorge)	3. Acxomucuil (Waterbird?)
4. Acxotlan (Place of the Fir Tree)	4. Nacxitl (Four Foot)
5. Tepetitlan (Beside the Mountain)	5. Cochimetl (Sleeping Agave)
6. Itztulco (In the Obsidian Reed)	6. Yacapitzahuac (Pointed Nose)

Tzonmolcotemple
Ixcozauhqui-
Xiuhtêcuhtli

City quarter Cuepopan

petlatl Atlauhco
in the calpolli
Chililico
Acxomucuil

petlatl Pochtlan
in the calpolli
Coatlan
Yacatêcuhtli

City quarter Atzacualco

City quarter Moyotla

City quarter Teopan-Zoquiapan

Petlatl Tepetitlan
in the calpolli
Yopico or Cihua-
têcpan
Cochimetl

Petlatl Acxotlan
in the calpolli
Molonco itlillan
Nacxitl

Petlatl Ahuachtlan
in the calpolli Atempan
Chalmecacihuatl,
Chiconquiahuitl

Petlatl Itztulco
in the calpolli
Coatlxoxouhcan
Yacapitzahuac

temple

petlatl

Fig. 7.3. *Placement of the* petlatls *over the four quarters of Tenochtitlan.*

ably the only goddess, or perhaps the chief goddess, of the *pochtecacihuâ*, the female *pochtecâ*, whose principal temple may have been in Ahuachtlan. In the *petlatl-teotl* chart above, numbers three and four are separated.

Now for the hypothetical part of my conclusions. The two principal *petlamê* (seats) Pochtlan and Acxotlan were in the first and fourth places respectively in the enumeration, each being followed by two other *petlamê*. This suggests that each, together with the two other *petlamê*, formed a group of three. Having made this assumption, one might conclude that this division was connected with the terms *pochtecâ* and *oztomecâ*. However, after a comparison of available texts that mention the two terms jointly or separately, it is apparent that both were used to refer to the organized merchants in general. But there is one striking detail: the merchants who traveled into unconquered territory were frequently called *nahualoztomecâ* (*oztomecâ* in disguise), never *nahualpochtecâ*.

Further, there is a sentence in the *Florentine Codex* that begins as follows:

Auh in yêhuantin pochtecâ,	But those who were merchants,
in motenehuâ acxotecâ,	who were called *acxotecâ*
in oztomecâ,	and *oztomecâ*,
in motlacamatî.[20]	the wealthy men.

Now there are two criteria, the one of which is not very clear, by which to distinguish the *pochtecâ* from the *oztomecâ*: only the *oztomecâ* acted as merchants in disguise and, if necessary, served somewhat as commandos in usually hostile foreign regions; the *pochtecâ* in the strict sense of the word were, of course, associated with Pochtlan, and the above text suggests a similar association between the *oztomecâ* and Acxotlan.

One interpretation of the first criterion could be that the *pochtecâ* were the real traders, whose main purpose was to carry out their tasks peacefully. This explanation is supported by the following passage dealing with the merchants' involvement in warfare:

niman iciuhca	Then he [the king] quickly
yaotlanahuatiaya	proclaimed the state of war
in ic yaoquixohuaz,	wherefore they marched out on campaign,
yêhuantin teyacantihuiâ	those who commanded the troops
in oztomecâ	were the *oztomecâ*,
tlaixquetzayâ	the men chosen
in puchtecâtlâtoque.[21]	by the chiefs of the merchants.

Fig. 7.4. *Aztec merchants being attacked.* Codex Mendoza, *fol. 66.*

This survey of the structure of the merchant's guild in the capital city can now be completed with two partly hypothetical conclusions. The term *pochetecâ* was used to indicate merchants in general, nonmilitant merchants in particular, and, in specific cases, the subjects of the *petlatl* of Pochtlan only. The term *pochtecâ* in a limited sense referred to the members of half of a dual hierarchy, at the head of which was a high official with the title *pochtecâtlailotlac*. It is likely that in each of the six *petlamê* there were always *pochtecâ*, in the limited sense of the term, together with a group of *oztomecâ*. The term *oztomecâ* was used for the militant merchants, who were armed and defended the caravans and their merchandise. They formed the other half of the dual hierarchy of both the regional association of merchants and the capital city. Their chief was the *acxotecatl*. The *acxotecatl* was therefore the supreme external chief of the merchants, and the *pochtecâtlailoltac* was their supreme internal leader.[22]

The Pochtlan-Acxotlan opposition can also be studied from another perspective, which will bring us back to the division of the six *petlamê* into two groups of three. Pochtlan (Place of the

Pochotl, or Ceiba Tree), is ritually associated with the east, the *pochotl* being the tree of the east. According to Acosta Saignes, the name of the god of Pochtlan, Yacatêcuhtli is a pun on Ce Acatl-Têcuhtli (=Lord One-Reed), the calendar name of Quetzalcoatl as the god of Venus. As god and as a calendar sign, he was associated with the east.[23] Acxotlan, the seat of the chief of the *oztomecâ* (people from Oztoman, Extensive Cave), was ritually associated with the west because the extensive cave is the place where the sun disappears when it sets in the west; and the god of Acxotlan is Nacxitl (Four Foot), Quetzalcoatl's name as god of the west and of wizards. This aspect of Quetzalcoatl is associated with the calendar sign of Nahui Ehecatl (Four Wind), which is worshiped in Chalco. The Acxotecâ were once an important population group in Chalco.[24]

The fact that both Yacatêcuhtli and Nacxitl are aspects of the great Toltec god and, therefore, also Aztec god Quetzalcoatl agrees with the higher status of Pochtlan and Acxotlan and seems to justify the supposition that Sahagún's informants mentioned the six *petlamê* and their corresponding gods in the correct order.

The governing board of the merchants' guild was composed of the two supreme chiefs mentioned above, the chiefs of the other *petlamê,* and some older males and females who, in the course of their careers as merchants, had fulfilled a number of ritual tasks that entitled them to hold certain offices (see below).

The members of the board were charged with special functions in the imperial regime:

1. They administered justice within their own groups (this was a privilege).

2. They kept peace and order in the marketplaces, adjudicated differences between market vendors, and inspected the merchandise and prices. There were special officers (male and female), called *tianquizpan tlayacanquê* ("men or women in charge of the market"). They saw to it that customers were not overcharged or cheated.

3. They might be sent abroad as ambassadors.

4. They collected information about foreign countries and passed it on to the authorities.

5. In times of war the chief *oztomecâ* served as military scouts.

6. They had a number of ritual duties to fulfill for the high military officers and the highest state officials.

The Cargo *Hierarchy of the Merchants*

Upward social mobility for the Aztec merchants—as it is for the members of many Mexican and Central American Indian communities today—depended on the successful performance of a number of set tasks *(cargos)* within the ceremonial religious system. Their upward social climb was largely determined by their ability to acquire wealth, since some degree of prosperity was indispensable for the performance of the increasingly expensive ceremonial duties.

The young sons of merchants and probably some of their daughters received training in commerce at home. Besides this the boys attended the *telpochcalli* ("house of youth"), and the girls the *ichpocacalli*, both part-time boarding-schools in the calpolli in which they lived. At school the boys learned how to use arms; were taught the principles of religion, history, and society; and were indoctrinated with the values and aims of the Mexican regime. The children of ambitious merchants and the more promising students were sent to the *calmecac* of Tzonmolco, a school run by priests. There they received much more extensive training. It was necessary to have a *calmecac* education to hold almost any high office in Aztec society—the exceptions were some strictly military ones. The *calmecac* were full-time boarding schools, whereas the students of the *telpochcalli* went home regularly to help their families at harvesttime or for special activities. At either school the youths continued their studies until the age of twenty. However, a student could interrupt his training to gain military experience by accompanying a warrior as arms bearer on an expedition. Similarly, the youth who wanted to succeed his father as a merchant could join a caravan as an apprentice. This first journey, made under the supervision of an experienced *pochtecatl* or *oztomecatl,* was his first *cargo,* or set task, and was necessary for admission to the ceremonial-religious hierarchy proper. Before undertaking their first journeys, these young men were called *pochtecatelpopochtin (pochteca* youths) or *oztomecatelpopochtin.* After they successfully completed the journeys, they were called *tlazcaltiltin* ("apprentices") and were henceforth allowed to join a caravan as ordinary members. At that time they began to make more costly offerings to the gods, such as birds, rubber balls, paper goods, and flowers, whereas before they had sacrificed their own blood drawn with agave thorns from their ears, tongues, and limbs.

After a young man had accompanied a few expeditions as a

tlazcaltilli and had married, when he returned home from a journey, he organized the Necxipâquiliztli (Washing of Feet ceremony; see Chap. 8). After this act he was considered to be a full-fledged merchant, either a *pochtecatl* or an *oztomecatl*, depending on his social position. Henceforth he could act as an independent merchant.

Having successfully completed a number of profitable expeditions, these young merchants might aspire to higher and higher rank in the social hierarchy of their group. Those fit for such positions began their ascent by giving the song feast (Cuicuicaliztli). This early *cargo* was an expensive undertaking. A banquet was held to which the merchant chiefs, the older male and female merchants, the high army officers, and the usually large group of kinsfolk were invited. The host hired seven professional singers and many servants and paid for all the food and drink—including turkey, maize, chocolate, and vanilla—and tobacco, as well as the cooking utensils and dishes.

The high-ranking army officers received "shield flowers" and "eagle flowers."[25] Sacrificial offerings of these and other flowers as well as tobacco were made at six different temples and before the house altar (see Chap. 8). All the guests performed dances except the merchant chiefs, who, since the feast was financed by one of their subordinates, assumed the responsibilities of hosts and hostesses.

After the banquet, as the singers sang their songs and the guests danced, intoxicating mushrooms and honey were served, and soon the guests experienced hallucinations and dreams. When they awoke, they told one another of their visions—whether they were to die on tropical coasts or to return as rich slave traders. Then chocolate was served, and at midnight there were offerings of paper and rubber, after which the singing and dancing resumed.

The next morning the guests ate, drank, and smoked again and were offered fresh flowers. Later all the widows and widowers living in the host's calpolli were invited to the feast, for which a large quantity of maize gruel and *tamalli* (a dish made from maize and turkey) was cooked. At noon on the second day the feast ended. The women paid the singers with cloaks of cotton (an Aztec currency), and everyone went home. The next day there was another dinner party to which a smaller number of people, with whom the host maintained special relations, were invited.

When the young merchant had thus completed all the obligations connected with the song feast, the older merchants returned for a

Fig. 7.5. *The* tianquiztli *(marketplace) of Tlatelolco. From* La Civilización Azteca, *p. 52 (National Museum).*

final assessment of his performance. If nothing was left of the food, the flowers, and the tobacco, they concluded that their god had bestowed, on this one occasion, all the favors he had in store for the young host. He would never be prosperous, he had reached the final stage of his career, and he would not be allowed to organize another feast or attain a higher social rank. If the old merchants found that there was plenty of everything left, they considered it a sign that the young merchant would give many more feasts and have a good chance of attaining a higher status in the social hierarchy, which might be appointment as a *têuhcnenenqui* (caravan leader).

A young merchant whose Song Feast did not bankrupt him could look forward to performing his next *cargo:* the sacrificial offering of one or more slaves to Huitzilopochtli during the fifteenth feast of the year, Panquetzaliztli (Raising of the Banners). After a number of profitable trading years he might consider himself able to sacrifice the slaves required by his *petlatl* for his own account, which would cost him much more than just the money to buy the slaves. He had to give clear evidence that he was not miserly and was willing to part with everything he possessed. He was expected to distribute between 800 and 1,200 large cotton mantles and about 400 loincloths, all richly decorated, among high-ranking military officers and civil servants. He was obliged to give similar gifts to the merchant chiefs, to those who had already sacrificed slaves before him, to all disguised *oztomecâ*, and to the slave dealers. Merchants in the other eleven cities who had already made sacrificial offerings of slaves also received gifts from him, as did their wives, to whom he gave costly clothing.

In the meantime, depending on his financial circumstances, he might have bought as many as four slaves, two men and two women, at the market in Azcapotzalco. He would have done this with the utmost care, giving special attention to the slaves' appearance and other special qualities.

After the distribution of presents he would leave at once for Tochtepec, where he would perform an elaborate ritual to the god Yacatêcuhtli (see Chap. 8) and invite the most prominent merchants of all twelve cities to dinner in the "guild hall" maintained by his local association. Back in the capital city, he would invite the three chiefs, either the three *pochtec* or the three *oztomec* chiefs of his association. On one occasion, reported by Sahagún's informants, the chiefs who were invited included Cuappoyahualtzin, who, according to other texts, was the *acxotecatl,* and Huetzcatotzin and

Zanatzin, who were apparently the chiefs of the *petlamê* of Tepeti-tlan and Itztulco, respectively. If the interpretations given above are correct, the example mentioned by Sahagún's informants must have concerned one of the three Oztomec *petlamê* who wanted to sacrifice slaves. The three chiefs sat down to a sumptuous meal and received personal gifts. The aspirant who intended to carry out the sacrifice informed the three chiefs that he desired to look the great Huitzilopochtli in the face. They told him the ramifications of what he intended to do, lest he should shame them. Then they inspected his possessions and, if satisfied, gave him permission for the sacrifice.

Before he could carry out the sacrifice, however, the merchant had to fulfill several duties. He had to give four banquets. The first was in conjunction with the Teyolmelahualiztli ceremony, which was aimed at "directing the minds of men," that is, draw-ing the attention of the people to their duties, after which there would be no turning back from them. He gave another banquet at the Tlaixnextiliztli ceremony, where he publicly displayed the goods and slaves that he had gathered for the sacrificial offering. He gave his third banquet at the Teteoaltiliztli (Holy bathing of persons) or simply Tealtiliztli (Bathing of persons), the ceremonial bathing of the slaves, when he received the title of *tealtiani* ("he who bathes others"). Finally he gave his last banquet, during the Tlamictiliztli ceremony, when the slaves were offered in sacrifice. To these ceremonies the *tealtiani* had to invite not only the nota-bles of his own city but also the merchant chiefs from the other eleven seats of the regional organization. After the slaves had been dispatched on the sacrificial stone, a ritual was held during which the flesh of the victims was consumed by the *tealtiani* and those of his neighbors who belonged to his *petlatl*. When all these duties had been carried out, the young merchant was eligible for even higher posts. Now he could become a slave trader *(tecohuani)*, after that *pochtecatlâtoani* (chief of the *pochtecâ*), and finally *poch-tecatlailotlac* (imperial minister of economic affairs). Regardless of his future career, in his old age he would belong to the highly respected group of *pochtecahuehuetquê*, for he had successfully undertaken each stage of the *cargo* hierarchy.

Among the *oztomecâ* the bravest men could reach the highest social strata in a slightly different way. Evidently an *oztomecatl* could avoid the expensive final *cargo* by going to foreign territories as a disguised trader *(nahualoztomecatl)*. In all the texts examined for this work, the *nahual-oztomecâ* are considered the equal of "slave bathers," slave dealers, and the *teyahualonimê,* the leaders of the merchants' commando troops. A *nahual-oztomecatl* might be elected *acxotecatl,* but probably he could not become *pochteca-tlailotlac.* To help the reader distinguish among the many offices and titles, the chart below shows the hierarchy of merchant *cargos* and ranks.

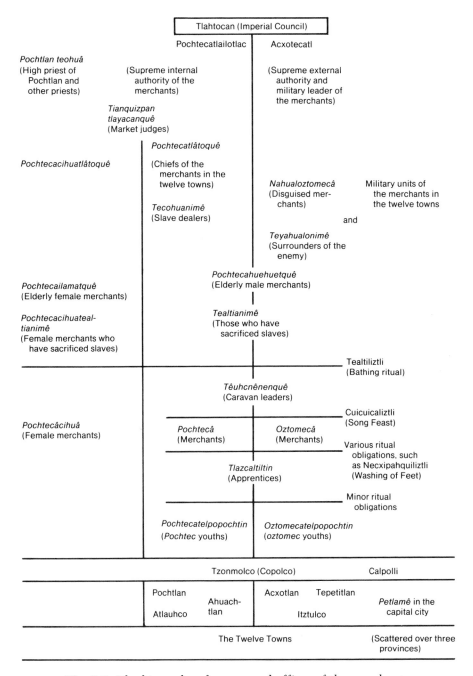

Fig. 7.6. *The hierarchy of cargos and offices of the merchants.*

CHAPTER 8

Ritual and Ceremonial Organization of the Merchants and Other Vocational Groups

AZTEC religion was governed by two different calendars: the *tonal-poalli*, or count of days, and the *xiuhpoalli*, or solar calendar. The *tonalpoalli* covered a period of 260 days composed of 20 day-signs combined with the numbers 1 to 13. The period was thus divided into thirteen intervals of 20 days, and also into twenty intervals of 13 days. The solar calendar was composed of 365 days. The solar year (*xihuitl*) consisted of eighteen intervals of 20 days plus the remaining 5 days (*nemontemi*, "useless fillings"), which were considered unlucky days. The day-signs and the associated numbers of the *tonalpoalli* were also used to indicate the days of the solar year. This resulted in the days shifting each new year, some days occurring twice in a given solar year of 365 (260 + 105) days, others only once. This yearly shift did not cause any confusion among *tonalpouhquê*, experts in the counting of days, because in addition to the number and the day-sign, every day had a *quecholli*, or night-sign. There were nine night-signs, which meant that a day associated with the same night-sign was never repeated in the same solar year. Whereas the combination of a number and a sign can refer to a day-name as well as to the name of a year, in this book I follow the practice of using a Roman numeral and a capital letter for the first letter of the sign-name for year denotations and using an Arabic numeral and small letters for the day-names. Of 20 day-signs, 4 were combined with the numbers I to XIII to refer to years, making a cycle of 52 (4 × 13) years of different names. The long-term calendar was therefore divided into periods of 52 years (for further details see chapter 11).

The Ritual of the Merchants According to the Tonalpoalli
(the count of days)

The first day of the first 13-day period was 1 cipactli (1 crocodile), an important day for the merchants in many respects. This day and the days 1 coatl (1 snake, the first day of the ninth 13-day period), 1 ozomâtli (1 monkey, the first day of the eleventh 13-day period) and 7 coatl (snake, the seventh day of the seventh 13-day period) were especially propitious for beginning a trading expedition. The first two of these days were associated with the east, the last two with the west (see fig. 8.1).

On the night before their departure the travelers bathed thoroughly and had their hair cut. In ritual abstinence, during the expedition they would wash their heads and limbs only and would let their hair grow. At nightfall trumpets were sounded as a signal to cut sacrificial papers. First they cut ritual papers to kindle the fire for Xiuhtêcuhtli (Lord of the Year). Then they cut paper banners with crosses shaped like the Maltese cross hanging from them and paper images of the fire god, Tlalxictenticâ (He Who Keeps Filling the Navels of the earth, i.e. volcanoes). Similar sacrificial papers were cut for Yacatêcuhtli (Lord of the Vanguard) and for the gods of their *petlamê* (Cochimetl, Yacapitzahuac, and so on). After all had been accomplished, they made a bundle of bamboo traveling canes that represented the god Yacatêcuhtli, to be carried on the expedition along with the sacrificial papers, which had been divided into four parcels, one for each of the four quarters.

Finally they cut sacrificial papers for the Ce Coatl Ohtlimelahuac (One Snake Marching Route) and for Tlacotzontli and Zacatzontli, the gods of the roads.

Each member caravan who made sacrifices began them at midnight. First, the papers for Xiuhtêcuhtli were burned in the fireplace. Then each participant went into the courtyard of his own house and made the offerings for Tlaltêcuhtli, Ce Coatl Ohtlimelahuac, Tlacotzontli, and Zacatzontli. The papers for Yacatêcuhtli and those for the gods of the *petlatl* were not burned but were used to cover the representations of these gods to be preserved. Afterward the merchants went inside, and in front of the fireplace they sacrificed quails and blood that had been drawn from their ears and tongues with maguey thorns. These offerings were cast into the hearth fire (the fire god as god of hearth fire was also the god of the center), after which they were taken to the courtyard and thrown into the air, first directly upward, then in the directions of the four quarters in order: east, west, south, and finally north. The sacrificial papers were also spattered with blood.

Then the merchants again stood before their hearth and raised

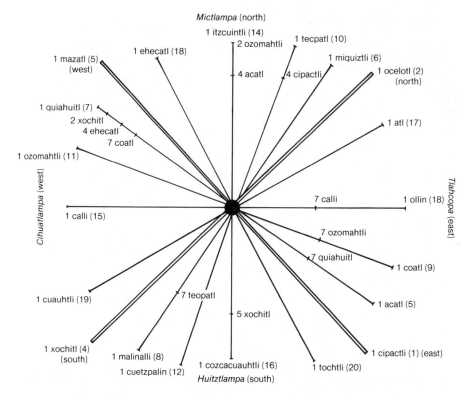

Fig. 8.1. *Chart of the merchants' religious feasts in the* tonalpoalli *(day count) and their relationship to the spatial divisions.*

the papers four times, saying: "Be strengthened, Thou, the unique One, who fillest the navels of the earth, Lord of the quadruple, receive thy property peacefully and benevolently. For I may have offended thee."[1]

Then each departing merchant threw his final paper offerings into the fire and cast white copal over them (copal is a high-quality resin used for incense). He watched the papers intently. If they merely smoked and scorched without producing flames, he would be much alarmed, for that portended that he might be taken ill on his journey. If the papers produced flames and burned well, he was relieved and said: "The princely Lord has favored me. I shall arrive safely at my destination."[2] For the final ritual of the night he reentered the courtyard to burn piled-up paper offerings to Tlacatzontli, Zacatzontli, and Ce Coatl Ohtlimelahuac. Then he collected the ashes of all the offerings made inside the house, carefully avoiding mixing them with wood ashes, and buried them.

At dawn a wealthy merchant leaving for an expedition would send invitations to a farewell feast to each of the chiefs of the six merchant *petlamê*, the disguised *oztomecs*, those who bathed slaves, and the slave dealers. He asked his guests to wash their hands and mouths and offered them food and drink. A poor merchant, or one who had just started his career, invited only the principal merchants of his own *petlatl*. After the meal speeches were made by different guests. They expressed to him the wish "that your feet may carry you farther in good condition, for you will be following the route of One Snake."[3] Then the departing merchants gathered to form the caravan and began their journey. Once the caravan had moved forward, none of the travelers was allowed to look back.

In combination with 7 ozomâtli, 1 cipactli was a suitable day for a merchant to give the Song Feast (Cuicuicaliztli). First a meal was served with the typical Aztec luxuries: chocolate, tobacco, and flowers. Then the seven hired singers prepared to sing their songs and perform dances. Meanwhile, offerings of flowers and tobacco were made at six temples. The first was made at the first gallery of the temple of Huitzilopochtli in the *cuauhxicalli* (eagle vessel); the second, at the temple of Huitznahuac, in the southern city quarter of Teopan; the third, at the Pochtlan temple, in the eastern city quarter of Atzacualco; the fourth, at the Xipe temple, called Yopico, in the western city quarter of Moyotla; the fifth, at the Tlamatzinco temple, in the northern city quarter of Cuepopan; and finally, in Momozco, in the center of the city. By the time the singing and dancing had begun, the sun was setting, but before it had completely disappeared, the participants whistled through their fingers. As the informants of Sahagún wrote in the *Florentine Codex* the host and his family, hearing this, "sighed and rose." Together with their guests they performed the Tlalcual-iztli ceremony "the eating of earth," which consisted of touching the ground with the outstretched hand and bringing the fingers to the mouth. This was the usual Aztec mark of honor to gods and rulers. Afterward a fire offering was made in the courtyard of the house. As the host beheaded a quail, everyone watched anxiously to see in what direction the reeling bird would fall. If it fell toward the north, the direction of death, it was an omen of evil. If it fell in any other direction, the departing merchant was greatly pleased. Then the merchant made offerings to the four quarters, after which the general of the field army, the commander of the arsenals, and all the other chief military officers performed dances. The merchant chiefs did not dance but stood side by side watching the performance. Then intoxicating mushrooms were served.

The first day of the third 13-day period, 1 *mazatl* (1 deer), was dedicated to the *cihuateteô* (goddesses) or *cihuapipiltin* (princesses), the female rulers of the crossroads. Small temples honoring them were found at all crossroads. They consisted of dangerous goddesses or of the no-less-ominous spirits of women who had died in childbirth and who, because they had died heroic deaths, lived on as companions of the setting sun. They accompanied the sun from noon, when they relieved the escort of warriors who had been killed in battle and had accompanied the rising sun until it reached its zenith. After the sun had set, the *cihuapipiltin* went to the crossroads,where they tried to seduce men and lead them to ruin. The merchants, therefore, wanted to appease them and made regular offerings to them, especially on the five special days dedicated to them. These were the first days of each of the following 13-day periods: the third period, the first day of which was 1 mazatl (1 deer); the seventh period, 1 quiahuitl (1 rain); the eleventh period, 1 ozomahtli (1 monkey); the fifteenth period, 1 calli (1 house); and the nineteenth period, 1 cuauhtli (1 eagle).

The first day of the fifth 13-day period, 1 acatl (1 reed), was the special feast day of the eastern aspect of Quetzalcoatl. On that day the *pochtecâ*, along with many other social groups, made sacrificial offerings in the Mexîco Calmecac, the central priests' school in the capital city.

The seventh day of the same period was 7 quiahuitl (7 rain), the feast day of the goddess Chalmecacihuatl in the *petlatl* of Ahuachtlan. This was probably an important feast day for the women merchants, but nothing else is known about this ceremonial.

At the beginning of the sixth 13-day period, on 1 miquiztli (1 death), the merchants and all other population groups commemorated the end of the god Huitzilopochtli's life on earth as leader of the people.

As has been seen before, the seventh 13-day period began with one of the days dedicated to the Cihuapipiltin, 1 quiahuitl (1 rain). The second day of the period was 2 xochitl (2 flower). Like 1 calli (1 house) and 2 ozomâtli (2 monkey), it was a suitable day for the Teyolmelahualiztli, the ritual acceptance of the obligation to sacrifice slaves. This ritual will be dealt with in connection with the celebration of the fifteenth feast of the year, Panquetzaliztli.

The fourth day of this period was 4 ehecatl (4 wind), which, according to the Aztec experts in the counting of days, had both favorable and unfavorable aspects. On this day the *hueyi tlâtoani* ("great ruler"), the supreme external authority in the empire, received new strength to recover from the adverse influences of the "princesses" on 1 rain. On this day, too, criminals and adulterers were executed, and evil wizards and the nahuals of people became active. Fear was pervasive, and special herbs were burned in the fireplace to keep away nahuals.[4] To the merchants, however, it was a very special day, and for the rich among them, it was a day of rejoicing. On that day they could show off their wealth in public.[5] They displayed their possessions on rich mantles in the temples of their city wards. The usual offerings of copal and quails were made, and people ate, drank, and smoked to their hearts' content. The old merchants especially, women as well as men, drank much too much during the night that followed and boasted of their riches. On the seventh day everyone, including the merchants, celebrated a feast for the *cihuapipiltin*, the goddesses of the west, the companions of the sun, in the temple of Aticpac.[6] It was also a suitable day, as were 1 cipactli, 1 coatl, and 1 ozomâtli, to set out on a trading expedition.

On the seventh day, 7 tecpatl (7 flintstone) of the eighth 13-day period, called 1 malinalli (1 very tall grass), the Aztecs celebrated the feast of Chicomecoatl (seven snake), the maize god. Since this god was special to the merchants, we may assume that they took an active part in his festival. We have no information about their ritual for that day, however.

On the first day of the ninth 13-day period, 1 coatl (1 snake), the merchants worshiped the god who guided their march, Ce Coatl Ohtlimelahuac. As mentioned earlier, his day was especially propitious for beginning a trade expedition. On this day the families, who would remain at home, began the rituals for the traveling merchants. As a mark of honor and as penance they washed their heads with soap only once every 80 days, until the merchants returned, but unlike the merchants they did wash the rest of their bodies.

When a merchant died on a journey, the sad news was first told to the old merchants, the *pochtecahuehuetquê,* whose duty it was to inform his relatives and the members of his household. Four days were set aside for mourning and eulogy. After the mourning period pine faggots were made into a bundle that symbolized the deceased. The bundle was covered with sacred papers, special kinds of paper ornaments. If the merchant had been killed in battle, the symbolic structure was placed in the temple of his calpolli for one day. It was burned at midnight in the courtyard of the temple near either the eagle vessel or the skull rack. If he had not been killed in battle but had died of disease or from some other cause, the image was burned in his house, not at midnight but shortly before sunset.

The day 1 snake was also a suitable day on which to start a war. As has been said before, the seventh day of this period, 7 ozomâtli (7 monkey) was a suitable day to hold the Song Feast.

The eleventh 13-day period began with 1 ozomâtli (1 monkey), one of the feast days of the goddesses of the west.

The seventh day of the thirteenth 13-day period, which began with 1 ollin (1 rolling movement), was 7 calli (7 house). Like 1 calli, the first day of the fifteenth period, it was another favorable day for the traveling merchants to return home with their merchandise. The Necxipâquiliz (Washing of Feet ceremony) was held (see below, under 1 calli).

The first day of the fourteenth 13-day period, 1 itzcuintli (1 dog), was also one of the important feast days of the merchants. It was dedicated to Xiuhtêcuhtli-Tlalxictenticâ (Lord of the Year, who filled the navels of the earth), the fire god, the major god of the calpolli of Tzonmolco. On this day the people of Tzonmolco made offerings to this god of resin and costly sacred papers entirely covered with pieces of jade and precious feathers. This ceremony was called Nextlahualli (Payment).[7] It was lavishly celebrated in the homes of the wealthy, especially among the merchants of the *petlatl* of Pochtlan, and the feather-mosaic workers of Amantlan who also belonged to that temple and who "held the fire god in particularly great veneration and made him great."[8] They held banquets and drinking bouts and were merry. At dawn they burned sacred papers; then they cast basketfuls of white copal into the fire. They sacrificed quails and sprinkled agave wine (*pulque* in Spanish, *octli* in Nahuatl) in the center and the four corners of the living room as sacrificial offering. The common people had nothing but small bits of broken resin to sacrifice. The poorest among the poor cast aromatic herbs and hemp onto the hearth as their offerings to the fire god. This was also the day of the election of new chiefs, new executives, and of meetings of government officials all over the land.

The second day of this period, 2 ozomahtli (2 monkey), was set apart for the Teyolmelahualiztli, the public acceptance of the obligation to sacrifice slaves (see below under the fifteenth feast of the year, Panquetzaliztli). Like 7 Calli, this was a propitious day for the merchants to return from their expeditions. It was said that on that day "the property of the omnipresent, the owner of the earth, invisible as the night, fleet as the wind (the supreme god), entered undamaged."[9]

When the merchants left Xoconochco or Xicalanco, in the far southern and southeastern parts of the empire, for the journey back, they had to fulfill many ritual obligations. They made sacrificial offerings at a temple in each place through which they passed. On the days when they did not travel through any village or town, they made their offerings in the fields. When they arrived at Itzyocan (today Izúcar de Matamoros), they remained there until by timing their march they reached their own city on 1 or 7 calli. They may have waited at Itzyocan "from ten to twenty days."[10]

When they arrived, they took care to reach the city after dark. The merchandise was well hidden in covered boats. They did not take their goods directly to their own homes but delivered it to the homes of relatives or other trustworthy persons, saying that the goods belonged to the chiefs of the merchants. This accomplished, one of the next acts they performed was to take their walking sticks, which had served them on the successful journey, to the temples of their calpollis, where the sticks, being sacred, were placed inside the buildings.

The feast celebrating the return of the merchants was organized by the junior merchants who had taken part in the expedition.

It was called Necxipâquiliztli (Washing of Feet), and the organizing of it was the first important task in the hierarchy of the *cargo* system of the Aztec merchants.

On his return the merchant at once reported to his local chief to inform him of his safe arrival. Then invitations were sent out, and at midnight offerings were laid before the fire god Xiuhtêcuhtli and before Yacatêcuhtli, the Lord of the Vanguard. After this the merchant and his helpers made preparations for the meal. It was still dark when the guests arrived. The guests were the inhabitants of the ward and their chiefs, the old *pochtecs* and *oztomecs,* and women merchants who had supplied sacrificial slaves at least once. The first dishes brought in were those to be served to Xiuhtêcuhtli, followed by the offerings to Yacatêcuhtli. Then came the food for the guests. Before and after the meal every guest washed his mouth and hands. The two gods were also offered the first two bowls of every drink. The guests drank chocolate and smoked tobacco. Each chief received two bowls of chocolate, the other guests one. Each guest had two hundred cocoa beans and one hundred aromatic teonacaztli plants (to flavor the cocoa drink) delivered to his home, as well as one stirring stick for every member of his household.

The day 1 calli was the most important of the five feast days dedicated to the western goddesses, the princesses, and the female rulers of the crossroads. The first day of the nineteenth 13-day period, 1 cuauhtli (1 eagle) was also dedicated to the goddesses of the west. The first day of the twentieth and last 13-day period of the tonalamatl, 1 tochtli (1 rabbit), was a feast day for Xiuhtêcuhtli, the fire god, and was therefore another important day for all merchants.

The Ritual of the Merchants During the Solar Year

During each of the eighteen 20-day periods of the solar year a great religious feast was held in which all Aztecs took part, though some of the feasts were dominated by specific groups. The major ceremonies and the celebration proper nearly always took place at the end of a 20-day period and often lasted for more than a day, sometimes even extending into the first few days of the next period. Only those feasts of the solar year in which merchants took part as members of their professional organization are dealt with in this chapter. General ceremonial rituals in which they participated are not discussed.

The second of the eighteen feasts of the solar year was Tlacaxipehualiztli (Skinning of Human Victims). The guild of the gold-smiths was the main occupational group celebrating this feast. On this occasion merchants could sacrifice slaves to Huitzilopochtli and Xipe Totêc. The *tealtianimê* ("Bathers of men") among them had already bathed their slaves during the previous eighteenth 20-day period, called Izcalli (Resurrection). If they participated in the Tlacaxipehualiztli, they probably did so because they had failed to complete their preparations for the ritual offering of slaves that was to have taken place during their great feast, the fifteenth feast of the year, Panquetzaliztli. The ritual and feast connected with the sacrifice of slaves is described below. It is necessary here only to state that the god Xipe Totêc was one of the principal manifestations of Tezcatlepoca. Xipe was in particular the god of spring, fertility, and renewal. His temple, Yopico, was situated in Moyotla, the quarter of Tenochtitlan associated with the west. He was the *calpolteotl* of the goldsmiths (the god of their calpolli).[11]

The fourth feast of the year, Hueyi Tozoztli (Great Vigil), was also of special significance to the merchants. It was the special feast of the maize god, sometimes represented as a goddess. His name was Cinteotl (Maize God), and his calendar name was Chicomecoatl (Seven Snake). During this feast youths between fifteen and twenty years of age visited the merchants' homes and the homes of high functionaries to weave pine twigs into mats, on which offerings made of reed and grass woven into hollow balls were laid. Between the offerings the youths laid maguey thorns stained with their blood. This was done just before sunset. Four days earlier there had been fasting in all the houses, and the youths had made sacrificial offerings of thick reeds with blood spattered on them. At night a special kind of *atolli* (maize gruel) was served inside the house, after which the youths swept all the temples in their calpollis. At dawn the boys and the priests called at every house to collect contributions for the feast.[12]

Of the eighteen feasts in the year, the fifth, Toxcatl (Chain of Dried, or Popped, Maize), was one of the most important. It was dedicated to the gods Tezcatlepoca and Huitzilopochtli, and all Aztecs took part. The texts give little suggestion of special participation by the merchants as a group. They say only that during the ceremony, called Toxcachocholoa (Jumping Dance of Toxcatl), the wives and daughters of merchants and other wealthy families sacrificed costly mantles to Huitzilopochtli, while other women and girls made offerings of paper.[13]

During the sixth feast of the year, Etzalcualiztli (Eating of

Fig. 8.2. *Ritual during the feast of Tlacaxipehualiztli.* Florentine Codex, *vol. 2.*

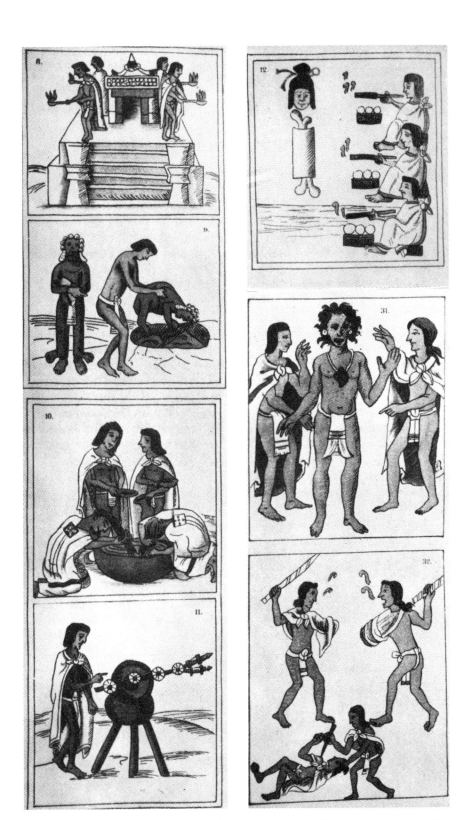

Fig. 8.3. *Ritual during the feast of Tlacaxipehualiztli and Panquetzaliztli.*
Florentine Codex, *vol. 3.*

Beans), slaves as well as prisoners of war could be sacrificed to the rain god, Tlaloc. This provided the merchants with another opportunity to compete publicly with one another and with military officers of high rank.[14]

The ninth feast of the year, Tlaxochimaco (Offering of Flowers), was celebrated in honor of Huitzilopochtli. Flower offerings were made at the home altars of all the chiefs and their subjects. In all the temples in each calpolli, in the *telpochcalli* ("houses of youth"), and in the houses of the tax collectors the images of Huitzilopochtli and all the local gods were decorated with garlands of flowers. In the temple of Tzonmolco the decoration was the responsibility of the merchants, as it was in the *telpochcallis* of their *petlamê,* and also in the tribute warehouses under their authority. At the conclusion of the feast the different groups in the capital city worshiped the gods of their own *calpoltin.*[15]

The tenth feast of the year was Xocotlhuetzi (Fruit Falls). From time immemorial it had been the great feast of Otontêcuhtli, the god of the Otomis. Among the Mexîcas it was a feast dedicated to Xiuhtêcuhtli. This period was also twenty days, during which the merchants could sacrifice slaves to their own god Yacatêcuhtli in their sanctuary in Pochtlan. Later the skulls of the slaves who had been sacrificed were added to the collection on the merchants' own skull rack *(tzompantli)* at Pochtlan.[16] Evidently the feast day of Yacatêcuhtli fell on the first day of this period, whereas the ceremonies in honor of Xiuhtêcuhtli took place at the end. The Fire God, as the *calpolteotl* of Tzonmolco and one of the chief gods of the merchants, was on this occasion honoured by them with the sacrifice of five slaves, four males and one female, who impersonated special gods of the pochtecâ.[17]

The eleventh feast of the year, Ochpaniztli (Sweeping of the Roads), was dedicated to the goddess Tocî Teteô Innan (Our Grandmother, or Mother of the Gods), who was also called Tlazolteotl (Goddess of Filth). This feast was chiefly organized by and for women, especially female healers. Healers, aged women, virgins, and prostitutes formed two separate groups. One group included the most important women healers, who carried the symbolic representation of the goddess Teteô Innan; they fought a ceremonial battle against the other group, which lasted four days. Then a woman who acted as a representation of the goddess Tocî was sacrificed. She was taken to the market square, where the healers stood around her. She was presented to the priests of Seven Snake (Chicome Coatl), the god(dess) of maize, and then led across the marketplace by way of farewell to it, since Tocî was also the goddess of markets. The healers reminded her that she was going to die and spoke words of comfort. Then she was quickly led to the temple and beheaded. She was flayed by a large, strong priest who covered himself with her skin except for that of her thighs, which was taken to Pochtlan, where the person who represented the goddess's child Cinteotl (the Maize god), covered himself with it. Finally the Tocî and Cinteotl priests went to the temple of Huitzilopochtli, where the feast assumed a more general character. Since part of the ritual took place at their main temple, the merchants must have been involved in it.

The twelfth feast of the year, called Teotlêco (Arrival of the Gods), was dedicated to all the gods of the Aztec pantheon, which included all the gods known to them, their own and those of other peoples. Although it was a general feast, some attention is given to it here for the special role the merchants' gods played in its celebration. At the beginning of the last 5 days of this twelfth 20-day period, young men laid wreaths of fir branches at house altars and at the foot of each temple, including the temples dedicated to the goddesses of the west. Maize cobs were also sacrificed. On the third day after the wreaths had been distributed, the god Telpochtli Tlamatzincatl (the Young Tezcatlepoca) arrived. Offerings were laid before him; on the fourth day (the nineteenth day of the period) the wreaths were thrown away. The 2-day ceremony of Quimicxipacâ in Teteô ("Washing of the Feet of the Gods") had begun the previous night. On the night before the last day the priests made a circular floor of crushed maize. An old priest with the title *teohuâ* ("possessor of the god") watched the maize floor closely until he saw a faint footprint in it. Then he rose, saying, "Yes, the ruler has arrived!" The priests immediately formed a procession that wound all over the city. They sounded their shell trumpets to proclaim the great news, the arrival of the god. The common people now made offerings in all the temples, for all the gods had come to the people, except those of the merchants:

Auh in imuztlayoc,	And it was the next day
ihcuac ehco in Yacapitzahuac,	that Pointed Nose arrived,
in Iyacatêcuhtli,	the Lord of the Vanguard,
pochtecâ inteouh catcâ,	he who was the god of the merchants,
ihuan in Ixcozauhqui,	and the Yellow-faced One,
yêhuatl in Xiuhtêcuhtli,	he who is the Lord of the Year,
zan no pochtecâ inteouh catca;	who was also a god of the

	merchants;
zan huallatzacuitihuiâ,	but they appeared after the others,
zan huallatoquilitihuiâ,	they only followed the others,
zan quihualcentzacuitihuiâ,	they were the last to arrive,
yehica ca yê huehuetquê.[18]	because they were ancient gods.

The gods of the merchants were commonly accepted as being the oldest among the gods. The *pochtecâ* were evidently one of the oldest occupational groups in the Aztec empire, or at least they were considered to be the heirs of such a group. The *Florentine Codex* indicates that in the fourteenth feast of the year, Quecholli (Crane), many slaves were sacrificed. Therefore we must assume that merchants had some opportunity to take part in the Quecholli rituals, however they are not particularly mentioned in this instance.

As mentioned earlier, the fifteenth feast of the year, Panquetzaliztli (Raising of the Banners), was an important feast for merchants and warriors as well, because it was the climactic event in the worship of Huitzilopochtli. In contrast to most of the other feasts of the year, it did not start halfway through or at the end of the twenty-day period but immediately followed the preceding feast of Quecholli. At dusk "Tlaxotecayotl" ("Hymn of Huitzilopochtli"), which may be considered a kind of Aztec "national anthem," was sung. It went as follows:

Tlaxotlan tenamitl	At the walls of Tlaxotlan
îhuitl macoc,	feathers were given,
mupupuxotiuh yauhtlâto.	the war chief proceeds to fulfil his task.
Noteouh Tepanquizqui	My god is called
mîtoa!	Dominator of Men!
Oya yêhua huel mamahuia	He who is from Tlaxotlan
in Tlaxotecatl	goes in rich array of sacrificial paper,
teuhtlan, teuhtlan	he circles around
milacatzoa![19]	in the places of dust!

The women also joined in the singing, even the *ahuianimê* ("daughters of joy") the state-recognized harlots, who slept with the young unmarried warriors. They danced and sang with the men from before sunset until midnight each night of the feast for twenty days.

The men and women merchants had, long before, bought one or more slaves in the Azcapotzalco market at a price of thirty or forty cotton mantles, depending on the quality of the slaves. But they did not begin the ritual of Panquetzaliztli before the fifteenth day, though they had made many preparations and had held many obligatory ceremonies. After they bought the slaves they distributed gifts to army officers of high rank and to both male and female merchant chiefs in their own city as well as those of the other eleven cities. Once this had been done, they traveled to Tochtepec, where they went to the temple of Yacatêcuhtli, the god of the merchants. For every slave he was going to sacrifice, each merchant placed one staff, hung with ritual papers, before the image of the god. He also displayed to Yacatêcuhtli the clothes that the sacrificial slaves would wear. Then he held the banquet described above, at which he told the merchant chiefs that he "wanted to look into the face and behold the presence of the portentous prince Huitzilopochtli."[20] When the aspirant "sacrificer of slaves" had returned to Mexico, he held two banquets, the first to announce his decision *(teyolmelahualiztli)* and the second to display his slaves *(tlaixnextiliztli)*. On the second occasion his slaves wore their finest clothes, and they danced and sang for the guests. This was an occasion of great significance to the young merchant. If the slaves were ill-favored or if they sang and danced badly, the merchant made a very poor showing that adversely affected his social career. If the slaves were handsome and proved to be good cooks and servants, the owners ran a risk of quite a different nature. There were sure to be high-ranking army officers and other government officials of noble birth among the guests who could demand that slaves of such good quality must be sold to them.[21] In this way slaves were saved from sacrifice, and they became personal servants of the dignitaries who had bought them. To the previous owner, however, this meant that advancement in the *cargo* hierarchy would have to wait at least until the next time for making ceremonial offerings if he happened to be at home and not in the far south on a trade expedition. This procedure afforded the highest authorities in the regime a mechanism for social control; by this means they were able to restrain the social career of too ambitious a merchant.

The third banquet held by the merchants was the occasion on which their slaves were "bathed" and underwent a ritual purification that took place on the eleventh day of Panquetzaliztli. The slaves were dressed in beautiful clothes and ornaments. They wore earplugs, noseplates, headgear made of variously colored feathers, epaulets made of kestrel wings, and sacred tunics decorated with feather mosaics in blue, black, red, and bluish-green belts. They also wore scarves around their left wrists and black sandals. The owners of the slaves also invited their helpers, those men who guarded and cared for the slaves and the elderly women who ceremonially washed their faces. All the helpers, both male and female, were present at the sacrificial ceremony, which took place on the twentieth day. On the day of bathing, however, they had received their reward when the owners had given them beautifully embroidered clothes and feather ornaments. On this day too the sacrificial slaves were presented in the temples of the appropriate calpollis, after which the "slave-bathers" danced and sang with their wives.

On the fifteenth day the slaveowners and all the aged men in their several calpollis began fasting; during the next four days they ate only one meal a day, at noon. In the evening they went to the calpolli temple and at midnight the males bathed in the House of Mist (Ayauhcalli), while the women merchants who wanted to sacrifice slaves bathed at the lake shore, and each sacrificed one maguey thorn with her own blood. The nineteenth day of the feast saw the beginning of the "joint dances." The slaves, their owners, the "catchers" of the slaves, the banner-bearers, the women who had washed the faces of the slaves, and the men who were to carry the slaves down the steps of the temple when they had been killed performed dances in one long row. The aged men who belonged to the calpollis of the sacrificing merchants beat their drums and sang. The male slave-bathers were not allowed to sleep with their spouses on that night. Just before sunset they took the slaves to the temple of Huitzilopochtli, where the slaves were offered holy wine, medicine of the sacrificial knife. The slaves became slightly intoxicated, so that they no longer feared death. They did not return to the houses of their owners, but were taken either to the temple at Pochtlan or to the temple at Acxotlan.[22] In the meantime, their owners, for the fourth time, entertained high army officers and chiefs and distributed gifts among them.

At midnight the sacrificial slaves sat on mats before a fire; then the slave-bathers arrived and put on their "sacred tunics," which resembled those which the slaves had worn. The fire was extinguished, and the slaves then received amaranth honey cakes to eat. After that, one lock of hair was cut from the crown of each of the slaves' heads. The slave-bathers kept the hair and the slaves' clothes and decorations in a sacred chest, which would be burned during the owner's funeral ceremony. Then the slaves waited the arrival of Paynal, the "counterpart being" of Huitzilopochtli. Now the twentieth day had begun. Heading a quickly moving procession, Paynal left Tenochtitlan in a northerly direction through Tlatelolco, proceeded along the western shore of the lake to re-enter the city from the south, through Xoloc.

When he returned, the sacrificial slaves were given arrows for hunting birds and taken to the part of the city called Coatlan, in the northeastern city quarter of Atzacualco. In Coatlan they stood facing the Huitznahuâ (Southerners), war captives who were also to be sacrificed. The prisoners of war wore coats of mail and carried shields and pine cudgels. The two groups of slaves fought a ritual battle, in which some might be killed or taken prisoner. This ritual was further evidence that warriors had a privileged social position, for army officers who wanted to help the Huitznahuâ could do so. If an officer captured a slave, he took him to the Huitzcalco temple, where a price was fixed at which the original owner could buy him back. If the merchant owner had insufficient means to do this, the officer who had captured the slave could sacrifice him to advance his own career. If an officer who had joined the battle was wounded, killed, or taken prisoner by a slave, he too was sacrificed by that slave on a drum, which served as an altar.[23]

When the master of the battle saw Paynal approaching, he ordered the fight to be stopped and the sacrificial ritual began. A procession formed, headed by the bearers of banners and other emblems, and marched to the temple of Huitzilopochtli, where first the war captives and then the slaves were sacrificed. Each time a slave's heart was cut out of the body, the shell trumpets were sounded. To many a merchant this was the greatest moment in his life. A married merchant would take his wife with him to accompany the slaves up the steps of the temple pyramid. If he was single, he would ask a relative or a friend to go with him. The slave bather and his male or female companion each carried a feathered staff up the steps, drawing the full attention of the crowd that had come to watch the ceremony. After the bodies of the sacrificed slaves had glided down the stairs, the merchant and his companion descended from the temple. Following this part of the ceremony the attendants took the bodies of the dead slaves to their homes, where they were cooked with a little salt and no chili. Small pieces of the flesh were sprinkled on cooked maize, and the dish was served to all the neighbors. Since the spirits of the sacrificial victims remained wandering about on earth for four more days the last ritual was performed on the fourth day of the next 20-day period, Atemoztli, on which day the sacrificial paper clothes of the slaves were burned and the ashes strewn over the earth.

The eighteenth feast of the year, called Izcalli (Resurrection), was dedicated to Xiuhtêcuhtli Ixcozauhqui, the Lord of the Year, Yellow Face, the fire god. As has been said before, he was the calpolteotl of Tzonmolco and one of the two most important special gods of the merchants; hence the merchants took a prominent part in this feast. In ordinary years it was an unpretentious celebration, only maize dishes being served in all the calpolli temples. But once every four years it was celebrated more lavishly. Then rich merchants and other well-to-do people in Tzonmolco sacrificed slaves, this time to Ixcozauhqui. In ordinary years the actual sacrifices had to wait until the second period of the next year, 45 days later, until the end of Tlacaxipehualiztli.

This has been a brief survey of the merchants' rituals. Of course, the merchants also had to fulfill other minor daily ritual obligations, and on trading expeditions priests who were in the merchants' permanent service made daily offerings of smoke.[24]

The Moral Code of the Merchants

A detailed discussion of the moral code of the merchants, their system of values and norms, is beyond the scope of this book. Yet a brief description is useful to demonstrate that the merchants not only followed prevailing Aztec standards but in addition had important rules of conduct for their own group. It goes without saying that a regime in which the young people were educated in boarding schools until their twentieth year would achieve a fair degree of indoctrination. Even after the young merchants had joined the guild, the older merchants and the chiefs continued to tell them what to do and how to do it.

From the ceremonial speeches delivered by the merchants in the course of their feasts and from the stereotyped descriptions of good and bad merchants by Sahagún's informants, the major values and rules of conduct governing this group can be deduced. The general Aztec values and norms appear to have been as follows:

1. Maintenance of control and discipline.[25]
2. Fluency of speech and good manners.[26]
3. A composed and reserved attitude.[27]
4. A sense of responsibility for the common people.[28]

5. Respect for one's elders.[29]

6. Interest in and knowledge of the gods.[30]

7. Courage, submission to one's fate, a desire to die a heroic death rather than to die without having made a serious effort to expand and strengthen the Aztecs's supremacy. According to Mexican teaching about a merchant who was killed on the battlefield, as well as about a warrior who died in battle, it was said that "quitoca in Tonatiuh, ilhuicac yauh" ("he follows the sun, he rises to heaven"), meaning that after death he did not go to the realm of the dead in the underworld as did an ordinary human being.[31]

The values and norms adhered to specifically by the merchants were as follows:

1. Loyalty and solidarity among all the members of the national association of merchants (between *pochtecâ* and *oztomecâ,* among the *petlamê* and among the cities); absence of envy.[32]

2. Respect and regard for others, including non-Aztec peoples within the empire and even foreigners outside it, respect for their property and their customs, etc.[33]

3. Responsibility for the apprentices, the young people learning to be merchants.[34]

4. Plain living, modesty, inconspicuous behavior, self-control, absence of pride.[35]

5. Absence of attachment to one's property; generosity without waste.[36]

6. Fairness in matters of trade; accurate description of the quality of merchandise; reasonable prices.[37]

7. Acquisition of wealth by working hard, not by taking great risks, gambling, or betting.[38]

8. Respect for other men's wives, including those of foreigners. The merchants were expected, during their long trade expeditions, to refrain from adultery, "for in every stone, in every tree the Omnipresent One (the supreme god) is watching you," the chiefs told them on their departure.[39]

9. Self-denial and staying power, qualities considered indispensable in every merchant.[40]

Several of the principles and rules of conduct for the merchants differed from those that the warriors followed. Number 1 of the merchant's code above certainly did not pertain to the warriors, since the military was divided into different contending units.

Rules 2, 4, 7, and 8 were also applied less stringently to the warriors. A sentence of death was usually pronounced by the merchant-judges for any violation of rule number 2.[41] On the other hand, a military court-martial would pronounce a sentence of death only for the more serious violations of the rule, though violations of any kind were frowned upon by high-ranking officers.

It is clear that the relationship between the merchants and the military, two powerful groups within Aztec society, illustrate the conditions of the Mexican regime. These relationships are perhaps nowhere more clearly seen than in the following comments by Sahagún's informants:

Motêuhczoma (the *Tlâtoani*) held the old merchants, the disguised traders, the slave bathers, and the slave traders in high esteem; he treated them as if they were members of his nobility. But, if they should forget their station in life, if their minds were corrupted and they indulged in evil thoughts, they were secretly condemned, under pretense, by means of false testimony and executed by the army officers.[42]

When merchants had gained a great victory over an enemy without support from the warriors, their chiefs would say to them: "Let no one be proud, let no one boast of his courage because of all the prisoners we have taken. For we sought land only for our prince, the great Huitzilopochtli."[43] In spite of the merchants' rivalry with the warriors, there was always the consolation offered them by the regime that once in every 260 days, on 4 wind, they could boast without let or hindrance, and they were officially recognized as the men who, "leading the caravans, made the Mexican state great."[44]

Other Vocational Groups

The merchants' guild formed the most prominent vocational group in Aztec society, but there were other more or less important organizations. In status the *amantecâ,* the feather-mosaic workers, were a close second to the merchants. They and the merchants lived and worked on the same streets. They originated from the Mexitin.[45] Their chief god was Coyotlinahual (Wolf Is His Animal Counterpart), whose temple was in Amantlan, an area adjoining Pochtlan in the calpolli of Coatlan. Their god Tizahuâ probably belonged to the group that lived in the city quarter of Teopan. Their earth god, Macuilocelotl (Five Ocelot), belonged to the *tlaxi-lacalli* of Yopico and consequently was worshiped by their colleagues in Moyotla. The fourth god of the feather-mosaic workers was Macuiltochtli (Five Rabbit), and since this god belonged to the *tlaxilacalli* of Têcpantzinco, he probably was worshiped also by members of the guild in Moyotla. The fifth and sixth deities on the list were the goddesses Xilo (Young Maize Cob) and Xiuhtlati (Burning Turquoise), both of whom were probably associated with Cuepopan. Tepuztecatl is mentioned as their seventh god, and, as god of pulque (agave wine), he belonged to Izquitlan and therefore to Cuepopan.[46]

Like the merchants, the *amantecâ* probably had sanctuaries in all four great city quarters. Their connection with Yopico and Izquitlan was in accordance with their Mexitin background. Probably they were the only guild of Chichimec origin in the city. During the celebrations of the yearly calendar they played an important part in the feasts of Tlaxochimaco and Panquetzaliztli.[47]

The *tlatecquê*, the precious-stone workers, had four sanctuaries, one in each of the city quarters. One was dedicated to the god Chicunahui Itzcuintli (Nine Dog) in Atempan, in the city quarter of Teopan. The second, dedicated to Nahualpilli (Magic Prince), was situated in Moyotla, near Yopico. The third was Macuilcalli (Five House), in Chililico, in the city quarter of Atzacualco. Their fourth god was Centeotl (Maize God), who was worshiped in Tlamatzinco, in Cuepopan.

The *teocuitlapizquê* were gold- and silversmiths whose guild was of Toltec origin. Xipe Totêc (Flayed One, or Our Lord) was the god of this group, as he was of all the precious-metal workers throughout Mesoamerica. No mention is made of any other gods associated with this guild. This is not to say, however, that the guild members resided only in Moyotla. According to Durán, smaller Xipe sanctuaries were scattered about the city. Their great religious center was the Yopico temple in Moyotla.

The *iztatlacâ* ("salt people"), or *iztachiuhquê* ("extractors of salt"), were another important vocational group living in the city. Their product was of great importance to the economy. The patroness of this group was Huixtocihuatl, who was looked on as a sister of the rain gods, Tlaloquê.[48] Her main feast fell in the seventh 20-day period, called Têcuilhuitontli (Minor Gentlemen's Feast). For ten consecutive days the salt extractors sang songs, "the way women sing," and in the afternoon they also danced. Their most important ceremony included a sacrifice of a human being representing the goddess of Huixtocihuatl. The sacrifice was held at the great temple in front of the chapel of the rain god,

Tlaloc. Broda believes that the importance of these salt workers is evident from the fact that their members were allowed to make sacrifices at the great temple.[49] In my opinion that is a doubtful argument for their importance. The relationship of this group's goddess to the rain god, Tlaloc, whose chapel stood next to that of Huitzilopochtli, probably made their presence at the great temple acceptable.

The hunters *(anquê)* held their most important public performance during Quecholli, when the yearly feast of their patron Mixcoatl was celebrated.[50] Nothing more is known, however, about their corporate organization.

The largest vocational group in Tenochtitlan was probably that of the weavers *(ihquitquê),* who had Xochiquetzal as their chief patroness. The group was not, however, one of the most important corporate organizations. It had a mixed membership, ranging from imperial noblewomen to men and women of the poorest commoner group and little or no internal coherence.

In fig. 8.4, I indicate the most likely connections between *tlaxilacallis* (rows of thirteen small sanctuaries in the framework of the *tonalamatl,* or daily calendar (see chapter 11), and vocational groups with their respective gods and goddesses and the dates of their patron feasts in the *tonalpoalli.* The available data do not give much more than a general impression of the corporate vocational structure of Tenochtitlan.

The inclusion of old Toltec corporate groups, such as merchants and gold- and silversmiths, in the Aztec population of the capital city and to some extent even in its top social strata, was a remarkable phenomenon. Timal was the last great military leader in the Quetzalcoatl and Nonoalco tradition.[51] After his defeat the tradition survived only among the merchants, who succeeded in reviving it and making it prosper. With the successful incorporation of these groups into their society the Aztecs had, in a certain sense, completed the policy that Huemac had tried in vain to carry out, namely, the reunification of the two pillars of Toltec social order.

To make a judgment about the relative social positions of each vocational group, it would be necessary to know to what extent their members were admitted into Aztec institutions of higher education and high offices. We know that the merchants were allowed to send their children to the *calmecac,* an institution of higher education. Tzonmolco was one of the seven *calpultin* in the city that had such a school,[52] and the merchants probably sent their children there. The educational situation is unclear as far as the

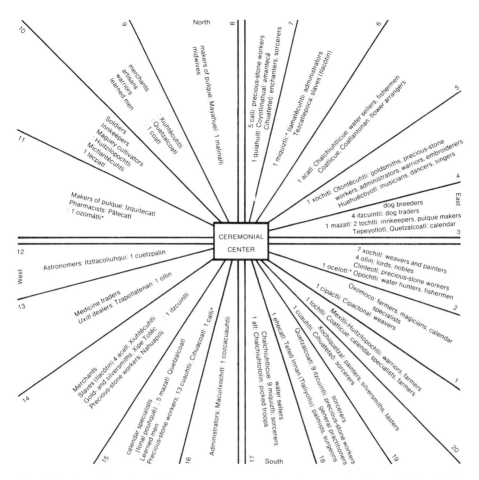

Fig. 8.4. *Participation of the corporate vocational groups in Tenochtitlan in the* tonalpoalli *rituals. The radiating lines indicate the approximate directions of the* tlaxilacallis *(see chap. 12). The day-names, patrons and patronesses, and vocational groups related to each other are listed together.*

*It is possible that the mat makers *(petlachiuhquê)*, with their god Nappatê-cuhtli, belonged to lines 2, 6, 11, and 15.

other guilds are concerned. The *calmecac* were boarding schools with rigid discipline in which boys and girls were strictly segregated. The lessons were given by priests and priestesses, and discipline was very strict. The pupils had to fulfill arduous ritual obligations each day as well as at night. In every calpolli there was a *telpochcalli* (house of youth) and an *ichpocacalli* (house of girls). These were a form of boarding school with a much more lenient policy and were attended by most of the young people. The schools gave the children training in agriculture, housekeeping, and ordinary military activities. Both schools provided courses until the twentieth year, which was indeed an impressive achievement for any society in the fifteenth and sixteenth centuries. A *calmecac* education was a prerequisite for appointment to the highest administrative ranks. To attain the highest priestly offices, it was even necessary to have been educated at a special high priests' school, the *tlamacazcalli*. The highest military ranks could be attained after a *calmecac* as well as a *telpochcalli* education, but only officers with a *calmecac* preparation were allowed in the highest ranks of the administration.

Membership in any of the vocational groups appears to have been based mainly on heredity. However, election to the top ranks in the guilds depended on an individual's education, ambition, and personal achievements. For example, it was impossible to become a *pochtecatlailotlac* without a *calmecac* education. It was also possible to become an *acxotecatl* (external chief of the central organization of merchants' guilds) without having attended a *calmecac*, but this required exceptional effort and ambition, and also barred the way to a post in the central government.

CHAPTER 9

Kinship Policy and "Ancestor Borrowing"

THE so-called Toltec tradition required that chiefs, male or female, who primarily exercised authority over internal affairs, must have descended through both mother and father from the families that traditionally had the highest status. "External chiefs," usually male but in special cases female, were responsible for relations between their group or community and other societies. It was necessary for these individuals to be related to the traditional aristocracy in only one line, preferably that of their fathers.[1] These elites were encouraged to marry out of their communities as part of the Aztecs' administrative policy of allying themselves with other groups or communities through marriage. As the external system gained power, the number of exogamous elite marriages grew. The increase in such marriages was stimulated by the custom of polygyny and by concubinage, which was acceptable among members of the aristocracy.

With an increase in the linkages of the external system the power exercised by the external chiefs came to exceed that of the internal chiefs. Their supremacy was confirmed by a combination of exogamous and endogamous marriages and by concubinage. Thus through alliances within the system they also gained direct influence in the internal power network, enhancing their authority at the expense of the internal chiefs. That the latter retained any important functions that they traditionally had held can only be ascribed to the ancient and pervasive system of ideological dualism that obtained in all Mesoamerican cultures. The dualistic system essential to the Mesoamerican concept of the cosmos and world view found expression at all levels of social organization and continues to do so in modern Mexican communities.[2]

Considerations of kinship were always an important part of Aztec policy and had been so among the groups from which the Aztecs originated. In early colonial times kinship ties were the primary means by which indigenous noble families acquired influence in colonial society. Pedigrees and genealogies dating from colonial times, composed out of a desire for power, were, of course, usually unreliable, and it is hardly surprising to find contradictions in ancestral claims in the sources from that time. Early colonial conditions not only affected family and group histories but also caused basic changes in the nature of the kinship system and the rules of succession governing it. Ambitious native nobles soon realized that they would have the best chance of success with the colonial authorities if they based their claims to material goods and rank on patrilineal descent through the mechanism of primogeniture. The system of testation and succession was quite complicated and differed from the Spanish system in several important respects. After the Conquest the Spanish colonial judicial administration generally applied Spanish rules, by which persons who in the indigenous system would have little chance of attaining high office could suddenly acquire some "legitimate" claim to it. They produced documents about their kinship relations in which the native system was represented as a model of the Spanish system. The few indigenous parties whose rights were adversely affected by such a procedure and who tried to defend themselves on grounds of pre-Spanish rules of legitimation were usually overruled by the colonial judges.

Three major circumstances profoundly influenced the Aztec kinship system. The first was the passing of administrative power from the calpolli chiefs to a rising Toltec or Aztec nobility. The second was the assumption of power by Itzcoatl and his followers. The third was the establishment of the colonial Spanish regime. In spite of the obscuring effect these three processes have had on data relating to the pre-Spanish kinship system, a number of basic rules governing this system can be traced:

1. The successor of an external chief was to be his brother or his offspring, depending on which was the more competent. The right to succession was based on primogeniture and the status of the mother's as well as the father's family; thus it was possible for a woman to be appointed to a high position ahead of her male relatives. In the matter of land inheritance the rule of primogeniture was apparently of little consequence.[3]

2. The brother of a chief was preferred as a successor to the

chief's son or daughter; however, the brother's descendants were rarely considered for succession, and after his death or retirement the office reverted to the heirs of his predecessor.[4]

3. A child born of a so-called official wife was preferred as a successor to one born of a concubine. For an external chief the rule was that his mother preferably should be from a society outside his father's group.[5]

4. The mother's rank as well as the father's determined the status of the child, but an individual's status was, to a considerable extent, also determined by his personal achievements.[6]

5. Inheritance of a noble title was restricted to only three or four generations of the descendants who were not eligible for certain offices or for the enfeoffment of landed property. Noble rank was lowered with each succeeding generation of persons not holding the offices related to their family.[7]

6. The predominant custom of patrilocality, in which a married woman lived with her husband's family, was supplemented by territorial kinship ties. That is, a daughter could inherit her father's house, house lot, arable land, and office. A niece could inherit the same from her uncle, but only in those instances where the niece's husband lived on one of the properties of the testator.[8]

7. Newcomers settling on a house lot or a piece of land were considered, after some time, to be kin of the people who were already living there when they arrived, and the newcomers came to consider the ancestor of the original owners as their own.[9]

8. A chief's child who because of his mother's low social status could not be considered for succession to his father's office could change his circumstances by marrying a kinswoman whose parents had high status.[10]

Before comparing these basic principles with the specific rules of the inheritance of offices and possessions among the Aztec elite, a discussion of the general background of the Mesoamerican kinship system is in order.

The most basic Mesoamerican idea of kinship is still recognizable in the Aztecs' concept of *tocî* or *teteô innan,* which literally means "our grandmother" or "mother of the gods." Both terms are commonly applied to the earth goddess in Tenochtitlan and also to the *calpolteotl* of Atempan, which actually refer to the following idealized kinship relations: earth goddess ("our grandmother"), gods ("our mothers," "our fathers"), and human beings. Sahagún's informants say that the Xiuhtêcuhtli, the fire god, was

regarded by the Aztecs as the Old God and as *teteô innan* and
teteô intâ, ("the mother and father of the gods")[11] Fire and earth
were evidently seen as the first ancestors of both the gods and
human beings. All over Mesoamerica the gods regarded as the
more direct ancestors were those who lived in the sacred mountains near the long-established agricultural communities, such as
those in Chiapas. The seminomadic groups carried with them the
remains of their ancestors in sacred bundles.[12]

Before the creation of the people of the Fifth Sun, the god of
motion (Ollintonatiuh), the wind god (Quetzalcoatl), and the sun
god had made essential contributions to cosmic creation. This resulted in a complicated situation whereby mankind had celestial,
earthly, and underworld ancestors or creators.

The mythology of the Nahua peoples, to which the Mexîcâ
belonged, mentioned another special pair of ultimate ancestors,[13]
but this addition did not change the basic premise that man is
descended from ancestral gods who were descended from the ancient gods. The oldest Toltec god and creator, who probably dated
from pre-Toltec times, was Ometeotl (Two-God), a god with dual
male and female aspects and thus a creating god within himself.[14]
Many other individual deities of the Nahuatlacas were represented
sometimes as male and sometimes as female beings. Well-known
examples are Tlaltêcuhtli (the earth god or goddess), Cinteotl (the
maize god or goddess), and Metztli (the moon god or goddess).

The basic elements of Mesoamerican mythology and philosophy
invariably contain dual male and female elements. A unilinear
system would conflict with this structure; a kinship system based
on actual blood relations would be more appropriate. Thus it is
logical that the Aztecs included both their mother's and father's
ancestors in establishing descent. Attempts made by pre-Conquest
Aztecs to obscure or to emphasize certain blood relationships were
motivated not by the desire to prove their "direct" lineal descent
but rather by territorial circumstances or political, social, or religious considerations.

Genealogies of Toltec and other central Mexican royal or elite
families are found in the historical sources. An example is shown
in fig. 9.1, the genealogy of the royal Toltec family of Tollan, which
many colonial-period aristocratic families in Anahuac very much
wished to claim as their own.[15]

Figure 9.1 shows ten generations of Toltec monarchs, who were
said to have ruled on the central Mexican plateau for 520 years
(10 × 52). It is, of course, inaccurate from a Western historical

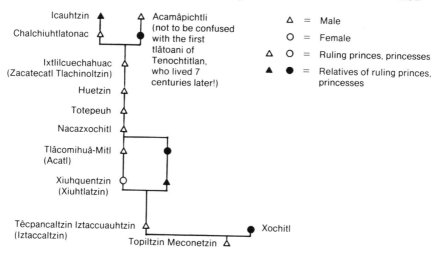

Fig. 9.1. *Genealogy of the royal family of Tollan, seventh to twelfth centuries. Compiled from Ixtlilxochitl and Torquemada.*

point of view but most interesting as a model. Note that the more common patrilineal succession is broken twice by a successor who was a "daughter" or other female. Since polygyny was common, it is unlikely that there were no brothers, uncles, nephews, or male cousins who could have inherited the office of chief. Any of the following circumstances (or a combination of them) may account for the deviation from the more normal patrilineal succession pattern:

1. The mother of the female successor was of higher rank than that of the mothers of any of the male relatives who could have been considered for succession.

2. The female successor was the first-born child of a mother of high rank (right of primogeniture).

3. The female successor had a husband of high rank who did not have the right to succession but had the qualities necessary for the office (dual chieftainship by marriage).

For a woman to succeed as chief in this manner, even when male candidates were available, was no rare occurrence in pre-Spanish Mesoamerican societies. Chimalpahin mentions a number of instances from his own family,[16] and Ixtlilxochitl gives both early and late Toltec examples, such as the succession of the princess Ilancueitl in Colhuâcan.[17]

In light of the above, it is not surprising that historical sources and oral traditions contain many contradictory data about the origins of the Aztec royal families. In the first place, certain names could belong to men as well as women, as, for example, the names Ilancueitl and Axolohuâ.[18] Moreover, the purposes of the indigenous historians had a bearing on the accuracy of their work, depending on whether they were more interested in descent as such or in establishing the right to succession.

Finally, apart from any political aims or desire for power, they could simply have made mistakes or drawn the wrong conclusions. In chapter 3 I have mentioned the contradictions in the sources about the ancestry of Huehuê Huitzilîhuitl. Torquemada says in one place that he was the son of Ilhuicatl, a son of the chief Tochpanecatl of Tzompanco, and Tiacapantzin, (Firstborn Daughter), a daughter of one of the Mexitin chiefs,[19] and, as appears from her name, the oldest daughter. In another place he seems partly under the influence of Acosta, assuming that Huehuê Huitzilîhuitl was a son of Coatzontli, who married a daughter of Acxocuauhtli of Colhuâcan.[20] Chimalpahin in his second *Relación* gives yet another story: There the mother of Huehuê Huitzilîhuitl is said to have been the princess Tlaquilxochtzin of Tzompanco, a daughter of Tlahuizcalpotonqui Têuhctli, *tlâtoani* of Tzompanco, even though his father was merely a Mexîcatl Chichimecatl.[21] Chimalpahin adds significantly to the data about the election of Huehuê Huitzilîhuitl:

ic niman contlâtocatlalliquê	and therefore they then elect as their
in Huehuê Huitzilîhuitl,	king the Old Hummingbird Feather,
auh yehica ipampa ca	and the reason was that
huey tlâtocatlacamecayotl	his much esteemed mother,
quipiaya in inantzin	Tlaquilxochtzin, had a great royal
Tlaquilxochtzin,	pedigree
ipampa ca iichpochtzin	because she was the daughter
in tlâtoani Tzompanco.[22]	of the king of Tzompanco.

Elite families from Tzompanco were Toltec. They may have been the first Toltecs with whom the Mexitin became closely allied in central Mexico. It is likely that the elites of the two groups commonly intermarried, which may be one reason for the confusion among later historians about the descent of Huehuê Huitzilîhuitl. The historical sources explain in various ways that there were kinship ties between the Mexitin royal family and the later Aztec royal house of which Acamâpichtli was the progenitor. As mentioned earlier the sources provide many backgrounds and important ancestors of this first Aztec king.

Here is a list of all the men and women who have been named as the parents of Acamâpichtli of Tenochtitlan:

NAMED AS FATHER:

1. Opochtli Iztahuâtzin[23]
2. Huehuê Huitzilîhuitl[24]
3. Cuauhtzin of Colhuâcan[25]
4. Huehuê Acamâpichtli of Colhuâcan[26]
5. Aculhuâ of Azcapotzalco[27]

NAMED AS MOTHER:

1. Atotoztli of Colhuâcan[28]
2. Ilancueitl of Colhuâcan[29]
3. Iztahuâtzin of the Mexitin[30]
4. Ixxochitl, daughter of a Mexîca chief[31]
5. Cuetlaxoch, daughter of Amacui Xolotl[32]

On the first page of the *Codex Izhuatepec* a nobleman named Cuauhxayaca(tl) is mentioned as the father of Acamâpichtli. His mother is depicted as a noblewoman, but no name glyph is given for her. Both parents are represented in a group of noble Colhua kinsfolk that includes Coxcox, Ilancueitl, and another personage. This confusing enumeration of ancestors makes Acamâpichtli's origin obscure enough; yet still another source says that he was an adopted son as well as a blood relative of Huehuê Acamâpichtli of Colhuâcan and Ilancueitl and that his name was originally Xilechoz.[33] These claims imply a strong need to represent Acamâpichtli as a scion of a Colhuâ royal family, which he would no doubt have been. But he was also considered to be a descendant of the Mexitin, Têcpanecs, and Chichimecs. It is the Tetzcocan sources that emphasize the Têcpanec-Chichimec relationship. Veytia, who on the whole follows the Tetzcocan historians, finds an elegant intermediate solution by ascribing the Tetzcocan representation of Acamâpichtli's descent to the fact that Huehuê Acamâpichtli was confused with the later Acamâpichtli of Tenochtitlan. Thus he arrives at the kinship relations shown in fig. 9.2, which indicate a Têcpanec as well as a Colhuâ background.[34] The interpretation

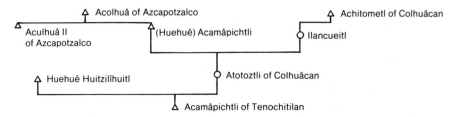

Fig. 9.2. *Ancestors of Acamâpichtli. Based on Torquemada.*

in fig. 9.2 creates the desired connection with the royal family of
the Mexitin by showing Atotoztli married to Huehuê Huitzilîhuitl.
It is, of course, too good to be true. Huehuê Huitzilîhuitl came
to Colhuâcan as a prisoner of war, and, although hypergamy was
not uncommon in Mesoamerica, it seems most unlikely that under
those circumstances he would have married a princess of the victorious Colhuâ.

It is remarkable, however, that Chimalpahin should mention an
Acamâpichtli as *tlâtoani* beside Huehuê Huitzilîhuitl, the latter
exercising a priestly office.[35] At first sight this claim seems to be
strengthened by Mendieta's information that, "according to some,"
Acamâpichtli's father had the same name and ruled for some time
after Tenoch. From the particulars that Mendieta adds to his statement, however, it appears that the story refers to Huehuê Acamâpichtli of Colhuâcan, who was also killed by a "tyrant," whereafter
his small son was taken to a safe place either by his mother or by
a wet nurse.[36] Yet Mendieta's version is, of course, very important
because it is further proof that the Colhuâ-Chinampanecâ are historically associated with the Mexîcâ. A closer look at the purported
parents of Acamâpichtli of Tenochtitlan indicates the following
group relationships:

1. Mexîcâ and Colhuâ: When Opochtli Iztahuâtzin is mentioned
as father, he is always said to be married to the princess Atotoztli
of Colhuâcan. Clavijero says that Opochtli Iztahuâtzin is a descendant of Tochpanecatl of Tzompanco,[37] which also provides a connection with the first Mexican royal house. When Iztahuâtzin is
taken to be a woman from the Mexitin, she married Cuauhtzin, a
prince of Colhuâcan and a son of Coxcoxtli and Ilancueitl. When
Huehuê Acamâpichtli of Colhuâcan is mentioned as father, his
wife, and thus the mother of Acamâpichtli of Tenochtitlan, is
always a Mexican woman. But if the Mexican king Huehuê Huitzilî-

huitl is given as the father, the mother is a woman from Colhuâcan. In all these instances Acamâpichtli of Tenochtitlan is represented as being born of Mexîca and Colhuâ parents, though the various sources give different personal names for them; and, as in the case of Huehuê Huitzilîhuitl, the two ethnic groups are alternately associated with the father and the mother.

2. Mexîcâ and Têcpanecâ: Only the oldest writings from the Aztec state of Acolhuâcan represent Acamâpichtli of Tenochtitlan as a direct descendant of the royal families of Azcapotzalco and Tenanyucan, that is, those of the Têcpanecs and the Chichimecs of Xolotl. The original Chichimec royal house of Acolhuâcan-Tetzcoco considered itself to have been descended, through the male line, from the Xolotl dynasty.[38] It is noteworthy that the *Codex Xolotl,* and also Ixtlilxochitl and Veytia, which are analogous to it, represent the progenitor of the royal family of the Mexîcâ-Tenochcâ as being closely related to their own royal families as well as to the royal house of the Têcpanecs. This genealogical reconstruction in the *Codex Xolotl* is historically untenable. Acamâpichtli of Tenochtitlan could never have been a grandson of Amacui Xolotl because Acamâpichtli lived at least two hundred years later. Further, he was a contemporary of Techotlalatzin of Tetzcoco, who according to the *Codex Xolotl* was a great-great-grandson of Amacui Xolotl.[39] Even if we follow Veytia and assume that the *Codex Xolotl* confuses Aculhuâ I with his son Aculhuâ II of Azcapotzalco, there would still be a gap of one generation between Acamâpichtli of Tenochtitlan and Techotlalatzin of Tetzcoco, as the kinship diagram in fig. 9.3 shows.

This gap of one generation is not an insurmountable problem if Acamâpichtli of Tenochtitlan was born not much later than Techotlalatzin. Furthermore, all the historical sources that contain more detail about Acamâpichtli of Tenochtitlan emphasize his Colhuâ descent (of course, all these discussions by no means exclude the existence of another Acamâpichtli in the Têcpanec royal line). Thus the Acamâpichtli of *Codex Xolotl* was probably not the same person as Acamâpichtli of Tenochtitlan. Moreover, the name was originally not Têcpanec but Toltec. This means that if the name had occurred among Têcpanec royalty it would probably have been given to the son of a Toltec princess who had married a Têcpanec prince. In that case the woman would most likely have come from Colhuâcan.

However, one may ask whether the name Acamâpichtli, which according to oral tradition was the name of one of the first two

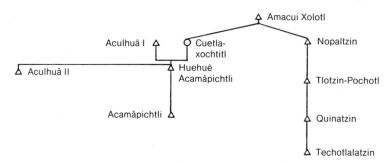

Fig. 9.3. *Genealogy of Acamâpichtli and Techotlalatzin. Based on Vey-tia, 1944, 1:349; and* Codex Xolotl.

Toltec chiefs, was being used in attempts to restore "Toltec" society. If so, it may well have been that the political aspirations of several young Toltec chiefs led them to adopt the name. This might explain the existence of an Acamâpichtli who was a contemporary of Huêhuê Huitzilîhuitl in Chapoltepec and Acamâpichtli of Tenochtitlan, who was first called Xilechoz, or, more likely, Chilatlexochtzin (see chapter 5). Huêhuê Acamâpichtli of Colhuâ-can, who was killed by "Chichimec" warriors in his territory who were supported by the Mexitin, would also fit this version.[40]

So the historical puzzle of Acamâpichtli remains unsolved. A few conclusions, however, can be drawn. The historical sources of Acolhuâcan-Tetzcoco are unreliable as far as the origin of the Mexican royal house is concerned, and two motives may have been behind this presentation of the facts: the desire to deprive the Mexican royal house of early Toltec ancestors or to present the Mexican royal house to the Spanish rulers as a "collateral branch" of the Chichimec royal house of Acolhuâcan-Tetzcoco. Further, historians of the Mexîcâ-Tenochcâ assume that Acamâpichtli of Tenochtitlan was a prince in whose veins ran the noble blood of the Méxitin, the Chinampanecs, and the Toltecs. If my theories about the formation of Aztec society are correct, he must have been an "Aztec" par excellence. Although Aztec politicians and historians have co-opted ancestors for their own Acamâpichtli, the fact of his "marriage" to Ilancueitl alone would have convinced them that his Toltec background was real (chapter 5).

The kinship relations of the Aztec kings after Ilancueitl and Acamâpichtli remain confused until the reign of Itzcoatl, and even for the period after Itzcoatl the historical documents contain contradictory information. Confusion and contradiction are most abundant with regard to female relatives. Everywhere descent through the male line shows more consistency, except that sometimes Chimalpopoca is presented not as Huitzilíhuitl's brother but as his son. If, for a start, we look at the most reliable kinship diagram of these monarchs through the male line, we are immediately struck by the fact that it mentions two women in key positions, the princesses Atotoztli and Têcuichpo, who may be looked upon as the actual heirs, though their sons or husbands probably exercised the duties of external chief.

Figure 9.4 presents the kinship relations of the holders of the offices of *tlâtoani* and *cihuacoatl* in Tenochtitlan, based on the sources used in this chapter. It would seem that to be considered for election to the highest government offices in Tenochtitlan and the Aztec empire as a whole a candidate must be related to Acamâpichtli. In most instances succession to the office of *tlâtoani* was through the male line; rarely did a daughter inherit her father's position. With Atotoztli this was significant because she had a brother, Iquehua(ca)tzin, who held the important office of *tlacateccatl*.[41] Was the right of primogeniture applied in her case? It is possible, but in Tenochtitlan this right was obviously not customarily a guarantee of inheritance since one of her sons, Axayacatl, ruled before his older brother, Tizoc.[42] It is also possible that Tezozomoc, Atotoztli's husband, was a more capable ruler than was her brother Iquehua(ca)tzin. Now the question arises why Tezozomoc—as son of Itzcoatl—was not elected. It may have been that after the appointment of the suitable brothers of Huitzilíhuitl the system dictated a return to the primary line. This happened, too, when Motêuhczoma Ilhuicamina was elected. Tezozomoc tells us that after Motêuhczoma's death the office of *tlâtoani* was offered to Tlacayelel, who, however, preferred to remain *cihuacoatl*.[43]

Following Tezozomoc, like most other authors I have interpreted Tlacayelel's decision to be a consequence of his zeal for the office of internal chief *cihuacoatl*. This dedication has been thought to have been an expression of Tlacayelel's political ambition to structure the internal order of Aztec society according to his own ideas. It is conceivable, however, that he wished to create a "dynasty" of his own. If Tlacayelel had accepted the office of *hueyi tlâtoani*, after his death it would probably have passed to a descendant of Motêuhczoma Ilhuicamina, and the position of even the

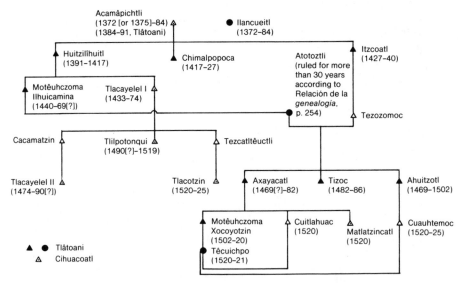

Fig. 9.4. *Kinship relations of the Aztec rulers. Note the two series of four rulers* (tlâtoquê), *each preceded and followed by a female ruler* (cihuatlâtoani). *This would fit a structure in which four rulers always symbolized the four quarters of the compass and the female ruler symbolized the center.*

best of Tlacayelel's own heirs would remain uncertain. Since, however, he chose to remain as internal chief, he could secure that post for his progeny.

In this connection it is interesting to look at the royal intrigue that took place as a consequence of the succession of Motêuhczoma Ilhuicamina. As mentioned earlier, he had at least one son of high rank, the prince Iquehua(ca)tzin. The prince held the high office of *tlacateccatl,* which was considered to be excellent preparation for the position of *hueyi tlâtoani* ("grand ruler"), the highest external imperial ruler. There were, however, influential persons in the Aztec regime who did not want Iquehua(ca)tzin to succeed his father. The documents of the Tenochcas do not mention it, but the *Annals of Tlatelolco* tell us that shortly before the civil war between Axayacatl and Moquihuix, in the year VI Tecpatl (VI Flintstone), which more or less corresponds with the year A.D. 1472, the Tenochcas "killed Iquehuacatzin, who should have been the king of Tenochtitlan."[44] After that Axayacatl, a nephew of Iquehuacatzin, became king of Tenochtitlan. Axayacatl was a younger son of Atotoztli and Tezozomoc, who were, respectively, a daughter of Motêuhczoma Ilhuicamina and the son of Itzcoatzin. Thus through both his father's and his mother's families Axayacatl was closely related to the primary royal line. His father's father had been the fourth king of Tenochtitlan, his mother's father had been the fifth king, and his mother was the sixth member of the Acamâpichtli-Itzpapalotl-Chalchiuhtlatonac family to come to power.

Motêuhczoma Ilhuicamina, a son of the princess Miyahuaxihuitl of Cuauhnahuac, was married to Chichimecacihuatzin, a princess of his mother's family.[45] Of this marriage Atotoztli, mentioned above, was born. We do not know whether Iquehuacatzin was her full brother or whether he had another mother. At any rate, his mother must have been of high rank; otherwise, under normal circumstances he would never "have been destined to rule in Tenochtitlan," as the statement in the Annals of Tlatelolco says (cf. note 44). The question why Atotoztli was preferred over her brother is not fully explained by the vague allusions to her succession in the historical documents. What is clear is that it was a disputed choice and caused serious controversy in the highest circles of the imperial nobility.

Chimalpahin tells us more about it in his third *Relación:*

Auh in oc ic ayamo	And in the days when the respect-
motlahtocatlaliaya	able Axayacatl [Water Face]
in Axayacatzin,	did not yet rule,
auh yêhuatl quixquetzayâ	they appointed to a [lower] office
tlahtocatizquia ce ipiltzin	a respectable son
in Huehuê Motêuhczoma	of Old Motêuhczoma [Serious Lord],
Itoca Iquehuac,	whose name was Iquehuac [Therefore He Has Risen],
inic ome quixquetzayâ	in the second place they appointed
itoca Mâchimallê.	[to another such office] Mâchimallê [Possessor of a Forearm Shield, a brother of Iquehuac].
Auh in onmotlahtocatlali	But when Axayacatzin had
in Axayacatzin,	already come into office,
niman no quicocoliquê	these two wanted to harm him, and
oquinamoxquê	they embezzled
in intlacallaquil	the tax revenue
in Coaixtlahuaquê	of the inhabitants of Coaixtlahuacan;
ihuan otlanamoxquê	and after that their aunts

in innanhuan,	secretly took possession of it,
in têcpancihuâ,	it was the women of the palace
otlaquixtiquê,	who brought it all out,
auh in onezquê,	and when they made it public
ic ocholoquê yahquê	they [the two brothers] therefore
in campa opolihuitô,	fled and met their doom
ic oquipoloquê	and thus lost
in inpillô in inmahuizô.[46]	their noble titles and their honor.

In the seventh *Relación,* Chimalpahin provides more detail and says that after the Axayacatl's accession to the throne two sons of old Motêuhczoma, the first called Mâchimallê and the second Iquehuacatzin (who was *tlacatecatl*), were appointed to lower offices, "which prevented them from becoming rulers." Therefore they conspired against the young king, their nephew, and they illegally seized the tax revenues from the province of Coaixtlahuacan, which had been their father's most spectacular conquest.[47] It is significant that the rebellion of the two brothers was not the cause but rather the result of their exclusion from the highest external imperial office. It was clear that they disapproved of the election of their nephew Axayacatl and possibly even with the earlier election of their sister Atotoztli, though at the time they did not cause much trouble.

Further, Tezozomoc shows that Axayacatl's brothers were also displeased by his election:

Auh in yêhuantin in	And those who were the older brothers
tetiachcahuan in	of Axayacatzin thought
inteicauh in Axayacatzin	nothing of their younger brother;
âtle ipan quittayâ	he did not count with them, and
âtle ipan compoayâ	they did nothing but subject
zan quitlapinahuiliayâ	him to ridicule
in ihcuac canapa ontepehuayâ	when the Mexicans
Mexîcâ ompa tehuan	made conquests somewhere,
ontlamaya in Axayacatzin;	and Axayacatzin together with others took prisoners
quimonaya imalhuan.	and carried them off.
Auh in itiachcahuan,	But his older brothers,
ye omîto, zan quipopoloyâ	as has been said, only spoke
zan quîtoayâ:	unfavorably about him, saying:
"Cuix nelli in oquichtli	"Or is it really true that Axayaca
Axayaca, cuix nelli	is a brave man? is he really
in tlamaniyaoc	the maker of prisoners of war
in iuh machizti,	that he pretends to be?

amo zan iztatlacâ
tlacôtin in quimonomococohuia
in quinhual-
huica nican Mexîco,
inic oquichneci Axayaca";
ocaiuhqui in inic
quipapatzahuaya
Axayacatzin
in itiachcahuan.[49]

or does he only buy slaves for
himself from among the extractors
of salt,[48] taking them back here
to Mexico?
in that way Axayaca only seems
to be a brave man";
in this way his older brothers
spoke evil of Axayacatzin

As I have explained in notes to *Los Anales de Tula* in 1979, there are reliable indications that the princess Atotoztli ruled between 1466 and 1472. A woman acting as chief of the external administration of the empire was uncommon, and many historians have neglected to mention it, stating instead that Motêuhczoma Ilhuicamina lived until 1469 and that he was succeeded immediately by his grandson. Owing to lack of further information, the details surrounding the succession of the princess Atotoztli have remained rather obscure. It is possible that they involved the political ambitions of Cihuacoatl Tlacayelel and his followers. Although Tlacayelel refused to be elected, it is possible that, as internal chief of the empire and chief of the part of the royal family that was connected with that office, he would not have wanted a strong personality occupying the most powerful seat of the tripartite throne. That may explain why the young, inexperienced, and at that time evidently not very brave Axayacatl was preferred to his older brothers and also to his experienced uncles Iquehuacatzin and Mâchimallê.

For Têcuichpo, the circumstances were different from those of Atotoztli's succession. Her brothers had already been killed when, after the Spaniards had been driven out of Tenochtitlan, the succession to her father's throne had to be arranged. Her uncle Cuitlahuac and after him her cousin twice removed Cuauhtemoc "legitimized" their rule by "marrying" the young princess, who was still under age. After the Conquest she married successively several Spanish noblemen and was granted valuable rights in Tlacopan. In those early-colonial times both Aztecs and Spaniards looked upon her as the highest-status member of the indigenous nobility.[50] The special position of women in the Mesoamerican systems of succession gave political and social value to a marriage that far exceeded the simple ties between two groups normally created or strengthened by marriage. For this reason if for no other it is understandable that women could also play an important role in the external area of the dual social organization. This sociopolitical role could be strengthened by economic and religious factors. A clear example of the latter is given in the *Annals of Cuauhtitlan*. When a group of Colhuâs arrived at Cuauhtitlan in the fourteenth century, they were regarded with some suspicion because of hostile activities committed by the Colhuâs against the Mexitin, who had been friends and even relations of the Chichimecs of Cuauhtitlan. The Colhuâ immigrants, worshipers of the goddesses Tocî and Xochiquetzal and of Chiucnahui Ozomahtli, set out to Xaltocan to take prisoners for the Chichimecs of Cuauhtitlan. When they returned with three prisoners, enough to enable them to perform the inaugural fire-drill ritual, the Chichimecs gave them land and wives from Cuauhtitlan.[51]

When landless strangers obtained land by marrying women from the landowning population, their children would then belong to the families of their fathers-in-law. This is an ancient Mesoamerican tradition so persistent that it still exists today. Nutini has described its occurrence in modern San Bernardino Contla,[52] and I have come across it in many Nahua villages, even in the strongly acculturated village of Milpa Alta, less than twenty miles from the outskirts of Mexico City. Mexican Indians do not regard this arrangement as a deviation from their usual system of succession. Although inheritance of land usually takes place along patrilineal lines, descent is never an exclusive criterion; people living on the testator's land may also be heirs. The indigenous peoples of Mesoamerica and those of the Andes show a strong inclination to express their social relations in terms of blood relationship. This implies that long-established communities are regarded as large kinship groups. By pursuing a certain kinship policy, such groups soon achieve the realization of the model.

As Carrasco and I have said before, one of the basic elements of the internal hierarchy of a calpolli was the degree of relationship existing between the members and the ruling nucleus of the aristocratic family in the calpolli.[53] Calpolli chiefs who were effective administrators, pursued a kinship policy aimed at keeping the status of their own families high and increasing, as much as possible, the external status of the calpolli. To attain the first goal, it was necessary for them to have good connections not only with all traditionally important families in the calpolli but also with the other upwardly mobile members of the calpolli, whose military achievements, success in trade, or religious devotion had won them great esteem. It was in the interest of the ruling chiefs to have these upwardly mobile persons marry their daughters or nieces, and usually their interest was consistent with that of the nonaristocratic status seekers.

To raise the status of the calpolli as a whole, the chiefs had to enter into good marriages outside the calpolli. Sometimes they might ally themselves with foreign noblemen, but that could be a dangerous strategy since it might force the original aristocratic family into second place. Hypergamy, "marrying above oneself," often provided a solution with fewer hazards. A calpolli chief might marry a girl of higher status from a calpolli more important than his. It is not surprising that this was a desirable play for the calpolli chief in question, but why should it be attractive to the girl and her family? The explanation lies in the Aztec system of patrilocality.

As a rule, when a woman married, she went to live in or near the house of her husband's parents. Thus she was under the daily supervision of her mother-in-law, and was dominated by older unmarried sisters-in-law. The custom was then, as it still often is today in many Indian communities, that the mother of an eligible young man chose the girl who would be her daughter-in-law. If the woman was of lower status or of the same status as her husband, her position in her new surroundings would, at least in the beginning, be lower than that which she had enjoyed in her parental home. Only later, when she had borne at least four children, would she enjoy an elevated position and then only if she was a "lawful" wife, not a secondary wife or a concubine. If the status of a newly married woman's parents was higher than that of her husband and his family, her position in the new surroundings would be much better because then it was her line, not her husband's, that would determine the status of the next generation. From the very beginning this gave her high prestige in the family, and she was treated with respect. Many upper-class parents thus preferred to ensure a pleasant life for their daughters rather than subjecting them to the whims of mothers-in-law. Moreover, close ties with a group of somewhat lower status proved to have other advantages as well, such as political and military loyalty and economic cooperation. Within the Aztec society, which I have characterized as strictly hierarchical, hypergamy had a more or less equalizing effect. Of course, a few calpolli chiefs were able to pursue a policy aimed at expansion of power and rise in status. Among the chiefs there existed many different interests and many different ambitions. Many of these were closely connected with the relationship be-

Fig. 9.5. *Huitzilopochtli.* Manuscript Tovar, *pl. 19.*

tween status and land-ownership or at least the usufruct of land. Relations of the chiefs in the collateral line, therefore direct descendants of former chiefs, lost their rights to land after three or four generations and finally could become "mâyequê." But through exceptional achievements these "poor" relations could raise their status. However, if they could not or would not do so they were usually supported by their more powerful relatives, who facilitated them the means to hold up the status of the family. These "poor" relations were usually assisted by influential kinsmen who occupied intermediate positions between them and relatives in administrative positions. If, however, too many "poor relations" encumbered a calpolli chief's household, they no doubt hampered the family's social promotion and that of their calpolli.

Another important aspect of the Aztec social system that could retard the attainment of a higher status was the considerable in crease in burdens that accompanied it: the higher the status, the stricter the administration of justice and the heavier the religious duties and other representative duties to the community, or, in short, the more conscientious the observance of the puritanical norms of the Aztec system.

On the other hand, more or less accidental events might result in a rapid change of status. Acquiring a calpolli god of great importance, taking a stranger or foreigner of great respectability into the group, successfully undertaking a new industry or even composing a new song might result in a rise in status and even yield entirely new ancestors. A description of all facets of this subject requires a thorough study of the Aztec kinship system that is beyond the scope of this book.[54] A study of Mexican name-giving traditions is also revealing. It is clear that name giving had implications beyond the individual upon whom they were bestowed. Such names as Chalchiuhtlatonac in the royal house of the Colhuâ-Mexîcâ and Acolmiztli in that of Acolhuâcan-Tetzcoco almost assume the character of family names. Naming offspring after ancestors on both the father's and the mother's sides occurred with both sexes, and the names of the parents might also be passed on to the children. Giving the names of nonrelatives seems to have been just as common. It was not unusual for a successful warrior to name his son after a captive taken by him in a flower war. Use of calendrical and god names makes the picture even more complicated. The identification of persons or groups who have little or no relationship to each other, despite identical names, calendar signs, or god or goddess names, simplifies the picture of the past and makes it possible to structure apparently complex interethnic communal connections into rather simple kinship models. An interesting example is the network of kinship relations attributed to the Aztec founding father and god Huitzilopochtli shown in fig. 9.6.

As we have seen earlier, Coatlicue, the mother of Huitzilopochtli, was the *calpolteotl* of Coatlan, a dependency of Tlacatêcpan. The unknown father of Huitzilopochtli must have been associated with the calpolli of Huitznahuac. Perhaps he was, like the feather that fluttered to the ground, the symbol of one of the three stones of the fireplace. Huitzilopochtli's uncles and aunts—or according to other sources, his own brothers and sisters, among whom was his sister and rival Coyolxauhqui—, were also reckoned to belong to the calpolli Huitznahuac. Another sister and rival, Malinalxochitl, belonged to Chalman, apparently because she was married to the chief of Malinalco, a dependency of Colhuâcan. The marriage of

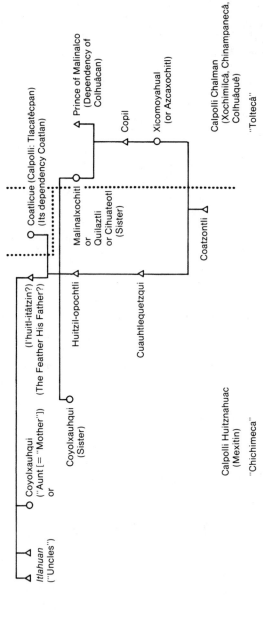

Fig. 9.6. *Family relations of the "historical" Huitzilopochtli. Based on* Florentine Codex *and Cristóbal del Castillo.*

Huitzilopochtli's descendant Cuauhtlequetzqui to the granddaugh-
ter of Malinalxochitl merged the families of the "Chichimec" and
"Toltec" gods and gave rise to Aztec society. Yet it was thought
necessary to declare Malinalxochitl the "sister" of Huitzilopochtli,
or, perhaps we should say, to identify the Toltec god Huitzilopochtli
with the god Mexitli Tlaltêuhctli of the Mixitin. Even in later times,
during the growth of the empire, the kinship model was strictly
applied to political relationships: Aztec and colonial historians
mention "ancestor relationships" with the ethnically different
Tarascans of Michoacan.[55] It appears that upon the arrival of the
Spanish conquerors the native chiefs even tried to incorporate
these strangers into their own kinship systems from the beginning
by offering their sisters, daughters, and nieces to them in marriage.[56] Kinship meant peace; the lack of it might lead to war.

Even prisoners of war became "sons" of the men who had captured them, and the ancestors of beheaded enemies were adopted
as ancestors of the conquerors; otherwise, their land could not be
permanently occupied.

CHAPTER 10

Tenochtitlan: Base of an Empire

In the previous chapters I have described several principles and systems of organization in the society of Tenochtitlan. It is clear that even before 1433 Tenochtitlan had developed rapidly from a rather insignificant Toltec-Chichimec rural community to a major center of trade and industry, equipped with a powerful defensive and offensive military force. The canoe fleets of Tenochtitlan and Tlaltelolco made it possible to transport troops nearly anywhere in the vast lake area. Economic and military development was accompanied by such far-reaching social and political change that it is difficult clearly to imagine what conditions had been like in an earlier time, especially since these social changes also influenced the Aztecs' own ideas about their past. As has been said before, political developments also meant that the calpolli nobles had lost some of their traditional power to a rising imperial nobility. This process illustrates the direction in which Aztec society was going, yet explains only part of it. The shift in political power was accompanied by another no less important power shift. The priests, who had been influential in administrative affairs, lost much of their political power to the military and the merchants, though they remained an important group in society. It was the task of the rising imperial elite to integrate these three social forces in their young regime. It is no exaggeration to say that the success of this task was an indispensable condition for the considerable growth of the Aztec empire. Further, the new imperial elite had to reform old social institutions or combine them with entirely new ones to form one functionally integrated system. The priests and their calpolli temples and the traditional nobility and their calpollis must be fused into one coherent structure that recognized the authority of the new central imperial institutions. This process must have begun when Tenochtitlan, after the conquest of Acolhuâcan, became one of the three Têcpanec administrative centers and obtained direct administrative control of Tetzcoco. This circumstance entitled the new state to one-eighth of all the tax revenues derived from the conquered territories.[1] Information about these adjustments in the governing elite of Tenochtitlan is extremely scarce. Moreover, it is conceivable that the early imperial elite, who probably had a noble "Toltec" ancestry, or at least had appropriated it, disappeared for the most part after the failure of Chimalpopoca and his army chief.[2] But after the overthrow of the Têcpanec regime in 1430, the gradual expansion of central power can be seen in the historical sources. When land was redistributed among the Mexican army leaders after the conquest of Coyohuâcan, a new hierarchy was formed in which some of the traditional calpolli nobility and a newly formed nobility who had acquired status through personal achievement performed the central functions. The members of the new imperial elite had a difficult task ahead. Besides a difficult integration policy within their own society they had to pursue a similar policy on a wider scale in areas from which Têcpanec authority had rapidly disappeared and must be replaced quickly to avoid a dangerous administrative vacuum. An important start was made in 1433, when Tetzcoco and Tlacopan were designated the second and third imperial administrative centers. Imperial organization also had to be imposed within Tenochtitlan itself. Moreover, Tlaltelolco, which was economically very powerful and a potentially dangerous political rival, had to be kept under control. On the other hand, Tenochtitlan could profitably use Tlaltelolco's relations with the outside world to expand its own power. As early as the second half of the fourteenth century Tlaltelolco had exercised considerable commercial influence in a vast area in central Mexico. This influence had been considerably strengthened by Tlaltelolco's conquest of Cuauhtinchan, an important market center in the present-day state of Puebla. However, as an important Têcpanec administrative center, Tlaltelolco also had great political influence.

A great deal is known about the external policy of the governments of Itzcoatl and Tlacayelel. That aspect of government policy, however, falls outside the scope of this book and has been dealt with in detail by Nigel Davies.[3] Far less direct information is available about internal policy, especially during the first six years of the Aztec regime (1427-33), which are of primary interest here.

No clear description of the internal organization of Tenochtitlan at that time is to be found. Only the titles of twenty-six military and priestly executives of the period have been preserved. Although the titles provide information about calpollis and their social organization, they offer little help in forming a clear overall picture.

Even so, by combining this information with what Tezozomoc has to say about the dedication of the great temple of Tenochtitlan in 1487, it is possible to enhance our insight into the city's social organization. Of course, Tezozomoc's account is concerned with an event that took place more than fifty years after the first days of the Aztec state. Yet we should be able to use the account to understand the earlier development of Aztec society, for the dedication ceremony contained many old customs and traditional elements and represented symbolically the fusion of the social and imperial organization of Tenochtitlan. Therefore, Tezozomoc's account is invaluable for a thorough understanding of Aztec society. The symbolic representation emphasizes the basic characteristics of the social system that dates from well before 1487.

Tezozomoc's description covers nearly forty pages of text and contains a wealth of data on the organizational model for Tenochtitlan and for the empire as a whole. It is, in fact, astonishing that this large collection of data has not been thoroughly studied before. The many difficulties involved in interpreting it are probably responsible for its neglect.

The Mexican temple pyramids served various functions in the Aztecs' religion and their world view in general. First, the temples were sanctuaries in which important rituals were celebrated. In popular religious thought they represented the sacred mountains where the spirits of the ancestors of the Aztecs' progenitors lived. They were also used as burial temples for important persons.[4] The temple pyramids also symbolized the concept of *altepetl* and as such were "the mountains filled with water," the heart of society.[5] Finally, in the more "priestly" experience of religion, the great temple pyramids expressed the entire celestial order as conceptualized by the Mexicans. For them the cosmos was divided into thirteen sections, each of which was associated with particular superhuman phenomena. In accordance with this belief, the great temple pyramid of Tenochtitlan, consisted of four platforms built steplike one atop another. Corresponding to the four points of the compass the three lower platforms comprised a total of twelve (3×4) sections; the top platform, the smallest, was the thirteenth section, on which was built the dual temple of Huitzilopochtli and Tlaloc. Like other societies, the Aztecs had discovered that the pyramid form is extremely suitable for expressing hierarchical order.

The Historia de los mexicanos por sus pinturas, an early colonial translation of the indigenous pictorial writings and an authentic work, depicts in detail the order of the first eight heavens but remains vague about the upper five.[6] By comparing these data with those of Tezozomoc, the *Codex Ramírez,* and Durán, we can draw several conclusions about the Aztecs' perception of the universe and its relationship to the early division of Tenochtitlan into eight geographic sectors. Tezozomoc begins his description of the completion and dedication of the great temple as follows:

Llamó Cihuacoatl a todos los mayordomos, y preguntóles si habrá entre todos los tributos abundancia de ropas para los señores comarcanos y los mexicanos	The Cihuacoatl summoned all tax collectors and asked them whether there was among the tributes an abundance of woven textiles for the chiefs of the surrounding territories and for those of the Mexicans.
Dijeron que estaban represados tributos de dos años. . . . [*Cihuacoatl*] hizo llamar luego a los embajadores para que fuesan a Acolhuâcan y Tlalhuacpan,	They said that the taxes for two years had been saved [for the purpose]. . . . [The *cihuacoatl*] then ordered the ambassadors to be called so that they would go to Acolhuâcan and to the Tlalhuacpan
Tabuca y los demas pueblos	of Tlacopan and to the other neighboring
comarcanos para que viniesen indios, y subiesen los dioses, signos y planetas al templo alto que llamaban tzitzimimê, y asentáronlos alrededor del dios Huitzilopochtli;	villages to call up native people to carry the gods, calendar signs, and celestial bodies to the top of the temple and give all these, which they called *tzitzimimê*, a place around the god Huitzilopochtli;
y le pusieron al dicho Huitzilopochtli en la frente un espejo relumbrante; también añadieron una diosa	and on the forehead of the said Huitzilopochtli they put a glittering mirror; and they also added a goddess representing the sister

más, a imitación de la hermana
de Huitzilopochtli, que se llamaba
Coyolxauh(qui),
pobladora de los
de Mechoacan . . . :
asimismo los antiguos
deudos y abuelos
que vinieron primero de las
partes de Aztlan
Chicomoztoc, Mexitin
Chanêquê, la antigua casa
de donde descienden y
salieron que llaman
Petlacontzitzquiquê,[7]

tenedores de la silla y
asiento del señor, y de
los otros llamados
(Cen)tzonhuitznahuâ y
Huitzitzilnahuatl y
Coatopil,
los cuales estaban en
piedras figurados con
rodelas, alrededor del
cerro del templo. . . .[8]

of Huitzilopochtli,
whose name was
Coyolxauhqui [Bell Face],
she was the founder of the people
of Michoacan . . . :
they did the same with the
distant relatives and ancestors
who had been the first to arrive
from the region of the White Land, or
Land of Herons, the Place of
Seven Caves, those who were
the family heads of the Mexitin,
who originated from and descended
from the ancient house and are
   called Petlacontzitzquiquê,
holders of the throne and the
seat of the lord [*sic*],
and of the others, who are called
Innumerable Southerners and
Talking Hummingbird and
Snake Staff,
who stand there carved in stone,
provided with shields and gathered
around the temple pyramid. . . .

This interesting passage expresses the connection between heavenly order, which is symbolized by the temple, and the social
organization of the original calpollis, represented by the images
of their mythical progenitors. It is important to make a further
study of this connection to see whether there are other details
that might deepen our insight.

The *Historia de los mexicanos* relates a traditional story about
the restoration of the cosmos after the fourth sun. The four principal gods, Tlatlauhqui Tezcatlepoca, Yayauhqui Tezcatlepoca,
Quetzalcoatl, and Huitzilopochtli, see that "heaven has fallen upon
the earth." They order four roads to be built through the middle
of the earth to make it possible to raise heaven again. They create
four men to help them: Cuauhtemoc (Falling Eagle), Itzcoatl (Knife
Snake), Ezmali (Blood Catcher, or He Catches Blood) and Tenexxuchitl (Ashes Flower). Tezcatlepoca transforms himself into the
mighty Tezcacuahuitl (Mirror Tree), and Quetzalcoatl changes
himself into the great tree Quetzalhuexotl (Feather Willow, or
Beautiful Willow). The men, the trees, and the gods then lift up

Fig. 10.1. *Recent discoveries at the site of the Great Temple of Tenoch-titlan. The stone images in the foreground are probably the* petlacontzitz-quiquê *("holders of the mats and urns").*

the sky with all the stars as we know them now. The primary god Tonacatêcuhtli then rewarded the four by making them gods of heaven.[9]

The four sky lifters have solar names. Tenexxuchitl (Ashes Flower) points to the creation narrative of the present sun, which tells how the insignificant leprous god Nanahuatzin bravely jumps into the divine oven in Teotihuâcan and emerges in the eastern sky as the sun.[10] This is, therefore, the sun of the east. Itzcoatl, Knife Snake or Obsidian Snake, is the sun of the north. Cuauhtemoc, Descending Eagle, is the setting sun, the sun of the west.

Ezmali, Blood Catcher, is the southern sun and war god and is thus closely linked with Huitzilopochtli.

The nature of different "heavens" or parts of heaven is also explained by the *Historia de los mexicanos por sus pinturas,* which contains the following description:

These Indians of Mexico thought that there was a star in the first heaven called Citalnine [Citlalicue, Star Skirt], which was female, and Tetallatorras [Citlallatonac, Brilliant Star], which was male, and that Tonacatêcuhtli made them guards of heaven, and he did not show himself because his position was on the road of heaven. They say that in the second heaven there are a number of women who have no flesh, only bones, and they call them *tetzauhcihuâ* ["horrifying women"] and by another name *tzitzimimê* ["apparitions"]; and they were there because, if the world should be destroyed, it was their task to devour all people.

When asked when this end of the world would be, these ancient people would say that they did not know but that it would come when the gods perished and Tezcatlepoca stole the sun. . . . In the third heaven were the four hundred men created by Tezcatlepoca, and they were of five colors: yellow, black, white, blue, and red, and they guarded that heaven.

In the fourth heaven were all kinds of birds, and from there they came down to the earth.

In the fifth heaven were the fire serpents created by the fire god, and they produced the falling stars and the signs of heaven.

In the sixth heaven were all the winds.

In the seventh heaven everything was full of dust, and from there dust fell down to earth.

In the eighth heaven all the gods gathered, and from there no one rose higher up to Tonacatêcuhtli and his wife. And they did not know what there was in the other heavens.[11]

The manner in which the Aztecs conceived the spatial order of these heavens or parts of heaven can be deduced from their ritual. Sahagún's indigenous informants provided a clear description of how the directional symbolism was applied in ritual blood sacrifice:

Niman ye ic hualquiza	There he soon appears
in ithualnepantla.	in the middle of the inner court.
Achtopa ontlatlaza in	First he repeatedly throws
ilhuicac	up to heaven,
contlaza in yezzo.	he throws his blood.
Niman ye ompa in tonatiuh	Then to the direction where the
iquizayan mîtoaya tlapcopa	sun rises, called the east,

nauhpa in contlaza yezzo.

in that direction he throws his blood four times.

Niman ye ompa in tonatiuh
icalaquiyan mîtoaya
cihuatlan,
no nauhpa in contlaza

Then to where the sun sets, called the west [women's resort],

in that direction too he throws his blood

yezzo.

four times.

Niman ye ompa in mâopuchcopa
tlalli mîtoaya huitznahuacâtlalli,

Then to the land on his left,
which is called the land of the southerners,

no nauhpa in contlaza yezzo.

in that direction too he throws his blood four times.

Niman ye ompa
in imâyauhcampa
tlalli mîtoaya mimixcoâ
intlalpan;
no nauhpa in contlaza

Thereafter to the land on
his right,
which is called the land of the
cloud snakes,
in that direction too he throws his blood

yezzo.
Zan ompa ommocahua
in ic nauhcampa
ommihzo.[12]

four times.
But that was the end;
thus in four directions has
blood been sacrificed.

If we assume that the blood that was "repeatedly thrown up to heaven" was also thrown four times, the whole ritual must have taken place exactly five times four, that is, twenty times, in which case it could have been connected with the twenty calpolli temples and with the twenty day-signs of the *tonalpoalli* or "counting of days" (the sacred almanac). We shall deal with this in detail in chapter 11.

We have now gained more background information to help evaluate the information provided by Tezozomoc regarding the plan and arrangement of the new temple of Huitzilopochtli. In the sources quoted above, the names of at least twelve *petlacontzitz-quiquê* ("keepers of the mat and the urns") are mentioned, those of the eight chiefs of the seven large calpollis and the four priests of Huitzilopochtli who were assumed to have been among those who left the legendary land of Aztlan, or Aztatlan.[13]

The following survey of the temple pyramid of Huitzilopochtli gives the symbolic meanings of its sections and attributes as far as they can now be deduced from the known sources. The thirteen heavens or parts of heaven are represented by the thirteen platforms of the pyramid. The data from the *Historia de los mexi-canos* clearly lead to the conclusion that the third heaven must be in the south because it is there that the four hundred *huitzna-huâ* (southerners) created by Tezcatlepoca belong (see fig. 10.2). In accordance with the ritual of the blood sacrifice described above, the first heaven must be in the east, the second in the west, the third in the south, the fourth in the north, the fifth again in the east, and so on. It is now feasible to connect the eight original calpolli chiefs with the first eight parts of heaven. The four bearers of Huitzilopochtli, one of whom was the high priest Cuauhtle-quetzqui, probably were related to the remaining four parts of heaven that were a mystery to the writer of the *Historia de los mexicanos.*

We have already mentioned the relationship of both Cuauhtle-quetzqui and Axolohuâ to the quarters of the compass.[14] There are good reasons to associate Ococaltzin with Moyotla,[15] which would make the eastern part the only place left for the god bearer Cha-chalaitl. It is quite likely that the four god bearers, or *teomama-quê*, who were positioned on the pyramid to correspond with the positions of the four central calpollis in the city were actually associated with those calpollis. The other sixteen calpollis, in eight pairs, would then have been associated with the eight other parts of heaven in such a way that two calpollis from two different city quarters always shared one part of heaven. This is exactly the principle applied in the scene depicting the founding of Tenoch-titlan in the *Codex Mendoza,* though there the native scribe drew only the pictures of the ten most important chiefs, and the two half city quarters that fell within one sector of heaven were not pictured separately. So it can be seen, for example, how the scribe of *Codex Mendoza* put Ahuexotl and Xomimitl in one southern sector, though they belonged to distinct city quarters (cf. fig. 4.5).

A close examination at the survey of the temple platforms that represent the thirteen parts of heaven reveals a number of striking features:

1. The hierarchical positions of the "military" calpollis of Tla-cochcalco, associated with the otherwise important chief Tenoch, and Huitznahuac, associated with the chief Ahuexotl, are low in this "priestly" classification system. Moreover, the third and fourth heavens are given the symbols of the realm of the dead. The four hundred southerners were destined by Tezcatlepoca to be sacri-ficed, and the four hundred cloud snakes had been created for the

same purpose by Camaxtli.[16] Moreover, the birds of the fourth heaven are the spirits of the warriors who died in battle.[17] A low position is also awarded to the calpollis of Chalman and Izquitlan, represented by their chiefs, Tenzacatetl (Tzompan) and Huicton (Xiuhcaquê), respectively. Izquitlan is connected with the *tetzauhcihuâ* (horrifying women), women who died in childbirth and whose spirits accompany the sun on its daily journey to the underworld. This also shows a clear connection with the realm of the dead. Chalman is associated with the first heaven and with the gods within it, who are called "guards at the entrance to heaven."[18] In this system Chalman is evidently connected with the eastern exit of the underworld, from which the sun makes his daily entry into heaven; here, therefore, "door of the underworld" and "gate to heaven" are one and the same. The function of the Cihuacoatl, who came from Chalman as chief of the ceremonial center, seems to support this interpretation (see below). The four lowest parts of heaven thus appear to contain the symbols of the underworld and represent the underworld, as it were, in a tripartite as well as quadruple celestial system.

2. In the fifth heaven we find Ocelopan (or perhaps Acacihtli) of Tlacatêcpan in the company of fire snakes and comets, that is, celestial bodies falling to earth. The sixth heaven contains Aatl Mexitzin of Cihuatêcpan, the chief of the "female," internally directed side of the overall administration of all the calpollis. In this heaven are found the *ehecamê* (winds), which are the dynamic aspect of the activities of the gods of earth. Trade and science as well as magic and medicine are associated with them. And Four Wind (Nahui Ehecatl) is the calendar name of Quetzalcoatl. The dust in the seventh heaven is the preeminent symbol of the earth in heaven. It is Xomimitl of Yopico, who, by catching and sacrificing a high officer of Colhuâcan, "rightfully" takes possession of the territory for the Aztecs.[19] In the eighth heaven are found the *teteô* (gods). Evidently these are the gods who play an active role on earth, for the celestial gods belong to the five upper heavens. The eighth heaven has Acacihtli (or perhaps Ocelopan), the lord of the Chichimecs, the chief of the external administration, and also the chief of Tlacatêcpan or of one of its dependencies. Some sources say that Acacihtli is a progenitor of the ruling Aztec royal family.[20] His comparatively high position in this "priestly" system is in accordance with these data. The four parts of heaven represented on the second level of the temple platforms therefore represent the earthly aspect within the celestial order.

3. The five upper parts of heaven naturally symbolize the heavenly aspect of the cosmos. The real or spiritual progenitors of the priestly calpollis were thought to reside there, and they were assumed to be connected with the highest celestial deities. Here again we see, as always, that a fundamental principle of the whole is repeated in each of those elements. The universe is divided into heaven, earth, and underworld, and each of these three shows a similar tripartite division.

Now for Tezozomoc's description of the dedication of the temple. The inhabitants of Tetzcoco and Tlacopan placed on the pyramid the images of the gods important to the progenitors. After that, Tezozomoc goes on, the high-ranking administrators of Tenochtitlan set out for the imperial territories to collect contributions for the dedication feast, which would also celebrate the coronation of the grand ruler Ahuitzotzin. The imperial subjects who lived in the south of what is now the state of Puebla gave, in addition to their usual taxes, Tlaxcaltec prisoners of war, namely, the brave Otomi warriors from the town of Tecoac. Acapetlahuâcan supplied tribute and slaves, as did Atlatlahuâcan. Twenty-eight tax-collecting locations supplied more than two thousand slaves and prisoners of war to be sacrificed to Huitzilopochtli. Thirty-two tax-collecting districts in the west and north of the empire provided a similar number. The inhabitants of the Chinampa area, of Acolhuâcan, and of the Têcpanecapan, that is, the people of the three central states, also supplied 1 million loads of *ocote* (wood for torches), 4 million loads of firewood and charcoal, 50,000 fanegas of maize, 20,000 fanegas of brown beans, and large quantities of turkeys, quails, and mountain game.

After that, ambassadors were sent out to all the provinces connected with the flower wars and to foreign rulers to invite them to the dedication and coronation feast. The governments of the independent states of Metztitlan, Michhuâcan (the Tarascan empire), and Yopitzinco accepted the invitation, but of the province rulers connected with the flower wars only those of Cholullan were at first willing to come. The imperial government then sent another delegation, and those who had originally refused accepted the "invitation" after they were threatened with military intervention.[21] The foreign guests and those from the provinces of the flower wars were secretly led into the city, where they were received by Tlâtoani Ahuitzotl and Cihuacoatl Tlacayelel.

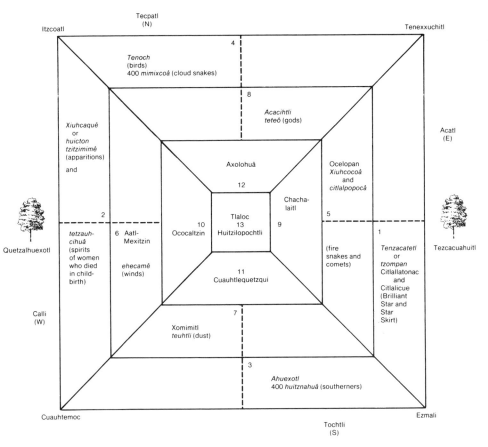

Fig. 10.2. *Positions of the* petlacontzitzquiquê *on Coatepetl (Snake Mountain) of Tenochtitlan.*

The climax of the feast was to be the sacrifice of prisoners. The Aztec imperial leaders decided that

the ceremonial day should be divided into four equal parts, one fourth at the place were the sun rises, one fourth in the west, and the two remaining parts in the north and south respectively. Also the prisoners should be offered one by one to the gods, so that, because of the large number of them, the ceremony would last four days, and on those days many favors and gifts should be presented to the important men and nobles of all the population groups, especially to those from the nine hostile peoples, who were also to have the seats with the best view.[22]

Fig. 10.3. *The Great Temple of Tenochtitlan. Photograph of scale model.*

A few days before the feast the priests were summoned to prepare for it. They gathered all the sacrificial knives from the imperial stockrooms, and guild artisans were employed to make two thousand beautifully painted incense burners. The potters were told to make spoons for the offerings of incense, and the feather-mosaic workers had to apply the finishing touches of costly feathers on the gold bracelets, feather headgear, and ornamental fans, as well as on the gold shields and standards of noblemen and chiefs.

The next day the kings of Acolhuâcan and the Têcpanecapan arrived in the city and went to their palaces, which were now decorated with flowers and triumphal arches. Immediately after that, the delegations from the various parts of the empire were told to arrange the prisoners in rows in the four directions.

The Tlillancalqui, a chief connected with the southwestern city quarter of Moyotla, was ordered to bring the prisoners who came from Acolhuâcan, the northeastern central federal state, to Coyonacazco along the north thoroughfare through the northeast part of the sister city of Tlaltelolco.

The prisoners from Tlacopan were brought up in rows at Mazatzintamalco, an islet off the western causeway. The Tocuiltecatl, a chief connected with the southeastern city quarter of Teopan-Zoquipan-Xochimilcâ, had to bring the prisoners from Matlatzinco and those from the Chinampanecs at Acachinanco along the southern causeway. These last two groups were the prisoners of the Mexican federal state, also called Culhuâcan. In accordance with the previous data given by Tezozomoc dealing with the arrangement of the prisoners into four sections, we must assume these last two groups were to have been later divided over the southern and eastern causeways so that the prisoners from Matlatzinca remained on the southern avenue and those of the Chinampa area were taken to the eastern one.

In an article written in 1963, "Principios organizadores de los Mexicas," I showed that the northeastern quarter of the world was associated with Tetzcoco, the northwestern quarter with Tlacopan, and the southwestern and southeastern quarters with Mexîco-Tenochtitlan. The division of prisoners described above is in complete agreement with this model.

Next came the Tlacateccatl and the Tlacochcalcatl. They gathered the selected troops of the Cuacuachictin and of the Otomis and told them to "decorate the temple and the mountain (pyramid) of Ziteocalli and Ayauhcalli."[23] Ziteocalli is probably a corruption or an orthographic error in the writing of Xiuhteocalli (Blue

Temple). Blue was Huitzilopochtli's color as sky god, and the term
Xiuhteocalli may have been used for the calpolli temple of Huitznahuac, the original *calpolco* of Huitzilopochtli. This assumption
becomes almost a certainty since it appears that Ayauhcalli, mentioned at the same time, also lies in the ceremonial center of
Huitznahuac.[24]

People from the four quarters of the capital city itself were
employed to give the great temple a thorough final cleaning so
that it would look radiantly white and be clearly visible from afar.
Then came the chiefs of the city quarters, the Tlacatêcco *teachcauh,* the Yopico *teachcauh,* the Cihuatêcpan *teachcauh,* the Huitznahuac *teachcauh,* and the Tezcacoac *teachcauh,* all of whom
acted as "absolute rulers"[25] and gave orders for all the chapels
and temples of the gods to be put in good condition. These included the Cihuateocalli (the temple where aristocratic girls served)
and the Telpochcallis (the boys' schools). Also the *tlenamacaquê*
(fire sellers) were called upon. They were the calpolli priests
charged with the burning of incense and with the care of the ritual
objects used for it. They had to prepare for the responsibilities
they would assume when the "children of the Sun and of the
Earth" (human sacrifices) were to die.[26]

The Cihuacoatl Tlacayelel also ordered that all elderly people
and boys and girls from the most important places in the three
central federal states come to the feast.

On the eve of the dedication the Cihuacoatl directed the chief
of the tribute storerooms to lay out the garments, regalia, ornaments, banners, and weapons of the kings and chiefs in the order
of their respective ranks. Then the temple priests began to dress
in accordance with their individual functions. One high priest
wore the garments and symbols of Huitzilopochtli, the other those
of Quetzalcoatl. Other priests dressed to represent the following
gods: Tezcatlepoca, Tlalocantêuhctli, Yuhualahuan (corrected for
Yuhualcihua), Chalchiuhtlicue, Izquitecatl, Ilamatzin (corrected
for Mamatzin), Apantêuhctli, Mictlantêuhctli, Itzpapalotl, Opochtli, Chicunahui Ehecatl, Cihuacoatlicue, and Tocîhuatl. Thus there
were fifteen priests in all who represented fifteen *calpolteteô* of
Tenochtitlan. Tezozomoc says that they "imitated the ancient gods
of the Mexicans."[27]

At dawn the following day the coronation and dedication feasts
began. The great temple pyramid, including the 360 steps that
approached the top, were decorated on all sides with a great

variety of flowers. Tezozomoc then relates something that, at first
reading, seems puzzling: "The effigy [of Huitzilopochtli] faced
south, in the direction the Indians call Mictlampa, he looked at
the Marquisage [the area south of Mexico City, which, with the
title of Marqués del Valle, was bestowed on the conqueror Hernán
Cortés]."[28] Mictlampa means "in the direction of the realm of the
dead (the underworld)," a word which in Nahuatl is a common term
for the north. It is almost inconceivable that Tezozomoc, whose
mother tongue was Nahuatl, should have misinterpreted it. Therefore, as we shall see below, there must be an acceptable explanation for the words he used in this particular passage.[29]

Beginning early in the morning all the main streets of the city
filled with people, and the princes and priests as well as the
guests who had come from far and near took their seats in accordance with the roles they were to play in the coming events.
Grand Ruler Ahuitzotl, assisted by the priests of Huitzilopochtli,
Tlalocantêuhctli, Quetzalcoatl, Opochtli, and Itzpapalotl, went to
offer human sacrifices at the great temple of Huitzilopochtli.[30]
Cihuacoatl Tlacayelel took up his position for the same purpose
at the Cuauhxicalli, behind the great temple and between it and
the so-called Colhuâcan temple, which was considered to be the
oldest temple in Tenochtitlan. He was assisted by the priests of
Apantêuhctli, Zacailamatzin ("Zactlamatzin"), Tocî, Izquitecatl,
and Chicunahui Ehecatl.[31] The king of Tetzcoco, Nezahualpilli,
took up his position at the Yopico temple and was accompanied
by the priests of Mixcoatl ("Mixcuahuac"), Yohualahuan, and Totoquihuaztli—not to be confused with the Têcpanec king of the same
name.[32] The king of Tlacopan took up his position at the temple
of Huitznahuac (the calpolli temple of Huitzilopochtli in Teopan).
Tezozomoc calls him Totoquihuaztli. There have, indeed, been two
Têcpanec kings of this name, the first was the grandfather of the
second. But at the time of the temple's dedication, it was the son
of the first who ruled in Tlacopan, and his name was Chimalpopoca.[33] Tezozomoc must have made a mistake in recording the
name, possibly because his own parents had personally known
the second Totoquihuaztli, who began his reign only three years
after the dedication.

The king of Tlacopan was assisted by the two priests of Coatlicue and Ometêuhctli.[34] These and other priests sounded their
trumpets and beat their drums to begin the ritual. Human sacri-

fices were made at the temples mentioned above and in fifteen other calpolli temples (the names of these fifteen temples are given in fig. 10.5).

Then the grand ruler Ahuitzotl mounted the sacrificial stone and "ate earth" with his middle finger (the customary Aztec ceremonial manner of greeting superiors) in honor of the gods; he looked from east to west and from north to south, holding the sacrificial knife in his hand. He then cut out the heart of the first sacrifice and held it to the four directions. It is noteworthy that here too the customary order of north and south is reversed (see above).

When Ahuitzotl tired of making the offerings, he was relieved by the priest of Huitzilopochtli, who in turn was relieved by the priest of Tlalocantêuhctli. After the Tlaloc priest came the priest of Quetzalcoatl-Tlahuizcalpantêcuhtli, and he made more offerings than the others.[35] Now the Opochtli priest wielded the obsidian blade, and the last to make offerings was the priest of Itzpapalotl. In the three other major sacrificial locations, where Tlacayelel, Nezahualpilli, and the king of Tlacopan had opened the ritual, it proceeded in a similar way. In the end the four temples dripped with blood, and Tezozomoc writes that the other eleven calpolli temples, where no king began the ritual, were also covered with blood.

The guests from the provinces who took part in the flower wars and those from abroad had been given seats on the topmost gallery of the temple of Cihuatêcpan. This afforded them the best view of the sacrificial ritual, while, on the other hand, they were invisible to the Aztec people who might be hostile toward them. Apart from the logistical considerations mentioned by Tezozomoc there was a symbolic reason for the choice of the Cihuatêcpan temple as the place for the guests. Cihuatêcpan, the calpolli of Aatl-Mexitzin, was associated with internal authority, which was subject to a higher authority. The Aztec government thus emphasized that it considered itself to be the supreme authority over the provinces of the flower wars and to dominate the regimes outside the empire. The importance of the acknowledgment of Aztec authority is shown by the fact that a refusal to accept the invitation to attend the dedication and coronation feast was reason enough to declare war. It is also evident from the fact, mentioned by Tezozomoc, that at the end of the celebrations the grand ruler and the *cihuacoatl* proceeded to the temple of Cihuatêcpan to present costly gifts to the noble guests from abroad. Then the

Fig. 10.4. *Nezahualpilli, the* tlâtoani *("king") of Tetzcoco.* Codex Ixtlil-xochitl, *fol. 106; Boban, pl. 69.*

guests were returned to the borders of their domains under military escort.

After this, gifts were distributed to the Mexicans themselves. First the nobles and the members of the military elite received their rewards. Then came the *calpixquê* (the imperial civil servants of middle rank). Finally Ahuitzotl ordered two hundred loads of valuable textiles to be brought for the priests, and each one received five loads. So, there were apparently forty priests to be rewarded, and we may assume that this was the number who were functionaries in the ritual.[36]

What do these data tell us about the social organization of Tenochtitlan? More than meets the eye. A systematic examination of the data supplied by Tezozomoc leads to some significant conclusions. In columns 1, 3, 5, and 6 of the following diagram (table 10.1) are shown all the priests, gods, and calpolli-temples mentioned in this connection by Tezozomoc. On the basis of the conclusions discussed in previous chapters, columns 2 and 4 give the calpollis that were associated with the priests or gods shown in columns 1 and 3. The diagram shows that all twenty of the ritually and ceremonially important calpollis of Tenochtitlan, that is to say, the twenty inhabited by the actual population of the city, were involved in the dedication feast.

Since Grand Ruler Ahuitzotl, as supreme imperial external leader, had a predominant position in the empire, he was associated on one hand with the direction that is "to the right of the sun" (the Aztec way of indicating the north), but, on the other hand, as leader of the celestial aspect in the worldly regime he was also associated with the south. This posed a problem of ritual order which was solved by having the southern heavenly agents portrayed in the north and the northern agents of the underworld portrayed in the south. It is notable that the assistants of the four kings always symbolize the four points of the compass, while the direction associated with the group of each king is represented twice according to the principle of vertical tripartition. Therefore, the group of priestly aides of Ahuitzotl, which was associated with heaven, had two delegates from Teopan, the city quarter identified with the south, and one delegate from each of the other city quarters. The priestly aides of Tlacayelel, which was associated with the earth, had two representatives from Atzacualco, identified as the "eastern" city quarter, and again one representative from each of the other three city quarters.

The aides subject to the kings of Tetzoco and Tlacopan formed the underworld group of five representatives. Two came from Cuepopan, the "northern" city quarter, and three came from each of the other three city quarters.

In regard to the twenty calpollis, we see that the priests of the four central calpollis, Acatliacapan, Tezcacoac, Têcpantzinco, and Cuauhquiahuac, did not take a direct part in the feast. This agrees with what I have said before, namely, that these four calpollis had a more "imperial" character and were not included among original Aztec-Mexican calpollis. Evidently the same can be said of the calpolli of Xochicalco, which also had no priests in the fifteen-part tripartite vertical system.

These five calpollis, however, with their calpolli temples did play a part in the dedication feast. The people of Xochicalco were probably an indigenous population group, perhaps of Otomî origin. Among the names of the *calpolteô*, the calpolli gods, we sometimes find a certain god Otontêuhctli (the tribal god of the Otomîs), and it is possible that he was worshiped here along with Chalchiuhtlicue. The calpolli of Coatlxoxouhcan had a priestly representative at the sacrificial ritual, though the god represented by this calpolli was not one of the "ancient gods of the Mexicans." It is possible that the original Mexitin or Chinampanec nature of this Huitznahuac dependency was a decisive factor in this arrangement. But because of the original ancient nature of this calpolli, it was identified with subjection and was placed in the underworld segment of the vertical tripartite division.

The difference between the columns 5 and 6, enumerating the calpolli temples where sacrificial offerings were made, is exactly four calpollis. Among these temples were those of Yopico and Huitznahuac, where the kings of Tetzcoco and Tlacopan made their offerings, and Atempan, with which, as far as we know, Tlacayelel was closely connected. It seems logical to assume that the fourth calpolli missing from the second list was the calpolli of Ahuitzotl, for it was also the calpolli of Tlalocantêcuhtli, and the identification of this Mexican king's name with the rain god is well known. Sahagún's informants told about it as follows:

. . . ca nel nozo quiteumatiâ	. . . for they considered this little animal
in yolcapil,	[*ahuitzotl*] as it were to have a godly nature,
quilmach Tlaloc,	it was looked upon as Tlaloc,
quil tlamacazqui[37]	it was said to be a priest.

1	2	3
Priests Assisting the Four Kings During the Sacrificial Ritual	The Priest's Calpollis	The Fifteen "Original" Gods of the Mexicans
With Ahuitzotl, the grand ruler: Huitzilopochtli	(Heaven) Huitznahuac	Heaven: Huitzilopochtli
—	—	—
Tlalocantêuhctli	Chililico	Tlalocantêuhctli
Quetzalcoatl	Tzonmolco	Quetzalcoatl
Opochtli	Chalman	Opochtli
Itzpapalotl	Cihuatêcpan	Itzpapalotl
—	—	—
With the Cihuacoatl: Apantêuhctli	(Earth) Apantêuhctlan	Earth: Apantêuhctli
(Zaca)Ilamatzin	Tlacatêcpan	Ilamatzin
—	—	—
Toci	Atempan	Tocîhuatl
Izquitecatl	Izquitlan	Izquitecatl
Chicunahui Ehecatl	Molonco itlillan	Chicunahui Ehecatl
With the king of Tetzcoco: Mixcoatl	(Underworld) Tlamatzinco	Underworld: Tezcatlepoca
Yohualahuan	Yopico	Yohualahuan
Totoquihuaztli	Tlacochcalco	Mictlantêuhctli
—	—	—
With the king of Tlacopan: Coatlicue	(Underworld) Coatlan	(Cihua)coatlicue
Ometêuhctli	Coatlxoxouhcan	—
Separately: —	—	Chalchiuhtlicue (= Atlatonan)

4	5	6
e Gods' Calpollis	The Fifteen Calpolli Temples Involved, According to Tezozomoc	Tezozomoc's Enumeration of Eleven Temples
aven:	Heaven:	Heaven:
Iuitznahuac	Huitznahuac	—
—	Cuauhquiahuac	Cuauhquiahuac
Chililico	Chililico	—
'zonmolco	Tzonmolco	Tzonmolco
Chalman	—	—
Cihuatêcpan	—	—
—	Têcpantzinco	Têcpantzinco
th:	Earth:	Earth:
Apantêuhctli	Apantêuhctli	Apantêuhctli
'lacatêcpan	—	—
—	Acatliacapan	Acatliacapan
Atempan	Atempan	—
zquitlan	Izquitlan	Izquitlan
Molonco itlillan	Molonco itlillan	Molonco itlillan
lerworld:	Underworld:	Underworld:
'lamatzinco	Tlamatzinco	Tlamatzinco
'opico	Yopico	—
'lacochcalco	—	—
—	Tezcacoac	Tezcacoac
Coatlan	Coatlan	Coatlan
—	—	—
Xochicalco	Xochicalco	Xochicalco

The second enumeration, therefore, differs from the first only in the omission of the four calpollis that were represented by the four kings.

A hypothesis that is of great significance for clear insight into the original Aztec social organization of Tenochtitlan can now be formulated.

Of the twenty calpollis the ten that took part in the dedication feast with their priests and temples were inhabited by that part of the population considered to be "real" Aztecs and to have high status in the ritual life of the city.

The five calpollis that participated through their priests but not their temples were also "genuinely" Aztec. Four of these were represented by a dependent satellite temple, the fifth by a co-ordinate satellite temple (see the survey).

The five calpollis that took part in the central dedication feast with their temples but not with priestly agents[38] represented "alien" groups within the society of the capital city. Four of these were the so-called central calpollis. Their members were most probably *têcpanpouhquê* and other "adopted" foreign nobles. And in the case of the fifth of this group, the calpolli of Xochicalco, they may have been indigenous Otomis from Toltzalan-Acatzalan.

In chapter 6 we saw that after the conquest of Coyohuâcan the twenty-six chiefs who received land and titles probably belonged only to twenty calpollis, and in any case not to twenty-six calpollis. After the explanation of the lack of ritual importance of the four central calpollis it is to be expected that the four supreme chiefs among the twenty-six chiefs did not belong to any of these four. These four supreme chiefs are reckoned to belong to the oldest, original calpollis. The *tlillancalqui,* for instance, belonged to Molonco Itillan, a dependency of Cihuatêcpan, and therefore also to the city quarter of Moyotla. We have already seen that the personage who held this position was in charge of the care and the disposition of all human sacrifices from Acolhuâcan. Thus a chief from the southwest section of the city was in charge of the sacrifices from the northeast part of the empire. Later on, in the expanded Aztec empire, the *tecocyahuacatl,* who, according to the *Codex Izhuatepec,* also came from Moyotla, was charged with the division of land and other affairs of the empire in Acolhuâcan. Then again, the principle of opposition was applied in assigning a chief from a particular sector the responsibility for administering affairs concerning the geographically opposite one.

Apparently the office of *tecocyahuacatl* did not yet exist when Coyohuâcan was conquered; at any rate, it was not very important. This may be because, when the title was introduced, Acolhuâcan had not yet been retaken from the Têcpanecs. The prestige of the *tecocyahuacatl* coincided with the rise of the military hierarchy.

The *tlillancalqui*, however, was one of the twenty-six chiefs at the time of the foundation of the empire, and he was one of the four most important. Originally his function was a predominantly religious one connected with the worship of the goddess Cihuacoatl. Therefore, it is to be considered as an extremely traditional measure that this office in 1487 was charged with the care and disposition of the sacrifices from Acolhuâcan.

The king of Tetzcoco made offerings in Moyotla, and the personage who looked after these human sacrifices and disposed of them came from the same city quarter. The king of Tlacopan made offerings in TeopanZoqui(a)pan. Tezozomoc does not say who received and disposed of the human sacrifices at the western causeway, but we may assume that it was a functionary from Teopan, probably the Huitznahuacatl or the Ezhuahuacatl. The principle of ritual opposition, is at any rate, another of the factors that determined an individual's position in the inauguration ritual.

As has been said before, the chiefs of each of the city quarters had titles associated with Tlacatêcpan, Tezcacoac, Cihuatêcpan, Yopico, and Huitznahuac. Here, therefore, a chief from one central calpolli acted with four chiefs from the oldest calpollis of the Aztecâ-Mexitin.

The roles played by the various calpollis in the temple dedication form a complex system of mutual hierarchical relationships. As has been said before (see chapter 4), these hierarchies cut across each other. There was the tripartite order of calpollis, ranking from those that were associated with the celestial part of the cosmos to those concerned with the earthly part and, finally, to those that were connected with the underworld. Each of these three groups of five calpollis had an internal hierarchy of its own. Furthermore, we may assume that the calpollis that sent priests as their representatives to the four most important sanctuaries enjoyed greater prestige and, thus, were of higher status than those that were allowed to celebrate the feast only in their own calpolli temples. In the more prestigious group ten calpollis performed the sacrificial ritual in their own calpolli temples as well, and five others did not. This was also because of a difference in status. Huitznahuac, Chililico, Tzonmolco, Apantêuhctlan, Atempan, Izquitlan, Molonco Itlillan, Tlamatzinco, Yopico, and Coatlan appear, in a religious sense, to have been the most important calpollis. Huitznahuac and Tzonmolco are known to have been powerful in other respects, the former for its military functions, the latter for its role as a ceremonial and social center of merchants. This again emphasizes the importance of these two pillars that supported the Aztec-Mexican empire.

From the frequently applied principle of opposition it appears that the ritual of the dedication had a dual structure as well as a quadruple and tripartite structure. This means that the groups of the Grand Ruler Ahuitzotl and the Cihuacoatl Tlacayelel formed a division opposite that of the kings of Tetzcoco and Tlacopan. This again shows that the acting priests for the celestial-terrestrial part were those from the following pairs of opposite calpollis: Tzonmolco-Atempan, Chililico-Molonco Itlillan, Cihuatêcpan-Tlacatêcpan, and Chalman-Izquitlan. Only the priest of Tlacochcalco officiated in this case without his opposite counterpart.

It is notable that the opposite pairs were always divided between two of the four most important sanctuaries so that they were integrated, as it were, to form two pairs. This expresses a dual division of the corporate groups to which great importance was evidently attached in Tenochtitlan and the empire as a whole. At a higher level the whole is again held together by the Tlacochcalco-Huitznahuac axis, which was the pivot on which everything turned. Both groups were closely associated with the worship of Huitzilopochtli and symbolized the unity of Aztec society. In this regard we can say that Tlacochcalco, which was connected with the original Otomî population, had an overall regulating function in the dedication ritual along with the retinues of the kings of Tetzcoco and Tlacopan. Therefore, Tlacochcalco represented the remote parts of the empire, whereas Huitznahuac represented the central Mexican region.

Only Apantêuhctlan occupied a solitary position in this system, a kind of tail-end position within a group of fifteen. But then Apantêuhctlan was strongly connected with the original pre-Aztec Otomî population and thus to so-called ancient gods like Huehuêcoyotl (Old Wolf) and Apantêuhctli (Lord of the Water Surface) —in short, to phenomena and aspects that did not belong to the heart of the Aztec system.

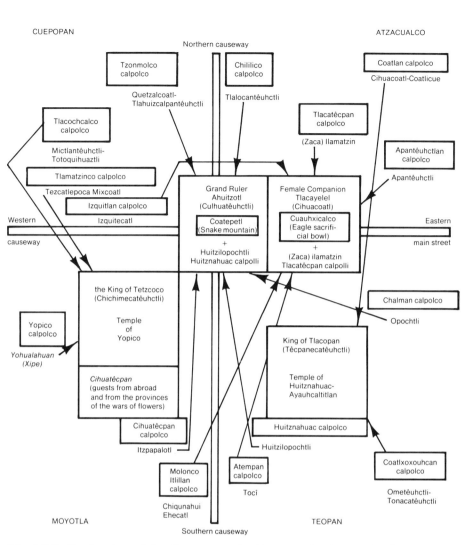

CUEPOPAN

ATZACUALCO

Northern causeway

Tzonmolco
calpolco

Chililico
calpolco

Coatlan calpolco

Cihuacoatl-Coatlicue

Quetzalcoatl-
Tlahuizcalpantêuhctli

Tlalocantêuhctli

Tlacochcalco
calpolco

Tlacatêcpan
calpolco

Mictlantêuhctli-
Totoquihuaztli

(Zaca) Ilamatzin

Apantêuhctlan
calpolco

Tlamatzinco calpolco

Apantêuhctli

Tezcatlepoca Mixcoatl

Grand Ruler
Ahuitzotl
(Culhuatêuhctli)

Female Companion
Tlacayelel
(Cihuacoatl)

Izquitlan calpolco

Western

Izquitecatl

Coatepetl
(Snake mountain)

Cuauhxicalco
(Eagle sacrifi-
cial bowl)

Eastern

causeway

+
Huitzilopochtli
Huitznahuac calpolli

+
(Zaca) ilamatzin
Tlacatêcpan calpolli

main street

the King of Tetzcoco
(Chichimecatêuhctli)

Chalman calpolco

Opochtli

Yopico
calpolco

Temple
of
Yopico

Yohualahuan
(Xipe)

King of Tlacopan
(Têcpanecatêuhctli)

Cihuatêcpan
(guests from abroad
and from the provinces
of the wars of flowers)

Temple of
Huitznahuac-
Ayauhcaltitlan

Cihuatêcpan
calpolco

Huitznahuac calpolco

Itzpapalotl

Huitzilopochtli

Molonco
Itlillan
calpolco

Atempan
calpolco

Coatlxoxouhcan
calpolco

Toci

Chiqunahui
Ehecatl

Ometêuhctli-
Tonacatêuhctli

MOYOTLA

TEOPAN

Southern causeway

Fig. 10.5. *Dedication of the Great Temple (Coatepetl) of Tenochtitlan in 1487.
Based on Tezozomoc.*

CHAPTER 11

"We Look Huitzilopochtli in the Face . . .

This and the next chapters in this social history of the Aztecs verify the data that have been collected and used thus far by analyzing them against a background of the spatial systems represented in the different Aztec and other Mesoamerican calendars.[1] This analysis is a complex, difficult, and often tiresome job, and it may possibly tax the reader's patience. But those who are really interested will be amply rewarded for their perseverance. The result of this work is a detailed outline of the social organization of the city of Tenochtitlan as well as an entirely new concept of Aztec historiography and the extent to which it was determined by social relationships. Before considering the spatial association of groups, their gods, and temples with reference to the spatial divisions of day-signs and the thirteen-day cycles as they are known from the pictorials, we must first understand the principles of the Mesoamerican almanacs.

In pre-Hispanic Mesoamerica—and also in some present-day areas in that region—two systems of time count were commonly used. The Aztecs and other Nahuatl speakers called one kind *tonalpoalli* (counting of days), and the calendar for that system was called *tonalamatl* (sheet of days). The *tonalpoalli* was a system in which twenty different day-signs were successively combined with the numerals 1 to 13. This combination yielded 260 different day names, the 261st day sign being the same numeral and sign as that of the first day. The following survey of a complete *tonalamatl* (table 11.1) shows how the counting of days worked.

The four day-signs with asterisks are the so-called year-bearers. Only these four, combined with the numerals 1 to 13, could successively designate a solar year. The day count was the same in

Table 11.1. Tonalamatl (To be read from top to bottom)

Day-sign	Count													Next Count	
cipactli (crocodile)	1	8	2	9	3	10	4	11	5	12	6	13	7	1	8
ehecatl (wind)*	2	9	3	10	4	11	5	12	6	13	7	1	8	2	and so on
calli (house)*	3	10	4	11	5	12	6	13	7	1	8	2	9	3	
cuetzpalin (lizard)	4	11	5	12	6	13	7	1	8	2	9	3	10	4	
coatl (snake)	5	12	6	13	7	1	8	2	9	3	10	4	11	5	
miquiztli (death)	6	13	7	1	8	2	9	3	10	4	11	5	12	6	
mazatl (deer)	7	1	8	2	9	3	10	4	11	5	12	6	13	7	
tochtli (rabbit)*	8	2	9	3	10	4	11	5	12	6	13	7	1	8	
atl (water)	9	3	10	4	11	5	12	6	13	7	1	8	2	9	
itzcuintli (dog)	10	4	11	5	12	6	13	7	1	8	2	9	3	10	
ozomâtli (monkey)	11	5	12	6	13	7	1	8	2	9	3	10	4	11	
malinalli (prairie grass)	12	6	13	7	1	8	2	9	3	10	4	11	5	12	
acatl (reed)*	13	7	1	8	2	9	3	10	4	11	5	12	6	13	
ocelotl (ocelot)	1	8	2	9	3	10	4	11	5	12	6	13	7	1	
cuauhtli (eagle)	2	9	3	10	4	11	5	12	6	13	7	1	8	2	
cozcacuauhtli (vulture)	3	10	4	11	5	12	6	13	7	1	8	2	9	3	
ollin (rolling movement)	4	11	5	12	6	13	7	1	8	2	9	3	10	4	
tecpatl (flintstone)*	5	12	6	13	7	1	8	2	9	3	10	4	11	5	
quiahuitl (rain)	6	13	7	1	8	2	9	3	10	4	11	5	12	6	
xochitl (flower)	7	1	8	2	9	3	10	4	11	5	12	6	13	7	

*Year-bearers.

all of Mesoamerica, but the year bearers differed. In some regions of South Mexico for instance, year bearers were not the same as those in Central Mexico.

The second time count was called *xiuhpoalli* ("counting of years") by the Aztecs and related peoples. The complete cycle was fifty-two years of 365 days each, that is 18,980 days in all, which is exactly seventy-three *tonalpoallis*.

The Aztec year was divided into eighteen 20-day cycles, plus 5 days that were called *nenmontemi* ("useless fillings"). Therefore, if the first day of a new year was the day-sign ocelotl (ocelot), all 20-day cycles in that year began with that day-sign but usually combined with different numerals, and all the 20-day cycles ended in days with the sign acatl (reed). This means that the 360th day of the year was a day acatl and the 365th day bore the sign tecpatl (flintstone). Thus the new year started with a day quiahuitl (rain), which is exactly 5 days after ocelotl (ocelot). It should now be clear that only a specific 4 of the 20 day-signs could coincide with the beginning of the year and that only 4 other day-signs could designate the final day of each of the 20-day cycles. If either the first or the last day of a specific 20-day period was used to mark a year — it could only be one of no more than 4 day-signs and 13 numerals, or 52 names. After each 52 years the cycle was repeated. In Tenochtitlan and central Mexico in general the day-signs Acatl, Tecpatl, Calli, and Tochtli served as year-bearers, so that the 52 year cycles were as shown in table 11.2.

The Aztecs "bundled" their years in periods that were designated as II Acatl (II Reed). That is to say, after a 52-year cycle had ended in a year I Tochtli (I Rabbit). The "bundling of years" (*xiuhmolpiliztli* or *xiuhtlalpilli*) was celebrated with elaborate rituals, which reached a climax in the drilling of the new fire on the *Huixachtepetl* near Colhuâcan. This was carried out by the fire priest of the calpolli of Tzonmolco that was the calpolli of Xiuh-têcuhtli, the fire god; then the new fire was taken to the temples of Tenochtitlan and from there to all important temples in the country.[2]

Usually at the end of each of the eighteen 20-day cycles, which in most of the existing literature are rather confusingly called "months," an important religious feast was celebrated. During the fourteenth cycle, Quecholli (Spoonbill), and the eighteenth cycle Izcalli (Revival), there were also great feasts halfway through the cycle. The names of the eighteen 20-day cycles differed from region to region. The names of some of the cycles in Tetzcoco, for instance,

Table 11.2. Year-Bearers (To be read from top to bottom)

Year-Bearer	Count													
Acatl (Reed)	2	6	10	1	5	9	13	4	8	12	3	7	11	2
Tecpatl (Flintstone)	3	7	11	2	6	10	1	5	9	13	4	8	12	
Calli (House)	4	8	12	3	7	11	2	6	10	1	5	9	13	
Tochtli (Rabbit)	5	9	13	4	8	12	3	7	11	2	6	10	1	

were different from those in Tenochtitlan. Table 11.3 gives the names most commonly used by the Aztecs for these eighteen cycles with the deities associated with them.

This system of "counting of years," or some similar method, was used nearly everywhere in Mesoamerica and almost always in close conjunction with the "counting of days." The ways in which the "counting of years" and "counting of days" were made to coordinate differed, however, from one region to another and even from one town to another. In Tenochtitlan, for instance, the conjunction between day names and the dates in the "counting of years" was different from that in its sister city, Tlatelolco. Both used the same day-signs for the same days, but the accompanying numerals differed.[3] If two such closely related Aztec communities showed such differences in their calendric systems, it is understandable that less closely related population groups could show much greater differences.

Tenochtitlan numbered the "counting of days" and the "counting of years" in such a way that the 360th day of the year, the twentieth day of the eighteenth 20-day cycle, was the year-bearer. Thus if the cycle Izcalli in a specific solar year ended, for instance, on the day 2 acatl (2 reed), that year was called II Acatl.

As has been said, in other towns and in other regions other systems were used. There were, for instance, calendars in which the first day of the year was the year-bearer, and others in which the 365th day was so designated.[4]

Besides this difference there were others. Not everywhere did the year begin with the same 20-day cycle. In the official calendar of Tenochtitlan, the first day of Cuahuitlehua was also the first day of the solar year. In Tlatelolco the year probably began with Izcalli, and in Tetzcoco with Tlacaxipehualiztli.[5] This, of course, implies that the "useless fillings" (the five extra days) could, in different locations, be added to different 20-day cycles. Furthermore, it even happened that in some larger towns there were several ways of counting years.[6] All this has led to the great confusion found in the colonial historical records and to the rise of an extensive field of investigation that can be called "Mexican calendric studies." The problems relating to it that are of importance here have to do mainly with the differences in the beginnings

Table 11.3. Eighteen 20-Day Cycles and Associated Deities

Names of 20-Day Cycles	Deities
1. Cuahuitlehua (Trees Are Rising Up) or Atlcahualo (Lack of Water)	Tlaloquẽ (rain gods)
2. Tlacaxipehualiztli (Flaying of Men)	Xipe Totêc (Our Lord the Flayed One, fertility god)
3. Tozoztontli (Little Vigil)	Coatlicue (Serpent Skirt, earth goddess)
4. Hueitozoztli (Great Vigil)	Chicomecoatl (Seven Snake, maize goddess)
5. Toxcatl (Cord of Atonement, Drought)	Huitzilopochtli and Tezcatlepoca
6. Etzalcualiztli (Eating Beans)	Tlaloquê (rain gods)
7. Têcuilhuitontli (Little Feast of Lords)	Huixtocihuatl (salt goddess) and Tlaloc (Wine of the Earth, rain god)
8. Hueitêcuilhuitl (Great Feast of Lords)	Xilonen (maize goddess) and Cihuacoatl (earth goddess)
9. Tlaxochimaco (Presentation of Flowers)	Huitzilopochtli
10. Xocotlhuetzi (Fall of the Fruit)	Otontêcuhtli (god of the Otomis and Têcpanecs)
11. Ochpaniztli (Sweeping)	Teteô Innan (mother of the gods)
12. Teotlêco (Coming of the gods)	All the gods
13. Tepeilhuitl (Mountain Feast)	Xochiquetzal
14. Quecholli (Spoonbill)	Mixcoatl and Xochiquetzal
15. Panquetzaliztli (Raising of the Banners)	Huitzilopochtli
16. Atemoztli (Coming Down of the Water)	Tlaloc and Chalchiuhtlicue
17. Tititl (Wrinkle, Narrowed Passage)	Ilamatêcuhtli (old earth goddess)
18. Izcalli (Revival)	Xiuhtêcuhtli (Lord of the Year, fire god)
Nenmontemi ("useless fillings")	Five mountain gods

and ends of the varying forms of "counting of years" *(xiuhpoalli).* It is now apparent that this *xiuhpoalli* is not the most appropriate starting point for our study of the connections between social organization and systems of spatial order as they are found in the calendars. Since the solar year did not begin on the same day in Tetzcoco or Cholullan as it did in Tenochtitlan, data from the year counts in those cities are not unconditionally applicable to the circumstances in Tenochtitlan. Therefore, it seems sensible that our study should be primarily directed at the larger connections with the *tonalpoalli,* or "counting of days." This would be simpler since there are only local differences in the labeling of time and not in the form of the system to consider. When data about the "counting of years" undeniably originated in Tenochtitlan, of course, the above-mentioned difficulties do not arise. Therefore, we shall use one such calendric monument from this city extensively.

Many historical records say that the twenty day-signs of the *tonalpoalli* were arranged in accordance with the four points of the compass. Although it can be assumed that colonial sources were not free of Spanish influences, no such influence attends the world-famous "calendar stone." This calendar, or "solar," stone (the "Stone of Axayacatl") is an elaborately worked fifteen-century sacrificial stone that was found in the center of Mexico City at the site of the great pre-Hispanic temple (fig. 11.4). Huitzilopochtli, as ruling god of the fifth sun, is depicted in the center of the stone. It is possible that this image of the supreme Aztec god represents his particular earthbound form of Mexîtli, but that would not interfere with the argument offered here. His face is set in the day-sign 4 ollin, which indicates the fifth sun. The four "wings" of the ollin day-sign show the four signs for the other four suns.[7] This center is encircled with a band containing the glyphs of each of the 20 day-signs. From this circle emanate eight lines indicating the eight directions. Four of these are conspicuous, while the other four are half-hidden behind another, larger ring in which forty small rectangles each with five points have been sculptured ten times in each of the four directions.[8] Below the half-hidden rays are the four day-signs that serve as year-bearers, meaning that in combination with the numerals 1 to 13 they designate the fifty-two years of a complete Mesoamerican cycle. These four important day-signs are Acatl (Reed), east; Tecpatl (Flintstone), north; Calli (House), west; and Tochtli (Rabbit), south. These relations with the main directions are borne out by the celebration of the Hueyi Têcuhilhuitl, when the year-bearers were worshiped at Tetamazolco on the eastern causeway, at Necoquixecan (on the northern causeway), at Atenchicalcan (on the western causeway), and at Xolloco (at the junction of the southern causeways).[9]

In Tenochtitlan the year-bearers were evidently associated with the directions of these four causeways, which means that the four partly obscured lines can be associated with each of the main streets and, therefore, with the boundaries of the four city quarters. Another conclusion is that the four conspicuous lines represent the four diagonal sacred streams, since the stone was made primarily for religious purposes. Huitzilopochtli as sun god (or Mexîtli, as earth god) is depicted ·with a projecting tongue that is to be regarded as a token of (or the exercise of) authority and at the same time forms his calendar sign l-tecpatl. His tongue points in the direction of the ray pictured below him, which is partly obscured by the open jaws of two feathered dragons that face each other. The two dragons form the outermost ring of the elaborate stone. Between their tails, which meet above the god Huitzilopochtli, we see the sign XIII Acatl. Over most of the length of each of the two feathered serpents this sign is made another eleven times. From their mouths emerge the heads of two gods which coincide with the top of the lowest line. Looking out from the mouth of the left dragon is the face of the god Xiuhtêcuhtli, the fire god; Tonatiuh, the sun god, is looking out from the mouth of the right one. The symbolism depicted here means that the two dragons, the eternally competing fires of heaven and the underworld, bring war and death before the eyes of Huitzilopochtli, that is to say, the places where the sacrificial blood was offered and channeled to the thirsty Huitzilopochtli through one of the holy canals.

If we can discern to which of the sacred canals Huitzilopochtli is pointing his tongue, we shall have another clue to the hitherto mysterious connections among the calpollis, the calendrical day-signs, and their relevant deities. We can assume that the twenty calpollis were related to the twenty day-signs and therefore that every city quarter is connected to five different day-signs. Furthermore, on the basis of its individual connection to one of the points of the compass and a god or goddess, each separate day-sign can be reckoned to belong to one of the original calpollis, whose relative positions in each city quarter are known to us. On the inner side of the snake wall around the ceremonial center of Tenochtitlan there were twenty calpolli sanctuaries where the calpolli chiefs

vista de frente

vista lateral

Fig. 11.1. *Stone of Axayacatl (calendar stone). National Museum.*

performed their ritual fasts.[10] Here would be a good place to start. Each of these sanctuaries represented, within the temple premises, a calpolli with all its relevant god(s) and calendar signs. This implies that, as a rule, there was more than one connection between a calpolli and the calendar, in other words, that more than one calendar date was associated with a single calpolli. It is, however, highly probable that within this complicated system, which was perhaps fully known only to the priests, there was a simpler more direct connection between each of the twenty calpollis and a specific one of the 20 day-signs irrespective of its accompanying numeral. The simpler system was one of the factors that determined the religious practice of the common people, the majority of the calpolli members, who were thus reminded of their obligations at least once every 20-day cycle. It has already been seen how the four year-bearing day-signs are associated with the points of the compass in most of the colonial sources as follows: Calli, west; Tochtli, south; Acatl, east; and Tecpatl, north. The greatest problem with these records, however, is that on the whole they show European influences in their representation of Mesoamerican calendars. This is clear in the form of the presentation and in the attempt to represent the multiplicity of temporal systems as a single calendar, all fitting the same rules. Therefore, almost none of the colonial historians considered the possibility that the *tonalpoalli* and the *xiuhpoalli* might have entirely different rules for directions, deities, and associated social groups. A happy exception is the native historian Cristóbal del Castillo, who in his *History of the Mexicans* has included the following clearly expressed and, for our purpose, very significant passage:

. . . Auh câ in xiuhtlapoalli ca nanahui intentiuh: in ic ce câ Calli, in ic ome câ Tochin, in ic ei câ Acatl, in ic nahui câ Tecpatl, ca in ye mochi câ ompoalli ommatlactli omome xihuitl. ca matlactli omein Calli in iquizayampa in Tonatiuh pohui; auh no matlactli omei in Tochin mictlancopa	. . . And that is the counting of years for four by four it fills itself up, the first is Calli [House], the second is Tochin [Rabbit], the third is Acatl [Reed], the fourth is Tecpatl [Flintstone], for all together they are [4 × 13] fifty-two years. For the thirteen signs House belong to the direction where the Sun rises [east] and the also thirteen signs Rabbit belong to the direction

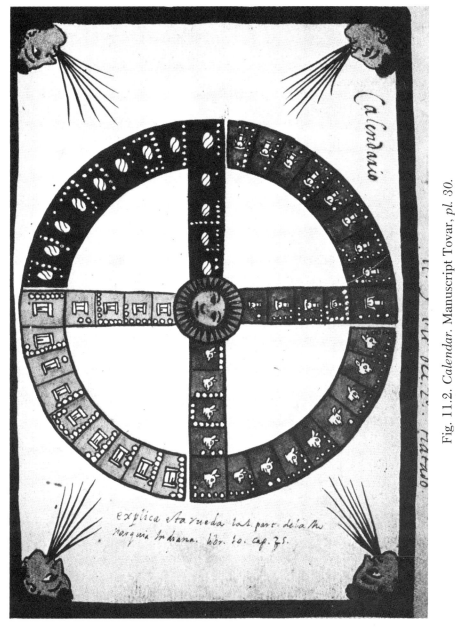

Fig. 11.2. *Calendar.* Manuscript Tovar, *pl.* 30.

pohui;
auh no matlactli omei
in Acatl icalaquiyan
in Tonatiuh pohui,
auh no matlactli omei
in Tecpatl iz Cihuatlan
pohui, in ye mochi
52 años in xihuitl
molpia.[11]

of the realm of the dead [north]
and the also thirteen signs
Reed belong to the place
where the sun sets [west]
and the also thirteen signs
Flintstone here belong to
the place of women [south],
all together they are fifty-two years,
joined together into a bundle of
years.

This preserved fragment of an originally much larger work gives clear evidence that in the *xiuhtlapoalli,* or solar calendar, the four important day-signs that lent their names to the years were associated with the four points of the compass in an order just opposite that of the *tonalpoalli,* the priestly or 260-day count. In the *xiuhpoalli* the thirteen Calli years were identified with the east, whereas in the *tonalpoalli* the day 1 calli and the next 12 days were associated with the west. The Tochin or Tochtli years of the solar calendar were all associated with the north, whereas in the *tonalpoalli* the day 1 tochtli and the next 12 days, which form the 13-day cycle 1 Rabbit were associated with the south. Likewise, Acatl in the solar year belonged to the west but in the *tonalpoalli* to the east, and Tecpatl was associated with the south in the solar year but in the day count with the north. The calendar stone of Axayacatl is, without doubt, a predominantly *xiuhpoalli* monument. The picture of the god Huitzilopochtli is, indeed, set in a day sign (4 ollin) that contains four other day-signs, but these 5 are all used in the Mexican calendars to designate cycles of many years. Moreover, the calendar stone shows all 20 day-signs in one ring without any accompanying numerals; only the four year-bearers have been given special emphasis by a bolder line. The conclusion is that the day-signs are meant to designate days in general as well as parts of the solar year. This means that Cristóbal de Castillo's data can also be applied to this calendar stone.

   We know now that Huitzilopochtli (Mexîtli) sticks out his tongue —in the form of a sacrificial knife that is the Tecpatl sign—in the direction of the symbolic canal that ran between the northern causeway (with the sign Tochtli) and the western one (with the sign Acatl). That is the sacred canal that traverses the northwestern city quarter, Cuepopan Tlaquenchiuhcan. On either side of this symbolic line were the sanctuaries of the calpollis Tlacochcalco and Tzonmolco. The calpolli gods of those two temples were Tona-tiuh and Xiuhtêcuhtli, the same gods who are depicted in the mouths of the dragons.

The above conclusions indicate a provisional connection between calpollis and their day-signs. There will be a preliminary survey of these associations since their relationships must be compared with the gods that relate to the day-signs as well as to the calpollis. Only when this triple connection is proven to be systematic will there be a good reason to assume that our identifications are the same as those of the Aztecs. Apparently the following signs and their directional associations belong to the northwestern city quarter of Cuepopan: Tochtli, south; Atl, east; Itzcuintli, north; Ozo-mâtli, west; and Malinalli, south.

As has been said, the following five calpollis belonged to the city quarter Cuepopan: Tlacochcalco and Tzonmolco, in the north-west and northeast; Tlamatzinco and Izquitlan, in the west and south; and Tezcacoac, at the center, and thus in the south of Cue-popan. In this way we can associate the day-sign tochtli with Tez-cacoac, atl with Tzonmolco, itzcuintli with Tlacochcalco, ozomâtli with Tlamatzinco, and malinalli with Izquitlan. Tochtli has been associated with Tezcacoac and not with Izquitlan on the assump-tion that the four year-bearing day-signs would probably have been connected with the four central calpollis. Two considerations have led to this assumption. In the first place, the four central calpollis that adjoined the main ceremonial center had a special ritual status. Furthermore, they were the only four calpollis each of which was situated on either side of one of the four causeways leading into the city. As stated above, it was on these main cause-ways that important rites relating to the four year-bearers were carried out. This leads us to the following connections in the other city quarters:

In Moyotla: Acatl (east), Têcpantzinco; ocelotl (north), Xochicalco; cuauhtli (west), Yopico; cozcacuauhtli (south), Cihuatêcpan; and ollin (east), Molonco Itillan. In Teopan—Zoqui(a)pan—Xochimilcâ: Tecpatl (north), Cuauhquiahuac; quiahuitl (west), Atempan; xo-chitl (south), Huitznahuac; cipactli (east), Coatlxoxouhcan; and ehecatl (north), Chalman. In Atzacoalco: Calli (west), Acatliaca-pan; cuetzpalin (south), Apantêuhctlan; coatl (east), Coatlan; mi-quiztli (north), Tlacatêcpan; and mazatl (west), Chililico.

The social organization of the Aztec capital city will be apparent once we succeed in discovering one logically integrated system of the deities associated with each of the calendar signs and cycles and with the calpollis. Fortunately there are several original Mexican pictorials that give us an overview of the various ways in which the twenty calendar signs and the thirteen-day cycles, individually or collectively, were associated with particular deities. The most important of these codices are *Borgia, Cospi, Laud, Féjervary-Mayér, Vaticanus A* and *B, Telleriano-Remensis, Borbonicus,* and *Tonalamatl Aubin.* About half of these codices, namely, those of the Borgia group, are not Aztec but deal with the Mixtecs and other cultures in Puebla and Veracruz. The *Codex Borbonicus* and the *Tonalamatl Aubin* are Aztec works, though not necessarily from Tenochtitlan. We are well aware of the many local differences in Mesoamerican religious ritual and ceremony and of the many different aspects of the various gods and goddesses. It is understandable then that the gods shown in these pictographs, or rather their special forms, need not always agree with those of comparable positions in the ritual and social arrangement in Tenochtitlan. Therefore, the absence of codices that relate specifically to conditions in Tenochtitlan presents us with a major problem. Nevertheless, let us see what a comparison of the ritual arrangement in Tenochtitlan with those mentioned in the codices will bring. *Borgia* and *Vaticanus* show us which gods and goddesses were considered to be regents of the twenty day-signs, as shown in the following list:

cipactli (crocodile): Tonacatêcuhtli
ehecatl (wind): Quetzalcoatl
calli (house): Tepeyollotli
cuetzpalin (lizard): Huehuêcoyotl
coatl (snake): Chalchiuhtlicue
miquiztli (death): Tecciztecatl—Metztli—Coyolxauhqui
mazatl (deer): Tlaloc
tochtli (rabbit): Mayahuel
atl (water): Xiuhtêcuhtli
itzcuintli (dog): Mictlantêcuhtli
ozomahtli (monkey): Xochipilli—Centeotl
malinalli (prairie grass): Pâtecatl
acatl (reed): Tezcatlepoca—Iztlacoliuhqui
ocelotl (ocelot): Ixcuinan—Tlazolteotl
cuauhtli (eagle): Xipe Totêc, Tlatlauhqui Tezcatlepoca
cozcacuauhtli (vulture): Itzpapalotl
ollin (rolling movement): Xolotl

tecpatl (flintstone): Tezcatlepoca—Chalchiuhtotolin
quiahuitl (rain): Chantico or Tonatiuh
xochitl (flower): Xochiquetzal

A preliminary comparison of this list with the provisional connections between day-signs and calpollis quickly shows that they agree on some points. We know from many historical records that Xipe Totêc (Our Lord the Flayed One, also called Red Brilliant Mirror) was the patron or ancestor god of the calpolli Yopico. Therefore, the main center for his worship was the Yopico temple.[12] The fact that the day cuauhtli (eagle) was associated with the calpolli of Yopico as well as with the god Xipe provides us with a necessary connection of day-sign, calpolli, and calpolli god that fits well in our system. We also know that there is a connection between Xiuhtêcuhtli, the fire god, and the calpolli of Tzonmolco. A comparison of the two lists shows that the day-sign atl (water) was indeed connected with Tzonmolco and with the fire god. These two points of agreement give the impression that the model drawn from a comparison of Cristóbal del Castillo's data and those found on the Stone of Axayacatl was indeed the system used by the Aztecs. Let us take a further look at the other day-signs, gods, and calpollis and their connections.

In the pictographs cipactli (crocodile) is combined with the god Tonacatêcuhtli (Lord of Our Existence), one of the oldest gods of creation. He and Tonacacihuatl (Lady of Our Existence) are the primordial divine couple from whom all other gods originated.[13] As such they, in fact, correspond exactly with the Toltec primordial god Ometêcuhtli (Lord of Duality, literally, Two Lord). This ancient deity also played a part in the dedication ceremonies of the Great Temple of Huitzilopochtli, and, as noted in the previous chapter, the priest of this god probably belonged to the calpolli of Coatlxoxouhcan. The day-sign cipactli was also associated with this calpolli, as shown in the data from various sources.

The day-sign ehecatl (Wind) was an aspect of the well-known god Quetzalcoatl, and, if our model is correct, they should both be associated with the calpolli of Chalman. But the calpolli god of Chalman appears to be Opochtli (Southern Rain), one of the forms of Tlaloc.[14] However, we have pointed out above that in the Toltec religion Tlaloc and Quetzalcoatl were so closely associated that it is not surprising that in different local systems one should be substituted for the other. Thus the fact that, in the pictorial writings of the Nahua-Mixtecs of south and central Puebla, a representation of Quetzalcoatl takes the place occupied in Tenochtitlan by one of Tlaloc need not disqualify our model.

The day-sign calli (House), one of the four year-bearers, is controlled by the god Tepeyollotl (Heart of the Mountain or Life Principle of the Mountain), a primordial form of Tlaloc, the rain god who is often represented by the form of a jaguar. If we assume that each of the four year-bearers belonged to one of the four central calpollis, calli represents Acatliacapan in the east, which must have regarded Tepeyollotl as its calpolli god.

The day-sign cuetzpalin (lizard), according to the old pictographs, is associated with the god Huehuêcoyotl (Old Coyote), who was recognized as a god of the Otomis.[15] As such he was closely related to Otontêcuhtli (Lord of the Otomis) and the Têcpanec god Cuecuexin, both of whom share with Huehuêcoyotl the nature of a phallic fire god.[16]

The *Leyenda de los Soles* mentions the god Apantêcuhtli as one of the *mimixcoâ* (cloud snakes, aspects of the god Mixcoatl).[17] As has been indicated, the goddess Itzpapalotl was one of the cloud snakes, and, according to the descriptions given by Sahagún's informants, her day-sign adorns both the front and back of the headdress of the god Otontêcuhtli.[18]

Thus there is a line connecting Huehuêcoyotl with Apantêcuhtli, and there is every reason to assume that both gods, who perhaps may be regarded as different aspects of the same god, were associated with the calpolli of Apantêuhctlan. The day-sign coatl (snake) has Chalchiuhtlicue (Jade Is Her Skirt), the symbol of earthly waters, as patroness.[19] The calpolli temple of Coatlan in Tenochtitlan appears to have been dedicated to Coatlicue (Serpent Skirt), the mother, or earth, goddess, rather than to Chalchiuhtlicue, the "spouse" of the rain god Tlaloc.[20] However, both are mother goddesses and therefore related to one another.[21] Moreover, the connection between the day-sign coatl and the calpolli of Coatlan is so obvious that here too our hypothetical model is substantiated.

The day-sign miquiztli (death) belongs to the moon god(dess) who, like many other Aztec deities, is known by a great many different names and aspects, Metztli, Tecciztecatl, Coyolxauhqui, Tetzauhteotl, and Ilamatêcuhtli being the most common ones. In the previous chapter it was noted that her priest was Zacailamatzin, who represented the calpolli of Tlacatêcpan in the dedication of the great temple. It is possible that the personal name of Ilancueitl, which shares with Ilamatêcuhtli and Zacailamatzin the stem *ilama* ("old woman"), was in fact a priestly title or indicator of an office that relates to this goddess and "her" calpolli. As we have seen, in the early days of Tenochtitlan the "princess" Ilancueitl, according to the *Codex Izhuatepec*, held an office that was connected with the calpolli of Tlacatêcpan. Both the sun and the moon are associated with miquiztli. Among the peoples of indigenous America the sun and the moon are often depicted as being closely related and as being in competitive opposition.

The day-sign mazatl (deer) belongs to the rain god, Tlaloc (Wine of the Earth), and at the dedication ceremonies of the great temple his priest came from the calpolli of Chililico. This fact also supports our provisional model.

The day-sign tochtli (rabbit), one of the four year-bearers, is the sign of the goddess of the agave, Mayahuel, who was patroness of midwives. She is sometimes named Ayopechtli or Ayopechcatl (Sitting on the Tortoise).[22] One of the hymns that the Aztecs sang during their rituals, the "Song of Ayopechtli," was dedicated to her.[23] Sahagún's Aztec informants clearly indicate that she was associated with the calpolli of Tezcacoac, for they called her Tezcacoac Ayopechtli.[24]

The day-sign atl (water), as said above, was connected with the god Xiuhtêcuhtli and the calpolli of Tzonmolco. The day-sign itzcuintli (Dog) was associated with Mictlantêcuhtli (Lord of the Realm of the Dead), and at the dedication of the great temple a priest of that name represented the calpolli of Tlacochcalco. This again corresponds to our provisional model.

The day-sign ozomâtli (monkey), according to the pictographs, is the sign of the god Xochipilli (Flower Prince), who was also called Macuilxochitl (Five Flower).[25] He was regarded as the patron of those who lived in palaces. The maize god Centeotl was also associated with ozomâtli. According to our provisional model this day-sign should belong to the calpolli of Tlamatzinco, but we must assume that this calpolli was particularly connected with the god Tlamatzincatl, one of the aspects of Tezcatlepoca and also a form of Mixcoatl.[26] Two hymns that fortunately have been preserved in the *Florentine Codex* were dedicated to Xochipilli and Macuilxochitl. Both hymns express close ties with the maize god(dess), but the "Song of Macuilxochitl" also expresses an identification with "Tetzauhteotl Tezcatlipuca," which provides a direct link with our provisional model.[27]

The day-sign malinalli (prairie grass) is given in the pictorials as the sign of the god Pâtecatl (Medicine Man), one of the many gods of pulque (agave wine). Izquitecatl was another of the well-

known pulque gods, and in Tenochtitlan he was, of course, the calpolli god of Izquitlan. It is likely that in Tenochtitlan it was the god
Izquitecatl rather than Pâtecatl who was associated with the day-
sign malinalli. In that case, there is again complete agreement with
our provisional model.

The day sign acatl (reed), another of the four year-bearers, is
connected with the nocturnal, northern aspect of Tezcatlepoca,
often referred to as Itztlacoliuhqui (Curved Obsidian). On the
basis of the rites described in the *Florentine Codex* it has been
assumed that each of the year bearers was connected to one of the
four central calpollis. The fact that Têcpantzinco, as one of the
four, had one of the forms of the principal god Tezcatlepoca as calpolli god, further reinforces the special character of these calpollis.

The days designated by the sign ocelotl (ocelot) belonged to the
goddess Tlazolteotl or Ixcuinan. Like Xochiquetzal, Coatlicue, and
Chimalman she is an aspect of the earth and mother goddess in the
form that symbolizes sexual power and reproduction. The priests
and priestesses of this goddess were known as specialists in the
counting of days and in predictions for new born infants.[28] Chalchiuhtlicue Chalchiuhtlatonac, another aspect of this same mother
goddess, was primarily associated with earthly waters.[29] Chalchiuhtlicue also played an important role in the ritual performed for
newborns.[30] As noted in the previous chapter, a Chalchiuhtlicue
priest appears to have represented the calpolli of Xochicalco. It
is not surprising, therefore, to find the goddess Tlazolteotl-Ixcuinan
as patron deity of this calpolli. It is difficult to determine from
these data which of her aspects was actually the most common
in Tenochtitlan, but, in any event, some form of the earth or
mother goddess was worshiped in Xochicalco.

The day-sign cuauhtli (eagle) was the sign of Xipe Totêc, who,
as we know, was patron of the calpolli of Yopico.

The day-sign cozcacuauhtli (vulture) was associated with the
goddess Itzpapalotl (Obsidian or Black Butterfly). As we have seen
before, this goddess was also called Mexîtli, Tetzauhteotl, and
Cihuacoatl. We have already made her acquaintance as calpolli
god of Cihuatêcpan, and, in accordance with the calendric system,
we meet her again.

The day-sign ollin is connected in the pictographs with Xolotl
(Monster or Twins), an important aspect of the Toltec god Quetzalcoatl. The connection between him and the calpolli of Molonco
Itillan is confirmed by several sources, which also supports our
provisional model.[31]

The day-sign tecpatl (flintstone), one of the four year-bearers, is shown in the pictorials combined with Tezcatlepoca in the form of Chalchiuhtotolin (Jade Turkey). Here again we see a fully acceptable patron god for the southern central calpolli of Cuauhquiahuac.

The day-sign quiahuitl (rain) belongs to the goddess Chantico Cuaxolotl, the major goddess of the Colhuas and the chinampa dwellers. We have seen that Malinalxochitl was only another aspect of this goddess. If the provisional model places Chantico-Cuaxolotl and her day-sign with the calpolli of Atempan, it would be in complete agreement with all the data accumulated so far. Atempan was a dependency of Chalman and, furthermore, was the calpolli to which Tlacayelel belonged—who as Cihuacoatl occupied in the Aztec political organization a position comparable to that of Huitzilopochtli's "sister" Malinalxochitl in the tribal organization as described in the migration myth. However, the day-sign quiahuitl is associated not only with Chantico but also with Tonatiuh (Sun). Here again we see the close sun-moon relationship that was so important in pre-Conquest times. This association again implies a close relationship as well as competitive opposition, as in the case of Tlacatêcpan and its connection with the day-sign miquiztli.

In the pictographs the day-sign xochitl (flower) is connected with the goddess Xochiquetzal (Ornamental Flower), another form taken by the earth and mother goddess. As such she is closely related to Coatlicue, the mother of Huitzilopochtli.[32] One ancient source names Xochiquetzal herself as mother of Omitêcuhtli-Maquizcoatl (Tetzauhteotl) Huitzilopochtli.[33] We can assume that the day-sign xochitl actually belonged to Huitznahuac, since pictorials recorded far from Tenochtitlan use the day-sign xochitl for Xochiquetzal, who in Tenochtitlan was the mother of the patron god of that calpolli.

A comparison of all twenty day-signs and their associated deities with our provisional model shows no essential contradictions. On the contrary, there is overwhelming agreement. These data lead to the obvious conclusions:

1. The monumental calendar stone is an idealized symbolic representation of the Aztec cosmos in general and of the ceremonial center of Tenochtitlan in particular.

2. While on the calendar stone the god Huitzilopochtli is surrounded by eight partitions and twenty day-signs, in the ceremonial center he is surrounded by the four gates of each of the

major causeways and the four lines (symbolizing the four sacred
streams) that emanate from each corner of his temple pyramid
and lie diagonally between the causeways. Furthermore, he is surrounded by images of the *petlacontzitzquiquê* (holders of the mat
and the urns) and by the twenty calpolli sanctuaries. With the
Aztecs all these phenomena belonged to a complex symbolic arrangement in which the two terrestrial horizontal quadripartitions
as well as the vertical tripartition into heaven, earth and underworld were represented.

CHAPTER 12

Further Observations on the Aztec Arrangement

WE CAN considerably enhance our insight into the social organization of Tenochtitlan by comparing the results gained so far with
two other systems of spatial partition of calendric dates used by
the Aztecs. These systems are concerned with the thirteen-day
cycles and their patron gods and goddesses. Fortunately the associations between the 13-day cycles and their patrons have been
more fully described in the pictorial sources. Some of these codices
have come from the immediate surroundings of Tenochtitlan and
perhaps even from the city itself.

The *Codex Fejérváry-Mayer* shows a depiction of the two systems of spatial arrangement that were most commonly used in
central Mexico with regard to the 13-day cycles. One was a system in which the 13-day period that started with 1 cipactli (1
crocodile) and the 12 succeeding days were represented as in a
specific direction. The next 13-day period, beginning with ocelotl
(ocelot), is turned to the left. This pattern is repeated until all
twenty 13-day cycles have been shown, the final 13-day period
being 1 tochtli (1 rabbit), which ends the sequence. This continuous order of 260-day cycles consisting of twenty 13-day periods
is magnificently represented on the first folio of the *Codex Fejérváry-Mayer* in the shape like that of the cross of the Order of Saint
John. Each of the four diagonals is crowned with the glyph of one
of the four year-bearers (see fig. 4.2).

The other system, in which the 13-day cycles do not form a continuous sequence but are divided over the four quarters of the
ring, is shown on the same folio. Here 1 cipactli is placed in one
direction; the next 13-day period, 1 ocelotl, 90 degrees to the left;
the third period, 1 mazatl (1 deer) 180 degrees to the left of 1
cipactli; the fourth period, 1 xochitl (1 flower) 270 degrees to the

left; the fifth period, 1 acatl (1 reed), falling in the same quadrant as 1 cipactli, and so on. The final result is four groups of five 13-day periods, whose initial signs are shown on the *Codex Féjerváry-Mayer* next to the diagonal arms of the cross so that the correct order is apparent when they are read from the middle out to the circumference. Each 13-day period is accompanied by thirteen different aspects of gods or goddesses, since every individual combination of numeral and day-sign belongs to a specific deity. But among those thirteen deities there is always one who is more important than the others, or at any rate is given a more prominent position within the group. This deity, sometimes accompanied by another, is the patron of the entire 13-day period.

Table 12.1 lists the patron gods and goddesses of the 13-day periods as they appear in the pictorials and codices from the central Mexican plateau southeast of the Valley of Mexico and then as they appear in codices from the Valley of Mexico itself. It goes without saying that the sources from the valley are of the most importance for our purposes. They are the *Codex Borbonicus,* the *Florentine Codex* and the *Tonalamatl of Aubin,* plus additional data taken from Cristóbal del Castillo. Another important source is the *Codex Telleriano Remensis,* probably from the Cholullan area, which provides an identification of the special feast day of the patron deity within each 13-day period.

The two lists show a number of discrepancies; however, these are mainly the result of Eugène Boban's rather pretentious interpretation of the *Tonalamatl of Aubin.*[1] Most of the names that are different in the second list are actually no more than aspects or local manifestations of the gods and goddesses named in the first list. When we compare this system of periods and their patron gods with the system of days, a remarkable shift is apparent. The calpolli gods who are associated with the first ten day-signs are also the ruling gods of the first ten 13-day periods. But the eleventh god, Xochipilli, of the calpolli of Tlamatzinco and patron of the eleventh day-sign, ozomâtli, is not the ruling deity of the eleventh 13-day period. The patron of the eleventh 13-day period is the calpolli god of Izquitlan who is associated with the twelfth day-sign, malinalli (prairie grass). His name is Izquitecatl, the pulque god, also known by the names Ometochtli and Pâtecatl. The list continues regularly through the goddess Xochiquetzal, patroness of the twentieth day-sign and the ruling goddess of the nineteenth 13-day period. The twentieth and final 13-day period, like the nineteenth, is associated with gods of the calpolli of Huitznahuac, for both Huitzilopochtli and the deified sacrificial knife Itztapaltotêc were among its major gods.[2]

Tlamatzinco has been omitted from this system, but I shall explain below why this was done and how this calpolli will be compensated in the ritual ceremonial organization of Tenochtitlan. In the nineteenth century Eduard Seler attempted a calendric solution to this problem, but it is not a satisfying one.[3] Before this remarkable feature can be explained, it is necessary to integrate the different organizational systems of gods, dates, directions, and social groups that were ritually important in Tenochtitlan. We know that every calpolli except Tlamatzinco and Huitznahuac was directly associated either with two 13-day periods of the 260-day *tonalamatl* or in two ways with one of these periods. In the 260-day cycle every calpolli was combined thirteen times with the day-sign (independent of the accompanying number) of its own patron god(dess), and every calpolli, except Tlamatzinco and Huitznahuac had, during that period of time, one complete 13-day period dedicated to its god or goddess. Tlamatzinco was not associated with a specific 13-day period, but Huitznahuac had two periods and thus an extra 13 days. Therefore the other eighteen calpollis recognized 25 or 26 days to be of great ritual significance, namely the 13 days of its own 13-day period augmented by the 12 or 13 times that the one calpolli day (without a number) occurred in the other nineteen 13-day periods. The one-day variation occurred because the day-signs of some calpollis were repeated once within the 13-day period dedicated to their own patron god or goddess. Therefore, one day with a specific numeral and day-sign coincided with one of the thirteen times that its own day-sign appeared in the 260-day *tonalpoalli*. This was not the case in some calpollis whose day-signs did not appear in their own 13-day periods. The reader who finds it difficult to understand this must realize that the Aztecs used twenty different day-signs. Therefore there are seven signs more than the thirteen that belong to a particular 13-day period. The specific calpolli day (without a number) could belong to the 13 days of "its own" period or to the 7 other days.

It is also important to remember that a single calpolli was rarely the only one to have ritual associations with a particular day but almost always shared the day with another calpolli. When, for instance, the calpolli of Tzonmolco celebrated the day 1 coatl, the day of Ohtlimelahuac, the god of the merchants, the calpolli of Coatlan also had a feast day because the day-sign coatl belonged

Table 12.1. *Survey of the Patron Gods and Goddesses of the Twenty 13-Day Periods of the Tonalpoalli*

First Days of the 13-Day Periods	Patron Gods and Goddesses		
	According to *Borgia, Cospi, Telleriano-Remensis*, and *Vaticanus-Rios* Codices	According to *Borbonicus, Tonalamatl of Aubin, Florentine* Codices, and *Castillo*
1. 1 cipactli (1 crocodile)	Tonacatêcuhtli, Tonacacihuatl	Quetzalcoatl*
2. 1 ocelotl (1 ocelot)	Quetzalcoatl	Titlacahuan, Quetzalcoatl, Tonatiuh, Chicomexochitl
3. 1 mazatl (1 deer)	Tepeyollotli	Tezcatlepoca, Tepeyollotli, Cihuapipiltin, Izquitecatl
4. 1 xochitl (1 flower)	Huehuêcoyotl, Ixnextli	Huehuêcoyotl, Macuilxochi-quetzalli
5. 1 acatl (1 reed)	Chalchiuhtlicue, Tlazolteotl	Atl-Chalchiuhtlicue, Tlazolteotl, Ehecatl-Quetzalcoatl
6. 1 miquiztli (1 death)	Nahuiollin (Tonatiuh) Metztli (Tecciztecatl)	Tonatiuh-Piltzintêcuhtli Tetzauhteotl (Tezcatlepoca)
7. 1 quiahuitl (1 rain)	Nahuiehecatl (Tlaloc)	Hueyi Tlaloc-Xopancalê Chicomecoatl, Cihuapipiltin
8. 1 malinalli (1 prairie grass)	Mayahuel, Cinteotl	Ometochtli, (Xochi) Meichpochtli Tetzauhteotl, Mayahuel, Omacatl
9. 1 coatl (1 snake)	Tlahuizcalpantêcuhtli, Xiuhtêcuhtli	Tlahuizcalpantêcuhtli, Quetzalcoatl, Quetzalmalinalli Xiuhtêcuhtli
10. 1 tecpatl (1 flintstone)	Tonatiuh, Mictlantêcuhtli	Mictlantêcuhtli, Teotlamacazqui, Tonatiuh, Huitzilopochtli
11. 1 ozomâtli (1 monkey)	Pâtecatl, Cuauhtliocelotl	Pâtecatl, Cuauhtliocelotl, Tonatiuh, Tlaltocaocelotl, Tepoztecatl, Cihuapipiltin

12. 1 cuetzpalin (1 lizard)	Itztlacoliuhqui-Tezcatlepoca	Itztlacoliuhqui, Teonexquimilli Tlazolteotl, Tlaltêcuhtli
13. 1 ollin (1 rolling movement)	Ixcuinan, Tezcatlepoca (as eagle)	Teoiztactlachpanqui, Ixcuinan, Tezcatlepoca
14. 1 itzcuintli (1 dog)	Xipe Totêc, Quetzalcoatl	Tlatlauhqui Tezatlepoca Xipe, Tonatiuh Piltzintêcuhtli, Coatlicue, Quetzalcoatl, Xiuhtêcuhtli
15. 1 calli (1 house)	Itzpapalotl	Itzpapalotl, Teoyaotlâtoa Huitzilopochtli, Teoyaomiqui-Cihuacoatl
16. 1 cozcacuauhtli (1 vulture)	Xolotl, Maculxochitl, Tlalchitonatiuh	Xolotl, Maculxochitl, Tlalchitonatiuh, Tlaloc, Citlalimicueyê
17. 1 atl (1 water)	Chalchiuhtotolin-Tezcatlepoca	Chalchiuhtotolin-Tezcatlepoca, Ahuilteotl-Tezcatlepoca, Quetzal-huexolocuauhtli, Chalchiuhtlicue
18. 1 ehecatl (1 wind)	Chantico-Cuaxolotl, Quetzalcoatl-Ceacatl	Chantico-Cuaxolotl-Chicunauhitzcuintli, Piltzintêcuhtli, Tlazolteotl, Xochiquetzalli, Tlaloc
19. 1 cuauhtli (1 eagle)	Xochiquetzal, Tezcatlepoca	Xochiquetzalli, Tlâtocaocelotl (Tezcatlepoca)
20. 1 tochtli (1 rabbit)	Itztapaltotêc, Xiuhtêcuhtli	Tetzauhteotl-Huitzilopochtli, Teotecpatl-Itztapaltotêc, Xiuhtêcuhtli

*It is disputable whether in this particular case the *tlâcuilo* ('writer') of the codex indeed meant to represent Quetzalcoatl in one of his better-known aspects as wind god or as introducer of culture. Here the god is more likely to be a representation of the god-creator, who as such completely corresponds with Tonacatêcuhtli.

to its calpolli goddess Chalchiuhtlicue (Jade Skirt). This gives us a much broader background for understanding a casual remark made by Sahagún's informants in their description of the *teucualo* ritual ("God is eaten") during the celebration of the Panquetzaliztli feast in honor of Huitzilopochtli:

Niman ye ic quixitiniâ	Then they immediately dissected
in inacayo in tzoalli;	his body made of maize dough;
in iyollo itech pohuia	his heart belonged to
in Motêuhczoma;	Motêuhczoma;
auh in occequi in imimillo	and some other parts of his body
in iuhqui yomiyo muchihua	which were served as his skeleton
tepan moyahua nemamaco;	were distributed among the people and given away;
omolotl in maco in Tlatilulcâ	two maize-cobs were given to the Tlatelolcas
ihuan ume in ipepechiuhca,	and also two lower limbs;
no omolotl maco in calpul-	two maize cobs were also
huehuetquê in Tlatilulcâ,	given to the calpolli elders in Tlate-lolco, the same things were also given
in Tenochcâ	to the people of Tenochtitlan,
auh zahtepan quimomamaca	and after this everything was given away
zan têcpantiuh,	in small pieces in a very orderly way;
cecexiuhtica in quicuâ,	every year again they eat it,
ce xihuitl ontlaxilacalli in quicua	in one year it is eaten by two tlaxilacallis
no oncalpoltin in calpolhuehuetquê	and also by the calpolli elders of two calpollis;
auh inacayo in tzoalli,	his [Huitzilopochtli's] body of maize dough
cenca zan achitoton	into very small parts,
zan tepitoton piztlatoton	only very little pieces and
yêhuan in telpopuchtin	parts of the body are eaten by
in quicuayâ	the young men
auh inin quicuaya	and he who is eating
mîtoa "teucualo"	is called "God is eaten"
auh in ye oquicuaquê	and those who have finished eating
motenehuâ "teupia,"[4]	are said to be "god-possessing."

The culminating point of the annual celebration of the Panquetza-liztli feast was at the end of the 20-day period of that name. The celebration began a few days before the end of the period and lasted until sometime in the following period. In a fifty-two-year cycle, the last day of Panquetzaliztli was each of the four year-bearers in turn, with one of the numbers I to XIII, so that not for another fifty-two years would the same number occur in combination with the same day-sign.

In a year II Acatl (II Reed), for instance, the fifteenth 20-day period Panquetzaliztli always ended in a day 7 acatl. This day belonged at the same time to the 13-day period that began with the day 1 mazatl and, as has been said before, belonged to Acatliacapan. The day 1 mazatl is then the fourteenth day of Panquetzaliztli. The 13-day period preceding 1 mazatl, which begins with the day 1 ocelotl, still belongs to Panquetzaliztli, and, as we know, this 13-day period was associated with Chalman. Thus in a year II Acatl, Acatliacapan and Chalman had many ritual obligations during Panquetzaliztli. It is very likely that in that year members of these two calpollis took part in the *teucualo* ritual.

Sahagún's informants say emphatically that every year each of two *tlaxilacallis* ate a maize cob representing a "human bone" and a lower limb, while two other cobs were given to the elders of two calpollis. Probably this is to be understood in the sense that the term *tlaxilacalli* (structures of the flank, belly houses) was used to refer to the group connected with the small sanctuaries of a 13-day period. When the same group emphasized the socioeconomic and administrative aspects as well as the general religious association with one or more calpolli gods and one particular day sign, it was termed calpolli. This would mean that Chalman, for instance, was both a *tlaxilacalli* and a calpolli. In early colonial records both terms occur in reference to similar groups in local communities and were evidently used as synonyms.[5] Then in colonial times, when the distinction between the pre-Spanish religious and ritual meanings of the two terms had diminished, either term was used to signify the colonial successors of the indigenous social groups. If the *tlaxilacalli* serving at the end of Panquetzaliztli and the preceding one were indeed the two groups performing the *teucualo* rites, then the succession of each of the twenty *tlaxilacallis* must have been an intricate one. This complexity is shown in table 12.2 the succession of ritual obligations during one bundle of fifty-two years. Within a single bundle of years all twenty *tlaxilacallis* were called on more than once to perform the *teucualo* rites. Each of the *tlaxilacallis* Huitznahuac, Coatlan, Tlacochcalco, and Cihuatêcpan was on duty six times, each of the others, five times. The four privileged *tlaxilacallis* were those of the gods Huitzilopochtli, Coatlicue-Chalchiuhtlatonac, Tonatiuh-Mictlantêcuhtli, and Mexîtli-Itzpapalotl, who are four aspects of the same Aztec god(dess) given in the order of their association with the four main points of the compass. Together they form the symbolic representation of heaven, earth, and underworld. This was an omnipresent expression of the foundation on which Mexican culture rested. The four special groups also included four of the *petlacontzitzquiquê*, ("keepers of the mat and the urns"), the progenitors of the calpollis. These are the sacred, almost divine ancestors Ocelopan, Tenoch, Mexîtzin, and Ahuexotl, who played important roles in the sagas about the founding of Tenochtitlan and Tlatelolco and represent the east, north, west, and south respectively (see chapters 4, 10). The first comparison of our tentative interpretation of the concept of *tlaxilacalli* and the relevant system of twenty *tlaxilacallis* in Tenochtitlan has thus produced an altogether satisfactory result (see fig. 12.2). Of course, a single comparison is insufficient for an acceptable degree of certainty about the correctness of the proposed system. Therefore, I shall now compare it with a number of calendar dates on which, according to historical sources, rituals for the consecration of a temple or some other important ceremonies took place. For this purpose it will be best not to go too far back in time. This elaborate system was probably not fully evolved before the establishment of the Aztec empire; so, for the purposes of this study, I shall not consider data from the time before the rule of Motêuhczoma Illuicamina. Further, a larger amount of pertinent data is available to us for the later period.

The first important date, then, is the final day of the 20-day period Hueyi Têcuilhuitl (Great Feast of the Lords) of the year I Tochtli (I Rabbit), the notorious year of famine (1454), in which the harvest was badly affected by prolonged drought. In the calendar of Tenochtitlan, the last day of the Feast of the Lords in a year I Tochtli is always the day 9 tochtli. This means that, according to our system, during the Feast of the Lords of 1454, the *tlaxilacallis* Acatliacapan and Apantêuhctlan had ritual obligations in the day count. For 9 tochli was the ninth day of the 13-day cycle beginning with 1 xochitl, which was dedicated to the god Huehuê-coyotl (Old Coyote) and thus was associated with Apantêuhctlan. The eleven days preceding 1 flower, which still were part of the Feast of the Lords, then belonged to the preceding 13-day cycle, which started with 1 mazatl and was associated with the god Tepe-yollotl (Heart of the Mountain) and the *tlaxilacalli* Acatliacapan.

Table 12.2. *The* Tlaxilacallis *and the* Teucualo *Ritual*

Year	Last Day Panquetzaliztli	Two *Tlaxilacallis*
II Acatl	7 acatl	1 ocelotl (Chalman); 1 mazatl (Acatliacapan)
III Tecpatl	8 tecpatl	1 tecpatl (Tlacochcalco); 1 ozomahtli (Izquitlan)
IV Calli	9 calli	1 ehecatl (Atempan); 1 cuauhtli (Ayauhcaltitlan)
V Tochtli	10 tochtli	1 miquiztli (Tlacatêcpan); 1 quiahuitl (Chililico)
VI Acatl	11 acatl	1 itzcuintli (Yopico); 1 calli (Cihuatêcpan)
VII Tecpatl	12 tecpatl	1 ocelotl (Chalman); 1 mazatl (Acatliacapan)
VIII Calli	13 calli	1 tecpatl (Tlacochcalco); 1 ozomahtli (Izquitlan)
IX Tochtli	1 tochtli	1 cuauhtli (Ayauhcaltitlan);* 1 tochtli (Huitznahuac)
X Acatl	2 acatl	1 quiahuitl (Chililico); 1 malinalli (Tezcacoac)
XI Tecpatl	3 tecpatl	1 calli (Cihuatêcpan); 1 cozcacuauhtli (Molonco Itlillan)
XII Calli	4 calli	1 mazatl (Acatliacapan); 1 xochitl (Apantêuhctlan)
XIII Tochtli	5 tochtli	1 ozomahtli (Izquitlan); 1 cuetzpalin (Têcpantzinco)
I Acatl	6 acatl	1 cuauhtli (Ayauhcaltitlan); 1 tochtli (Huitznahuac)
II Tecpatl	7 tecpatl	1 quiahuitl (Chililico); 1 malinalli (Tezcacoac)
III Calli	8 calli	1 calli (Cihuatêcpan); 1 cozcacuauhtli (Molonco Itlillan)
IV Tochtli	9 tochtli	1 mazatl (Acatliacapan); 1 xochitl (Apantêuhctlan)
V Acatl	10 acatl	1 ozomahtli (Izquitian); 1 cuetzpalin (Têcpantzinco)
VI Tecpatl	11 tecpatl	1 cuauhtli (Ayauhcaltitlan); 1 tochtli (Huitznahuac)
VII Calli	12 calli	1 quiahuitl (Chililico); 1 malinalli (Tezcacoac)
VIII Tochtli	13 tochtli	1 calli (Cihuatêcpan); 1 cozcacuauhtli (Molonco Itlillan)
IX Acatl	1 acatl	1 xochitl (Apantêuhctlan); 1 acatl (Coatlan)

Table 12.2 continued

Year	Last Day Panquetzaliztli	Two *Tlaxilacallis*
X Tecpatl	2 tecpatl	1 cuetzpalin (Têcpantzinco); 1 ollin (Xochicalco)
XI Calli	3 calli	1 tochtli (Huitznahuac); 1 cipactli (Coatlxoxouhcan)
XII Tochtli	4 tochtli	1 malinalli (Tezcacoac); 1 coatl (Tzonmolco)
XIII Acatl	5 acatl	1 cozcacuauhtli (Molonco Itlillan); 1 atl (Cuauhquiahuac)
1 Tecpatl	6 tecpatl	1 xochitl (Apantêuhctlan); 1 acatl (Coatlan)
II Calli	7 calli	1 cuetzpalin (Têcpantzinco); 1 ollin (Xochicalco)
III Tochtli	8 tochtli	1 tochtli (Huitznahuac); 1 cipactli (Coatlxoxouhcan)
IV Acatl	9 acatl	1 malinalli (Tezcacoac); 1 coatl (Tzonmolco)
V Tecpatl	10 tecpatl	1 cozcacuauhtli (Molonco Itlillan); 1 atl (Cuauhquiahuac)
VI Calli	11 calli	1 xochitl (Apantêuhctlan); 1 acatl (Coatlan)
VII Tochtli	12 tochtli	1 cuetzpalin (Têcpantzinco); 1 ollin (Xochicalco)
Viii Acatl	13 acatl	1 tochtli (Huitznahuac); 1 cipactli (Coatlxoxouhcan)
IX Tecpatl	1 tecpatl	1 coatl (Tzonmoloco); 1 tecpatl (Tlacochcalco)
X Calli	2 calli	1 atl (Cuauhquiahuac); 1 ehecatl (Atempan)
XI Tochtli	3 tochtli	1 acatl (Coatlan); 1 miquiztli (Tlacatêcpan)
XII Acatl	4 acatl	1 ollin (Xochicalco); 1 itzcuintli (Yopico)
XIII Tecpatl	5 tecpatl	1 cipactli (Coatlxoxouhcan); 1 ocelotl (Chalman)
I Calli	6 calli	1 coatl (Tzonmolco); 1 tecpatl (Tlacochcalco)
II Tochtli	7 tochtli	1 atl (Cuauhquiahuac); 1 ehecatl (Atempan)
III Acatl	8 acatl	1 acatl (Coatlan); 1 miquiztli (Tlacatêcpan)
IV Tecpatl	9 tecpatl	1 ollin (Xochicalco); 1 itzcuintli (Yopico)

Table 12.2 continued

Year	Last Day Panquetzaliztli	Two *Tlaxilacallis*
V Calli	10 calli	1 cipactli (Coatlxoxouhcan); 1 ocelotl (Chalman)
VI Tochtli	11 tochtli	1 coatl (Tzonmolco); 1 tecpatl (Tlacochcalco)
VII Acatl	12 acatl	1 atl (Cuauhquiahuac); 1 ehecatl (Atempan)
VIII Tecpatl	13 tecpatl	1 acatl (Coatlan); 1 miquiztli (Tlacatêcpan)
IX Calli	1 calli	1 itzcuintli (Yopico); 1 calli (Cihuatêcpan)
X Tochtli	2 tochtli	1 ocelotl (Chalman); 1 mazatl (Acatliacapan)
XI Acatl	3 acatl	1 tecpatl (Tlacochcalco); 1 ozomahtli (Izquitlan)
XII Tecpatl	4 tecpatl	1 ehecatl (Atempan); 1 cuauhtli (Ayauhcaltitlan)
XIII Calli	5 calli	1 miquiztli (Tlacatêcpan); 1 quiahuitl (Chililico)
I Tochtli	6 tochtli	1 itzcuintli (Yopico); 1 calli (Cihuatêcpan)
II Acatl	7 acatl	Again: Chalman and Acatliacapan, etc. —next bundle of years

*It is obvious that the two *tlaxilacallis* belonging to the calpolli of Huitznahuac were also called by two different names. Huitznahuac is, indeed, also called Ayauhcaltitlan.[38] Probably this name belonged to *tlaxilacalli* 1 cuauhtli (eagle) with the gods Ahuitzotl and Xochiquetzal. The *tlaxilacalli* 1 tochtli (rabbit) of Huitzilopochtli will then have been called Huitznahuac, like the calpolli.

According to Tezozomoc, by order of the king a great ceremony was held at the great temple, which was still under construction to persuade the gods to improve the bad weather conditions.[6] It can be assumed that such a ceremony was mainly addressed to the rain and fertility gods. And, indeed, the goddess of young maize, Xilonen, was worshiped during the Feast of the Lords. But a remarkable and, in fact, very convenient condition in that particular year was that the two groups charged with the rituals of the day count were also connected with the same gods and goddesses. The 13-day period 1 deer was dedicated to the rain god Tepeyollotl, a primordial guise of Tlaloc, who symbolized the clouds that clustered around the summits of the mountains of the ancestors. Fur-

thermore, the god Quetzalcoatl in his variant appearance of wind
was associated with this period because it was the force of the
wind that gathered the clouds around the mountaintops. Quetzalcoatl and Tlaloc were worshiped on the day 7 acatl of this period,
and in a year I Tochtli that day would be the fifth day of the Feast
of the Lords. The sixth day of that same 20-day period was 8 ocelotl,
which was dedicated to Tepeyollotl. In that year the day 12 tecpatl
was the tenth day of the Feast of Lords and was associated with
the earth god. The twelfth day of the Feast of the Lords was the
first day of the next 13-day period and with it began the responsibilities of the *tlaxilacalli* Apantêuhctlan. Their service began on
a day 1 xochitl, dedicated to the maize god Cinteotl, on which
the Feast of Flowers was celebrated. The day 8 mazatl, which
then coincided with the nineteenth day of the Feast of the Lords,
was another day for Tepeyollotl, and it was on 9 tochtli, the
twentieth and last day of the 20-day period, that the Feast of
the Lords proper was celebrated. The 13-day period 1 xochitl
belonged to the gods Huehuêcoyotl (Old Coyote), Ixnextli (Eye
of Ashes), and Xochiquetzal (Beautiful Flower), who respectively
symbolized dancing, intoxicating power, and power of rich growth.
The *Codex Telleriano Remensis* says about the god Huehuêcoyotl
and his 13-day period, 1 xochitl, that if, on the day 1 flower, in
the year I Rabbit, a rosebud opens on earth and then withers it is
considered to be a bad omen.[7]

Summarizing the above, we see that the *tlaxilacallis* whose responsibilities, according to my interpretation, fell during the Great
Feast of the Lords of 1454 were associated with both rain, earth,
and fertility gods and goddesses. Thus the day 1 xochitl in a year
I Tochtli appears to be of special significance for relief of the
drought conditions that apparently prevailed in years of the Rabbit. All this implies that the Feast of the Lords in 1454 must have
been a most appropriate time to hold a great religious ceremony
that would ensure a favorable crop. And that is exactly what happened, according to Tezozomoc.

Five years later there was another important dedication, that
of the *temalacatl*, the round sacrificial stone used in the ritual
contest in which brave and prominent prisoners were allowed to
fight Aztec officers. One foot of the prisoners was tied to a hole
in the center of the *temalacatl*; they were equipped with a wooden
bat that was used to ward off the attacks of their well-trained
opponents, who used weapons fitted with razor-sharp obsidian
blades. This *temalactl* and its *techcatl* (sacrificial altar) were the

focus of the so-called sacrificial offerings of gladiators. Orozco y Berra dates the inauguration of these attributes in 1459, which was a year VI Acatl. The dedication and the ritual itself took place at the Yopico temple and therefore in the calpolli of Yopico with its patron god, Xipe Totêc.[8] Therefore, the ceremony must have been held in the second 20-day period, Tlacaxipehualiztli (Flaying of People), which was dedicated to Xipe. But in the year VI Acatl, Tlacaxipehualiztli ends on 11 acatl. This means that in such a year this 20-day cycle partly coincides with the 13-day periods 1 itzcuintli and 1 calli, which in our system belong to the *tlaxilacallis* Yopico and Cihuatêcpan. Apart from the fact that here, too, Yopico and its god Xipe are involved, these *tlaxilacallis* are the two most important in the city quarter of Moyotla. The Yopico temple also belonged to this city quarter. In the year XIII Tochtli (1466), Motêuhczoma Ilhuicamina, or perhaps his successor, Atotoztli,[9] gave orders to lay the foundation for a large new temple of Huitzilopochtli. The work began on a day 1 tecpatl.[10] In our proposed system this is the first day of the 13-day cycle that belongs to the *tlaxilacalli* Tlacochcaloco and, therefore, to the gods Mictlantêcuhtli (Lord of the Realm of the Dead), Teotlamacazqui (Divine Maker of Offerings), and Tonatiuh (Sun). The day 1 tecpatl was a feast day dedicated to Huitzilopochtli within the *tonalpoalli*. Furthermore, any day tecpatl, no matter its number, always had to do with the southern calpolli of Cuauhquiahuac, for which one aspect of Tezcatlepoca was calpolli god. The Sun, the Divine Maker of Offerings, Death, and the Southern Tezcatlepoca can all be regarded as variant aspects of Huitzilopochtli. As noted above, Tlacochcalco was closely related ritually to the worship of Huitzilopochtli, and the calpolli of Cuauhquiahuac was a dependency of Huitznahuac. All these divine manifestations refer to aspects of Huitzilopochtli as Tetzauhteotl which were associated with the northern sun and the moon; that is to say, they refer to symbols having to do with projections of the underworld in heaven. It is natural that these attributes should be associated with the foundations of the temple and not with the structure itself. This comparison also seems to confirm our provisional system, a confirmation that is greatly strengthened by Chimalpahin's statement that the actual construction of the temple pyramid was not begun until the year I Acatl (1467).[11] In that year the 20-day period Panquetzaliztli, which was dedicated to Huitzilopochtli, ends in a day 6 acatl. That is the sixth day of the 13-day period 1 tochtli which was dedicated to Huitzilopochtli and his *tlaxilacalli* Huitznahuac. The day 1 tochtli was separately dedicated to Coatlicue (Serpent Skirt), the mother of Huitzilopochtli. In that year the previous 13-day period 1 cuauhtli, with its patron gods Tezcatle-poca-Ahuitzotl and Xochiquetzal, mainly associated with the other *tlaxilacalli* of the calpolli of Huitznahuac, Ayauhcaltitlan, also fell in Panquetzaliztli. This 13-day period contained the day 7 cipactli, on which the Feast of the Coming of the Eagles took place. The eagle was regarded as the *nahualli* of Huitzilopochtli.[12] One can hardly imagine a larger collection of variant aspects of Huitzilo-pochtli and his attributes. Therefore, the year 1467 was extremely suitable for the introduction, extension, and enrichment of the worship of this preeminent Aztec god.

In the year VIII Acatl, which approximately coincides with the year 1487, Ahuitzotl began a campaign against the independent region of Tziuhcoac, situated on the northeastern borders of the empire. Besides economic and military motives, the operation had a religious-ceremonial purpose: the Aztecs had to gather victims to be sacrificed during the consecration of the great temple in Tenochtitlan. Chimalpahin says that the conquest of Tziuhcoac took place on the day 1 miquiztli (death).[13] In a year VIII Acatl (1487) this day fell on the thirteenth day of the fifth 20-day cycle, Toxcatl, an annual feast in honor of the gods Tezcatlepoca and Huitzilopochtli. Moreover, that day was the first day of the ritual responsibilities of the *tlaxilacalli* Tlacatêcpan, which had the moon and the sun as its major gods. These two deities are important as-pects of Tezcatlepoca and Huitzilopochtli. The calpolli of Tlacatêc-pan, which belongs to the *tlaxilacalli* of the same name, was iden-tified with the administration of the empire and imperial authority; therefore, in that respect also 1 miquiztli was an appropriate day, even more so because the day miquiztli, whatever its accompany-ing numeral, was always associated with that calpolli.

The grand consecration ceremony of the great temple took place during the Raising of the Banners, the fifteenth 20-day period in which the important annual feast in honor of Huitzilopochtli was held. In 1487 (VIII Acatl) this feast fell between the days 7 ocelotl and 13 acatl, when the *tlaxilacallis* Huitznahuac and Coatlxoxouh-can were on duty. These two *tlaxilacallis* were associated with Huitzilopochtli and Tonacatêcuhtli, Lord of Our Existence. Ac-cording to the *tonalpoalli*, the day 13 acatl was a feast day for the Sun God, a well-known manifestation of Huitzilopochtli.

After the foregoing considerations, I believe that a comparison of the proposed system of twenty calpollis and twenty *tlaxilacallis*

Fig. 12.1. *Gladiatorial fighting on the temalacatl. Manuscript Tovar, pl. 27.*

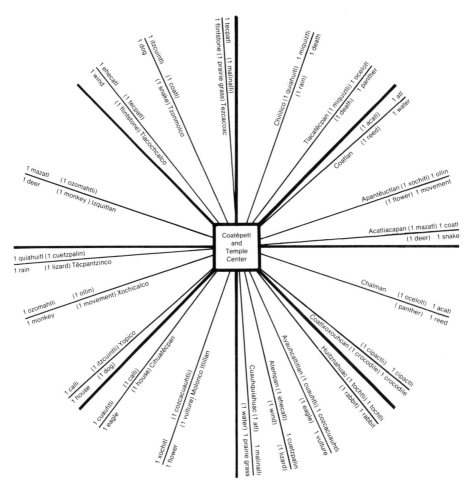

Fig. 12.2. *The* tlaxilacalli *feasts according to systems 1 and 2 of* Codex Fejér-váry-Mayer. *The inner circle gives the names of the 20* tlaxilacallis; *the middle circle gives their 13-day cycles according to system 1; the outer circle gives their 13-day cycles according to system 2.*

in Tenochtitlan, together with the scanty information available on the day dates of socioreligious historical events found in central Mexican sources, will demonstrate that the proposed system is valid. Such a comparison yields an overwhelming number of relationships that could be expected among the active groups, patron gods, and goddesses as mentioned in the system and their calendar dates. It corresponds not only with the above-mentioned dates but also with Chimalpahin's terminology in regard to social groupings, which further supports the conclusions.

Chimalpahin indiscriminately uses the terms *calpollis, tlaxilacallis,* and *calpollaxilacallis.*[14] These three different groups all occur in the system described above. Tlamatzinco is a calpolli, not a *tlaxilacalli;* Ayauhcaltitlan is a *tlaxilacalli,* not a calpolli, while eighteen other groups are designated as both calpollis and *tlaxilacallis;* therefore, according to a rule of word formation in Nahuatl, they would have been called *calpollaxilacallis.*

The survey below clearly shows the connections and relationships of the *tlaxilacallis:*

1. Coatlxoxouhcan	1
2. Chalman — Coatlan — Tlacatêcpan	3
3. Acatliacapan — Tzonmolco — Izquitlan	3
4. Apantêuhctlan — Xochicalco — Molonco Itlillan	3
5. Coatlan — Cuauhquiahuac — Chalman	3
6. Tlacatêcpan — Chililico — Chalman	3
7. Chililico — Têcpantzinco — Tlacatêcpan	3
8. Tezcacoac — Tlacochcalco — Cuauhquiahuac	3
9. Tzonmolco — Yopico — Acatliacapan	3
10. Tlacochcalco — Atempan — Tezcacoac	3
11. Izquitlan — Xochicalco — Acatliacapan	3
12. Têcpantzinco — Atempan — Chililico	3
13. Xochicalco — Apantêuctlan — Izquitlan	3
14. Yopico — Cihuatêcpan — Tzonmolco	3
15. Cihuatêcpan — Ayauhcaltitlan — Yopico	3
16. Molonco Itlillan — Ayauhcaltitlan — Apantêuhctlan	3
17. Cuauhquiahuac — Coatlan — Tezcacoac	3
18. Atempan — Tlacochcalco — Têcpantzinco	3
19. Ayauhcaltitlan — Cihuatêcpan — Molonco Itlillan	3
20. Huitznahuac	1
Total	56

Until now we have not dealt with the second system, that of the spatial order of 13-day periods, which is also represented in the *Codex Fejérváry-Mayer.* It probably served three ceremonial purposes. First, it gave each *tlaxilacalli* its own association to a particular direction within the city quarter to that it belonged, which could also be applied in the first, continuous system. Second, this second ordering system created pairs of *tlaxilacallis,* a significant factor in the strongly dualistic Mesoamerican world view. Third, the combination of the two systems into a single system yields eighteen groups of three *tlaxilacallis* and two independent *tlaxilacallis,* namely, those of Huitznahuac and Coatlxoxouhcan. Thus this integrated system shows $3 \times 18 + 2 = 56 = 8 \times 7$ ceremonial positions, which may have been associated with the eight sectors of the city (see fig. 12.3). The ritual importance of the three hearth stones is well known,[15] and it is possible that the Aztecs associated the groups of three *tlaxilacallis* with this basic pattern.

Finally, there is another important connection between the specific social groups and time count, namely, that which existed within the counting of years *(xiuhpoalli).* Eighteen of the twenty annual feasts held during the eighteen 20-day cycles fell each completely at the end of its cycle. The remaining two were held also at the midpoint of a cycle. Each of these annual feasts was associated with particular deities and the calpollis, *tlaxilacallis,* and vocational groups associated with them, and it seems that the imperial nobles played a relatively more important role in them than they did in the celebrations and ceremonies connected with the day count. Other corporate groups in Aztec society, such as vocational groups, and social groups such as *macehualtin* and poor people, also played an important part in these feasts. In general it can be said that the rites and ceremonies of the annual feasts were externally directed and symbolized the relationship of the population of Tenochtitlan to the outside world whereas the feasts of the day count were mainly internally directed. To put it another way, the annual feasts related mainly to the external system, and the feasts of the day count related mainly to the internal system.

The most important historical sources for all kinds of particulars about the feasts connected with the counting of years are the *Florentine Codex,* Sahagún's great work, the *Codex Telleriano-Remensis,* the *Codex Vaticanus-Ríos,* and the works of Diego Durán. The descriptions in these sources of the feasts and their rites differ in many respects. They are not contradictory, but they emphasize different gods, groups, and activities and consequently have different perspectives. Thus none of the descriptions that have been preserved can claim to be complete, notwithstanding the fact that they often go into great detail. On one level these different perspectives given to the subject make them more difficult to compare; on another level they greatly enhance our knowledge of the Aztec social system by complementing each other in many respects.

In the following surveys I represent the ways in which, according to the sources used, the calpollis, guilds, and other groups in and outside Tenochtitlan cooperated in the feast celebrations of the solar calendar. There is little reason to assume that the enumeration of the events discussed is complete in all these sources, but even so the material is extensive enough to draw some important conclusions. Twelve accounts mention some group from outside Tenochtitlan participating in an annual ritual. These accounts refer to the following population groups: Têcpanecs, mentioned four times; Tlatelolcas, three times; Xochimilcas, two times, and Acolhuas (Tetzcocas), Tlaxcaltecas, Huexotzincas, Otomis, and perhaps Huaxtecs (Cuextecâ), each mentioned once. It is worth noting that the Otomis are mentioned only once as a specific group. As for the Cuextecâ (Huaxtecs), it is unclear whether the Cuextecâ mentioned in the *Florentine Codex* and by Durán were the ethnic group or individuals who had particular functions. In twenty-five instances the sources mention special participation by a vocational group in the celebration. Military officers and merchants each participated six times; the organization of pulque makers had obligations three times; medicine men and midwives, twice. The following eight groups apparently had only one ritual obligation: flower arrangers, carpenters, cabinet makers (shrine workers), painters, draftsmen, scribes, jewelers, female weavers, female embroiderers, salt extractors and sellers, and hunters. Military officers and merchants are cited as participating occupational groups in almost half of the celebrations.

Rarely in early colonial records were the participating calpollis and *tlaxilacallis* mentioned by name. Their specific participation must be inferred in most cases from references to the calpolli temple, the deities, or priests serving that calpolli or *tlaxilacalli*. However, a number of calpollis and one *tlaxilacalli* are specifically mentioned: the four central calpollis, Huitznahuac, Ayauhcaltitlan, Chalman, Atempan, Coatlan, Chililico, Tzonmolco, Tlacochcalco, Tlamatzinco, Izquitlan, and Yopico. If we count each time the name of a temple, god, or priest is mentioned in the historical sources, we arrive at a total of eighty-three instances of participating calpollis or *tlaxilacallis*. Chalman, for instance, is mentioned ten times as having an annual function in the celebration of one of the calendar feasts. Huitznahuac, Coatlan, and Tlamatzinco are each men-

Table 12.3. *The Corporate Groups and Their Involvement in the Feasts of the 20-Day Cycles*

Calpollis and/or *Tlaxilacallis*	Number of the Feast	Number of Rites
I. 1. Huitznahuac	II, V, VIII, IX, XI, XII, XV	7
2. Ayauhcaltitlan	I, V, XIII, XV, XVI	5
3. Coatlxoxouhcan	IX	1
4. Cuauhquiahuac	VIII, XI	2
II. 5. Chalman	I, II, IV, VIII, IX, X, XVI(2×)	8
6. Atempan	IX, XI(2×), XIII	4
7. Tecanman*	II, V	2
Total, Zoqui(a)pan—Teopan—Xochimilcâ		29
III. 8. Tlacatêcpan	II,XVII	2
9. Apantêuctlan	—	—
10. Acatliacapan	VI, VIII, X, XIII, XVI	5
11. Coatlan	I, III, VI, X, XIII, XIV, XVI	7
12. Chililico	I, II, III, VI, XVI, XVIII	6
Total, Atzacoalco		20
IV. 13. Tlacochcalco	V	1
14. Tzonmolco	II, VIII, X, XII, XVIII(2×)	6
15. Tezcacoac	II, VIII, IX, XIII, XVIII	5
V. 16. Izquitlan	X, XIV, XV	3
17. Tlamatzinco	IV, IX, X, XII, XIV(2×), XVII	7
Total, Cuepopan—Tlaquenchiuhcan		22
IV. 18. Yopico	I, II, III	3
19. Xochicalco	V	1
VII. 20. Cihuatêcpan	V, VIII, IX, XIII	4
21. Molonco Itlillan	II, VII	2
22. Têcpantzinco	VIII, IX	2
Total, Moyotla		12

Vocational Group	Number of the Feast	Number of Rites
1. *Pochtecâ-oztomecâ* (merchants)	II, IV, X, XII, XV, XVIII	6
2. *Tiacahuan* (regular soldiers)	V, VIII, IX, X, XI, XV	6
3. *(Têcu)tlachicquê* (wine-makers)	XIV, XV, XVIII	3

Table 12.3 continued

Calpollis and/or *Tlaxilacallis*	Number of the Feast	Number of Rites
4. *Titicî, Tepâtin* (midwives, medicine men)	II, XI	2
5. *Xochimanquê* (flower arrangers)	III	1
6. *Cuauhxinquê* (carpenters)	X	1
7. *Cuauhtlâcuiloquê* (cabinet workers)	XIII	1
8. *(Tlâcuiloquê* (painters, clerks)	XIII	1
9. *Iztachiuhquê, Iztatlacâ* (extractors of salt, sellers of salt)	XII	1
10. *Teocuitlachiuhquê* (gold- and silversmiths)	XIII	1
11. *Ihquitquê* (weavers)	XIII	1
12. *Tlamachihuanimê* (embroiderers)	XIII	1
13. *Aminimê, anquê* (hunters)	XIV	1
Total		26

Group from Outside the City	Number of the Feast	Number of Rites
1. Têcpanecâ	IV, IX, X, XI	4
2. Tlatelulcâ	II, VIII, XIV	3
3. Xochimilcâ	IV, VIII	2
4. Tetzcocâ, Acolhuâquê	IV	1
5. Tlaxcaltecâ	IV	1
6. Huexotzincâ	IV	1
7. Otomî (Otoncâ)	XIV	1
8. Cuextecâ	XI	—
Total		13

Source: Based on *CF, CFM, CVR,* and Durán.
*The name of a *calmecac* and temple belonging to Chalman-Atempan.

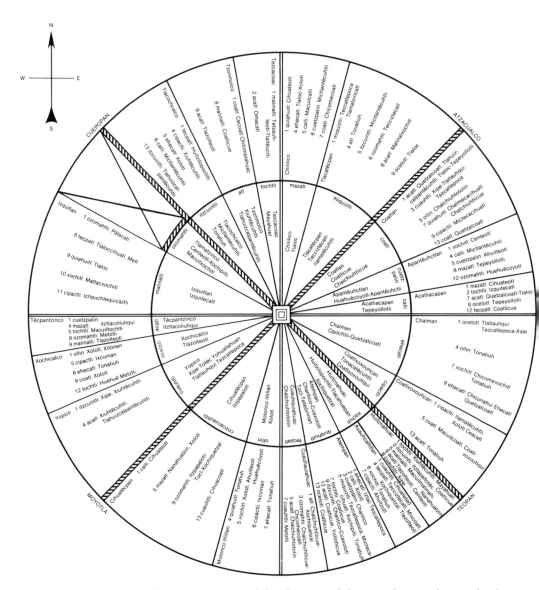

Fig. 12.3. *Spatial representation of the division of the population of Tenochtitlan into twenty-one corporate groups (calpollis and/or tlaxilacallis) and their relevant gods and goddesses. In the inner circle are the calpollis and their gods and goddesses. In the outer circle are the tlaxilacallis and their main tonalpoalli celebrations. According to AC, p. 52, Mixcoatl, Tozpan, and I'huitl are the gods who symbolize the three hearthstones. This statement suggests that the social groups in Tenochtitlan were divided into three larger groups of seven, of which Tlamatzinco Cuauhquiahuac and Apantêuhctlan were the last and most important. Apantêuhctli belongs to the Mimixcoâ; cf LS, p. 352.*

tioned seven times and thus share second place. The *calpollaxila-calli* Apanteûctlan is not mentioned at all and thus comes last. The following survey includes the nineteen *calpollaxilacallis,* the calpolli Tlamatzinco, and the *tlaxilacalli* Ayauhcaltitlan organized according to their original ethnicity. Although Ayauhcaltitlan was a dependency of the "Mexitin" calpolli of Huitznahuac, this tlaxila-calli was so bound up with the worship of Tlaloc and Tezcatle-poca-Xochiquetzal that, in my opinion, it pertains especially to the Toltec-Chinampanec minority of Huitznahuac. Using as a basis previous explanations given in this book I have placed Cihuatêc-pan, which is often represented as being "Toltec-Aztec," with the Mexitin groups.

It is notable that the Toltec-Chinampanec groups had twice as many ritual obligations as the Mexitin groups. About one-sixth of all the above-mentioned duties that belonged to these groups were performed by the four central *calpollaxilacallis.* Since ritual systems are usually conservative, the important part played by the four central *calpollaxilacallis* reveals the considerable influence of these comparatively young corporate groups of multiethnic composition.

Almost one-tenth of the roles were performed by the originally Têcpanec calpolli Tlamatzinco, which more than makes up for its exclusion from the *tlaxilacalli* system. At first glance the insignificant representation of the Otomi groups in the calendar feasts seems remarkable, especially in the case of the important *calpolla-xilacalli* Tlacochcalco. One explanation might be the prejudice held by highly advanced Mesoamerican cultures against the more "primitive" religion of the Otomis. Another possible reason is the close identification of this ethnic group with commoners, particularly the poor.

As we know, the fact that the Otomi were poorly represented can hardly be the result of neglect and suppression, for on the whole relations between Nahuatlacas and Otomis were good, and they were almost always on friendly terms. Moreover, the Aztecs applied the term "Otomi" to a brave warrior, which indicates that they were respected in battle. It is possible, however, that the calpolli of Tlamatzinco had an Otomi minority connected with the worship of Mixcoatl; in that case the Otomis would have been better represented in the celebration of the annual feasts than is apparent.

Table 12.4. *Participation of the City's Ethnic Groups in the Annual Feasts (According to* Florentine Codex, Codex Telleriano-Remensis, Codex Vaticanus-Ríos, *and Durán)*

Group	No.	Percent
Toltec-Chinampanec		
Chalman (including Tecanman)	10	
Atempan	4	
Coatlan	7	
Chililico	6	
Tzonmolco	6	
Molonco Itlillan	2	
Ayauhcaltitlan	5	
Total	40	48.2
Mexitin		
Huitznahuac	7	
Coatlxoxouhcan	1	
Tlacatêcpan	2	
Izquitlan	3	
Yopico	3	
Cihuatêcpan	4*	
Total	20	24.1
Têcpanec		
Tlamatzinco	7	8.4.
Otomî		
Tlacochcalco	1	
Xochicalco	1	
Apanteûhctlan	—	
Total	2	2.4
Central calpollis (mixed)		
Acatliacapan	5	
Tezcacoac	5	
Têcpantzinco	2	
Cuauhquiahuac	2	
Total	14	16.9
Total all groups	83	100.0

*Two are doubtful.

CHAPTER 13

Conclusions and General Characteristics of the Aztec Arrangement

FROM the foregoing analysis it is clear that Aztec historical perceptions were greatly influenced and even partly shaped by the Mesoamerican concepts of the symbolic interrelationships of gods, social groups, places, directions, and units of time. Early in the development of the empire, when Itzcoatzin and his corulers ordered the destruction of the old historical records, they undertook the task of rewriting the history of their people. After what has been said above, one would expect that the system of social and religious organization and its models were the starting points for writing that new history. Moreover, it was necessary that historiography must serve a political purpose. The various corporate groups in the young Aztec society, with their often divergent ethnic backgrounds, had to be integrated to form a single new social, religious, and administrative hierarchy. The history written for that purpose had suppressed, as a matter of course, the varied origins of the groups with some kind of Toltec background who participated in one way or another in the formation of the new Aztec empire. Therefore, the Aztecs integrated some completely different origin myths in one single narrative, the so-called pilgrimage from the obscure and mystical land of Aztlan which still lay before Chicomoztoc, the seven legendary caves of origin of the Mesoamerican peoples.

To achieve this, the traditions of the Chinampanecs, for example, who originated in the south, were drastically changed. By identifying the god Tetzauhteotl with Mexîtli and Huitzilopochtli, the Otomis, the Mexitin, and the Chinampanecs, the latter being partly of Toltec origin, found themselves combined into one rather complicated origin myth. The god of the Mexitin was also the god of the Chichimecs, the Chinampanecs, and the Toltecs, and he led them all from the north to the Valley of Mexico. The goddess Malinalxochitl (also named Cihuacoatl or Chantico) of the Chinampanecs became the sister of Mexîtli-Huitzilopochtli, although at first the goddess of the Mexitin (Itzpapalotl-Cihuacoatl) was in fact more closely related to Mexîtli. It is amusing to see how the Aztecs in their attempt to formulate their history conscientiously tried to retain important "actual events," handling them in a way that served their political aims. The historical opposition between Chinampanecs and Mexitin, for example, was not ignored; on the contrary, it was elaborated on in the Copil legends and at the same time represented as a struggle between the important calpollis of Chalman and Huitznahuac. However, Copil's daughter became the wife of the high priest of Huitzilopochtli, which in official Aztec history put an end to the violent struggle about a century earlier than was actually the case. Copil's mother, Malinalxochitl, had already been "left behind" in the vicinity of Malinalco, whereas in actual fact she and her followers originated in this area, which was a dependency of Colhuâcan.

Official Aztec history also had to find a reasonable explanation for the contradiction between the descent of the royal family and the historical importance of the Mexitin groups. Moreover, great emphasis had to be put on the "Toltec" origin of the royal house, for which purpose a model of the four points of the compass was applied to their past. The Otomis formed the earliest (autochthonous) part of the population whereby chief Tenoch ruled with Aatl-Mexitzin of the Mexi calpolli of Cihuatêcpan, who at the same time was the high priest of Itzpapalotl. Chief Opochtli Itztahuâtzin of Chalman had a son by a Toltec princess who was to become the future Acamâpichtli of Tenochtitlan. Acamâpichtli, as chief of Chalman, also became a priest of Itzpapalotl and consequently took over the role played by Aatl-Mexitzin. His rather obscure "aunt" (a term commonly used to indicate ceremonial kinship) Ilancueitl superseded the aristocratic Acacihtli family in the calpolli of Tlacatêcpan by virtue of her high Toltec status. But she was barren, and the daughter of Acacihtli, who was Acamâpichtli's second spouse, became, after all, the progenitress of the royal line. This ingenious solution provides for everyone and everything except historic fact. An ancient myth about the gods Quetzalcoatl (Chalman), Itzpapalotl (Cihuatêcpan), Metztli and Tonatiuh (Tlacatêcpan), and Mictlantecûhtli (Tlacochcalco) seems to have been applied to explain Aztec prehistory.[1] The writers of the "official history" did not always succeed in composing a totally integrated story. In Tenochtitlan, for instance, two tales about the pilgrimage remained in circulation with either Iztacmixcoatzin or Huitziltzin as the mythical hero. Probably the Aztecs found little fault with such anomalies because their entire social system, even their whole society, abounded in such organizational contradictions. Realizing that the official Aztec history is not always true to historic facts, we should, however, bear in mind that it represented the historic developments much better than the later histories of Mesoamerica written or influenced by Europeans. If the Aztec historians tampered with the actual order of events and sometimes reversed causes and their effects, they at least pointed up that the most essential historic development in Mesoamerica was the rise and decline of separate corporate groups and their struggles for power. In the personalistic approach of western historians to Aztec history this overall theme was largely lost.

The Stone of Axayacatl shows an intricate network of groups inhabiting the most important city in the Aztec empire and together forming the most important part of Aztec upper social strata. But what does it tell us about the essential nature of that society? In fact, many things, and although there are still questions to be answered and new ones arising, a number of long-term controversies among Mesoamericanists can now be resolved or at least viewed in a new perspective. It is now possible to still the debate over whether Aztec society was composed of clans, as Bandelier and others would have it,[2] or whether, as Katz puts it, it was a class society in the process of formation.[3] Neither argument is valid. Kinship played an important part in Aztec society, as it did in all other Mesoamerican societies, but it never was the only, and seldom the decisive, factor determining social position. We have shown with historical examples that membership in a calpolli could be changed. In the formation of new calpollis it was usual for people to be involved who were not related to each other, even if a system of kinship afforded the models that were applied to the new organization.

Apart from the terms which referred to kinship and membership in corporate groups such as calpollis and *tlaxilacallis,* the Aztecs held a number of socioeconomic concepts that implied involvement with means of production, centers of power, and ceremonial centers. Within this context they used such terms as *macehualtin* (farmers, citizens), *mâyequê* ("right hands"), *têcpanpouhquê* (people connected with the local government center), *tlacohtin* ("bought ones"), and *cuauhpipiltin* (war nobles). These terms were not indications of "class" or "social rank," as Katz and others have claimed, but indicated a person's relationship to other individuals, groups, or institutions.[4] A person living in a central federal state of the Aztec empire was called *macehualli* if he did not belong to the nobility but was a member of a calpolli, and he was entitled to cultivate or lease a piece of arable land in the *calpollalli* (calpolli land) for his own profit. A person who belonged to a rich and powerful calpolli might have productive agricultural land at his disposal, hold a high office, and live in a comfortable house and yet still be a *macehualli*. Another *macehualli* might belong to a calpolli that was unimportant, lacking fertile land, and not connected with a high office, and he might hold a field that was too small for his needs and not very fertile. He held no important office in his *altepetl* (regional or local community) and probably lived in a poor *xacalli* (straw hut). Elsewhere in the Aztec empire the concept of *macehualli* might have still other implications, almost the same as those conveyed by the middle Mexican term *tlalmaitl, mâyectli* or even *têcpanpouhqui*.[5] A *mâyectli* (plural: *mâyequê*) or *tlalmaitl* was somebody who cultivated land or had it cultivated under the instructions of the landowner or the person who held it in usufruct. The *mâyequê* were often former *macehualtin* who, by subjugation after a conquest or a rebellion, had lost their rights as holders in usufruct of calpolli land, perhaps because the right of usufruct had been divided among the military nobles among the conquerors or because the fields had been taken as special tributary land, such as *yaotlalli* (war grounds to be used by the army), *teotlalli* (land of the gods, to be used by the temples and priests), *tlâtocatlalli* (land belonging to the state and to be used by the central government), *teûhctlalli* (land to be used by the local government) etc.[6]

The *mâyequê* could also be descended from *macehualtin* or even from noble families. Here and there, though certainly not everywhere, the scarcity of land was a result of the prolonged process of inheritance which created unprofitable smaller and smaller plots of land. In some places this problem was solved by applying the right of primogeniture or sometimes ultimogeniture or by some other restrictive system to exclude an ever-increasing number of people from the inheritance in the usufruct or ownership of limited land. These were not only descendants of *macehualtin* but also those of noble families who were further removed from the progenitor. However, the latter usually did inherit some items of value: mantles, art objects, houses, royalties, offices, trading or marketing rights, and so on.[7] This made it possible for *mâyequê* to become much richer and more powerful than *macehualtin* who simply had the right to cultivate or lease out land, and even to become more influential and powerful than the members of somewhat poorer noble families who had inherited land. Before the coming of the Spanish conquerors, the *mâyequê* in central Mexico numbered about 30 percent of the total population.[8]

The *têcpanpouhquê* (people connected with the local government center) were usually descendants of the indigenous nobility of subjugated territories. They were given power in the village and regional administrative centers as officials of lower and middle rank, and they cultivated the *têcpantlalli* (land belonging to the local government) allotted to the *têcpan* (local government center). Individual prestige and influence varied greatly, depending on the importance of one's *têcpan.*

The *tlacohtin* (bought ones) were a class of slaves who had not been able to meet their obligations. They could "sell" their labor to creditors of their own free will or be forced to do so by judicial verdict. There was a close relationship, precisely defined by law, between the "bought one" and his owner. We may assume that the *tlacohtin* were often exploited, but they could not be resold without their own consent, unless they had frequently violated the rules, in which case, they eventually ended up on the block of a recognized slave market. Many *tlacohtin* were domestic servants, estate managers, artisans, farm laborers, and so on. Sometimes they stayed on in the service of their masters or mistresses long after they had repaid their debt. Some of these *tlacohtin,* who had become heads of domestic staffs of noblemen or supervisors on estates, had tenant farmers, *mâyequê,* or *tlacohtin* of their own and occasionally attained great prosperity.

The *cuauhpipiltin* (eagle's sons) were commoners, who by exceptional feats of arms or by distinguishing themselves in the flower wars were rewarded with a noble title and often with the usufruct of an estate, including the *mâyequê* belonging to it. Of these categories the *cuauhpipiltin* came closest to forming a separate social class. Among them there must have been great differences in power and prosperity, and generally their nearest relatives were commoners.

Although the above-mentioned social and economic categories did not form real social classes, yet in Aztec society there existed different status groups. There were the traditional landed and calpolli nobility and a high imperial nobility, both groups being hereditary. There were the high-status merchants and specialized artisans, the lower-status priests, the experts in the counting of days, and other specialized groups. Finally there were the lower-status groups, the farmers, hunters, fishermen, and members of other occupational groups of lesser importance. It is noteworthy, however, that the pre-Hispanic Aztecs regarded class and status distinctions as far less important than did the Spaniards and the indigenous noble families who came under European influence during colonial times. Class and status distinctions determined the character of Aztec society to a far less important extent than did corporate groups, such as calpollis, *tlaxilacallis,* and vocational groups. One might say that the Aztecs "hid" their class structure within their corporate social system. Since the calpollis formed a hierarchical system, the higher classes could "hide" in the high-status calpollis and so be designated by the same or similar titles as were their less prosperous compatriots in the less important calpollis.

Thus in Aztec society identification with one's own corporate group was much stronger than identification with one's class. The effectiveness of this system, with its built-in multifaceted ability to obscure and regulate contrasts, prevented class struggle. In Aztec society the greatest threat to the balance of power stemmed not from strong class distinctions and contrasts among the various ranks in society but from conflicting interests and rivalry among various corporate groups. A similar situation is still prevalent in many traditional Indian communities in Mesoamerica.[9] Within the nobility a certain degree of conflict existed between the state nobles with their imperialistic pretensions and the more indigenous nobility with their parochialism. Conflicts also arose in relations between the imperial nobility and the powerful vocational groups, particularly the merchants. I do not know of any example from Aztec history in which such distinctions alone led to large-scale violent clashes, but competition and conflicting interests between corporate groups often led to outbreaks of violence.

On the other hand, I must acknowledge that the marginal groups in the Aztec empire are underrepresented in the historical sources. During the Spanish conquest, Cortés's troops were joined by masses of Indian auxiliaries whose main objectives were plundering and marauding.[10] Therefore Jerome Offner may be right when he says that the significance of the private sector of the Aztec economy has been underestimated and that the governmental impact on society was more limited than others have claimed.[11]

In pre-Hispanic times, as from the Conquest until now, problems concerning the ownership, use, and management of land have greatly contributed to the growth of conflicts between groups. Historical records mention many instances of land dispute, yet this is only a minor representation of the total number and degree of such tensions between competing corporate groups or between such groups and between individuals and their dependents. Most such disputes were between nobles and those in their service.[12] The population density of the Aztec empire by the time of the Conquest plus the fact that the empire's natural resources had been almost exhausted suggest that the scope and seriousness of the land problem can hardly be exaggerated. A broader insight into this serious complex of tensions in Aztec society can be gained by considering the arrangements and regulations concerning the ownership and use of land in the empire. As early as 1955, Kirchhoff, in a publication that has often been overlooked, showed that the Aztecs recognized three main types of land.[13] Torquemada had recorded them in his description of Aztec maps of agricultural plots in which he identified three categories of land: calpolli lands *(calpollalli),* lands of the principals *(pillalli),* and lands that produced income for the king and his court *(têcpantlalli).*[14]

The historical sources mention at least six other types of land (some of which have already been discussed), but these should be regarded as subdivisions of the three major types. The obvious conclusion is, therefore, that the total acreage under cultivation in the Aztec empire was divided into communal land, land belonging to the nobility, and land belonging to the state.

To understand the prevailing conditions, it is essential to know how land was distributed and what rights and privileges the members of the corporate communities, the nobility, and the state had in the use of it. Much research has been done on this question in recent years, and from a number of excellent publications we can form a fairly clear picture of the distribution of economic power in some parts of the Aztec empire.[15] It is difficult to draw general conclusions, however, since in the sixteenth century there were apparently striking differences in the control of land in Cuauhtinchan, Huexotzinco, and the Valley of Mexico. In the Valley of Mexico the management of the *calpollalli* (communal land), was a widespread economic institution on which about half of the population depended for subsistence. In Toltec times the calpolli was probably the major form of land use for the whole region, but with the passage of time various conquering groups gradually encroached upon it. However, the calpollis continued to assert their power and acquired at least a share of the war profits, since some of the confiscated lands were added to the holdings of the calpollis and were not designated *pillalli* or *têcpantlalli.* Thus in the central Aztec states the administrative unification and expansion of the central government system did not result in such a rapid decrease of calpolli land as it did in the more remote regions, where the calpollis of the conquerors were not given a share of the land captured from the enemy but had to be satisfied with the war spoils they could carry, because the lands in the remote provinces were too far away to be tilled from the Valley of Mexico. Moreover, recent ethnohistorical studies of the Cuauhtinchan area prove that the introduction of calpolli control and use of land occurred only in Toltec or strongly "Toltecized" communities and was, therefore, far more common in the Valley of Mexico and other areas with a strong "Toltecized" administration.[16]

It is remarkable, however, that the Aztec imperial administration generally supported claims to land made by the nobles who belonged to ethnic minorities such as the Chochos or Pinomê in what is now south Puebla at the expense of the interests and claims of Toltec groups.[17] The Aztec central government, which had always claimed a Toltec background, preferred to take the side of noblemen who were of foreign extraction instead of supporting the related corporate Toltec calpollis. This indicates that the imperial administration was not entirely happy with the traditional institution. Furthermore it agrees with my assessment of the rise in power of imperial noblemen and the simultaneous decline of the traditional calpolli nobility. . . . Clearly the increase in the land holdings of the government and of the imperial nobility in the conquered territories was at least partly at the expense of the calpollis, steadily reducing farmers to a position of dependence on an administrative body or a noble family. This dependence may have been of a very direct nature; that is to say, it was imposed on the people concerned as a consequence of conquest, and in such instances the people became *têcpanpouhquê* (people connected with the local government center), *mâyequê* (right hands connected with a noble estate) or *têccalêquê* (members of manors belonging to noblemen).

Dependency may also have evolved without being directly imposed. Loss of land or expropriation of land as a result of conquest forced many farmers to enter the service of administrative bodies as tenant farmers or as servants in noble households if they did not have enough land of their own or calpolli land. Servitude was usually agreed to in exchange for the right to cultivate a small piece of land for private use. The tenant would also undertake various obligations, such as working as a farm laborer on government land or that of a nobleman: helping produce articles of home industry, which the patron noble family delivered as tribute; doing various kinds of forced labor; or serving as a low-status official. The wife and other members of his family might also be involved in these conditions of dependency. In 1538 this pre-Spanish system was still existent in the province of Tlahuican (more or less the same as the present state of Morelos). Detailed colonial records provided Carrasco with the data needed to analyze social relations at the lowest levels of Aztec imperial society. In a census of 1551 carried out in the neighborhood of Yautepec 13,899 family heads were reported for one community. Of these, 35 percent were tenant farmers; 2 percent of this 35 percent worked the lands of the king—a kind of "government land"—17 percent worked on the estates of noblemen, and another 16 percent worked the fields of other *macehualtin*. Only 2 percent of the ordinary citizens had no part in land cultivation. The other 63 percent were taxpaying farmers with their own land.[18]

In archival documents tenant farmers were referred to by several different terms that probably related to the various ways they were involved with land use. There may also have been local differences in the terms used. The Aztec term *momilcohuiani* ("he who rents arable land for his own use") was almost the same as our concept of tenant farmer, but there were several other classifications, such as *itech pouhqui* ("belonging to him or her," i.e., the noble lord or lady), *iicniuh* ("his or her friend"), *initla nemi* ("he or she who lives in his or her house"), and *itequitcauh* ("he or she who pays taxes to him or her"). The picture becomes even more complex when we consider the distinction between local government institutions relating to land use and *têccalli*, agricultural estates belonging to noble families. Some of these *têccalli* were also local or regional centers of administration and were usually continuations of autochthonous pre-Aztec administrative systems. Of course, other administrative bodies had been introduced by the central government, for example, the *calpixcacalli* (tax collector's building).

The staff of the *calpixcacalli* usually consisted of officials whose family line had originated in one of the three central federal states. In the area studied by Carrasco, the *calpixqui* himself, his staff, the *motititlanquê* (investigative officers), and the *tlayacanquê* (leaders) were individuals from Mexîcayotl.[19] There were exceptions, for instance, the wife of the defeated king of Coaixtlahuacan was appointed *cihuacalpixqui* (female tax collector) soon after the capture of that important market town by Motêuhczoma Ilhuicamina in the year 1458.[20]

The *calpixcacalli* was sometimes also called *texancalli* (building of the bricks of the people or building of papers made of tree leaves) when it was the administrative center for public works that were carried out by forced labor for the communities.[21] According to Aztec practice, physical labor was a form of tax payment.

The smallest unit larger than a nuclear family dwelling *(calli)* was the *ithualli* (court), which consisted of a group of houses built around a courtyard or on a common plot. Usually an *ithualli* was occupied by the head of an extended family, who lived there with relatives and others who were in his service or dependent on him.

A number of *ithuallis* formed a small calpolli, or *chinamitl.* Several *chinamitl* formed one large- or medium-sized calpolli, and some of these formed a large calpolli or village quarter. A number of large calpollis together might be called an *altepetl* (regional community). The officials connected with the lowest units above family level, that is, the *chinamitl* or small calpolli, were the lowest in the administrative hierarchy and were called *centecpanpixquê* (chiefs over twenty families) and *macuiltecpanpixquê* (chiefs over one hundred families). These units were organized on the principle that a *centecpanpixqui* could normally mobilize twenty adult men for military service or forced labor. The number twenty was a typical number. The actual number of families in service might vary. The same is true for the "chiefs over one hundred." Under them could serve three, four, six, or even seven chiefs over twenty instead of the ideal five. In the medium-to-large-size calpollis there were many officials, such as *tetêuctin* (local or regional administrators), *achcauhtin* (military commanders), *tequihuâquê* (imperial office-bearers charged with specific tasks), and *calpixquê* (tax collectors)—in short, offices that also occurred at the *altepetl* level or at least had equivalents at that level.

In the *altepetl* organization there were in addition to the functionaries above many others, and together they formed the regencylike, oligarchical, dualistic administrative system characteristic of the traditionally Toltec form of government. The relation-ship between nobles and commoners in the administrative system is not clear; probably here too there were important regional differences.

The *Florentine Codex* suggests that the central federal state of Mexîco knew a system of dual representation of hereditary nobility and others at nearly all levels of the hierarchy. In the flower-wars province of Huexotzinco, however, most of the ad-ministrative offices from the level of "chiefs over a hundred" up-wards were held exclusively by noblemen.[22] There tenant farmers made up at least 69 percent of the population, but the province had to cope with a situation similar to that found on a larger scale in the entire Aztec empire. In the central area of the prov-ince only half of the population consisted of "tenant farmers," but in more remote areas the percentage varied from 85 percent in the Valley of Tetzmolocan in the north to almost 100 percent in the Valley of Atlixco in the south. The other half of the popula-tion of the central area and the remaining 15 percent in the north-ern part of the province were calpolli members. In 1560 there were still 120 calpollis in these two areas.[23]

Usually there were large groups of immigrants among the "tenant farmers." During the period between the Toltec disintegration and the establishment of the new Aztec central government, the migration of many small population groups was a rather common phenomenon that continued after that period, partly as a result of the central government's policy.

In Huexotzinco 20 percent of the working population depended partly or wholly on some form of home-craft industry. At least two-thirds of these artists were also tenant farmers, except among the *amantecâ* (feather-mosaic workers). Most of the merchants lived in Axcotlan, where there were about four hundred of them, fifty-four of whom were also tenant farmers. The village of Axcotlan had the lowest percentage (15 percent) of tenant farmers in the province. Most merchants had no other occupation, since their work as *quetzalhuaquê* (driers of ornamental feathers) was di-rectly connected with their vocation as traders.

In the flower-wars province of Huexotzinco, 14 percent of the population belonged to the nobility. This comparatively high per-centage is related to the special function of this province as a partner in the flower wars of the central Aztec states. The nobility was most strongly represented in the central area (19 percent of the population) and had little representation in the outlying territories (7 percent in Tetzmolocan and 4 percent in Atlixco). This leads to the following rather unexpected generalization: the higher the percentage of tenant farmers within a section of the population, the lower the percentage of nobles. Within the hierarchical order of the nobility the *tetêuctin* ranked higher than the *pipiltin* who were dependents and lived on the estates of the *tetêuctin (têccallis)* or in large houses *(pilcalli)* outside but still dependent on these estates. A third category of *pipiltin* in this area consisted of lower-ranking officials of noble birth in the calpollis. Finally there were *pipiltin* who had lost their connection with any of the above-mentioned institutions and had become almost indistinguishable from the *macehualtin*.[24]

Now that the nature and composition of Aztec imperial society has been viewed against a broader background, it can be analyzed in greater detail. It is evident that Aztec imperial society was not sharply divided into categorical strata as is found in a caste society. Movements of individuals between different social strata appear to be gradual; again and again we come across instances of social roles falling between categories that are arranged according to a model of class stratification. This illustrates the fact there were no clear-cut class boundaries.

On the other hand, there were evidently groups or institutions which controlled the various means of production, especially the distribution of land. There were some large groups which were dependent on others for their share in the means of production. Some actual cases of rebellion by *macehualtin* against exploiting nobles and merchants have been recorded. This might be interpreted as the tentative beginnings of class struggle, but, in fact, these were rebellions against individuals who, even in the eyes of the ruling elite, had abused their power. Resistance was not directed against the institutions nor the upper class as such. The *Codex Huichapan* tells about a rebellion of ordinary farmers in 1432:

When the *macehualtin* spoke, they said that they had nothing anymore to eat, and that was why they had risen in rebellion, had taken up arms, and had killed the bad noble lords; that was what they said. As soon as the noble merchants had given them food to eat, they could pass freely through the area, said the impoverished farmers, who had risen in rebellion.[25]

One might consider such situations as the beginnings of a class society. But of what use is such a statement? Historical records do not justify the conclusion that such class relationships were a recent development in Mesoamerican societies, and other than these isolated examples there is hardly any indication of real class struggle. Most of the frequent conflicts over land took place between corporate groups or between traditional institutions that cut across class distinctions. Therefore, introducing the concept of class will not be sufficient to clarify the Aztec situation.

A much more productive approach is to direct attention to the concept of social mobility. An understanding of this process will deepen our insight into these pre-Hispanic societies particularly if it is considered against a greater sociohistorical background. Chimalpahin gives special insight into social relations at the end of the fourteenth century when Tenochtitlan had barely become a new administrative center:

I Tecpatl [1376]:
Ipan inin âcito Xochiyaoyotl
in ompa Chalco Atenco,
in iuh quîtoâ Amaquemequê,
chicuexihuitl in zan oc
Xochiyaoyotl in manca
in quimâciâ in Mexîcapipiltin,

zan oc quincahuayâ in Chalcâ,
mocuepayâ in inchan Mexîco.

Auh no ihui in quimâciâ
in Chalcâ pipiltin,
zan oc quincahuayâ in Mexicâ,
mocuepayâ in inchan Chalco;

ca zan oc in celtin
in macehualtin in miquiyâ.[26]

I Flintstone [1376]:
In this year the war of flowers
came to Chalco Atenco,
as those from Amaquemecan say,
only eight years it lasted
as a war of flowers;
the Mexican noblemen they had
    captured
were set free again by the Chalcas,
and they returned to their homes
    in Mexico.
And likewise when they captured
noblemen from Chalco,
the Mexicans let them go,
and they returned to their homes
    in Chalco;
for those who died
were only a few *macehualtin.*

One of the fundamental misconceptions about the Aztecs was created in the nineteenth century by Bandelier and other evolutionists who classified Aztec society as "clan democracy." This put them at the same level of social development in the theoretical model of the evolutionists as Iroquois society. Although it was not long before the model of social evolution was challenged, it continued to greatly influence later ethnologists and historians. This led to the rather generally accepted view that in the beginning Aztec society was strongly egalitarian or, if you like, "democratic," and that only later did tendencies arise leading to a more hier-

archical society and autocratic power. But Chimalphin's text quoted
above describes the situation before 1376, in the early days of
the Tlâtocayotl of Tenochtitlan, as one in which the dominant
position of Mexican calpolli nobles, along with their colleagues in
Chalco, enables them to provide human sacrifices to one another
without risk to themselves. This suggests the existence of systems
characterized by Max Weber as "patrimonial."[27] Under such circumstances, instances of social mobility must have been rare. But
we have already seen that a change was brought about in the
days of Itzcoatl and Tlacayelel. The new model of waging flower
wars often took a high toll of lives, especially among noblemen.
Tezozomoc and others tell us that many victims were members
of the highest imperial nobility, including the royal family.[28] In
contrast to the situation half a century before, the elite of the
new regime had to assert themselves constantly: social mobility
had greatly increased, successful *macehualtin* could become imperial nobles, and hereditary nobles could lose their prestige or
even their lives. Aztec society retained its hierarchical structure,
but it was no longer certain who would achieve the various positions in the Aztec hierarchy, since there were now greater opportunities for social promotion. Increased social mobility became
one of the tools in the Aztec arrangement that prevented outbreaks of class struggle. In another work, about the nature of
authority in the Aztec empire, on the basis of the forms of Aztec
rhetoric I have been able to formulate the following essential
characteristics of the Aztec regime:[29]

1. Government authority was paternalistic and compelled respect.

2. Government authority had to be exercised by officials who
were well balanced persons with the guarded wisdom of old men.

3. Government institutions had a dual structure.

4. Good government did not depend exclusively on the quality
and devotion of officials but depended also on the magic of fate.

5. Descent was not the only criterion for appointment to a position of authority; skill and experience were also considered.

6. The power of the sovereign government was made manifest
by the power of imposing the death penalty (supreme justice).

7. The legitimacy of and justification for the authority of the
state lay in its Toltec origin.

It is clear that the Aztec regime aimed for a strong oligarchy
that was committed to strict rules and that protected its people,

as much as possible, from any form of arbitrariness at the hands of the government. Furthermore, it appears that the Aztec arrangement was based on an intricate complex of social, religious, economic, and political structures through which it pervaded the whole society. It regarded the position of every corporate unit and to a certain extent that of each individual as essentially valuable to the whole system. Therefore, the annihilation of any group would not fit in with Aztec political ideology notwithstanding the pressures of overpopulation. The greatest threat to Mesoamerican peoples was, therefore, to come from abroad.

A last important and controversial question in Mesoamerican studies, which, in the light of our findings, we can help resolve, concerns the application of the tributes levied by the Aztecs. Several ethnohistorians have described Tenochtitlan as a tax-consuming city and look upon the Aztec empire as a piratical state that looted subjugated territories as tributary provinces without giving anything in return.[30] A seemingly convincing argument used in support of this thesis is that the total annual tax revenue in foodstuffs that filled the warehouses in Tenochtitlan would feed about 350,000 people, which is precisely the estimated population of the city.[31] Since this argument is based on numerical agreement, it appears to suggest a direct relationship between the quantity of tribute received and the size of the population. However, the historic development of Tenochtitlan makes this supposition untenable. In fact, Tlatelolco and Tenochtitlan were already densely populated centers of trade, horticulture, and industry before the Aztec empire was organized, and it was a certain degree of overproduction that enabled the Aztecs to expand their military and political power.

Moreover, we have shown that only a small part of the spoils of war and tribute found its way to the calpollis, that is to say, to the common people. The greater part of tribute in foodstuffs was kept in the state warehouses as stores in case of poor harvests, as reserves for the army, and as gifts for politically favored groups. Other goods received as tribute went to the government: the greater part was distributed among high ranking dignitaries, administrators, and the military elite. Raw materials such as cotton, gold, and precious stones were given to the vocational groups to be processed into final products, most of which were exported by the merchants. There is no doubt that tribute greatly strengthened Tenochtitlan's economy; however, the economy was not primarily dependent upon it. The real basis of the city's economy remained chinampa horticulture, cottage industries, and to a lesser extent fishing.

The still unresolved question of the actual importance of chinampa horticulture and its relation to the size of trade and industry prevents us from gaining a clear picture of the social and economic development of the Aztec empire. In a study of historical depth Calnek has provided an accurate picture of the socioeconomic conditions in Tenochtitlan.[32] He traces the development of chinampa horticulture and trade over the course of time. His conclusion is that chinampa horticulture was not the only factor that enabled Tenochtitlan and Tlatelolco to develop into large urban communities. He explains that in the second half of the thirteenth century these two Aztec towns utilized the natural resources found in their swamps and waters and sold their products in the neighboring markets. The sale of fish, waterfowl, vegetables, and small quantities of industrial products formed the basis of their economy. We may add that, at that time, the greater part of the population of the two sister cities consisted of calpolli members, because the low economic level of the cities did not attract many immigrants. There was some chinampa horticulture in and around the two towns early in their development, but it did not amount to much, since the hydraulic works necessary for large-scale horticulture were almost entirely lacking. Rather, it seems that, from the very beginning, the economic development of the Aztec empire proceeded from the expansion of trade and industry, supplemented with revenues from warfare. This last source of income at first influenced the Aztecs to serve other groups as auxiliary mercenary troops; later they began to make more and more conquests for themselves until finally they too were able to mobilize ethnically related as well as auxiliary foreign troops. So it appears that even in their early development the Aztecs practiced chinampa horticulture, which is not surprising, since part of their population was Chalmec; but they soon applied themselves to other typically Mesoamerican economic activities such as trade and industry. In the year VII Tochtli (VII Rabbit) (A.D. 1382) the country was struck by disastrous floods caused by heavy rainfall which destroyed many chinampas in Tlatelolco and Tenochtitlan. Consequently in the next year VIII Acatl (VIII Reed) famine struck the Mexîcâ, who were forced to eat algae and snails. It was not until X Calli (X House), 1385, that the water in the lakes dropped to the normal level, and by then the chinampas were unfit for use.[33] Apparently the Aztecs' response to their plight was not to repair and expand their chinampas but to increase their trade and enlarge their markets. The result was that by about 1415 most of the basic necessities of life were brought from the mainland in exchange for handicraft products and some game, fish, and other goods gathered in the lakes. Only during the rule of Itzcoatl (1426-40) did the Aztecs acquire large agricultural and horticultural areas on the mainland and begin to use serfs and tenants as laborers. From then on they were able to mobilize the labor necessary for large hydraulic works. Not until the end of Itzcoatl's rule was the chinampa area around Mexico extended. Large-scale development of chinampa horticulture in this area took place during the rule of Motêuhczoma Ilhuicamina (1440-67), when great dams were constructed that reached from the cities to the lakeshore. Also during this period a dike or dam was built that let the water pass slowly through scuppers. The dike lay east of Mexico across Lake Tetzcoco, to protect the waters around Tenochtitlan from an influx of saline water. As a result, the quality of the water around the two cities was greatly improved. Contrary to the theory of Karl Wittfogel,[34] the necessity for "hydraulic works" in Mexico did not cause the development of an empire, but was the result of this development. It was possible to build the great hydraulic works only after the empire had begun to develop and the concentration of population and centralization of government had taken place. It was only after a rapid increase in the population that the need for such works was felt.

This meant that the people of Tenochtitlan and Tlatelolco depended to a great extent on imported food. Soon these imports were distributed through two important regional markets established in the sister cities. At first imported food came almost entirely from the Valley of Mexico, especially from the chinampas around Xochimilco, Cuitlahuac, and Chalco. Later subtropical and tropical produce was introduced, such as fruits and cocoa, sometimes from remote parts of the empire. It is very important to establish that trade and industry enabled the citizens of Tenochtitlan and Tlatelolco to purchase most of the agricultural and horticultural produce they needed for their own use. Before the disaster of 1383 and afterward, during the imperial era, these imports were *supplemented* in considerable quantity by the cities' own chinampa gardens.

From this information it is clear that the rulers in Tenochtitlan did not use the bulk of the tax revenues to support people of the capital, because, as a rule, they had sufficient means to support themselves. For what, then, were the agricultural products received as taxes used? Before answering this question, we must distinguish among three groups of taxes. The first group included the revenues acquired by forcing subjugated or dependent population groups to deliver certain quantities of products to tax collectors at regular intervals, usually once every eighty days. This method of raising taxes has been recorded in the *Matrícula*, the *Codex Mendoza*, and the *Información* of 1554.[35] The second group of taxes consisted of the market taxes, taxes on handcrafted products made by vocational groups, and trade tariffs.

There was a third, even more important, kind of tax involving the yield from state farms. These farms had been acquired by conquest and were fertile lands or chinampas taken from the estates of the nobility and calpollis of conquered peoples that were reserved for state use. The state gave the usufruct of these lands to noblemen and to commoners who had been raised to the nobility by distinguishing themselves in war. Occasionally merchants were rewarded with use of such lands. The distribution of the yields from Têcpanec lands was the first step in this development. It is worth noting that the state gave only usufruct to favored members of the Aztec aristocracy, not ownership or management. Ownership remained in the hands of the state, and management of the land was carried out by government officials, who leased the lands to tenants or had them cultivated by serfs and slaves.[36] These officials also collected the rents or the yield of the lands and saw to it that the beneficiaries were paid. Calnek has been able to identify 100 such state-owned estates in central Mexico, which varied in size from about 15 to 100 hectares.[37] It is interesting to learn that even the land rent was paid not to individual noblemen but to the corporate organizations of nobles. The Tlalixtacapan estate, for instance, which was about 20 hectares, was divided into four parts. The yield from each part was paid to a group of nobles by descent and members of the military nobility in one of the four city quarters. The part connected with Moyotla was subdivided into plots of 0.44 and 0.66 hectare each, the yield of each part being paid to *tetêuhctin* (administrators of noble birth) and to *tequihuâquê* (state officials, predominantly members of the military nobility) in that part of the city.[38]

In the beginning of the sixteenth century about 10 to 15 percent of the total population of Tenochtitlan must have consisted of hereditary nobility and warlords, between 30,000 and 40,000 persons. The yield of about 2,500 hectares of high-quality state-owned lands must have been sufficient to provide this group with the necessities of life, but there was certainly not an abundance of everything. In addition to these provisions the nobility undoubtedly had other sources of income. Partly on their own initiative noblemen drew income from the advanced textile industry in which the women engaged in their own households. Furthermore, they received a share of government tax revenues as special rewards. These, however, consisted of luxury articles, not foodstuffs.

The foodstuffs paid to the government as taxes were stored, for the most part, in warehouses for use by the army and in other warehouses as food reserves. Some surpluses were probably sold in the markets. From its relationship with the merchants' guild, we know that the Aztec government also carried on trade or made investments in trading enterprises.[39] All in all the Aztec empire proves not to have been the piratical state that Katz would have us believe.[40] On the contrary, it had all the characteristics of a great administrative and trading center for which the government provided safe trade routes and a well-organized market system and looked after the welfare of the subjects of the Empire. Recent investigations have shown that the Aztec authorities built a much more extensive and efficient irrigation system for their agricultural lands than had previously been thought.[41] Nearly all the land that could be cultivated with the available technology was put under cultivation. This makes more plausible the enormous population density in the central provinces of the Aztec empire shown by Cook and Borah in several of their studies.[42] These large population figures were received at first with great skepticism by other scholars. The heated debate over this issue following publication of the studies has quieted, and the differences in projected population numbers have dwindled to a margin of a few million, as we can see from the calculations of Slicher van Bath.[43] By 1520 the Aztec arrangement had created a base of existence for at least 20 million people in central Mexico, an achievement that was not to be equaled until four and a half centuries later by means of a greatly advanced technology. The words attributed to one of the high priests of Huitzilopochtli in the *Crónica Mexîcayotl* can be said to characterize the Aztec arrangement:

> For arrows and shields have been given to me
> and warfare is my task;
> I shall proceed and behold all lands
> and I shall wait for people and meet them
> in the four main directions
> I shall give them drinks and food,
> for here I shall unite all the different peoples.[44]

The face of the imposing Tetzauhteotl Huitzilopochtli has a more benign expression than many would have us believe.

Appendices

Chronology of Aztec History
(After the Dispersion of Chapultepec)

(For the approximate years of office of the Aztec rulers, see fig. 9.4.)

1300–18	Dispersion of the Mexitin in the Valley of Mexico.
1318–50	Various Mexitin groups reunite in the swamps of Toltzalan-Acatzalan, joining the autochthonous Otomi and Chinampaneca (or Chalmeca) groups. Formation of Aztec society. Flower-war relationships with the Chalco state.
1350–76	Two Aztec entities (Tlatelolco and Tenochtitlan) led by calpolli aristocracy manifest themselves as new political and military forces with modest yet increasing economic opportunities.
1376	End of the regime of the traditional aristocratic calpolli oligarchy in Tenochtitlan, followed by the foundation of a Toltec-like central administration led by local Chinampanec nobles and Chichimec (Mexitin) collaborators. Beginning of the so-called joint rule of Ilancueitl and Acamâpichtli. "Conquest" of Colhuâcan.
1384	Death of Ilancueitl. Beginning of Aztec dynastic history.
1384–90	Military campaigns in the chinampa districts under the Têcpanec aegis. Beginning of the long-term hostile confrontation with Chalco.
1390–1415	Military and political involvement of the Aztecs in the big war between the Têcpanec and Acolhua states, both of whom desired hegemony in the Valley of Mexico and the surrounding regions. Conquest of Tetzcoco and Huexotla by Aztec forces. Establishment of Têcpanec-Aztec joint rule patterned on the traditional Toltec administrative system. Guerrilla warfare of Prince Nezahualcoyotl of Acolhuâcan against the Têcpanec-Aztec regime.
1424	Through the intervention of Prince Nezahualcoyotl's Aztec aunts at the court of Azcapotzalco, reconciliation is

	achieved between the Têcpanec-Aztec rulers and the Acolhua resistance leaders.
1426	Death of King Tezozomoc, head of the Têcpanec state. Confrontation of the "Têcpanec" and "Aztec" political factions; the former led by Prince Maxtla and the latter by Prince Quetzalayatzin and Chimalpopoca of Tenochtitlan. Rebellion of the Chichimecs of Cuauhtitlan against the Têcpanecs.
1427	Execution of Quetzalayatzin and Chimalpopoca by Maxtla. Suicide of the Tlacochcalcatl of Tenochtitlan. Death of Tlacateotzin of Tlatelolco. Itzcoatl, Tlacayelel, Ilhuicamina, and Nezahualcoyotl take leadership of the "Aztec" faction and organize military resistance to the Têcpanec usurpation. Beginning of the Têcpanec War (1427-33).
1430	Military victory of the Aztec faction. Conquest of Azcapotzalco.
1431	Burning of ancient historical records on order of King Itzcoatl.
1433	Establishment of the tripartite Aztec imperial state with Tenochtitlan, Tetzcoco, and Tlacopan as capitals.
1433-40	As new Colhuatêcuhtli, Itzcoatl "reconquers" the center of the old Toltec empire.
1451-54	Starvation. Beginning of Flower Wars with Tlaxcala, Huexotzinco, Cholula, and Tliliuhquitepec.
1458	Motêuhczoma Ilhuicamina conquers the important Mixtec market town Coaixtlahuâcan and demotes the local Toltec royal family to the rank of tax collectors. Beginning of the commercial expansion of Aztec merchants over the whole of Mesoamerica.
1465	End of the Chalco wars. Annexation of the last independent Chalcan territories by the Mexican state. Construction of the Chapultepec aquaduct and other major hydraulic works.
1472	The Aztecs conquer Cuetlaxtlan (the central region of the present state of Veracruz).
1473	Rebellion of the Tlatelolcas and their defeat.
1478	Aztec conquest of Matlatzinco and Mazahuâcan during the rule of Axayacatl.
1487	Dedication of the great temple of Tenochtitlan.
1497	Conquest of Tehuantepec by Ahuitzotl. Aztec expansion in Chiapas, Xoconochco, and Guatemala.
1510-11	Important conquests of Motêuhczoma Xocoyotzin in the Mixtec highlands and lowlands.
1519-25	Spanish conquest of the Aztec empire.

The Codex of Otlazpan *and the* Tlaxilacallis

The *Codex of Otlazpan* can give us further insight into the meaning of the concept of *tlaxilacalli.* This colonial account, written partly in ideographs and partly in Roman script, describes a border conflict between the communities of Tepexic and Otlazpan. It contains the names and/or occupations, the villages and the *tlaxilacallis* of the 52 people who appeared as witnesses when the conflict was brought before a court of justice. The list below, in which 10 of the 52 witnesses appear twice, contains many titles and names which were also known in Tenochtitlan. Among the ten witnesses were two from Tenochtitlan who belonged to the *tlaxilacalli* of Temazcaltitlan. Temazcaltitlan was a neighborhood in Teopan, in the southeastern city quarter. It was already an important sanctuary at the time of the "founding": it is said that female chief Quetzalmoyahuatzin, who had given birth to a son at Mixiuhcan, took her first steambath after childbirth in a place that was later called Temazcaltitlan (see Chimalpahin, 1963, p. 67, and *Codex Azcatitlan,* plate 12). The list of witnesses mentioned in the *Codex of Otlazpan* seems to imply that in early colonial times the term *tlaxilacalli* was used for hamlets or neighborhoods and occasionally for small city wards. Probably in pre-Hispanic times parts of a larger *tlaxilacalli* also happened to be called *tlaxilacalli,* as was the case with the calpollis. Thus the term might have been used not only for a large population group belonging to 13 sanctuaries but also for the smaller groups which belonged to each of the 13 sanctuaries. This might account for the use of the term in colonial times.

Witnesses in the Dispute Between Otlazpan and Tepexic

Office or Name	Village or Town	*Tlaxilacalli*
1. Tlacatêuhctli	Tultitlan	Ahuacatitlan
2. Atêcpanecatl	Toltitlan	Tlilhuâcan
3. Mayatl	Xilotepec	Tlauhtla
4. Tlillancalqui	Xilotepec	Tlauhtla
5. Temilocatl	Tenochtitlan	Temazcaltitlan
6. Papalotecatl	Tenochtitlan	Temazcaltitlan
7. Tolnahuacatl	Tlatelolco	Tezcapa
8. Itzoctecatl	Tlatelolco	Amaxac
9. Huêcamecatl	Tlacopan	Tepantonco
10. Tlacochcalcatl	Tlacopan	Xalla
11. Huitzicpal governador	Tepexic	
12. Ticocyahuacatl(pilli)	Tepexic	Tianquiztenco
13. Tlacochcalcatl(pilli)	Tepexic	Tianquiztenco
14. Tlacateccatl (pilli)	Tepexic	Tianquiztenco
15. Tlacateccatl	Tepexic	Momoztitlan
16. Yaotl(pilli)	Tepexic	Tianquiztenco
17. Matlallaca(pilli)	Tepexic	Tianquiztenco
18. Icnotlacatl(pilli)	Tepexic	Atenco
19. Pâtli Tepexic(pilli)	Tepexic	Atenco
20. Tlacatêuhctli	Tepexic	Huitznahuac
21. Atempanecatl	Tepexic	Huitznahuac
22. Colliquitl(pilli)	Tepexic	Atenco
23. Tlillancalqui	Cuauhtitlan	Nepantla
24. Atempanecatl	Cuauhtitlan	Atempan
25. Acolnahuacatl	Cuauhtitlan	Nepantla
26. Axoxoc Chililicatl	Cuauhtitlan	Tequixquinahuac
27. Tolnahuacatl	Tzompanco	Hueyicalco
28. Têuhctlehuâ papaztac	Tzompanco	Tlamatzinco
29. Tocuiltecatl	Citlaltepec	Hueyicalco
30. Atêcpanecatl	Citlaltepec	Mizquititlan
31. Tezcaco(hu)acatl	Huehuetocan	Huehuetocan
32. Chalchiuhtepehuâ	Huehuetocan	Calmecatepotzco
33. Huêcamecatl	Itztapalapan	Tzonmolco
34. Tlacochtêuhctli	Itztapalapan	Ayacac
35. Atempanecatl	Tullan	Tetepetlapan
36. Tlailotlac	Tullan	Tetepetlapan
37. Atzacualcatl	Tullan	Nepancalco
38. Tezcacoac tiachcauh	Tullan	Huanalla
39. I'huipanecatl	Tepexic	Teopan
40. Cuauhnochcatl	Tepexic	Huitznahuac
41. [Atempanecatl]	Tullan	Tetepetlapan
42. [Atzacualcatl]	Tullan	Tetepetlapan(!; cf. no. 37)
	(Now for Nochtonco)	

Witnesses in the Dispute Between Otlazpan and Tepexic (Continued)

43. Tlacateccatl	Apazco	Têcpan
44. Coatecatl	Apazco	Têcpan
45. [Tlacatêuhctli]	Toltitlan	Ahuacatitlan
46. [Atêcpanecatl]	Toltitlan	Tlilhuâcan
47. Ezhuahuacatl	Chiapan	Tepeticpac
48. Tocuiltecatl	Chiapan	Tepeticpac
49. Tlillancalqui	Atotonilco	Zoyatla
50. Zacancatl	Atotonilco	Sanctiago
51. Tepallequi	Xiuhpacoyan	Tlaliztacapan
52. [Tlacatêuhctli]	Tepexic	Huitznahuac
53. Tozamilcatl	Nochtonco	Nahuapan
54. [Tolnahuacatl]	Tzompanco	Hueyicalco
55. [Papaztac(a)tiachcauh]	Tzompanco	Tlamatzinco
56. [Atempanecatl]	Citlaltepec	Mizquititlan
57. [Huêcamecatl]	Citlaltepec	Hueyicalco
58. Tezcatzoncatl	Huehuetocan	Colhuâcapan
59. Ollopantzincatl	Huehuetocan	Calmecatepotzco
60. Coyohuâ Otomitl	Xiuhpacoyan	Tlaliztacapan
61. Tlapaltecatl	Xiuhpacoyan	Tlaliztacapan
62. [Ezhuahuâcatl]	Chiapan	Tepeticpac

Names in brackets indicate repeated appearance of a witness.

Glossary of Names, Terms, and Titles

achcacauhtin: (sing.: *achcauhtli*), lit. meaning: "elder brothers," military chiefs of the calpollis.

acxotecatl: lit. meaning: "he who comes from the Place of Spruce," title of the external chief of the central organization of merchants' guilds.

ahuianimê: (sing.: *ahuiani*), "pleasure girls," female companions of the soldiers.

altepetl: lit. meaning: "water mountain." Nahuatl term for the local community (village, town or city).

amantecâ: (sing.: *amantecatl*), members of the guild of the feather-mosaic workers, specialists of Mexitin-Chichimec origin.

atempanecatl: title of an officeholder in Tenochtitlan belonging to the calpolli of Atempan.

ayauhcalli: "mist house," a ceremonial construction belonging to the calpolli of Huitznahuac in Tenochtitlan.

Aztecâ: (sing.: *Aztecatl*), term used to designate persons whose ancestors came from Aztlan or Aztatlan (Land of Herons, White Land)

calmecac: lit. meaning: "chain of buildings," term for the priestly schools for upper-class and highly talented children. There were seven *calmecacs* in Tenochtitlan.

calpixquê: (sing.: *calpixqui*), lit. meaning: "guardians of the building," term for Aztec tax collectors.

calpolco or *calpulco:* lit. meaning: "in the large building," usual Nahuatl term for the ceremonial center of a calpolli.

calpollalli: landed property of the calpolli community.

calpollaxilacalli: a local group with the ritual obligations of a calpolli and a *tlaxilacalli*.

calpolli or *calpulli:* a local group of family heads belonging to a common *calpolco* and using the same *calpollalli*.

calpolteteô: gods of the calpolli considered to be patrons of the calpolli and related *tlaxilacalli(s)*.

Chalmecâ: (sing.: *Chalmecatl*), 1. name of a Toltecized pre-Aztec population group in the southern parts of the Valley of Mexico; 2. term used for the members of the calpolli Chalman in Tenochtitlan.

Chichimecâ: (sing.: *Chichimecatl*), term used by Toltecs and Aztecs for various seminomadic population groups that originated in the northern parts of the actual Mexican territory. The translation of the term is uncertain; historical sources give different meanings, as "descendants of dogs" and "eagle people."

Chinampanecâ: (sing.: *Chinampanecatl*), inhabitants of the chinampa's in the lacustrine regions of central Mexico.

chinampa: reclaimed swamps used for horticulture and other forms of intensive agriculture.

cihuacoatl: lit. meaning: "female consort," "female companion," or "female snake," title of the head of internal government in each of the three central states of the Aztec empire.

Colhuâquê or *Culhuâquê:* (sing.: *Colhuâ*), lit. meaning: "they who have ancestors," 1. inhabitants of Colhuâcan. 2. name given by the non-Aztec inhabitants of the empire to its central peoples.

copal: fragrant resin for ritual burning.

Cuaochpanmê: lit. meaning: "swept heads," term used by the Aztecs for their Tarascan enemies.

cuauhpipiltin: (sing.: *cuauhpilli*), "eagles' sons," military nobles.

cuauhxicalli: "eagle's bowl" or "eagle's vessel," term for an important ritual bowl or vessel used in human sacrifice.

Cuextecâ: (sing.: *Cuextecatl*), "Huaxtecs," inhabitants of the province of Cuextlan in the northeastern part of the empire.

Cuitlahuacâ: inhabitants of the important *chinampanecâ* town of Cuitlahuac.

ezhuahuâcatl: title of an officeholder in the Teopan quarter of Tenochtitlan, related to the calpolli of Huitznahuac.

Huacuxecha: (sing.: *Huacux*), lit. meaning: "Eagles," the Tarascans' name for their Chichimec ancestors.

Hueyi Tlâtoani, Hueyi Tlahtoani: "grand ruler," title of the leader of the external government in the Aztec empire.

huitznahuatl: title of an officeholder and military chief related to the calpolli of Huitznahuac.

ichpocacalli: lit. meaning: "maiden's house," calpolli school for girls.

ihquitquê: (sing.: *ihquitqui*), male or female weavers.

ilhuicatl xoxouhqui: lit. meaning: "blue sky," 1. name of the shrine of Huitzilopochtli on top of the great temple in Tenochtitlan; 2. one of the names for the national Aztec god Huitzilopochtli.

macehualtin: (sing.: *macehualli*), "subjects," term used by the Aztecs in the Valley of Mexico to indicate the common members of the calpollis. In other parts of the empire the same term could refer to subjects of the estates of the nobles.

Matlalatl: Blue Water, a stream of water with important ritual meaning in the city of Tenochtitlan.

Matlatzincâ: (sing.: *Matlatzincatl*), ethnic group living mainly in a region south of Tolucan. When the Aztecs conquered the region, some of the Matlatzincâ took flight to the Tarascan state, where they established themselves in the neighborhood of the actual capital of Michoacán, Morelia. Their language belongs to the Otomian family.

mayequê: lit. meaning: "those who have right hands," term used by the Aztecs of central Mexico (or Anahuac) for the serfs of the estates of the nobles. In other parts of the empire they were sometimes designated *macehualtin.*

Mexîcâ: (sing.: *Mexîcatl*), name used for the inhabitants of Tenochtitlan and Tla(l)telolco and their immediate dependencies in the Valley of Mexico.

Mexitin or *Mexîtin:* (sing.: *Mexîtli*), name of a Chichimec tribe that lived at the northwestern frontier of the Toltec empire. In the thirteenth century this tribe was one of the principal constituent parts of the rising Aztec nation.

Mixtecâ: (sing.: *Mixtecatl*), lit. meaning: "they who come from the cloudy region," ethnic group living in the south of Mexico belonging to the Mixtec language family of the Olmec-Otomangue group.

Mizquicâ: (sing.: *Mizquicatl*), inhabitants of Mizquic (Place of Acacias), a Chinampanec town on the southern shore of Lake Chalco.

Nahualli: (pl.: *nanahualtin*), "counterpart," term referring to a companion in destiny, often an animal or an outstanding natural phenomenon. Sorcerers possessed the power to manipulate their own *nahualli* (or *nanahualtin*).

nahualoztomecâ: (sing.: *nahualoztomecatl*), "disguised merchants," Aztec merchants who penetrated foreign territory using the language and dress of the region where they operated. They constituted the backbone of the Aztec intelligence service.

Nahuatlacâ: (sing.: *Nahuatlacatl*), "people living under the law," term used by the Aztecs to designate related ethnic groups in their empire, speakers of the same Nahuatl language.

Nahuatlâtolli: Aztec for the Nahuatl language.

ne(n)montemi: "useless fillings," term used for the five (sometimes six) days that concluded the solar year after the celebration of the eighteen 20-day periods.

Nonoalcâ: (sing.: *Nonoalcatl*), 1. name of an important ethnic group in the center of the Toltec empire; 2. inhabitants of a ward of Tla(l)-telolco.

Ollin Tonatiuh: Sun of Movement, name for the fifth sun, the period of the fifth creation.

Olmecâ: (sing.: *Olmecatl*), "people from the *caoutchouc* region," term used by the Aztecs for an ancient Mesoamerican ethnic group originally from the coast of the Gulf of Mexico that in historic times rose to a politically dominant position in the region of Cholullan and Tlaxcallan. These historic Olmecs are not the people who created the impressive archaeological monuments in Tabasco and Veracruz and were called by that name by modern archaeologists.

Otomî or *Otoncâ:* (sing.: *Otomitl*), 1. name of an autochthonous ethnic group in central Mexico; 2. title given by the Aztecs to certain excellent soldiers.

oztomecâ: (sing.: *oztomecatl*), "people coming from the extended caves," term used for the members of the external organization of the national merchant guilds of the Aztecs.

petlatl: (pl.: *petlamê*), lit. meaning: "mat," sometimes used to refer to authority, government (mat = throne); *petlatl* was also used by the Aztecs to designate local organizations of merchants on the level of a calpolli.

petlacontzitzquiquê: "keepers of the mat and the urns," a term referring to the ancient ancestor gods of the calpollis of Tenochtitlan.

pipiltin: (sing.: *pilli*), lit. meaning: "sons," term used to designate the second-rank nobility.

pochtecâ: (sing.: *pochtecatl*), "people from the ceiba region," term referring to the traveling merchants trading in luxury goods.

pochtecatlailotlac: "the returned merchant," title of the supreme internal chief of the central guild of merchants, who was a member of the Tlâtocan, the central imperial government of the Aztecs.

quecholli: "spoonbill," "crane," 1. calendrical symbol for the second part of a space of 24 hours; 2. name of the fourteenth 20-day period.

tecocyahuacatl: title of an officeholder in Moyotla, the southwestern quarter of Tenochtitlan.

têcpan: "chiefs' office," administrative building, place where local government is exercised.

Têcpanecâ, Tepanecâ: (sing.: *Têcpanecatl, Tepanecatl*), in the first form, the term used to designate the ruling ethnic group in the Têcpanec state, originally probably related to the Matlatzinca's; later, however, the Têcpanecs were Toltecized and became Nahuatl-speaking. The second form *(Tepanecâ)* is a nickname invented by the Aztecs meaning "suppressors," "tyrants."

têcpanpouhquê: (sing.: *têcpanpouhqui*), "those belonging to the administrative building," persons of foreign origin, often relatives of submissive chiefs in conquered provinces, who served as inferior assistants in the Aztec local government.

têcpantlalli: land for which the *têcpan* held the usufruct.

tetêuhctin: (sing.: *têuhctli, tecuhtli*), "lords," title of the internal heads of a *têcpan*, or holders of an estate with the function of a center of local government.

têuhctlalli: land for which one or more *tetêuhctin* held the usufruct.

têcuhtlâtoquê: (sing.: *têcuhtlâtoani*), title of the members of the Tlâtocan, the Aztec imperial government.

telpochcalli: "house of youth," name of the calpolli school for boys.

telpochtlâtoquê: lit. meaning: "rulers of the youth," title of subordinate military officers who served as schoolmasters in the *telpochcallis.*

temalacatl: sacrificial stone of the gladiators.

Tenochcâ: (sing.: *Tenochcatl*), inhabitants of Mexîco-Tenochtitlan.

teocuitlapitzquê: (sing.: *teocuitlapitzqui*), gold- and silversmiths.

teomama: "god-bearer," title of a priest who bore an image of a god(dess) or his (or her) sacred bundle during pilgrimages, religious ceremonies, military campaigns, or migrations.

teotl: (pl.: *teteô*), term used to designate the gods and goddesses of the Mesoamerican pantheon.

teotlalli: land the usufruct of which served to pay for the ceremonies in honor of a certain god or goddess.

tequihuâquê: (sing.: *tequihuâ*), title of an inferior civil and military functionary.

Tetzcocâ: (sing.: *Tetzcocatl*), inhabitants of Tetzcoco, the capital city of Acolhuacan.

teocualo, teucualo: "god is eaten," a ceremony held in honor of Huitzilopichtli during the fifteenth feast of the solar year, Panquetzaliztli (Raising of the Banners).

tezcacoacatl: title of an important functionary in the government of the Aztec capital city of Tenochtitlan, related to the central calpolli of Tezcacoac.

tianquizpan tlayacanquê: "market leaders," special judges in the marketplace appointed by the chiefs of the guild of the merchants.

tianquiztli: market.

tlacateccatl: title of a high military official who also served as a civil functionary and as a judge.

tlachtli: court of the ball game.

tlacochcalcatl: "man of the spear-house," title of a high military official.

tlacôtin: (sing.: *tlacôtli*), lit. meaning: "bought ones," "slaves by debt."

Tlahuicâ: (sing.: *Tlahuicatl*), inhabitants of the province of Tlahuican, the western part of the present state of Morelos.

tlalcualiztli: "eating earth," ceremony of homage in the presence of gods, princes, and high-ranking functionaries.

Tla(l)telolcâ: (sing.: *Tla(l)telolcatl*), inhabitants of Mexîco-Tla(l)telolco.

tlamacazcalli: "house of priests," higher priests' school.

tlâtoani, tlahtoani (pl.: *tlâtoquê*), "princes," external leaders of government.

Tlâtocan, Tlahtocan: highest government council.

tlâtocatlalli: land the usufruct of which belongs to the government.

tlâtocayotl: "royalty," government.

Tlaxcaltecâ: (sing.: *Tlaxcaltecatl*), lit. meaning: people from the Tortilla region, a Nahuatl-speaking ethnic group living in the central and southern parts of the present state of Tlaxcala; one of the most important adversaries of the Aztecs in the ritual flower wars.

tlaxilacalli: social and ceremonial group organized in relation to the *tonalpoalli* ritual and in charge of a number of shrines of the patron deities of one of the 13-day periods.

tlazôpipiltin: "highly esteemed princes," members of the imperial nobility.

Tleatl-Atlatlayan: Fire Water, Burning Water, a ritually important stream in Tenochtitlan.

tlenamacaquê: (sing.: *tlenamacac*), "fire sacrificers," term for a certain class of priests.

tlillancalqui: "chief of the black house," term for a high-ranking functionary from the city quarter of Moyotla in Tenochtitlan and leading member of the Tlâtocan.

tocuiltecatl: "chief of the place of worms," title of a functionary related to the city quarter of Teopan in Tenochtitlan.

Toltecâ, Tultecâ: (sing.: *Toltecatl*), lit. meaning: "Those Who Come from the Place of Rushes, 1. name of the dominant ethnic group in central Mexico in the eleventh and twelfth centuries; 2. guardians of the Mesoamerican cultural tradition; 3. artists or excellent artisans.

tonalamatl: calendar on the base of the so-called day count.

tonalpoalli: "day count," time reckoning in units of 260 days.

totoquihuaztli: a priestly title.

Toxpalatl: a holy stream in Tenochtitlan.

tozpan: term for one of the three hearthstones.

tzitzimimê: (sing.: *tzitzimitl*), "spirits," particularly female spirits of women who died during confinement.

tzompantli: skull rack.

Xicalancâ: (sing.: *Xicalancatl*), companions of the historic Olmecâ, coming from the same coastal region.

xiuhmolpilli: a "bundle" of 52 solar years.

xiuhmolpiliztli: ceremony of bundling 52 solar years.

xiuhpoalli: counting of solar years.

Xochimilcâ: (sing.: *Xochimilcatl*), People from the Flower Fields, an important town south of Tenochtitlan.

Yaotlalli: lands the usufruct of which was held by the army.

Glossary of Gods, Goddesses, Priests, and Chiefs

Acacihtli (Reed Hare): 1. a chief of the Mexitin during their migration and their stay in Chapultepec; 2. Chichimecatêcuhtli of Tenochtitlan, external chief of the calpolli Tlacatêcpan, related to the Chichimec members of this social group.

Acamâpichtli (Hand Full of Arrows): 1. name of an early leader of the Toltecs; 2. name of a king of Colhuâcan; 3. name of the first *cihuacoatl* of Tenochtitlan, who a few years later became its first *tlâtoani.*

Acolmiztli (Cat Paw): 1. name of a *tlâtoani* of Coatlichan, a relative of princess Ilancueitl; 2. name of many princes of the royal house of Tetzcoco.

Ahuexotl (Water Willow): founder of Tenochtitlan, external chief of the calpolli Huitznahuac.

Ahuitzotl (Otter): 1. *hueyi tlâtoani* of Tenochtitlan (1486-1502); 2. name of a god related to the Tlaloquê (Rain Gods).

Amâcui Xolotl (Water-Taker Twin): founder of the Chichimec royal dynasty in the Valley of Mexico who exercised political power in Tenanyucan; later his descendants transferred their residence to Tetzcoco.

Apanecatl (Water Ensign): one of the four god-bearers of the Mexîtin.

Apantêuhctli or *Apantecuhtli* (Lord of the Shore): patron god of the calpolli Apantêuhctlan in Atzacualco; he was related to the god Huehuêcoyotl, and he belonged to the Mimixcoâ.

Atototl (Waterbird): a founder of Tenochtitlan, a secundary chief of the calpolli Cihuatêcpan.

Atotoztli (Water Parakeet): 1. princess of Colhuâcan, mother of Acamâpichtli Chilatlexotzin, *cihuacoatl* and *tlâtoani* of Tenochtitlan; 2. princess and *cihuatlâtoani* of Tenochtitlan, daughter of Motêcuhzoma Ilhuicamina and mother of the kings Axayacatl, Tizoc, and Ahuitzotl.

Axayacatl (Water Face, Water Fly): *hueyi tlâtoani* of Tenochtitlan (1472-82).

Axolohuâ (Possessor of Axolotls): "founder" of Tenochtitlan and priest of Tlaloc; related to the autochthonous Otomî population of Toltzalan Acatzalan.

Ayopechtli (Seated on the Tortoise): byname of the goddess of the maguey, Mayahuel, patron of the calpolli of Tezcacoac.

Camaxtli (Mouth Eye): patron god of several Chichimec groups in central Mexico, such as the Tlaxcaltecâ, the Huexotzincâ, and some ethnic
groups in the lacustrine regions.

Ce Coatl Ohtlimelahuac (One Serpent Straight Road): an important god
of the Aztec merchants and principal deity in the *tlaxilacalli* of Tzonmolco.

Centeotl or *Cinteotl* (Maize god'): with Mayahuel this god or goddess
was a patron(ess) of the *tlaxilacalli* of Tezcacoac; with Xochipilli he
(or she) was patron(ess) of the eleventh *tonalli* ozomahtli (monkey)
and therefore related to the calpolli Tlamatzinco.

Chalchiuhtlatonac (Brilliant Jade): 1. a Toltec prince before the founding
of Tollan; 2. a prince of Aztatlan; 3. the second name of some rulers
of Tenochtitlan.

Chalchiuhtlicue (Jade Is Her Skirt): goddess of the earthly waters;
patroness of the *calpollaxilacalli* Coatlan.

Chantico: goddess of the hearth, patroness of the calpolli of Atempan;
also called Cuaxolotl.

Chicomecoatl (Seven Snake): calendrical name of the goddess of foodstuffs; she was intimately related to Cinteotl and to the Cihuapipiltin.

Chicunahui Ehecatl (Nine Wind): one of the calendrical names of the god
Quetzalcoatl; patron of the *calpollaxilacalli* Chalman.

Chimalpopoca (Smoking Shield): 1. *tlâtoani* of Tenochtitlan (1415-26);
2. tlâtoani of Tlacopan (1469-87).

Cihuapipiltin (Princesses): goddesses related to the four directions and
to the crossings of roads; in Tenochtitlan there were shrines for these
goddesses in five *tlaxilacallis:* in Acatliacapan, Chililico, Izquitlan,
Cihuatêcpan, and Ayauhcaltitlan; the first two tlaxilacallis belonged
to Atzacualco; the three others, to Cuepopan, Moyotla, and Teopan,
respectively. The Cihuapipiltin were considered to be deified women
who had died in confinement.

Cihuateteô (Goddesses): another name for the Cihuapipiltin.

Coatlicue (Serpent's Skirt): patroness of the calpolli Coatlan; mother of
Huitzilopochtli, goddess of the earth.

Coatzontli (Serpents' Beard or Serpents' Hair): son of Cuauhtlequetzqui,
the high priest of Huitzilopochtli and Xîcomoyahual, Copil's daughter;
he was probably the father or a grandfather of Opochtli Iztahuatzin.

Copil (Crown): 1. son of Malinalxochtil; magician and adversary of
Cuauhtlequetzqui and Tenoch; also mentioned as one of the founders
of Tenochtitlan.

Coyolxauhqui (Face Painted with Bells): "sister" of Huitzilopochtli and
daughter of Coatlicue; adversary of her brother; associated with the
moon.

Cuauhcoatl (Eagle's Snake): god-bearer and priest of the Mexitin.

Cuauhtemoc (Descending Eagle): 1. *hueyi tlâtoani* of the Aztecs (1521-

25); 2. name of the setting sun; 3. the southwestern holder of the vault of heaven.

Cuauhtlequetzqui (Eagle Going into the Fire): high priest of Huitzilopochtli, founder of Tenochtitlan; opponent of Copil; one of the *petlacontzitzquiquê.*

Cuaxolotl (Twin Head): another name for the goddess Chantico.

Huehuêcoyotl (Old Wolf): patron of the *calpollaxilacalli* Apantêuhctlan; one of the gods of the Otomî.

Huemac (Great Hand or Old Hand): Toltec coruler of Quetzalcoatl.

Huicton (Little Digging Stick): chief of the calpolli Izquitlan; founder of Tenochtitlan.

Huitzil (Hummingbird): priest who persuaded the Aztecâ-Mexîtin to leave Az(ta)tlan.

Huitzilîhuitl (Hummingbird Feather): 1. ruler of the Mexîtin in Chapultepec; 2. *tlâtoani* of Tenochtitlan (1391–1415).

Huitzilopochtli (Sinistral or Southern Hummingbird): 1. most important god of the Aztecs, identified with the fifth sun, also called Mexîtli, Tetzauhteotl, Tepanquizqui, and Ilhuicatlxoxouhqui; 2. name given by some sources to the priest who persuaded the Aztecâ-Mexîtin to leave Az(ta)tlan and who was afterward deified.

Huixtocihuatl (Lady of the Huixtotin the Trembling Ones): goddess of the salt, patroness of the salt workers.

I'huitl (Feather): 1. name of one of the three hearthstones; 2. possible father of Huitzilopochtli.

Ilamatzin (Old Woman), also called *Ilamatêuhctli* (Female Chieftain Old Woman) and *Ilancueitl* (see below), sometimes called *Zacailamatzin* (Grass Old Woman): goddess associated with the earth, the moon, and the ending of the winter; copatroness of the calpolli Tlacatêcpan.

Ilancueitl (Old Woman's Skirt): 1. goddess, consort of Iztacmixcoatl; 2. princess of Coatlichan and Colhuâcan, "aunt" and first lady of Acamâpichtli Chilatlexotzin; female external ruler of Tenochtitlan, Colhuatêuhctli of the calpolli Tlacatêcpan.

Ipalnemoani (That by Which Men Live): the pantheistic deity of the Toltecs and the Aztecs.

Iquehuac(atzin) (Therefore He Has Risen): *tlâtocapilli* ("eligible prince") of Tenochtitlan, son of Motêuhczoma Ilhuicamina, brother of princess Atotoztli; *tlacateccatl* of Tenochtitlan; opponent of prince Axayacatl.

Itzcoatl (Obsidian Snake): 1. one of the raisers of heaven; 2. *hueyi tlâtoani* of Tenochtitlan (1427–40).

Itzpapalotl (Obsidian Butterfly): 1. goddess, patroness of the calpolli Cihuatêcpan; 2. priestly title of Acamâpichtli Chilatlexotzin.

Itztapaltetl (Smooth Flatstone) or *Itztapaltotêc* (Our Lord Smooth Flatstone): patron of the *tlaxilacalli* Huitznahuac, god of the obsidian.

Itztlacoliuhqui (Curved Obsidian): patron of the *calpollaxilacalli* Têcpantzinco; god of the ice.

Ixcozauhqui (Yellow Face or Yellow Eye): god of fire, also called Xiuhtecuhtli.

Izquitecatl (He Who Comes from the Popcorn Region or He Who Comes from the Region of Odoriferous Flowers): god of the pulque and patron of the *calpollaxilacalli* Izquitlan.

Iztac Mixcoatl (White Cloud Snake): 1. a cosmic god associated with the galaxy; 2. a chief of the early "Aztecs" in Az(ta)tlan.

Macuilxochitl (Five Flower): god of music and dance; one of the patrons of Tlamatzinco.

Malinalxochitl (Prairie-Grass Flower): sister and adversary of Huitzilo-pochtli; mother of Copil; closely associated with the goddess Quilaztli.

Mayahuel: goddess of the maguey, or agave; patroness of the calpolli Tezcacoac.

Mexîtli (Navel of the Agave): an aspect of Huitzilopochtli as an earth-god.

Mictlantêcuhtli (Lord of the Region of Death): patron god of the *cal-pollaxilacalli* Tlacochcalco in Tenochtitlan; with Mictecacihuatl (Lady of the Inhabitants of the Region of Death) he was the ruler of the underworld.

Mixcoatl (Cloud Snake), plural: Mimixcoâ: father of Quetzalcoatl closely related to Camaxtli; god of the clouds and patron of the hunters.

Motêcuhzoma, Motêuhczoma (He Who Makes Himself Lord by His Sever-ity): 1. ruler in Aztatlan in ancient time; 2. *hueyi tlâtoani* of Tenoch-titlan (1440-68), also called Ilhuicamina (Sky Shooter); 3. *hueyi tlâ-toani* of Tenochtitlan, Culhuateuhctli (1502-20), also called Xocoyo-tzin (the Younger).

Nacxitl (Four Foot): 1. also called Topiltzin (Our Prince), ruler of the Toltecs; 2. one of the names given to Quetzalcoatl.

Nezahualcoyotl (Hungry Wolf): *tlâtoani* of Acolhuâcan or Tetzcoco (1433-72).

Nezahualpilli (Hungry Prince): *tlâtoani* of Acolhuâcan or Tetzcoco (1472-1516).

Ocelopan (Ocelot Flag): one of the founders of Tenochtitlan, *culhua-têuhctli* of the calpolli Tlacatêcpan.

Omacatl (Two Reed): a calendrical name for Tezcatlepoca; his day was celebrated in the whole country and particularly in the *tlaxilacalli* of Tezcacoac.

Omecihuatl (Lady of Duality): goddess of creation.

Ometêcuhtli, Ometêuhctli (Lord of Duality): god of creation, creator.

Ometeotl (God of Duality): creator.

Ometochtli (Two Rabbit): god of pulque, a shrine of this god was main-tained by the *tlaxilacalli* of Acatliacapan.

Opochtli (the Left One): a rain god, related to Tlaloc and Quetzalcoatl; patron god of the calpolli of Chalman.

Opochtli Iztahuâtzin (the Left One, Possessor of Salt): mentioned in some sources as the father of Acamâpichtli Chilatlexotzin; probably a priestly chief of the Chalmecâ.

Otontêuhctli, Otontêcuhtli (Lord of the Otomîs): god of the Otomîs, who was also accepted by the Aztecs.

Pâtecatl (He Who Comes from the Region of Medicine): a god of pulque closely related to Izquitecatl.

Paynal (He Who Is Made to Run): companion of the god Huitzilopochtli.

Piltzintecuhtli, Piltzintêuhctli (Noble Lord): surname of the god Tonatiuh (Sun).

Quetzalcoatl (Precious Twin or Precious Feathered Serpent): one of the leading gods of the Toltecs; principal deity in Cholullan; important god in the Aztec pantheon.

Quilaztli: one of several names used for the mother goddess, also called Tonantzin (Our Mother), Cuauhcihuatl (Eagle Woman), Cihuacoatl (Female Serpent), Itzpapalotl (Obsidian Butterfly), etc.; she was patroness of the midwives.

Têquichpo (Lord's Daughter) or *Tequichpo* (Tribute Daughter): daughter of Motecuhzoma Xocoyotzin, married first to Cuitlahuac, then to Cuauhtemoc, and after the Spanish conquest to three Spanish noblemen successively.

Tenoch, Tenuch (Stone Cactus): founder of Tenochtitlan, probably chief of the calpolli Tlacochcalco.

Tenzacatetl (Lip Ornament): one of the founders of Tenochtitlan, chief of the calpolli Chalman; one of the ancestors of the Aztec royal family.

Tepanquizqui (Conqueror): surname of Huitzilopochtli.

Teteô Innan (Mother of the Gods), also called *Tocî* (Our Grandmother): goddess of earth; patroness of the calpolli Atempan.

Tetzauhteotl (Terrifying or Imposing God or Goddess or Ominous, Magic, Wonderful, or Marvelous God or Goddess): term used for some particular gods and goddesses, including Mixcoatl, Mexîtli, Huitzilopochtli, and Itzpapalotl, deities who produced a marvel or a wonder.

Tezcatlanextia (Radiant Mirror): surname of the god Tezcatlepoca.

Tezcatlepoca (Brilliant Mirror [not Tezcatlipoca, Smoking Mirror]): one of the most important gods in the Aztec pantheon; related to the moon but also closely related to the supreme pantheistic deity, Ipalnemoani.

Tezozomoc (He Who Is Frequently Angered): 1. ruler of the Têcpanecs (1367-1426); 2. royal prince (*tlâtocapilli*) of Tenochtitlan, consort of queen Atotoztli and son of Itzcoatl; 3. a son of Axayacatl; 4. well-known Aztec historian, son of the Aztec prince Huanitzin.

Tizoc(icatzin) (He Who Made People Bleed): *hueyi tlâtoani* of Tenochtitlan (1482-86).

Tlacahuepan (Human Beam): 1. surname of Tezcatlepoca; 2. one of the Aztec conquerors of Azcapotzalco; 3. one of the Aztec heroes in the Chalco war.

Tlacayelel, Tlacaelel (Clear Is His Liver, Clear Mind): 1. empire builder of the Aztecs, *cihuacoatl* ("supreme internal ruler") from the beginning of Aztec dominance until his death in 1474; 2. grandson and successor of the former, son of the prince Cacamatzin, the *tlacochcalcatl;* this Tlacayelel (II) was the second Cihuacoatl of the empire (1474-90).

Tlahuizcalpotonqui (Feathered Dawn): ruler of Tzompanco, ancestor of Huitzilíhuitl, the first prince of the Mexítin in the Valley of Mexico.

Tlaloc (pl.: *Tlaloquê* [Earth Wine]): god of rain and thunder, one of the principal deities in the Aztec pantheon; companion of Huitzilopochtli in the great temple; patron of the *calpollaxilacalli* Chililico.

Tlaltêcuhtli, Tlaltêuhctli (Lord or Lady of the Earth): god or goddess of the earth.

Tlazolteotl (Muck Goddess): goddess of sin and remission.

Tocî (Our Grandmother): earth goddess, mother of the gods.

Tonacacihuatl (Lady of Our Existence): goddess of subsistence.

Tonacatêcuhtli, Tonacatêuhctli (Lord of Our Existence): god of subsistence.

Tonantzin (Our Mother): goddess of the earth.

Topiltzin Meconetzin (Our Prince, Maguey Child): last king of the Toltecs before the disintegration of their empire.

Totoquihuaztli (Repeatedly Stirred Fire): 1. *tlâtoani* of Tlacopan (1430-69); 2. grandson of the former, *tlâhtoani* of Tlacopan (1487-1519); 3. a priest who participated in the inauguration ceremony of the Great Temple of Tenochtitlan.

Tzompan (Beard Flag): 1. chief of the calpolli Chalman in the early history of Tenochtitlan; 2. name of a noble family in Cuitlahuac.

Xipe Totêc (Our Lord the Flayed One): important Mesoamerican deity; also called Tlatlauhqui Tezcatlepoca (Red Brilliant Mirror) and Yohualahuan (Night Drunk), patron god of the gold- and silversmiths; patron of the calpolli Yopico in Tenochtitlan.

Xiuhcaquê (Owner of the Blue Sandals); a founder of Tenochtitlan, a chief of the calpolli Izquitlan.

Xiuhtêcuhtli, Xiuhtêuhctli (Lord of the Year): important Aztec god of fire, also called Ixcozauhqui (Yellow Face); one of the principal gods of the merchants; patron god of the *calpollaxilacalli* Tzonmolco.

Xochiquetzal (Flower Feather): goddess closely related to Tonacacihuatl; patroness of the artisans; goddess of Huitznahuac and its *tlaxilacalli* Ayauhcaltitlan.

Xocoyol (Ankle Bell): a founder of Tenochtitlan; a chief of the calpolli Tlacochcalco.

Xolotl (Monster, Twin): 1. Twin god of Quetzalcoatl; 2. name of a whole dynasty of Chichimec rulers.

Xomimitl (Lower-Leg Arrow): a founder of Tenochtitlan; a chief of the calpolli Yopico.

Yacatêcuhtli, Yacatêuhctli (Lord of the Vanguard): patron god of the Aztec merchants.

Yaocihuatl (Warrior Woman): surname of the goddesses Cihuacoatl, Quilaztli, etc.

Yohualahuan(i), Yuhualahuan(i) (Night Drunk): surname of the god Xipe Totêc.

Zacailamatzin (Grass Old Woman): surname of the goddess Ilancueitl or Ilamatêcuhtli.

Notes

Chapter 1

For abbreviations, see the list at the front of the book.

1. The term Mesoamerica is used by Kirchhoff and other Mesoamericanists to delimit the area in Central and North America in which highly developed indigenous cultures that had a number of essential characteristics in common arose before the coming of the Spaniards. This area stretched from present-day northern Mexico to present-day Costa Rica and is not, therefore, identical with the geographic limits of Central America. Consequently, a new term was needed for the above-mentioned cultural area.

2. See Keen, 1971.

3. López Austin, 1973.

4. Davies, 1973b.

5. Chimalpahin, 1973, 1:6.

6. Ibid., 1:5, 6, 9; 2:68-71.

7. *AC,* 1938, p. 111.

8. See Krickeberg, 1971, pp. 216-17; Jiménez Moreno, 1973; Bernal, 1972, p. 102; López Austin, 1973, pp. 80-85.

9. Kirchhoff, 1961b.

10. López Austin, 1973, chap. 7.

11. See *Codex Azcatitlan,* 1949, p. 110; Tezozomoc, 1949, p. 37.

12. Kirchhoff, 1961a.

13. Castillo, 1908.

14. Van Zantwijk, 1976.

15. *Codex Ramírez,* 1944, pp. 19, 27n.

16. Davies, 1973b, pp. 35-36.

17. Castillo, 1908.

18. *AC,* 1938, p. 353.

19. Van Zantwijk, 1973.

20. The term Nahua, or Nahuatlacâ (People Who Are Legitimate, People Who Speak Intelligibly), was used by the Aztecs for all peoples who spoke a dialect of Nahuatlâtolli (Official Language), the official language of the empire, and as such were immediately intelligible to the Aztecs without the help of an interpreter *(nahuatlâto).* The Toltecs, the Chinampanecs, the Acolhuas, the Tlax-caltecs, the Chalcas, the Tlahuicas, the greater part of the Têcpanecs, the

Huexotzincas, the Chololtecs, and many other Central American population groups, plus some living much farther away in northern Mexico and in the heart of Central America, such as Metztitecs and inhabitants of present-day El Salvador and Nicaragua, all belonged to the great Nahua people.

21. *Chinampa* ("in the *chinantli*"), in Nahuatl means an artificial garden plot reclaimed from swampy land. Rows of poles were driven in the lakeshore swamps of Central Mexico's freshwater lakes; canals and ditches were dug between the poles. The dug-up mud, mixed with water plants, was thrown into the sections of swamp surrounded by poles until they were completely filled and the fertile soil reached above the surface of the water. In this way extremely fertile horticultural land was obtained. The prevailing opinion found in popular books that the chinampas were "floating gardens" is based largely on a misunderstanding of an Aztec legend about Mexico's early days. See also Coe, 1964.

22. The Aztec word *chichimecatl* (pl. *chichimecâ*) can be translated, first, as "those who are descended from dogs" and, second, as "wire suckers" or "rope suckers." Both translations seem forced and are not quite acceptable from a linguistic point of view. It is more likely that the word is an Aztec corruption of an originally "Chichimec" word (that is, a word from a language spoken by a "Chichimec" group). This assumption is supported by the fact that Ixtlilxóchitl translated Chichimecâ as Eagles while the Tarascan word for Chichimecs is *huacúxecha*, which in the Tarascan language also means "eagles."

23. Van Zantwijk, 1973.

24. Zorita, 1941; Carrasco, 1964, 1970, 1972. *Calpolli* or *calpulli*, means literally "large house." The word was commonly used for socioeconomic as well as religious units within Aztec communities. Every calpolli had a *calpolco* ("in the calpolli"), a ceremonial center with a temple of its own. Most *calpoltin* (pl.) formed unbroken territorial units inhabited by descendants and relatives by marriage of one or more historical or legendary ancestors. In some *calpoltin*, however, neither the territorial nor the kinship criterion could be traced. Therefore, the general criterion of a family's calpolli membership was permanent association with a particular ceremonial center.

25. Chimalpahin, 1963, pp. 44-45; Tezozomoc, 1949, pp. 39-44; *AT,* 1948, pp. 34-35.

26. Tezozomoc, 1949, pp. 4, 65.

27. Ibid., p. 80.

28. *Codex Izhuatepec,* fols. 25v-33r.

29. Davies, 1973b, pp. 152-58.

30. Durán, 1951, vol. 1, chap. 27; Van Zantwijk, 1980a.

31. Van Zantwijk, 1971.

Chapter 2

1. *HT-Ch.,* 1947, pp. 81-86. Tlachihualtepetl is an ancient name for Cholullan.

2. Ixtlilxochitl, 1952, 1:25.

3. Recinos, 1951, pp. 171, 174; see also Carmack, 1981.

4. *HT-Ch.,* 1947, p. 75.

5. *HT-Ch.* (facs.), fol. 30, p. 28.

6. *AC,* 1938, p. 53.

7. Ixtlilxochitl, 1952, 2:35.

8. Ibid., 1:82.
9. Ibid., 1:12; according to Ixtlilxochitl, this date corresponds with the year A.D. 387 (ibid., 1:28).
10. Ibid., 1:23-29.
11. Ibid., 1:27-28.
12. Muñoz Camargo, 1892, chaps. 4, 5.
13. *ATl.*, 1948, p. 32.
14. *CMex.*, 1952, pl. 22-23. See also Martínez Marín, 1976; for a more remote origin of the Mexítin, see Jiménez Moreno, 1971.
15. Chimalpahin, 1963, p. 6.
16. Lehmann, 1949 *(Coloquios v Doctrina Cristiana)*, p. 100.
17. Chimalpahin, 1963, p. 5-6.
18. Torquemada, 1723, 1:78; see also Calnek, 1978.
19. Chimalpahin, 1963, p. 9.
20. Ibid.
21. Tezozomoc, 1949, p. 16.
22. *ATl.*, 1948, p. 32.
23. Kirchhoff, 1961a.

Chapter 3

1. See Castillo, 1908, p. 58: "Tetzauhteotl, quimilhui ca yêhuatl in Metztli" ("The Impressive God, he said to them that he was the Moon").
2. Many Mesoamericanists have incorrectly translated this as "that we shall return from here." *Ticuepazquê* would mean "we shall return," but *titocuepazquê* means "we shall change ourselves."
3. Chimalpahin, 1962, 1:11.
4. *AC*, 1938, pp. 65-66.
5. *LS*, 1938, pp. 351-57.
6. Garibay, 1958, pp. 65-66.
7. Ibid., pp. 136-38.
8. Torquemada, 1943-44, 1:80-81.
9. Tezozomoc, 1949, p. 21. The name Divine Array is also explained in "Song of the Female Serpent" (*xayahualli* is Old Nahuatl for *xahualli:* see Garibay, 1958, pp. 134-35).
10. Chimalpahin, 1963, 1:11.
11. Tezozomoc, 1949, pp. 22-23.
12. Ibid., p. 29; the palaces are said by Sahagún to belong to Quetzalcoatl.
13. Ibid., pp. 30-31.
14. Garibay, 1958, p. 134.
15. Muñoz Camargo, 1892, p. 19.
16. Chimalpahin, 1962, 1:1.
17. Tezozomoc, 1949, p. 31.
18. *CF*, bk. 3, chap. 1. But according to Chimalpahin (1958), Huitzilopochtli died in Coatepec; see 1:45.
19. Cf. Garibay, 1958, p. 29.
20. Tezozomoc, 1949, pp. 32-36.
21. *ATl.* (facs.), p. 65.
22. Tezozomoc, 1949, p. 37.

23. Torquemada, 1943-44, 1:82.

24. *ATl.* (facs.), pp. 65-66.

25. *HMP*, 1941, pp. 224-25.

26. Tezozomoc, 1949, pp. 39-45.

27. Chimalpahin, 1963, 1:44.

28. *CMex.*, 1952, fig. 38.

29. See Tezozomoc, 1949, pp. 53-61.

30. Van Zantwijk, 1965.

31. *HMP*, 1941, p. 223; see also Reyes, 1969, pp. 35-38.

32. *AC*, 1938, pp. 291ff.

33. See Cline, 1973; Davies, 1973.

34. Olivera Sedaño, 1954-55.

35. Ibid.

36. *AC*, 1938, p. 293.

37. Ibid.

38. Chimalpahin, 1963, 1:10; *AC*, 1938, pp. 291-93.

39. *Codex Ramírez*, 1944, p. 76.

40. *AC*, 1938, pp. 246-48.

41. Ibid., p. 295.

42. Ibid., p. 290; Durán, 1951, 1:514. See also Davies, 1977, p. 316.

43. For the ancient Mesoamerican or "Toltec" character of Huitzilopochtli, one should compare the creation narratives in *HMP* with those in *LS* (the latter document calls him by his surname Tepanquizqui (Conqueror). See also the Huitzilopochtli song "Noteouh Tepanquizqui Mîtoa" ("My God is Called 'Conqueror'").

Chapter 4

1. See Chavero, 1887, 1:620.

2. *CM*, 1938.

3. *CMex.*, 1952.

4. Chavero, 1887; Kingsborough, 1831-48.

5. Tezozomoc, 1944, 1949.

6. Chimalpahin, 1963, 1965.

7. *Codex Ramírez*, 1944.

8. Lafaye, 1972.

9. Durán, 1951.

10. *CFM*, 1901.

11. *CVB*, 1972.

12. Orozco y Berra, 1960, 3:144.

13. Ibid.; Chavero, 1887.

14. Moreno, 1962; Monzón, 1949; Caso, 1956.

15. See Caso, 1956, p. 19.

16. Ibid., p. 9.

17. Tezozomoc, 1949, pp. 62-64. Cf. also *CF* (Anderson and Dibble, 1950-69), 7:16: The king who has just been installed says to his corulers and high dignitaries:

". . . tê momac maniz   ". . . in thy hands will rest

in matlalatl in toxpalatl	the blue water the yellow water,
in ipapacoca	the place where is washed
in iahaltiloca	the place where is bathed
in cuitlapilli in âtlapalli . . ."	the tail and the wing (the common people) . . ."

That is, "Thou wilt determine and thou wilt control the human sacrifices that will come from the four directions."

18. See note 1 above.

19. Caso, 1956.

20. *CF*, 2:134.

21. *CMex.*, 1952.

22. Durán, 1951, 1:222.

23. *Codex Azcatitlan*, 1949, p. 118; Tezozomoc, 1949, p. 80.

24. See Orozco y Berra, 1960, 3:117-45.

25. See *Codex Sigüenza*, 1887; Tezozomoc, 1949, p. 76. Cf. also Monjarás Ruiz, 1977, pp. 58-63.

26. See Tezozomoc, 1949, p. 70.

27. Van Zantwijk, 1966.

28. Tezozomoc, 1949, p. 127.

29. *CMex.*, 1952, pl. 16, 17, etc.

30. Gibson, 1964.

31. Orozco y Berra, 1960, 3:144; Chavero, 1887.

32. The Yopico Tzompantli is the fifty-fifth building in the list of temples and sanctuaries given by Sahagún.

33. Chimalpahin, 1963, 1:44.

34. Garibay, 1940, p. 112.

35. See *Codex Ramírez*, 1944, p. 19.

36. See *Codex Aubin*, 1963, pp. 40-41; Chimalpahin, 1963, 1:66.

37. Tezozomoc, 1944, 1949; Durán, 1951; Veytia, 1944; *CFM*, 1901.

38. Tezozomoc, 1944, p. 8; here too we see the tripartition: a celestial god, an earth goddess, and a god of the underworld.

39. Durán, 1951, 1:20-21.

40. Ibid., 2:148-49.

41. Veytia, 1944, 1:287.

42. Garibay, 1958, pp. 40-41.

43. The names in brackets are my additions.

44. *Codex Ramírez*, 1944, p. 39.

45. *CVB*, 1972, fols. 15, 16.

46. *AC*, 1938, p. 353.

47. *Codex Ramírez*, 1944, pp. 27n.19.

48. These are Calpilco and Tolnahuac, mentioned by Chimalpahin as two of the four calpollis in Aztlan (1963, 1:9).

49. The *Codex Izhuatepec* has it that Chalman and Huitznahuac lie in Teopan Zoqui(a)pan, Tlacatêcpan in Atzacualco, Tlacochcalco in Cuepopan, and Cihuatêc-pan in Moyotla. The map of Alzate from 1789 shows Yopico as a ward in Moyotla. The pre-Spanish Yopico temple stood in the corner of the ceremonial center of the city that faced Moyotla. From the procession ritual of Paynal it appears that Izquitlan was on the west side of the city on the western causeway, so it was located in Cuepopan (see also chap. 3).

50. Durán, 1951, 1:42, 2:148-49.

51. Tezozomoc, 1944, p. 331; Tezozomoc, 1949, pp. 32, 74-75.

52. See Van Zantwijk, 1963.

53. Cf., for example, *CF*, 2:165-80.

54. Schoembs, 1949, pp. 97, 102; Sahagún, 1955, 1:243.

55. See Caso, 1956, pp. 44-45.

56. Tezozomoc, 1944, p. 284.

57. Caso, 1956.

58. Van Zantwijk, 1971, p. 248.

59. *CF*, 2:127.

60. Ibid., p. 195.

61. Durán, 1951, 2:186.

62. Tezozomoc, 1944, pp. 32, 33, 41.

63. *IS*, 1958, 1:90-91; *CF*, 2:173.

64. Caso, 1967, p. 191.

65. Soustelle, 1959, chap. 8.

66. Tezozomoc, 1949, p. 43.

67. Cf. Caso, 1956.

68. Díaz del Castillo, 1955, p. 203; we see a similar organization in the Mexican army, where one experienced warrior was always placed with four recruits (cf. Tezozomoc, 1944, p. 361).

69. *CF*, 2:103; Tezozomoc, 1944, p. 106.

70. Seler, 1901, p. 132; *CF*, 2:165.

71. *CF*, 2:165, 178.

72. *HMP*, 1941, p. 209.

73. According to Veytia (1944, 2:342), the *teucallis* (temples) of both Tlacochcalco and Huitznahuac were connected with Titlacahuan (We Are His Slaves), one of the names for Tezcatlepoca. Both temples played a part in the Miccailhuitl (Feast of the Dead). Thus it is reasonable to assume that both were also connected with Mictlantêuhctli.

74. Tezozomoc, 1944, p. 311n.

75. *LS*, 1938, p. 352.

76. Garibay, 1958, pp. 40-46.

77. *CF*, 2:55ff.

78. Cf. Caso, 1956.

79. Ibid.

80. For Tzapotlan see *CF*, 2:195, 200; *IS* (ed. León-Portilla), 1958, pp. 92-93, 106-107, 128-29, 134-35; Caso, 1956; Garibay, 1958, p. 178.

81. Tezozomoc, 1944, p. 60.

Chapter 5

1. These ideas are still found today among northern tribes such as the Tarahumares and the Huichols, both of whom belong to the Uto-Aztecan language family.

2. Cf. *AC*, 1938, pp. 79-90.

3. Ibid., p. 93.

4. Cf. Thompson, 1954.

5. *AC*, 1938, p. 93.

6. Traces of this are still visible today at Teotihuâcan and at Tula (Tollan, Tullan).

7. *HT-Ch.*, 1947, pp. 68-69.

8. Davies, 1977, pp. 397ff.

9. Ibid., p. 385.

10. Ibid., p. 390.

11. *AC*, 1938, p. 65.

12. Durán, 1951, 1:517-24.

13. *AC*, 1938, p. 290.

14. Cf. chaps. 4, 8.

15. Tezozomoc, 1949, p. 82.

16. *AC*, 1938, p. 65.

17. Ibid., p. 162; the goddesses of the Colhuas are mentioned here as Tocî (Our Grandmother), Xochiquetzal (Flower Ornamental Feather), and Chiucnahuiozomahtli (Nine Monkey), the calendar name of Itzpapalotl (cf. *CTR*, 1964, pp. 221-23).

18. *Relación de la Genealogía*, 1941, p. 249; *Orígen de los Mexicanos*, 1941, p. 268.

19. Veytia, 1944, 1:358.

20. Davies, 1973b, pp. 201-10.

21. *Orígen de los Mexicanos*, 1941, pp. 268-69; *Relación de la Genealogía*, 1941, pp. 249-51; *HMP*, 1941, pp. 227-28; *AC*, 1938, p. 174.

22. *CM*, 1938, fol. 3r.

23. *Codex Izhuatepec*; Chimalpahin, 1963, p. 77; Tezozomoc, 1949, p. 85.

24. *Codex Matritense*, 1906, fol. 51r (cf. Castillo and Victor, 1974, pp. 183-94); *CMex.*, 1952, pl. 53; *Codex Xolotl*, 1951, pl. 4, p. 69; Van Zantwijk, 1979; Ixtlilxochitl, 1952, 1:119-20; *ATL*, 1948, pp. 15, 51; *Codex Aubin*, 1963, pp. 42, 52; *CVR*, 1964, pp. 228-29; *Codex Ramírez*, 1944, pp. 40-43; Acosta, 1962, p. 322; Durán, 1951, vol. 1, chap. 6; Lafaye, 1972, p. 27; Mendieta, 1945, 1:163; Motolinía, 1971, p. 8; Torquemada, 1723, 1:95.

25. *Codex Ramírez*, 1944, p. 42; Durán, 1951, 1:48; Motolinía, 1971, p. 8; Torquemada, 1723, 1:96; Lafaye, 1972, p. 27.

26. Durán, 1951, 1:49.

27. Ibid., p. 50.

28. *AC*, 1938, p. 173.

29. Chimalpahin, 1963, p. 9.

30. Orozco y Berra, 1960, 3:153.

31. Probably someone who belonged to the same priestly family as that of Cuauhtlequetzqui and Cuauhcoatl.

32. *AC*, 1938, p. 174.

33. Chimalpahin, 1963, 1:76.

34. See, for example, Ixtlilxochitl, 1951, 1:23, 27, 29-30.

35. Chimalpahin, 1963, 1:79.

36. Cf. Motolinía, 1971, p. 7.

37. Van Zantwijk, 1973.

38. Cf. Tezozomoc, 1948, pp. 86-88.

39. Ixtlilxochitl, 1952, 1:184-86.

40. Cf. Coe, 1964.

41. *Codex Ramírez*, 1944, pp. 62-64.

42. *AC*, 1938, p. 216.

43. Durán, 1951, 2:240.

Chapter 6

1. *CM,* 1938, fol. 64-65.
2. Cf. López Austin, 1961, p. 57.
3. Ingham, 1971.
4. Tezozomoc, 1944, pp. 54-55.
5. Orozco y Berra, 1960, 3:153.
6. Chimalpahin, 1963, 1:82.
7. Orozco y Berra, 1960, 3:153.
8. Tezozomoc, 1944, p. 58.
9. Orozco y Berra, 1960, 3:153; *CMex.,* 1952, pl. 17.
10. Orozco y Berra, 1960, 3:153.
11. Tezozomoc, 1944, p. 58.
12. See chap. 4.
13. Tezozomoc, 1944, p. 58.
14. Chimalpahin, 1963, 1:79-80.
15. Tezozomoc, 1944, pp. 55, 27, 32, 33, 36, 41, 50.
16. Ibid., p. 57.
17. Ibid., p. 58.
18. Tezozomoc, 1949, pp. 132-33.
19. Ibid., pp. 90-95.
20. Tezozomoc, 1944, p. 58.
21. Ibid.
22. Ibid.
23. Ibid.
24. Ibid.
25. Ibid.
26. Ibid., p. 41.
27. Ibid.
28. Ibid.
29. Ibid., pp. 57-60.
30. Cf. Tlillan *calmecac* and Tlillancalco as institutions in Moyotla belonging to Molonco Itlillan, a dependency of Cihuatêcpan (see chap. 10).
31. E.g., *CM,* 1938, fol. 68, where the *ezhuahuacatl* acts as one of the four judges of Tenochtitlan in the company of the *mixcoatlailotlac* (Cuepopan), *tequixquinahuacatl* (Moyotla) and the *acatliacapanecatl* (Atzacoalco).
32. See note 30 above.
33. Garibay, 1958, pp. 40-41.
34. See chap. 12.
35. Chavero, 1887, 1:620.
36. Similar identifications occur in the original cultures of the Andes regions (personal communication from R. T. Zuidema).
37. *CF,* 2:69.
38. See chap. 4.
39. See *CMex.,* 1952, pl. 17; *ATl.,* 1948, p. 44; *Anales Históricos de la Nación Mexicana (Unos),* 1945, p. 73.
40. Tezozomoc, 1944, p. 187. Almost the same composition is repeated on

p. 194, but there the *tocuiltecatl* has been replaced by his calpolli colleague, the *huitznahuatlailotlac.*

41. See note 35 above; *CM*, 1938, fol. 67.
42. Garibay, 1961a, p. 180.
43. Caso, 1956, p. 25.
44. Garibay, 1961a, p. 180.
45. Ibid.
46. Ibid., p. 181.
47. Robelo, 1951, pp. 212–13.
48. *CF*, 8:55.
49. Sahagún, 1955, 1:185.
50. *CM*, 1938, fol. 65.
51. Tezozomoc, 1944, pp. 251–52; cf. Monjarás Ruiz, 1977, for a detailed description of the functions of these officials.
52. Van Zantwijk, 1962, 1965.
53. Tezozomoc, 1944, p. 61; in reality the conquerors received only usufruct of the landed estates, not the estates themselves (see chap. 13).
54. *AC*, 1938, p. 239.

Chapter 7

1. Seler, 1960; Schultze-Jena, 1952; Garibay, 1961a, 1956; Acosta Saignes, 1945; León-Portilla, 1962; Caso, 1961; *CF*, 9:1959; López Austin, 1961; Alba, 1949; Soustelle, 1955; Katz, 1966.
2. Soustelle, 1955, pp. 86–92.
3. Katz, 1966, pp. 71–84.
4. Indigenous sources use the terms Aztecâ and Mexîcâ to indicate the dominant population group in Mexico in pre-Spanish times (see also chaps. 2, 3).
5. Tlacayelel I reigned from 1427 until about 1474, beside Kings Itzcoatl (1427–40) and Motêcuhzoma Ilhuicamina (1440–66), during the reign of Queen Atotoztli (1466–70), and for a few years beside King Acayacatl (1470–82).
6. Cf. Seler, 1927; Garibay, 1961a; León-Portilla, 1958; Paso y Troncoso, 1906 (facs.).
7. In *AC* and other historical sources of indigenous origin, such as the *Relaciones de Cempoala* (Hidalgo), and in some places in Pomar's work (see Garibay, 1964) the name of this god is spelled Tezcatlepoca. This spelling makes for a more logical interpretation in the translation of the term than the usual one, in which Tezcatlipoca is translated as Smoking Mirror. Smoking Mirror, however, would be Tezcapopoca in correct Nahuatl. On the other hand, Tezcatlepoca can be analyzed as *tezcatl* ("obsidian mirror") and *tlepoca* ("he, she, or it beams, shines, glitters").
8. For this and other texts see Paso y Troncoso, 1906, fols. 2, 3, 1.
9. Garibay, 1940, p. 112.
10. See Seler, 1927; Paso y Troncoso, 1906, fol. 12.
11. See *ECN* 14 (1980):441–43.
12. Garibay, 1961a, 3:62, 126.
13. See chap. 1, note 24; chap. 4.
14. Van Zantwijk, 1966.
15. Veytia, 1944, 2:278.

16. Ibid., p. 321.
17. See Schultze-Jena, 1952, p. 116.
18. *CF*, 9:12.
19. Caso, 1961, p. 95.
20. *CF*, 4:45.
21. Garibay, 1961a, 3:74.
22. Van Zantwijk, 1967.
23. Acosta Saignes, 1945.
24. Chimalpahin Cuauhtlehuanitzin, 1963, vol. 1.
25. *Chimalxochitl*, "shield flower" (*Helianthus annus*, L.), and *cuauhxochitl* "eagle's flower" *(Plumeria rubra)*.

Chapter 8

1. "Ma ximehuiltitie moceloquichtlê, tlalxictenticâê, nauhyotêcuhtlê, ma ihuian xic-hualmanili im mococauh in maxcatzin, ahzo itla oic nimitznoyolitlacalhui" (Garibay, 1961, 3:48).
2. "Onechmocnelili in tlacatl totêcuhyo: ca huel nahciz in ompa niyauh" (ibid., p. 50).
3. "Ma iyolic xoconana im mocxi, ca yê toconnamiquiz in Ce coatl ohtli melahuac" (ibid., p. 52).
4. A "counterpart being" *(nahualli)* is a being, usually an animal, whose fate is connected with that of a human being; when the animal dies, the human being in question falls ill and usually dies too. Wizards can exercise control over their *nahualli*, and can use them to do harm to other people.
5. *CF*, 6:45.
6. Torquemada, 1723, 2:153.
7. *CF*, 5:87.
8. See also Sahagún, 1955, 2:167; *CF*, vol. 9, chap. 19; *CF*, vol. 2, chap. 120.
9. Garibay, 1961, p. 78: "ca ye ic cencalaqui in icococauh in tloquê nahuaquê, in tlalticpaquê in yoalli ehecatl."
10. "ahzoc matlac ilhuitia ahnozoc cempoalilhuitia in quichiê cualli tonalli" (ibid., p. 86).
11. Cf. *CF*, 2:155ff.
12. Ibid., pp. 59-63.
13. Ibid., pp. 71-72.
14. Ibid., pp. 11-12.
15. Ibid., pp. 16, 103.
16. See Garibay, 1:239; López Austin, 1965, p. 93.
17. See Durán, 1977, p. 204; "When these slaves had been presented and dedicated, one was given the name Yacatecuhtli; another, Chiconquiahuitl; another, Cuauhtlaxayauh; another Coatlinahual; and the woman was called Chalmecacihuatl."
18. *CF*, 2:118-20.
19. Garibay, 1958, p. 29.
20. Garibay, 1961a, p. 120; "Auh ca ixco icpac ontlachiaznequi in tlacatl in tetzahuitl in Huitzilopochtli."
21. See *Codex Matritense*, 1906, fol. 23; "Auh intla aca oittoc in cenca mimati

tlaaltilli, in cuicamatini, in yolizmatqui, in ixê in yollo quiquixtiayâ in pipiltin" ("But if one of "those who were bathed" proved to be a well-educated person, who could sing well and was otherwise well trained in the art of living, and made a good impression on account of his outward appearance and inward qualities, the nobles would take such a person aside").

22. Garibay, 1961a, p. 146. This probably means that the Pochtec owners took their slaves to Pochtlan whereas the Oztomec owners took theirs to Acxotlan.

23. Ibid., pp. 148-50; *CF*, 2:134-35.

24. López Austin, 1965, p. 92. Only incidentally Sahagún mentions an important sacrifice of the merchants during the seventeenth feast of Tititl, (1955, 1:252), but in his description of Tititl, Sahagún does not refer to any participation of the merchants.

25. Garibay, 1961a, p. 86.

26. Ibid., pp. 54, 56.

27. Ibid., p. 136.

28. Ibid., p. 74.

29. Ibid., p. 84.

30. Ibid., pp. 54, 70, 72, 138.

31. Ibid., pp. 76, 112; cf. Hinz, 1978.

32. Ibid., pp. 54, 72.

33. Ibid., pp. 70, 71.

34. Ibid., p. 58.

35. Ibid., p. 82.

36. Ibid.

37. Schultze-Jena, 1952, pp. 118-20.

38. Garibay, 1961a, p. 82.

39. Ibid., p. 138.

40. Ibid., pp. 160, 162.

41. Ibid., p. 72.

42. Ibid., p. 88.

43. Ibid., p. 34.

44. Ibid., p. 66.

45. "Quinhualnotztiâ in huehuetquê in achto huallâquê in êconi in tlacapixoani Mexiti(n)" (*CF*, 8:4).

46. See chap. 4; *Codex Magliabecchiani*, 1970.

47. "Oppa in quinmahuiztiliayâ, in ceppa îcuac in motenehua Panquetzaliztli, inic oppa îcuac in mîtoa Tlaxochimaco" (*CF*, 8:4).

48. Ibid., 2:86.

49. Carrasco and Broda, 1978, p. 236.

50. *CF*, 2:124-29.

51. *HT-Ch.*, 1947, pp. 44, 54, 66, 293; *ATl.*, 1948, pp. 35-36.

52. Van Zantwijk, 1966.

Chapter 9

1. Cf. Van Zantwijk, 1973.

2. Van Zantwijk, 1962, 1967.

3. See also López Austin, 1961, pp. 90-93; Zorita, 1941, pp. 89-90, 144.

4. Cf. Zorita, 1941, p. 198.

5. Ibid., p. 75.

6. Cf. the key positions held by several women in royal families and their considerable political influence, as, for instance, that of the Mexican "aunts" of Nezahualcoyotl (see Davies, 1973, p. 165).

7. Carrasco, 1964, 1970, 1972.

8. Nutini, 1962, and Van Zantwijk, 1967, describe modern examples of it.

9. For instance, Opochtli of Chalman and Itzpapalotl of Colhuâcan became ancestral gods of the Tenochcâ in this way. See also Muñoz Camargo, 1892, p. 105.

10. An example which may be considered historically reliable is that of Itzcoatl's son Tezozomoc, who acquired great political influence through his marriage to Atotoztli, the legitimate daughter of Motêcuhzoma Ilhuicamina Chalchiuhtlatonac.

11. Sahagún, 1955, bk. 9, chap. 3.

12. See Vogt, 1966; López Austin, 1973; *Codex Azcatitlan,* 1949.

13. See *Codex Borbonicus,* 1974, fol. 21, where Oxomoco and Cipactonal are depicted as the first ancestors of Mesoamericans.

14. León-Portilla, 1962.

15. Ixtlilxochitl, 1952; Veytia, 1944; Torquemada, 1723.

16. Chimalpahin, 1958, bk. 13.

17. Ixtlilxochitl, 1952, 2:78. This refers to the third case: dual chieftainship by marriage.

18. See Chimalpahin, 1958, pp. 150, 161, 104, 106, 107.

19. Torquemada, 1943-44, 1:82.

20. Ibid., p. 97; Acosta, 1962.

21. Chimalpahin, 1963, 1:20.

22. Ibid., p. 21.

23. Ibid., p. 76; Tezozomoc, 1949, pp. 79-82.

24. Veytia, 1944, 1:349.

25. *ENE,* 1940, 10:121ff.

26. Chimalpahin, 1963, 1:77.

27. *Codex Xolotl,* 1951, bks. 2-6.

28. See note 23 above.

29. *Relación de la Genealogía,* 1941, pp. 249, 251; see also Davies, 1973, pp. 61-64.

30. See note 25 above.

31. See note 26 above.

32. See note 27 above.

33. *Relación de la Genealogía,* 1941, pp. 249, 250.

34. Veytia, 1944, p. 349.

35. Chimalpahin, 1963, 1:52.

36. Mendieta, 1945, 1:163.

37. Clavijero, 1958, 1:206.

38. Cf. Van Zantwijk, 1973; Corona Sánchez, 1973.

39. Ibid.

40. *AC,* 1938, p. 159.

41. Tezozomoc, 1949, p. 111; and Chimalpahin, 1963, 1:109.

42. Chimalpahin, 1963, 1:109 (*Relación* 7, fol. 171v.). See also Motolinía (1971, p. 9), who mentions the election of Atotoztli. The uncertainty about the question of which of the children of a dignitary is to be the first to succeed him

is unequivocally expressed in the *Florentine Codex* in the words addressed by a nobleman to his children (*CF*, 7:92), referring to his office:

"... auh ac tê in tonmocneliz?   "... and which of you will be benefited?

cuix tê in titeyacapan?   will it be you, the first-born?

cuix tê in titeach?   will it be you, the older one?

cuix titlâcoehua?   will it be you, who grows up as the middle one?

cuix nozo têhuatl in tixocoyotl?   or will it perhaps be you, the youngest?

cuix tê titlachixcatzintli?   Perhaps you, who are the most attentive?

cuix tê titlacaccatzintli?   perhaps you, who are the most sensible?

cuix tê mîtoa teutl moyollo?   perhaps you, whose inner nature is said to be divine,

cuix tê titlacateuyollocatzin?   you, who clearly have a divine heart,

toconcuiz, toconanaz   will perhaps receive it, take it with you,

ticmopialtiz."   keep it for yourself."

43. Tezozomoc, 1944, pp. 174-75.
44. *ATl.*, 1948, p. 59.
45. *ENE*, 10:121ff.
46. Chimalpahin, 1963, p. 109 (*Relación* 3, fol. 100).
47. Ibid., p. 109 (*Relación* 7, fol. 171).
48. N.B.: *iztatlacâ* = "extractors of salt," but *ichtacaca* = "secretly"; if the former is an error in writing for the latter, the line would mean "Or does he only buy slaves for himself in secret?"
49. Tezozomoc, 1949, pp. 115-16.
50. Cf. Gibson, 1964, pp. 124-25.
51. *AC*, 1938, pp. 163-65.
52. Nutini, 1968.
53. Carrasco, 1964, 1970, 1972; Van Zantwijk, 1974.
54. See Rammow, 1964, for further information on the Aztec kinship system.
55. See, for example, Acosta, 1962, pp. 325-26; Lafaye, 1972, p. 14.
56. See, for example, Díaz del Castillo, 1955, pp. 154-56.

Chapter 10

1. See Van Zantwijk, 1973.
2. Cf. *AC*, 1938, pp. 194-95.
3. Davies, 1973.
4. López Austin, 1972; *Codex Ramírez*, 1944, p. 130.
5. López Austin, 1972.
6. *HMP*, 1941, pp. 234-35.
7. *Petlacontzitzquiquê* = literally "keepers of the mat and the urn(s)," i.e., the mat on which the chiefs or kings sat when they administered justice or ruled and the urn(s) containing the ashes of the ancestors.
8. Tezozomoc, 1944, p. 300.
9. *HMP*, 1941, p. 214. For similar ideas among the present-day Mayas see Girard, 1966, pp. 95-100.
10. Cf. Garibay, 1961b, pp. 131-35.

11. *HMP*, p. 194, 234. *CVR* 1964, p. 9, does give further information about the last five parts of heaven: ninth: Teotl Iztacan = Place of the White God; tenth: Teotl Cozauhcan = Place of the Yellow God; eleventh: Teotl Tlatlauhcan = Place of the Red God; and twelfth and thirteenth Omeyocan = Place of duality.

12. Garibay, 1961a, p. 48.

13. See chaps. 2, 4.

14. See chap. 4.

15. There appears to be a connection between Ococaltzin and the god Cinteotl which leads to a further connection with Moyotla (see chap. 4).

16. *HMP*, 1941, p. 216.

17. Cf. Soustelle, 1959, p. 61.

18. *HMP*, 1941, p. 234.

19. See Chimalpahin, 1963, p. 67.

20. E.g., ibid., p. 79.

21. Tezozomoc, 1944, pp. 302–305.

22. Ibid., pp. 307–308.

23. Ibid., p. 315.

24. Caso, 1956, p. 22.

25. Tezozomoc, 1944, p. 315.

26. Ibid., p. 316.

27. Ibid., p. 320.

28. Ibid., p. 330.

29. See the end of this chapter and chap. 11 below.

30. Tezozomoc, 1944, p. 331.

31. Ibid.; Zacailamatzin is apparently a special form of Ilamatzin, perhaps worshiped especially by the Tenochcas, who regarded the Zacatepec as their "ancestor mountain."

32. Ibid., pp. 331, 332.

33. Van Zantwijk, 1969, p. 131.

34. Tezozomoc, 1944, pp. 331–32. Ometêuhctli (Lord of Duality) is the ancient pantheistic supreme god of the Toltecs. He represents the same creative primordial force as that attributed to the two gods Tonacatêuhctli and Tonacacihuatl.

35. Ibid., p. 332.

36. In chapter 12, I shall explain that the population of Tenochtitlan was divided into twenty calpollis and into twenty *tlaxilacallis*. If each *tlaxilacalli* and the calpolli had a leading priest of its own, these would form a group of exactly forty priests.

37. López Austin, 1969, p. 110.

38. This does not mean that none of the priests of these calpollis participated in the feast. On the contrary, since forty priests in all participated, these calpolli priests were among the number. But they were not delegated to the four most important sanctuaries and evidently performed their duties only in their own calpolco or *tlaxilacalli* (see chap. 13).

Chapter 11

1. The expression used as the chapter title was employed by Aztec merchants,

who took the vow to sacrifice slaves (cf. Garibay, 1961a, p. 134). The title is paraphrased in this way because the reader must also look in the face of Huitzilopochtli, though in a quite different manner.

2. Cf. Veytia, 1944, 1:278.

3. See Cline, 1973.

4. Ibid.; Caso, 1967.

5. Caso, 1967; Veytia, 1944, 2:339. At Tetzcoco the annual feast of Tlacaxipehualiztli is also called Xilomaniliztli or Xilomaniztli, i.e., Presence of the Young Maize Cobs; see Durán, 1951, 2:270; Castillo, 1908, p. 77.

6. See Cline, 1975, for the so-called Axayaca calendar in Tenochtitlan.

7. Cf. *LS*, 1938.

8. It is possible that these little quadrangles are the symbols for the twenty calpollis and the twenty *tlaxilacallis* (see further on in this and the next chapter). The five points might refer to the presence of five sanctuaries or other objects connected with certain directions that were involved in the religious worship in each of these units.

9. See *CF*, 2:97-98.

10. Ibid., pp. 179, 180.

11. Castillo, 1908, p. 78.

12. See for instance *CF*, vol. 2, chaps. 21, 22.

13. See *HMP*, 1941, p. 209.

14. Cf. chap. 4.

15. See *CTR*, 1964, sheet 10v.

16. See Spranz, 1964, pp. 277ff.; López Austin, 1973; cf. also León-Portilla, 1958, p. 123.

17. *LS*, 1938, p. 352.

18. León-Portilla, 1958, p. 122.

19. E.g. *CVR*, p. 17r.

20. Cf. chap. 10.

21. Cf. Ruiz de Alarcón, 1953, chap. 3; León-Portilla, 1958, p. 136: Chalchiuhtlicue = Iztaccihuatl = Coatlicue (!).

22. Cf. Thompson, 1966, pp. 103-106.

23. Garibay, 1958, pp. 128-33.

24. León-Portilla, 1958, p. 144.

25. Sahagún, 1955, 1:40-43.

26. Ibid., p. 212.

27. Garibay, 1958, pp. 217-23.

28. Sahagún, 1955, 1:32.

29. Garibay, 1958, pp. 130-31.

30. Ruiz de Alarcón, 1953, p. 137; *CF*, 7:202.

31. See, e.g., León-Portilla, 1958, pp. 90-91; Seler, 1902, 2:956: Xolotl = 9 ehecatl (!).

32. Cf. Garibay, 1958, pp. 166-67.

33. HMP, 1941, p. 209.

Chapter 12

1. Cf. Boban, 1891.

2. I have already pointed to the significant ritual opposition of the calpolli

of Tlacochcalco, which was strongly associated with human sacrifice, and its
dependent calpollis on the one hand and Huitznahuac and its dependencies on
the other.

3. Cf. also Nowotny, 1961.

4. *CF*, bk. 3, sec. 2.

5. For this subject see appendix 2 and Carrasco's works listed in the References.

6. Tezozomoc, 1944, p. 166.

7. *CTR*, 1964, sheet 6, p. 189.

8. Orozco y Berra, 1960, 3:257-58, 262.

9. The background of this succession is dealt with in detail in Van Zantwijk, 1979.

10. Tezozomoc, 1944, p. 157; Orozco y Berra, 1960, 3:284.

11. Chimalpahin, 1963, pp. 108-109.

12. Cf. Horcasitas, 1973; C. Atezcatitlan, 1949, plates 2, 5, 6, 8.

13. Cf. Chimalpahin, 1963, p. 124.

14. Cf. ibid., pp. 145-78 (*Relación* 8). Besides the terms mentioned, he uses
for Tlailotlacan Têcpan, the administrative center of Tlailotlacan, the explanatory term *ce tlaxillacalyacatl* ("the beginning of a *tlaxilacalli*"); the use of the
latter term fits particularly well the concept of *tlaxilacalli* offered here.

15. Cf. *AC*, 1938, p. 52.

Chapter 13

1. Cf. the roles played by these gods in the various creation myths.

2. Bandelier, 1879.

3. Katz, 1966; cf. also Moreno, 1962; Keen, 1971.

4. Ibid.

5. Cf. Reyes García, 1977, pp. 106-13, 117.

6. See Van Zantwijk, 1967, for a more detailed enumeration of the various
methods of land management.

7. Cf. Carrasco, 1968, and, for the copyright, Chimalpahin, 1963, pp. 115-16.

8. Cf. Borah and Cook, 1960, pp. 60, 114; cf. Carrasco, 1964, 1967, 1968,
1972; Hicks, 1974, López Austin, 1961, pp. 73-74; Zorita, 1941; Borah and
Cook, 1960, pp. 60, 114; Molíns Fábrega, 1955.

9. Until about 1960, in a traditional Tarascan community, as, for example,
Ihuatzio, internal conflicts and rivalries were predominantly related to the fulfillment of functions in the cargo system and to membership of corporate groups
as the *huapanecuas* (a kind of *tlaxilacalli!*). Cf. Van Zantwijk, 1967.

10. Cf. Orozco y Berra, 1960, vol. 4.

11. Offner, 1983, p. 281.

12. Cf. *AC*, 1938, pp. 165, 168-69, 179, 246, 249, 273-75, 281; Chimalpahin, 1963, p. 137; *HT-Ch.*, 1947, pp. 117-21; Reyes García, 1977, pp. 88-94.

13. Kirchhoff, 1956.

14. Torquemada, 1943-44, 2:545-46.

15. Cf. Carrasco and Broda, 1976, 1978; Palerm, 1973; Prem, 1978; Reyes
García, 1977; Wolf, 1976.

16. Reyes García, 1977, p. 113.

17. Cf. in this context the attitude of the imperial administration in the province

of Chalco, where in 1486 the governor was given a free hand to deal with the calpolli nobles (see *AC*, 1938, pp. 274-75) and where in 1509 new state-owned estates were created at the expense of calpolli-owned land (see Chimalpahin, 1963, p. 137).

18. Carrasco and Broda, 1976, pp. 102-17.

19. Ibid.

20. *AC*, 1938, p. 254.

21. López Austin, 1961, p. 129.

22. Ursula Dyckerhoff and Hans J. Prem, La estratificación social en Huexot-zinco, in Carrasco and Broda, 1976, pp. 160ff.

23. Ibid., p. 163.

24. Ibid., pp. 171-73.

25. *Codex Huichapan*, 1976, p. 97.

26. Chimalpahin, 1963, p. 78.

27. Weber, 1957, pp. 244, 296, 297.

28. Tezozomoc, 1949, pp. 134, 135, 137, 138, 142; see also *AC*, 1938, pp. 126, 289.

29. Van Zantwijk, 1980a.

30. Cf. Keen, 1971, p. 47; Katz, 1976.

31. *CM*, 1938; *Informacíon Sobre los Tributos . . . de 1554*, 1957; Miranda, 1952; Soustelle, 1955; Chellet Díaz, 1962, pp. 101-105.

32. Calnek, 1976; Tezozomoc, 1949, p. 29 (translation of Aztec text).

33. *ATl.*, 1948, p. 52.

34. Wittfogel, 1955, 1957.

35. See *Matrícula de Tributos*, 1980; *CM*, 1938; *Información Sobre los Tributos . . . de 1554*, 1957.

36. Calnek, 1976, pp. 55-56.

37. Ibid., pp. 54-55.

38. Ibid., p. 55.

39. Molíns Fábrega, 1955, p. 334.

40. Katz, 1976.

41. See Palerm, 1973, pp. 16-19; Wolf, 1976, pp. 133-36, 176-78.

42. See Cook and Borah, 1957, 1960a, 1960b, 1963.

43. Slicher van Bath, 1978.

44. Tezozomoc, 1949, p. 29 (translation of Aztec text).

References

Acosta, J. de. 1962. *Historia Natural y Moral de las Indias.* Mexico City, Buenos Aires.

Acosta Saignes, M. 1945. Los Pochteca. *Acta Antropológica* 1, no. 1 (Mexico City).

———. 1946. Los Teopixque. *Revista Mexicana de Estudios Antropológicos* 8:147-206 (Mexico City).

Alba, C. H. 1949. *Estudio Comparado Entre el Derecho Azteca y el Derecho Positivo.* Special ed., no. 3. Mexico City.

Anales Históricos de la Nación Mexicana (Unos). 1945. Corpus Codicum Americanorum Medii Aevi, vol. 2. Copenhagen.

Anales of Cuauhtitlan [*Códice Chimalpopoca*], (abbr. *AC*). 1938. Explanation and German translation by Walter Lehmann: Die Geschichte der Konigreiche von Colhuacan und Mexico. Stuttgart.

Anderson, A. J. O., and C. E. Dibble, eds. 1940-69. *Florentine* Codex [*Codice Florentino; Codex of Florence*] (abbr. CF). 13 vols. Santa Fe, N.Mex.

Annals of Tlatelolco and Codex Tlatelolco [*Anales de Tlatelolco and Códice de Tlatelolco*], (abbr. *AT1.*). 1948. Edition prepared by Heinrich Berlin, with summary of annals and interpretation of codex by Robert H. Barlow. Mexico City.

Bandelier, A. F. 1879. *On the Social Organization and Mode of Government of the Ancient Mexicans.* Reports of the Peabody Museum, no. 12. Salem, Mass.

———. 1879. *On the Art of War and Mode of Warfare of the Ancient Mexicans.* Cambridge, Mass.

Bandelier, A. F. 1971. Organización Social y Forma de Gobierno de los Antiguos Mexicanos. In *Antología de Teotihuacan a los Aztecas: Fuentes e Interpretaciones Historicas,* ed. M. Leon-Portilla. Mexico City.

Barbosa-Ramírez, A. R. 1971. *La Estructura Económica de la Nueva España, 1519-1810.* Mexico City.

Barlow, R., ed. 1949. *Codex Azcatitlan.* Paris.

Bernal, I. 1972. *Tenochtitlan en una Isla.* Mexico City.

Beyer, H. 1965. *Mito y Simbolismo del México Antiguo.* Mexico City.

Blacker, I. R., and G. Eckholm. 1966. *Cortés en de Ondergang der Azteken.* The Hague.

Boban, E. 1891. *Documents pour servir au Histoire du Mèxique.* Paris.

Borah, W., and S. F. Cook. 1957. The Rate of Population Change in Central Mexico, 1550-1570. *Hispanic American Historical Review* 37 (November):463-70.

———. 1960a. The Population of Central Mexico in 1548: An Analysis of the Suma de Visitas de Pueblos. *Ibero-Americana* 43.

———. 1960b. The Indian Population of Central Mexico, 1531-1610. *Ibero-Americana* 44.

———. 1963. The Aboriginal Population of Central Mexico on the Eve of the Spanish Conquest. *Ibero-Americana* 45.

———, and S. F. Cook, 1974. Essays in Population History. *Mexico and the Caribbean.* Berkeley and Los Angeles.

Burland, C. A. 1974. *Montezuma: Keizer der Azteken.* Bussum.

Calnek, E. E. 1976. Organización de los Sistemas de Abastecimiento Urbano de Alimentos: El Caso de Tenochtitlan. In *Jorge E. Hardoy and Richard P. Schaedel, Las Ciudades de América Latina y Sus Áreas de Influencia a Través de la Historia.* Buenos Aires.

———. 1978. The Analyses of Prehispanic Central Mexican Historical texts. *ECN* 13:239-66 (Mexico City).

Carmack, R. M. *The Quiché Mayas of Utatlán: The Evolution of a Highland Guatemala Kingdom.* Norman, Okla.

Carrasco, P. 1964. Family Structure of Sixteenth-Century Tepoztlan. In *Process and Pattern in Culture: Essays in Honor of Julian H. Steward.* Chicago.

———. 1966. Documentos Sobre el Rango de Tecuhtli Entre los Nahuas Tramontanos. *Tlalocan* 5:133-60.

———. 1967. Relaciones Sobre la Organización Social Indígena en el Siglo XVI. *ECN* 7:119-54 (Mexico City).

———. 1970. *Las Clases Sociales en el México Antiguo: Proceedings of the 38th International Congress of Mesoamericanists, Stuttgart, 1968.* Vol. 2. Munich.

———. 1972. La Casa y la Hacienda de un Señor Tlalhuica. *ECN* 10:225-44 (Mexico City).

———. 1974. Sucesión y Alianzas Matrimoniales en la Dinastía Teotihuacana. *ECN* 11:235-42 (Mexico City).

Carrasco, P., J. Broda, et al. 1976. *Estratificación Social en la Mesoamérica Prehispánica.* Mexico City.

———. 1978. *Economía, Política e Ideología en el México Prehispánico.* Mexico City.

Caso, A. 1956. Los Barrios Antiguos de Tenochtitlan y Tlatelolco. *Memorias de la Academia Mexicana de la Historia* 15, no. 1 (Mexico City).

————. 1967. *Los Calendarios Prehispánicos.* Mexico City.

Castillo, C. del. 1908. *Historia de los Mexicanos.* Preserved fragments, translated and explained by Francisco del Paso y Troncoso. Florence.

Castillo, F., Victor. 1974. Relación Tepepulca de los Señores de Mexico Tenochtitlan y de Acolhuacan. *ECN* 11:183-226 (Mexico City).

Chavero, A. 1887. Historia antigua y de la Conquista. Part 1 of *México a Través de los Siglos.* Mexico City.

Chellet, Díaz, E. 1962. *El Derecho Tributario en la Nación Azteca.* Mexico City.

Chimalpahin Cuauhtlehuanitzin, D. F. de San Antón Muñón. 1958. *Memorial Breve Acerca de la Fundación de la Ciudad de Colhuâcan.* German translation by W. Lehmann and G. Kutscher. Stuttgart.

————. 1963. *Die Relationen Chimalpahins zur Geschichte Méxicos.* Vol. 1, edited by G. Zimmermann. Hamburg. [Aztec text.]

————. 1965. *Die Relationen Chimalpahins zur Geschichte Méxicos.* Vol. 2, edited by G. Zimmerman. Hamburg. [Aztec text.]

Clavijero, F. J. 1958-59. *Historia Antigua de México.* 4 vols. Mexico City.

Cline, H. F. 1973. The Chronology of the Conquest: Synchronologies in *Codex Telleriano-Remensis* and Sahagún. *Journal de la Société des Américanistes* 62:9-34 (Paris).

Codex Aubin. 1963. Translated by C. E. Dibble. Madrid.

Codex Azcatitlan. 1949. Edited by R. Barlow. Paris.

Codex Borbonicus [*Códice Borbónico*]. 1974. In *Codices Selecti,* vol. 44. Explanations by K. A. Nowotny and J. de Durand-Forest. Graz.

Codex Boturini, or Tira de la Peregrinación. 1944. Mexico City.

Codex Fejérváry-Mayer (abbr. *CFM*). 1901. Explanation by E. Seler. Berlin.

Codex Florentine (abbr. *CF*). See Anderson and Dibble, 1950-69.

Codex Huichapan [*El Códice de Huichapan*]. 1976. Edited by M. A. Guinchard. Pt. 1, Relato otomí del México prehispánico y colonial. Mexico City.

Codex Izhuatepec. Transcript and copies in Library of Instituto Nacional de Antropología e Historia, Mexico City, Chapultepec.

Codex Magliabechiano. 1970. In *Codices Selecti,* vol. 23. Introduction and summary by F. Anders. Graz.

Codex Matritense [*Códice Matritense del Real Palacio*]. 1906. Facsimile edition by F. del Paso y Troncoso. Madrid.

Codex Mendoza [*Códice Mendocino*], (abbr. *CM*). 1938. Edited by J. C. Clark. London.

Codex Mexicanus (abbr. *CMex.*). 1952. Bibliothèque nationale de París, nos. 23-24. Explanation by E. Mengin. Paris.

Codex Otlazpan. 1967. Explanation by B. Leander. Mexico City.

Codex Ramírez, [*Relación del Orígen de los Indios que habitan esta Nueva España según sus Historias*]. 1944. Edited by M. Orozco y Berra. Mexico City.

Codex Sigüenza. See Chavero, 1887.

Codex Telleriano-Remensis (abbr. *CTR*). 1964. In *Antigüedades de México*, 1:151-337. Based on collection of Lord Kingsborough. Mexico City.

Códice Vaticano-Ríos or *Codex Vaticanus 3738* [*Códice Vaticano Latino 3738*], (abbr. *CVR*). 1964. In *Antigüedades de México*, 3:7-313. Based on collection of Lord Kingsborough. Mexico City.

Codex Vaticanus B, or *Codex Vaticanus 3773* [*Códice Vaticano 3773*], (abbr. *CVB*). 1972. In *Codices Selecti*, vol. 36. Introduction and summary by F. Anders. Graz.

Codex Xolotl. 1951. Introduction and explanation by C. E. Dibble. Mexico City.

Coe, M. D. 1964. The Chinampas of Mexico. *Scientific American* 211, no. 1 (San Francisco).

———, and Gordon Whittaker. *Aztec Sorcerers in Seventeenth Century Mexico: The Treatise on Superstitions by Hernando Ruiz de Alarcón*. Institute for Mesoamerican Studies, State University of New York at Albany, Publication no. 7. Albany.

Collis, M. 1954. *De verovering van Mexico*. Dutch translation in Prisma edition. Utrecht.

Coloquios y Doctrina Cristiana. See Lehmann, 1949.

Cook, S., and W. Borah. See Borah and Cook, 1974.

Cooper Clark, J. See *Codex Mendoza*, 1938.

Corona Sánchez, E. J. 1973. *Desarollo de un Señorío en el Acolhuâcan Prehispánico*. Mexico City.

———. 1976. Formas de Organización Política en el México Prehispánico. In *Forum de Arqueología* (Mexico City).

Davies, C. N. 1973a. *Los Mexicas: Primeros Pasos Hacia el Imperio*. Mexico City.

———. 1973b. *De Azteken*. Baarn.

———. 1977. *The Toltecs Until the Fall of Tula*. Norman, Okla.

Días del Castillo, B. 1955. *Historia Verdadera de la Conquista de la Nueva España*. Mexico City, Buenos Aires.

Durán, D. 1951. *Historia de las Indias de Nueva España y Islas de Tierra Firme*. 2 vols. and atlas. Mexico City.

Espistolario de Nueva España, 1505-1818, (abbr. *ENE*). 1939-42. Recorded by Francisco del Paso y Troncoso. 16 vols. Mexico City.

Garibay K., A. M. 1940. *Llave del Náhuatl*. Otumba, 1961. 2d rev. ed. Mexico City.

———. 1953-54. *Historia de la Literatura Náhuatl*. 2 vols. Mexico City.

———., ed. 1956. *Historia General de las Cosas de Nueva España, por Fray Bernardino de Sahagún*. 4 vols. Mexico City.

———., ed. 1958. Veinte Himnos Sacros de los Nahuas. *Informantes Indígenas de Sahagún* (abbr. *IS*), no. 2. Mexico City.

———. 1961a. Vida Económica de Tenochtitlan, Pochtecayotl. *Informantes Indígenas de Sahagún* (abbr. *IS*), no. 3. Mexico City.

———. 1961b. Los Dioses se Mudan en Sol y Luna (MS in Royal Palace,

Madrid). Text and translation published in *Llave de Náhuatl.* 2d ed. Pp. 131-35, 215-20. Mexico City.

——. 1964. *Poesía Náhuatl.* Vol. 1. Mexico City.

——. 1965. *Poesía Náhuatl.* Vol. 2. Mexico City.

——. 1968. *Poesía Náhuatl.* Vol. 3. Mexico City.

Gibson, C. 1964. *The Aztecs Under Spanish Rule.* Stanford, Calif.

Giffen-Duyvis, Mrs. G. E. G. van. N.d. *De Azteken.* Amsterdam.

Girard, R. 1966. *Los Mayas.* Mexico City.

Graulich, M. 1974. Las Peregrinaciones Aztecas y el ciclo de Mixcoatl. *Estudios de Cultura Náhuatl* 11:311-54 (Mexico City).

——. 1976. Les Origines Classiques du Calendrier Rituel Mexicain. *Boletín de Estudios Latinoamericanos y del Caribe,* no. 20, pp. 3-16 (Amsterdam).

Heyden, D. 1973. What Is the Significance of the Mexica Pyramid? *Atti del XL Congresso Internazionale degli Americanisti* 1:109-16 (Genoa).

Hicks, F. 1974. Dependent Labor in Prehispanic Mexico. *Estudios de Cultural Náhuatl* 11:243-66 (Mexico City).

Hinz, E. 1978. Analyse aztekischer Gedankensysteme, Wahrsageglaube und Erziehungsnormen als Alttagstheorie sozialen Handelns. *Acta Humboldtiana, Sieries geographica et Ethnographica,* no. 6 (Wiesbaden).

Historia de los Mexicanos por sus Pinturas (abbr. *HMP*). 1941. In *Relaciones de Texcoco y de la Nueva España (Pomar-Zurita)* (Mexico City).

Historia Tolteca-Chichimec (abbr. *HT-Ch.*), 1942. Facsimile of pictorial manuscript from Cuauhtinchan. Copenhagen.

Historia Tolteca-Chichimeca: Anales de Quauhtinchan. 1947. Mexico City.

Horcasitas, F. 1973. "Aquí Iba a Ser México"—un cuento etiológico. *Notas Antropológicas,* vol. 1 (Mexico City).

Información Sobre los Tributos que los Indios Pagaban a Moctezuma, Año de 1554. 1957. Mexico City. [Contains statements by Miguel Huecamecatl, Pedro Tecpanecatl, Toribio Tlacuchcalcatl, Marcos Ybcotecatl, Cristobal Papalotecatl and Martín Teucutlavua.]

Informants of Sahagún (abbr. *IS*). See Garibay K., 1958, 1961a; León-Portilla, 1958.

Ingham, J. M. 1971. Symbolic Dimensions of Clanship in Middle America. *Man* 6:624-29.

Ixtlilxochitl, F. de A. 1952. *Obras Históricas.* 2 vols. Mexico City.

Jiménez Moreno, W. 1973. La Migración Mexica. *Atti del XL Congresso Internazionale Degli Americanisti* 1:163-73 (Genoa).

Katz, F. 1966. *Situación Social y Económica de los Aztecas Durante los Siglos XV y XVI.* Mexico City.

——. 1975. Comparación Entre Algunos Aspectos de la Evolución del Cuzco y de Tenochtitlan. In *Las Ciudades de América Latina y Sus*

Áreas de Influencia a Través de la Historia, (edited by Jorge E. Harday and Richard P. Schaedel), pp. 27-40. Buenos Aires.

Keen, B. 1971. *The Aztec Image in Western Thought.* New Brunswick, N.J.

Kingsborough, L. 1831-48. *Antiquities of Mexico: Comprising Facsimiles of Ancient Mexican Painting and Hieroglyphics.* 7 vols. London.

Kirchhoff, P. 1955. Quetzalcoatl, Huemac y el Fin de Tula. *Cuadernos Americanos* 16, no. 6:164-96.

———. 1956. Land Tenure in Ancient Mexico: A preliminary sketch. *Revista Mexicana de Estudios Históricos* 14. no. 1 (1954-55; Mexico City).

———. 1961a. Das Toltekenreich und sein Untergang. *Saeculum* 12, no. 3:248-65 (Bonn).

———. 1961b. *Der Beitrag Chimalpahins zur Geschichte der Tolteken; Sonderdruck aus: Veröffentlichungen des Museums für Völkerkunde zu Leipzig.* No. 11, *Beitrage zur Völkerforschung; Hans Dann zum 65. Geburtstag.* Berlin.

Krickeberg, W. 1956. *Altmexikanische Kulturen.* Berlin.

———. 1971. Del Mito a la Verdadera Historia. In M. León-Portilla, *Antología de Teotihuacan a los Aztecas.* Mexico City.

Lafaye, J., ed. 1972. *Manuskript Tovar.* Graz.

Leander, B. 1967. *Códice de Otlazpan.* Mexico City.

Lehmann, W. 1906. Traditions des Anciens Mexicains [*Leyenda de los Soles*], (abbr. *LS*). *Journal de la Société des Américanistes de Paris* 3, no. 2 (Paris).

———. 1938. *Die Geschichte der Königreiche von Colhuacan und Mexico (Anales de Cuauhtitlan of Codex Chimalpopoca).* Stuttgart.

———. 1949. *Sterbende Götter und Christliche Heilsbotschaft: Wechselreden Indianischer Vornehemer und Spanisher Glaubensapostel in Mexiko, 1524 (Coloquios y Doctrina Cristiana).* Stuttgart.

León-Portilla, M. 1958. Ritos, Sacerdotes y Atavíos de los Dioses. Vol. 1 of *Informantes Indígenas de Sahagún.* Mexico City.

———. 1961. *Los Antiguos Mexicanos a Través de Sus Crónicas y Cantares.* Mexico City.

———. 1962. La Institución Cultural del Comercio Prehispánico. *Estudios de Cultura Náhuatl* 3:23-54 (Mexico City).

———. 1971. *Antología de Teotihuacan a los Aztecs: Fuentes e Interpretaciones Históricas.* Mexico City.

———. 1978. *Mexico-Tenochtitlan, Su Expacio y Tiempo Sagrados.* Mexico City.

Leyenda de los Soles (abbr. *LS*). See Lehmann, 1906, 1938.

López Austin, A. 1961. *La Constitución Real de México-Tenochtitlán.* Mexico City.

———. 1965. El Templo Mayor de Mexico-Tenochtitlan Según los Informantes Indígenas. *Estudios de Cultura Náhuatl* 5:75-102 (Mexico City).

———. 1969. *Augurios y Abusiones: Textos de los Informantes de Sahagún.* Mexico City.

———. 1973. *Hombre-Dios:* Religión y Política en el Mundo Náhuatl. Mexico City.

Manuscript Tovar [*Manuscrito de Tovar*]. See Lafaye, 1972.

Martínez, H. 1906. *Repertorio de los Tiempos e Historia de Nueva España.* Mexico City. Reprint, 1948.

Martínez Marín, C. 1976. Historiografía de la Migración Mexica. *ECN,* p. 121-36 (Mexico City).

Matrícula de Tributos. 1980. In A. Peñafiel, *Monumentos del Arte Antiguo mexicano.* Berlin. [The original is in the library of the Museo Nacional de Antropología de Mexico.]

Mendieta, Fray G. de. 1945. *Historia Eclesiástica Indiana.* 4 vols. Mexico City.

Miranda, J. 1952. *El Tributo Indígena en la Nueva España Durante el Siglo XVI.* Mexico City.

Molíns Fábrega. N. 1954-55. *El Códice Mendocino y la Economía.* In *Revista Mexicana de Estudios Antropológicos* 14, no. 1:303-36 (Mexico City).

Monjarás Ruiz, J. 1977. *Nacimiento y Consolidación de la Nobleza Mexicana.* Mexico City.

Monzón, A. 1949. *El Calpulli en la Organización Social de los Tenochca.* Mexico City.

Moreno, M. M. 1962. *La Organización Política y Social de los Aztecas.* Mexico City.

Moriarty, J. R. 1968. Floating Gardens (Chinampas): Agriculture in the Old Lakes of Mexico. *América Indígena* 28, no. 2 (Mexico City).

Motezuma, D. L. de. 1914. *Corona Mexicana o Historia de los Motezumas.* Madrid.

Motolinía, T. de B. 1903. *Memoriales o Libro de las Cosas de la Nueva España.* Mexico City.

Muñoz Camargo, D. 1892. *Historia de Tlaxcala.* Mexico. Facsimile ed., Mexico City, 1966.

Nowotny, K. A. 1961. *Tlacuilolli, die Mexikanischen Bilderhandschriften, Stil und Inhalt.* Berlin.

Nuttall, Z. 1911. L'Évêque Zumárraga et les Idoles Principales du Grand Temple de México. In *Journal de la Société des Américanistes de Paris* 8:153-71 (Paris).

Nutini, H. G. 1961. Clan Organization in a Nahuatl-speaking Village of the State Tlaxcala, Mexico. *American Anthropologist* 63:62-78.

———. 1968. *San Bernardino Contla: Marriage and Family Structure in a Tlaxcalan Municipio.* Pittsburgh, Pa.

Offner, Jerome A. 1983. *Law and Politics in Aztec Texcoco.* Cambridge.

Olivera Sedaño, A. 1954-55. Cuitlahuac. *Revista Mexicana de Estudios Antropológicos* 14, no. 1:299-303 (Mexico City).

Orozco y Berra, M. 1960. *Historia Antigua de la Conquista de México.*

4 vols. Mexico City.

Palerm, A. 1973. *Obras Hidráulicas Prehispánicas en el Sistema Lacustre del Valle de México.* Mexico City.

Paso y Troncoso, F. del., ed. 1906. See *Codex Matritense.*

———. 1953. *Idolatrías, Supersticiones, Dioses, Ritos, Hechiceriás y Otras Costumbres Gentílicas de Razas Aborígenes de México,* by H. Ruíz de Alarcón. Mexico City.

Piho, V. 1972. Tlacatecuhtli, Tlacochtecuhtli, Tlacateccatl y Tlacochcalcatl. *Estudios de Cultura Náhuatl* 10:195-223 (Mexico City).

Pomar, J. B. de. 1941, 1964. Relación de Texcoco. In *Relaciones de Texcoco y de la Nueva España (Pomar en Zurita),* pp. 1-64. Mexico City.

Prem, H. J. 1974. *Matrícula de Huexotzinco.* Graz.

———, and U. Dyckerhoff. 1976. La Estratificación Social en Huexotzinco. In *Carrasco, Broda,* et al., 1976.

Rammow, H. 1964. *Die Verwandschaftsbezeichnungen im Klassischen Aztekischen.* Hamburg.

Recinos, A. 1950, trans. *Popol Vuh: The Sacred Book of the Ancient Quiché Maya.* English version by Delia Goltz and Sylvanus G. Morley from the translation of Adrián Recinos. Norman, Okla.

Relación de la Genealogía de los Señores que Han Señoreado Esta Tierra de la Nueva España. 1941. In *Relaciones de Texcoco y de la Nueva España (Pomar y Zurita),* pp. 240-56. Mexico City.

Reyes García L. 1969. Los Dioses Tribales. In *Religión, Mitología y Magia II, Museo Nacional de Antropología.* Mexico City.

———. 1977. *Cuauhtinchan del Siglo XII al XVI.* Wiesbaden.

Robello, C. A. 1951. *Diccionario de Mítología Náhuatl.* Mexico City.

Ruíz de Alarcón, H. 1953. See Paso y Troncoso, 1953.

Sahagún, Fray B. de. 1927. *Einige Kapitel aus dem Geschichteswerk des P. Sahagún, aus dem Aztekischem übersetzt von Eduard Seler.* Stuttgart.

———. 1955. *Historia General de las Cosas de Nueva España.* 3 vols. Mexico City.

Schoembs, J. 1949. *Aztekische Schriftsprache.* Heidelberg.

Schultze Jena, L. 1952. *Gliederung des Alt-Aztekischen Volks in Familie, Stand und Beruf.* Stuttgart.

Seler, E. 1901. *Codex Fejérváry-Mayer.* Eine altmexikanische Bilderhandschrift. Berlin.

———. 1927. *Einige Kapitel aus dem Geschichteswerk des P. Sahagún.* Stuttgart.

———. 1960. *Gesammelte Abhandlungen zur Amerikanische Sprach und Altertumskunde.* 5 vols. Graz.

Slicher van Bath, B. H. 1978. The Calculation of the Population of New Spain, especially for the period before 1570. *Boletín de Estudios Latinoamericanos y del Caribe* 24 (June; Amsterdam).

Soustelle, J. 1955. *La Vie Quotidienne des Aztéques a la Veille de la*

Conquête Espagnole. Paris.

——. 1959. *Pensamiento Cosmológico de los Antiguos Mexicanos.* Puebla.

Spranz, B. 1964. *Göttergestalten in den Mexikanischen Bilderhandschriften der Codex Borgia-Gruppe, eine ikonographische Untersuchung.* Wiesbaden.

Tezozomoc, H. A. 1944. *Crónica Mexicana.* Mexico City.

——. 1949. *Crónica Mexicayotl.* Mexico City.

Thompson, J. E. S. 1954. *The Rise and Fall of Maya Civilization.* Norman, Okla.

——. 1966. Ayopechtli: An Aspect of the Nahua Goddess of the Maguey. *Actas y Memorias del XXXVI Congreso Internaciona de Americanistas* 2:103–106 (Seville).

Torquemada, Fray J. de. 1943-44. *Monarquía Indiana.* 3 vols. Madrid. 1723. Facsimile edition. Mexico City.

Tovar, J. de. 1972. *Relación del Origen de los Yndios que Havitan en Esta Nueva España Según sus Historias.* Edited by J. Lafaye. Graz.

Veytia, M. 1944. *Historia Antigua de México.* 2 vols. Mexico City.

Vogt, E. Z., ed. 1966. *Los Zinacantecos.* Mexico City.

Weber, M. 1957. *Essays in sociology.* Edited by H. H. Gerth and C. W. Mills. Routledge and Kegan Paul Ltd. London.

Wittfogel, K. A. 1955. Development Aspects of Hydraulic Societies. In *Irrigation Civilizations: A Comparative Study,* ed. J. Steward. Washington, D.C.

——. 1957. *Oriental Despotism: A Comparative Study of Total Power.* New Haven, Conn.

Wolf, E. R., ed. 1976. *The Valley of Mexico: Studies in Pre-Hispanic Society.* Albuquerque, N.Mex.

Zantwijk, R. van. 1962. La Paz Azteca: Ordenación del Mundo por los Mexica. *Estudios de Cultura Náhuatl* 3:101–37 (Mexico City).

——. 1963. Principios Organizadores de los Mexica: una Introducción al Estudio del Sistema Interno del Régimen Azteca. *Estudios de Cultura Náhuatl* 4:187–223 (Mexico City).

——. 1965. Introducción al Estudio de la División en Quince Partes de la Sociedad Azteca y Su Significación en la Estructura Interna. *Journal de la Société des Américanistes de Paris* 54, no. 2:211–22 (Paris).

——. 1966. Los Seis Barrios Sirvientes de Huitzilopochtli. *Estudios de Cultura Náhuatl* 6:177–87 (Mexico City).

——. 1967a. *Servants of the Saints: The Social and Cultural Identity of a Tarascan Community in Mexico.* Assen.

——. 1967b. Unos Ejemplos de Supervivencias de Formas Autóctonas de Tenencia de la Tierra Entre Indígenas Mexicanos. In *Les Problèmes Agraires des Amériques Latines* (Paris).

——. 1967c. La Organización de Once Guarniciones Aztecas, una Nueva Interpretación de los Folios 17v y 18r del *Códice Mendocino.*

Journal de la Société des Américanistes de Paris 56, no. 1:149-60 (Paris).

———. 1969. La Estructura Gubernamental del Estado de Tlacupan (1430-1520). *Estudios de Cultura Náhuatl* 8:123-55. (Mexico City).

———. 1971a. La Organización Socioeconómica de los Mercaderes Aztecas. In *Comercio Exterior*, pp. 244-53. Mexico City.

———. 1971b. Aztecs and Mayas. In *Man and His Gods: Encyclopedia of the World's Religions*, ed. Geoffrey Parrinder. Hamlyn, London, New York.

———. 1973. Politics and Ethnicity in a Pre-Hispanic Mexican State Between the 13th and 15th Centuries. *Plural Societies* 4, no. 2: 23-52. 's Gravenhage (The Hague).

———. 1974. "La Organización Social de la Mexico-Tenochtitlan Naciente: una Interpretación de la Primera Pintura (Folio 2r) del *Códice Mendocino.*" Paper read to the 51st International Congress of Mesoamericanists, Mexico City.

———. 1975. El Origen de la Sociedad y del Estado Aztecas y la Historicidad de las Fuentes Autóctonas: una Introducción. *Boletín de Estudios Latinoamericanos y del Caribe*, no. 18:4-14. Special no. in honor of B. H. Slicher von Bath. The Hague.

———. 1979. *Los Anales de Tula.* Graz.

———. 1980a. El Carácter de la Autoridad en el Imperio Azteca y Su Expresión en la Retórica Oficial. In *Gedenkschrift für Walter Lehmann*. Berlin.

———. 1980b. Una Nueva Interpretación del Mito de Aztatlan—Colhuâcan—Chicomoztoc. In *Antropología Americanista en la Actualidad: Homenaje a Raphael Girard*, 2:217-34. Mexico City.

Zorita [Zurita], A. de. 1909. *Historia de la Nueva España.* Madrid.

———. 1941. Breve y Sumaria Relación de los Señores y Maneras y Diferencias Que Había en Ellos en la Nueva España. In *Relaciones de Texcoco y de la Nueva España (Pomar and Zurita).* Mexico City.

Zuidema, R. T. 1964. *The Cheque System of Cuzco: The Social Organization of the Capital of the Inca.* Leiden.

Index

The Aztec Arrangement,
designed by Bill Cason, was set in Caledonia by the University
of Oklahoma Press and printed offset on 55-pound Glatfelter B-31,
a permanized sheet, by Cushing-Malloy, Inc. with case binding by
John H. Dekker and Sons.